# Data-Centric Systems and Applications

Henk M. Blanken · Arjen P. de Vries
Henk Ernst Blok · Ling Feng (Eds.)

# Multimedia Retrieval

With 152 Figures and 11 Tables

 Springer

*Editors*

Henk M. Blanken
Henk Ernst Blok
Ling Feng
Database group
Faculty of EWI
University of Twente
P.O. Box 217
7500 AE Enschede
The Netherlands
{h.m.blanken,h.e.blok,l.feng}@ewi.utwente.nl

Arjen P. de Vries
Centrum voor Wiskunde en Informatica
Kruislaan 413
1098 SJ Amsterdam
The Netherlands
arjen@acm.org

Library of Congress Control Number: 2007929550

ACM Computing Classification (1998): H.3, H.5, I.4

ISBN   978-3-540-72894-8  Springer Berlin Heidelberg New York

Springer is a part of Springer Science+Business Media
springer.com

© Springer-Verlag Berlin Heidelberg 2007

Cover Design: KünkelLopka, Heidelberg
Typesetting: by the Editors
Production: LE-TᴇX Jelonek, Schmidt & Vöckler GbR, Leipzig

Printed on acid-free paper      45/3180/YL      5 4 3 2 1 0

# Preface

**Motivation for the Book**

Traditionally, the database group at the University of Twente researched problems of data retrieval, where there is no uncertainty about the relationship between the query and the results. In the 1990s, the group started to look into non-traditional database applications, with a focus on multimedia databases. A notable event from that time is the 1995 Multimedia Advanced Course, held in a very nice hotel in Boekelo, a village close to the university. This summer course, with famous lecturers like Christos Faloutsos, Karl Aberer and Wolfgang Klas, resulted in the book Multimedia Databases in Perspective (1997). This edited volume was however targeted at fellow researchers, and not very well suited for the average Master of Science program in computer science.

We quickly realized that one of the key problems in multimedia databases is search, and that the proposed solutions to the problem of multimedia information retrieval span a rather wide spectrum of topics outside the database area, ranging from information retrieval and human computer interaction to computer vision and pattern recognition. While we have taught our students a varied mix of these topics over the years, often teaming up with colleagues from the Human Media Interaction group, we never managed to find the MSc level textbook covering a sufficiently broad range of topics without getting superficial.

As a result, we have resorted year after year to collections of scientific articles selected on an ad-hoc basis. When the co-editors Henk Blanken and Ling Feng were faced to organize again a course to address a variety of topics related to multimedia search, they realized that more than 10 years passed by since the advanced course, but without a text book on multimedia retrieval suited for an audience of MSc students in computer science. So, we decided to create this text book ourselves! We gathered a group of researchers from University of Twente and colleagues affiliated to institutes with which we collaborated in research projects, to cover the full spectrum of relevant research.

## Goals of the Book

Let us return for a moment to traditional database systems. These systems allow queries to retrieve data by directly addressing the content of structured data. For obvious reasons, this is not possible for objects like images, songs, and video clips. The following figure pictures important steps in multimedia storage and retrieval:

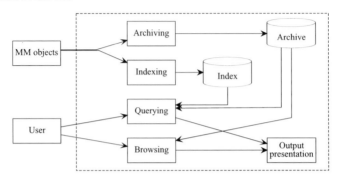

Multimedia objects are archived, but also undergo an indexing process. Indexing applied to a multimedia object generates metadata that is stored in an index. The major task of metadata is to describe the content of multimedia objects in a (semi)-structured way. Metadata play a very important part in multimedia retrieval. Instead of addressing the content of multimedia objects directly, a user queries metadata. When the metadata satisfies certain restrictions, the corresponding multimedia objects may, but also may not, satisfy the user's information need. User satisfaction is the key indicator for the quality of the retrieval process.

The goals of this book are to give state-of-the-art answers to the following questions:

- How can we describe the content of text, speech, images, and video?
- What quality of the retrieval process can be achieved by now?
- How can users interact with a system and how does interaction obey ownership rights?

## Our Approach

We keep the three questions in mind. The first question deals with metadata. Metadata describes the content of multimedia objects and can be derived manually or automatically. To the first class belong descriptive data, like name of author or creation date, and annotated text. In this book we explain information retrieval techniques to enable exploitation of annotated text. The second class consists of features and we distinguish low level features like color histograms and high level features like faces or trees. High level features are more meaningful to the end user and in this book we strongly emphasize the derivation and use of high level features. In fact, we deal with low level features only to capture high level features.

We apply mathematical techniques to extract features in media like image and audio. As known, video is composed of a sequence of images often accompanied by audio and subtitling (text). To derive high level features in video we use mathematics to combine evidence coming from three sources. So, mathematics plays a great part in feature extraction.

The second question addresses quality. We consider many aspects regarding the quality of a multimedia system. We observe that, in the end, it is the user who decides whether a retrieved object is relevant or not. So, when considering the quality of a system the end user must be strongly involved. As a consequence we explain how to perform user oriented experiments. Moreover, we report on the value of approaches by showing results of experiments.

Regarding the last question we mention the following. On one hand, users need to interact with systems to phrase their information need. In that respect we explain several interaction modes. But observe also that not every multimedia resource is freely available to everyone. So, we pay attention to certain standards, which are developed to guarantee the rights owners have. On the other hand, the system must consider the limitations of the output devices available to the user in order to present retrieved objects in a suitable way.

**Organization of the Book**
The book consists of thirteen chapters. After the Introduction we treat three languages to describe metadata (Dublin Core, RDF, MPEG-7). Chapter 3 gives an overview of important mathematical techniques in Pattern Recognition like Support Vector Machines, Hidden Markov Models, and Dynamic Bayesian Networks. The next chapter summarizes the state-of-the-art Information Retrieval techniques. Chapter 5 is a long chapter dealing with images and concentrating on image analysis. It gives a classification of objects occurring in images and explains detection algorithms. Chapter 6 offers a mathematical approach to detect features by combining evidence from text and images. Chapter 7 is devoted to audio processing, in this case mainly speech recognition. The Chapters 8, 9, and 10 cover video applications. Evidence for high level features in video may come from more than one source. The chapters describe approaches to combine evidence. Chapter 11 gives a description of interactions with a system and the presentation of results. Digital rights management is the topic of Chapter 12. The final chapter handles the difficult topic of evaluation of multimedia systems. Besides theoretical considerations, many evaluation efforts are described ranging from important test sets to evaluation procedures as pursued by, for instance, the Text Retrieval Conference (TREC).

**Intended Audience**
Writing the book, we had master students in computer science in mind. Maybe the mathematics part is a little heavy, but this difficulty is certainly manageable. We think also that the book is interesting for students of adjacent studies

like for instance electrical engineering, mathematics, and library sciences. Finally, PhD students and fellow researchers intending to broaden their scope and/or looking for a research topic in multimedia retrieval may find the book inspiring.

## Guidelines for Teaching

The book can be lectured from the first chapter to the last. It depends on the time available whether or not all chapters can be covered. When insufficient time is available we advice to skip Chapter 2 as other chapters do not actually use the languages for metadata too much. Chapter 6 gives a nice application of mathematics to combining evidence, but is not necessary to understand subsequent chapters. Chapters 8, 9, and 10 cover three video applications, one per chapter. If time is a scarce resource you can consider to skip a chapter. Depending on the interest of teacher and/or students, Chapter 12 (digital rights management) can be skipped also.

The Website `http://multimedia-retrieval.utwente.nl` presents exercises to help the students to master the material. The exercises range from simple questions to projects. We will improve the exercises year by year using results from our own course.

We are proud of the final result, and hope that this book will find its way into the classrooms of all these institutes struggling with setting up a course that gives credit to the diversity of expertise required for understanding multimedia retrieval.

## Acknowledgments

A preface is incomplete without thanking all of these contributors for their efforts. The draft book has been tested in practice on the students of the course Multimedia Retrieval, and we are grateful to their enthusiasm for a role as guinea pigs. One of these students, Sander Bockting, helped us create a set of exercises and answers that accompany the book (available from the Website). Maarten Fokkinga has lectured this course with the draft book, and above that provided invaluable technical as well as theoretical support. Peter Apers deserves the credits for moderating a somewhat heated debate among the large group of authors about the table of contents and scope of the book. We also would like to thank Springer-Verlag and especially Ralf Gerstner, who was always very helpful to solve our problems.

Enschede, the Netherlands

*Henk Blanken*
*Arjen P. de Vries*
*Henk Ernst Blok*
*Ling Feng*
May, 2007

# List of Contributors

**Henk M. Blanken**
University of Twente, Centre for
Telematics and Information Technology
P.O. Box 217
7500 AE Enschede, The Netherlands
h.m.blanken@ewi.utwente.nl

**Henk Ernst Blok**
address: see Blanken
h.e.blok@ewi.utwente.nl

**Erik Boertjes**
TNO
Information and Communication
Technology
P.O. Box 5050
2600 GB Delft, The Netherlands
e.m.boertjes@telecom.tno.nl

**Rogier Brussee**
Telematica Instituut
Postbus 589
7500 AN Enschede, The Netherlands
rogier.brussee@telin.nl

**Ling Feng**
Dept. of Computer Science &
Technology, Tsinghua University
Beijing, 100084, P.R.China
fengling@tsinghua.edu.cn
(Work done at the Univ. of Twente)

**Jan-Mark Geusebroek**
address: see Snoek
mark@science.uva.nl

**Ferdi van der Heijden**
University of Twente
Faculty of EEMCS
PO BOX 217
7500 AE Enschede, The Netherlands
f.vanderheijden@utwente.nl

**Djoerd Hiemstra**
address: see Blanken
d.hiemstra@utwente.nl

**Mark Huiskes**
Universiteit Leiden
LIACS
Niels Bohrweg 1
2333 CA Leiden, The Netherlands
Mark.Huiskes@liacs.nl

**Franciska de Jong**
address: see Blanken
f.m.g.dejong@utwente.nl

**Willem Jonker**
Philips Research Europe
High Tech Campus 34
5656 AE Eindhoven, The Netherlands
willem.jonker@philips.com

**Maurice van Keulen**
address: see Blanken
m.vankeulen@utwente.nl

**Dennis C. Koelma**
address: see Snoek
koelma@science.uva.nl

**Paul Koster**
address: see Jonker
r.p.koster@philips.com

**Wessel Kraaij**
TNO Information and Communication
Technology
P.O. Box 5050
2600 GB Delft, The Netherlands
wessel.kraaij@tno.nl

**David van Leeuwen**
TNO Defence, Security and Safety
Postbus 6006
2600 JA Delft, The Netherlands

**Vojkan Mihalovic**
address: see Jonker
vojkan.mihajlovic@philips.com

**Anton Nijholt**
address: see Blanken
a.nijholt@utwente.nl

**Roeland Ordelman**
address: see Blanken
r.j.f.ordelman@utwente.nl

**Milan Petković**
address: see Jonker
milan.petkovic@philips.com

**Elena Ranguelova**
address: see de Vries
Elena.Ranguelova@cwi.nl

**Frank J. Seinstra**
address: see Snoek
fjseins@science.uva.nl

**Arnold W.M. Smeulders**
address: see Snoek
smeulders@science.uva.nl

**Cees G.M. Snoek**
University of Amsterdam
Informatics Institute
Kruislaan 403, 1098 SJ Amsterdam,
The Netherlands
cgmsnoek@science.uva.nl

**Luuk Spreeuwers**
University of Twente
Faculty of EEMCS
PO BOX 217
7500 AE Enschede, The Netherlands
l.j.spreeuwers@utwente.nl

**Mettina Veenstra**
Telematica Instituut
Postbus 589
7500 AN Enschede, The Netherlands
mettina.veenstra@telin.nl

**Arjen P. de Vries**
Centrum voor Wiskunde en Informatica
(CWI)
P.O. Box 94079
1090 GB Amsterdam, The Netherlands
arjen@cwi.nl

**Thijs Westerveld**
address: see de Vries
thijs@cwi.nl

**Marcel Worring**
address: see Snoek
worring@science.uva.nl

# Contents

# 1

# Introduction

Henk Blanken, Ling Feng, Maurice van Keulen, and Henk Ernst Blok

University of Twente

## 1.1 Introduction

People interact with multimedia every day: reading books, watching television, listening to music, etc. For quite some time we have faced astonishing technological developments causing an explosion of digital multimedia information. Large amounts of text, images, speech, and video are converted to digital form. Think of catalog information of libraries, information about museums with nice pictures of paintings or famous speeches that are available on DVD. Moreover, much information is produced directly in digital form: TV programs, audio-visual data from surveillance cameras, photos. Major advantages of digitized data over analog data are easy storage, processing and sharing of data. Multimedia applications influence our daily life. Consider for example the following scenarios.

### 1.1.1 Journalism

This scenario is based on a field study by Markkula and Sormunen [12]. A journalist has to write an article about the influence of drinking alcohol on driving. Of course, she does some investigations. She collects news paper articles about accidents, scientific reports, television commercials broadcasted on behalf of the government, and interviews with policemen and medical experts.

After the article has been written, she has to illustrate it with one or more photos. She searches in the publishers' photo archives, and probably tries the archives of some stock footage companies as well. The selection of "good" photos from the candidate set is very subjective, and depends mainly on visual and emotional attributes like "shocking", "funny", and so on.

### 1.1.2 Watching a TV program

Large digital video libraries will become more and more publicly available as a result of recent technology developments in digital video, Internet, and computers. The presentation of already recorded TV programs is possible. This implies the storage and use of huge collections of TV programs in digital libraries. Consider a viewer who wants to see a movie. Sometimes she may be able to identify the movie precisely by providing the title and the name of the director. Another time the viewer may not be so sure. She is, however, able to define the type of movie (e.g., adventure). If the library "knows" her taste, "knows" the movies she has already seen, then some sensible suggestions can be made to her. Still another time the viewer intends to explore science fiction, a type of movie unfamiliar to her. However, her friend Cathy is very familiar with science fiction. So, she states that she would like to see a science fiction movie her friend Cathy favors.

### 1.1.3 Searching on the Web

Finding relevant information on the World-Wide Web is often a frustrating task, partly due to the unstructured character of the data involved. Consider the Australian Open web-site (see http://www.ausopen.org/) that contains multimedia objects like text-fragments, images, and videos. These multimedia data show the latest results of players competing at this international tennis tournament. We would like to access the Australian Open site in a user friendly way using terms like player, match, and profile. Related to these entities are attributes, like a player's name, photo, age, and history, etc. Furthermore, interesting events can be extracted from the multimedia data. Think of players approaching the net or smashing the tennis ball. The integration of conceptual terms and interesting events delivers the necessary ingredients to effectively answer a content based query such as "*Give information about female American tennis players and include video-segments showing the player going to the net*".

## 1.2 Retrieval problem

Retrieval of multimedia data is different from retrieval of structured data. Retrieving data from a (relational) database is rather "easy". The database structure is given and using a language like SQL a user can specify which data she requires. Suppose that there is a relation which keeps information about employees:

        EMPLOYEE (Name: char(20), City: char(20), Photo: image)

Selecting employees living in the city of Amsterdam results in a query in which the condition WHERE City = "Amsterdam" appears. Use is made of the fact that the city of Amsterdam is identified by the text "Amsterdam". A problem arises when you want to select employees having a certain value for the attribute Photo: specifying an image value is practically impossible. So, for attributes with data type image, sound, video, etc. the "normal" way of retrieving data does not work. *This book concentrates on techniques that enable retrieval of multimedia data.* We start with taking a more detailed look at various types of multimedia data.

## 1.3 Characteristics of Media Data

What are the characteristics of text, audio, image, and video? It would take a lot of space to describe these media. In this introduction we confine ourselves to briefly giving some basic characteristics.

### 1.3.1 Medium

The general meaning of medium is a means to communicate. Here we define a medium to be a type of information representation, like alphanumeric data, audio, images, and video. Alphanumeric data are the data normally occurring in SQL-like databases containing numeric and alphabetic (text/string) data. Media types like audio, video, and image have traditionally analog representations. We are interested in digital representations and further on we pay some attention to conversion of analog to digital data.

### 1.3.2 Static versus Dynamic Media

Media types can be classified according to the relationship with time, which leads to two classes of media types: *static* and *dynamic* (or *time continuous*).

Static media do not have a time dimension, dynamic media do. Examples of static types are alphanumeric data, images, and graphics. Audio, animation, and video are examples of dynamic types. Presenting dynamic media puts time requirements. When the human eye sees a video played at a rate of at least 25 frames a second, then it perceives a smooth movement. Playing back music puts even stronger requirements: only playback rates in a very strict region make sense. Other rates are perceived as unnatural.

### 1.3.3 Multimedia

Multimedia refers to a collection of media types used together. (Notice that a collection may have only one member.) At least one of the media types must be non-alphanumeric. As stated before we are not interested in analog audio or video representation: we deal with digitized, computer readable representation. In this book we concentrate on images, video, and speech, but we also devote a chapter to text only. Text may contain alphanumeric data only. The term "multimedia" is mostly used as an adjective in phrases like multimedia information, multimedia system, and multimedia applications. We use the term *multimedia object* to refer to multimedia data to which a certain meaning has been attached, like a video of a football match Ajax–Arsenal, or an image of a Van Gogh painting.

### 1.3.4 Representation of Multimedia Data

Multimedia data are often represented in an analog way. Below we briefly discuss the problem of obtaining a digital representation.

**Text**

Plain text consists of alphanumeric characters. Optical character recognition (OCR) techniques are applied to convert analog text to digital text. The most common digital representation of characters is the American Standard Code for Information Interchange (ASCII). For each character seven bits are needed (often eight bits are used, where the eighth bit is reserved for a special purpose). Notice that Chinese characters need more space. The required storage space for a text document is equal to the number of characters. A text document of say 15 pages of about 4000 characters requires 60 kilobytes. This is quite moderate.

Structured text documents are becoming more and more popular. Such a document consists of titles, chapters, sections, paragraphs, and so on. A title may be presented to the user in a format different from a paragraph or a sentence. Standards like HTML [20] and XML [19] are used to encode structured information.

There are some techniques, e.g., Huffman and arithmetic coding [23], to compress text, but as storage requirements are not too high, the compression techniques are in general less important for text than for multimedia data.

**Audio**

Audio is caused by air pressure waves having a frequency and amplitude. When the frequency of the waves is between 20 to 20,000 Hertz a human hears a sound. For example, elephants are able to hear wider ranges. Besides frequency, also the amplitude of a wave is important, see Figure 1.1a (Figure 1.1 has been taken from Lu [11]). A low amplitude causes the sound to be soft.

How to digitize these pressure waveforms? First, the air wave is transformed into an electrical signal (by a microphone). This signal is converted into discrete values by processes called *sampling* and *quantization*. Sampling causes the continuous time axis to be divided into small, fixed intervals, see Figure 1.1b. The number of intervals per second is called the sampling rate. The determination of the amplitude of the audio signal at the beginning of a time interval is called quantization. So the continuous audio signal is approximated by a sequence of values, see Figure 1.1c. If the sampling rate is high enough and the quantization is precise enough the human ear will not notice any difference between the analog and digital audio signal. The process just described is called analog-to-digital conversion (ADC); the other way around is called digital-to-analog conversion (DAC).

To give an indication of storage requirements, consider a CD-audio using 16 bits per sample, having 44,000 samples per second and two (stereo) channels. This gives rise to about 1.4 Mbit per second required storage capacity. This is a lot, so compression techniques are welcome. To compress sound within the entire audible range of 20 kHz a masking technique is often used. The idea is that one sound can make it impossible to hear another as is the

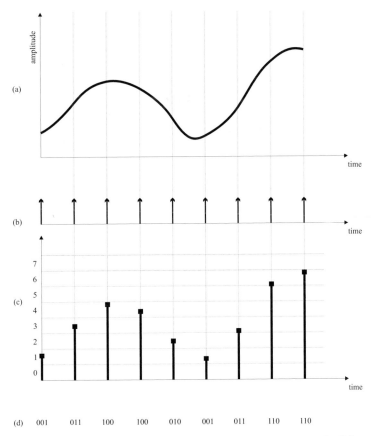

**Fig. 1.1.** Analog-to-digital conversion: (**a**) Original analog signal; (**b**) sampling pulses; (**c**) quantization; (**d**) digitized values.

case with a loud and a soft sound. The soft sound is supposed to be masked. Because masked sounds are not audible, they can safely be discarded. For speech (frequency lower than 7 kHz) other techniques are available. One technique uses the fact that low frequency speech is more important than high frequency. The coding accuracy has to be accordingly.

Moving Pictures Expert Group, abbreviated as MPEG, is a standardization group of ISO aimed to develop standards for coded representation of moving pictures, associated audio, and their combination for storage on devices (e.g., CD-ROMs) as well as telecommunication channels, e.g., LANs. MPEG has defined many standards, among others MPEG-Audio [18]. MPEG-audio is a general audio compression standard that exploits among others masking.

**Image**
Digital images can be obtained by scanning (analog) photos and pictures using a scanner. A scanner works according to the same principles as the ADC for

audio: the analog image is approximated by a rectangle of small dots. In digital cameras the ADC is built in. Another source of digital images is formed by the frames of a digitized or digital video.

Images can be in gray-scale or in color. An image displayed on a screen consists of many small dots or picture elements (pixels). To describe the gray-scale of a pixel we need say one byte of eight bits. For a color pixel we need three colors (e.g., Red, Green, and Blue) of one byte each. So, for a rectangular screen we can compute the amount of data required for the image using the formula

$$A = xyb$$

where $A$ is the number of bytes needed, $x$ is the number of pixels per horizontal line, $y$ is the number of horizontal lines, and $b$ is the number of bytes per pixel. For a screen with $x = 800$, $y = 600$, and $b = 3$ we get $A = 1.44$ Mbyte.

This amount of data is quite substantial, so compression is needed. Image compression is based on exploiting redundancy in images and properties of the human perception. It appears that pixels in a certain area are often similar; this is called *spatial redundancy*. Think of the yellow sand on a beach or the blue of a sky on a sunny day. Humans looking at images are tolerant regarding some information error or loss meaning that the compressed image does not need to exactly represent the original image. A compressed image with some error may still allow effective communication. Notice that this does not hold for alphanumeric data, where exact match is used for selecting data.

Several compression techniques are available, among others transform coding [5], and fractal image coding [10].

## Video

A digital video consists of a sequence of frames or images that have to be presented at a fixed rate. Digital videos can be obtained by digitizing analog videos or directly by digital cameras. Playing a video at a rate of 25 frames per second gives the user the illusion of a continuous view. It takes a huge amount of data to represent a video. For example a one second video with image size of 512 lines and 512 pixels per line, 24 bits per pixel and 25 frames per second amounts to $512 \times 512 \times 3 \times 25 = 19$ Mbytes of storage. Imagine what it takes for a movie of one hour. So, compression techniques are a must!

In general the image compression techniques can also be applied to the frames of videos. The same principles as with images are used: reducing redundancies and exploiting human perception properties.

Besides spatial redundancy we also have *temporal redundancy*. This means that neighboring frames are normally similar. This redundancy can be removed by applying the motion estimation and compensation where each image is divided into fixed-size blocks. For each block in the current image the most similar block in the previous image is determined and the *pixel difference* is computed. Together with the *displacement* between the two blocks, this difference is stored and if needed transmitted. This is in general more efficient than manipulating the current block by itself. (By the way: shot detection in a video uses the same pixel difference: as soon as this pixel difference is high a shot change is supposed to be detected.) Using compression a gain of a factor 10–100 can be achieved, which is quite substantial.

MPEG-1 [3], MPEG-2 [4], and MPEG-4 [9] deal with coding of video data of up to a speed of 1.5, 10, and 40 Megabits per second respectively. The intention of MPEG-1 is to code VHS quality video; MPEG-2 is an extension of MPEG-1 and provides high quality audio-visual encoding. MPEG-4 covers storage, transmission, and manipulation of multimedia data. It provides tools for decoding and representing atomic units of image and video objects, called "video objects", like a person in an image. While MPEG-1 and MPEG-2 perform pixel-based coding, MPEG-4 bridges the gap to object-based coding. Object-based coding makes content-based indexing and retrieval of multimedia data achievable.

## Summary of Storage Requirements

The storage requirements (without compression) of some media can be roughly estimated in the following way:

| | |
|---|---|
| a book of 500 pages | 2 Mbytes |
| 100 color images | 144 Mbytes |
| 1 hour of CD audio | 635 Mbytes |
| 1 hour of video | 68.4 Gbytes . |

## 1.3.5 Language for Composite Multimedia Documents

Multimedia documents contain data of different types. A scientific paper may consist of text, figures, and tables. A financial document on the Internet may have, besides text, also a spoken message and/or a video. There have been developed languages to describe "real" multimedia objects, e.g., SGML [1] together with HyTime [14]. We briefly describe the above mentioned language XML.

XML is an international standard and derived from SGML. The language enables the description of structured information; the description is independent of the presentation of the information. With the help of XML the type of a text document can be defined in a Document Type Definition (DTD). A document is "marked up" according to a DTD and an XML processor can check whether a document satisfies the type definition of the corresponding DTD. If true, the document is said to conform to the DTD. The DTD deals only with the structure of documents. To govern the presentation of documents that conform to a DTD, we relate structured elements of a DTD to output specifications. This happens in a separate specification expressed in the language DSSSL [6]. Roughly speaking the specification can be compared with the style sheet of an MS-Word document.

## 1.4 Metadata of Multimedia Objects

Let us return to the example in which we tried to find all employees having
a certain value for attribute Photo. The type of attribute Photo is image.
The question arises: how to search for images, or, in general, for multimedia
objects? Analyzing all employee photos one by one is mostly no option as it
takes too long. The standard way is to add information that describes in one
way or another the multimedia object; we call this information *metadata*. Of
course, these metadata have to be stored somewhere. So, instead of searching
for a multimedia object directly, we search for the metadata that have been
added to it. To be valuable in searching for multimedia objects, metadata
have to satisfy certain requirements:

- a description of a multimedia object should be as complete as possible;
- storage of the metadata must not take too much overhead; and
- comparison of two metadata values has to be fast.

Below we distinguish several kinds of metadata.

### 1.4.1 Descriptive Data

Descriptive data give some format or factual information about the multimedia object. Think of author name, creation date, length of the multimedia
object, used representation technique, and so on. There is a standard for descriptive data called Dublin Core [8] that gives many possibilities to describe
a multimedia object. Let us assume we are looking for a certain movie and
we know the name of the director and the year of release. Then we can address the metadata and formulate an SQL query in which this knowledge is
represented as conditions in the WHERE-clause.

### 1.4.2 Annotations

Text annotation is a textual description of the contents of the object. Think of
text added to photos in an album. Annotation can be a free format description
or a sequence of keywords. Text is added mostly manually making it time consuming and expensive. Another disadvantage of annotation is its subjectivity
and incompleteness. Later on we elaborate on so-called information retrieval
techniques. These techniques can be used to find multimedia objects based
on text annotation. The techniques are powerful and much used, especially
in combination with techniques addressing the content of multimedia objects
directly.

Besides text, also structured concepts can be used to describe the contents of multimedia objects [24]. This results in a kind of Entity-Relationship
schema, which gives concepts, their relationships to each other and to multimedia objects. The advantage is that use can be made of query languages with
an SQL like power. This can be a useful approach, especially in the realm of
a certain company where a tight control of the schema can be realized. Conceptual annotation is manual, so, again, slow and expensive.

### 1.4.3 Features

Now we turn our attention to approaches which try to derive characteristics from the multimedia object itself. These derived characteristics are called *features*. To describe features a kind of language is needed. MPEG-7 [13] is by now the most important standard. In Chapter 2 we treat MPEG-7 in some detail. The process to capture features from a multimedia object is called feature extraction. This process is often performed automatically, sometimes however with human support. Two feature classes are distinguished, namely low-level and high-level features.

### Low-Level Features

*Auto Extracted from image via usual process*

Low-level features grasp *data patterns and statistics* of a multimedia object and depend strongly on the medium. Low-level feature extraction is performed automatically. Let us start with the well-known text documents. Which "content" can be derived automatically? During the indexing process, words like "the", "it", "a", etc. are neglected: they do not bear any relevance for the meaning of the document. In Chapter 4 the indexing process will be explained. The result is essentially a list of keywords with frequency indicators, which is supposed to describe the content of the text document.

An audio signal can be represented by an amplitude–time sequence: for each sample value the air pressure is quantified. The amplitude belonging to the air pressure of silence is represented as 0, an air pressure higher than the silence pressure means a positive amplitude, and a lower air pressure implies a negative amplitude. We derive some low-level features from this amplitude–time sequence, among others average energy (indicates loudness of signal), zero crossing rate ZCR (indicates the frequency of sign change in signal amplitude), and silence ratio. A low silence ratio often indicates music, while a high ZCR variability often indicates speech. The Discrete Fourier Transform (DFT) of the amplitude–time representation is also used to derive low-level features. In Chapter 7 more attention is paid to these features.

What about images? When processing images you can count the number of pixels that have a color in a certain color range, giving rise to so-called *color histograms*. We can use color histograms to distinguish images. In an image also *spatial relations* may hold: we observe a spatial relation when, e.g., a blue area appears above a yellow area in a beach photo. If an image has many dark spots neighboring light spots, then it has a high score regarding the feature *contrast*. Many other features (e.g., shape, circularity) have been defined [7]. Chapter 5 deals with images.

Videos are sequences of images, so low-level features of images also apply to video. Video is a continuous medium and has as such a *temporal dimension*. Let us define a shot as a sequence of images taken with the same camera position. The end of a shot can be determined by computing the pixel difference between subsequent images. As soon as the pixel difference between two images is higher than a certain threshold we assume to have observed a shot change. Chapters 8, 9, and 10 cover video.

Note: Domain knowledge helps a ton in analysis - Domain knowledge is vital
Consider Beach example

## High-Level Features

Low-level features often have not too much meaning for the end user. Consider for instance images. What does a color histogram really mean? Much green may indicate many things: a golf course, or maybe a forest? With high-level features (or high-level concepts) we mean features, which are meaningful for the end user, like forest or golf course. There is obviously a gap between low and high level features. This gap is called the *semantic gap*. High-level feature extraction attempts to bridge this gap and tries to recognize concepts that are meaningful for the user.

An important part of this book tries to answer the question: How can we derive high-level features from low-level features? Low-level features in a text document are keywords. Luckily enough, keywords have a strong relationship with concepts in the human mind. When a document contains words like "football", and "referee" then this gives an indication of the content of the document.

It also appears that in speech recognition much progress has been made. For many languages reasonable speech to text translators have been built. Suppose we know that a certain data source contains speech. Extractors can automatically derive low-level features from speech and apparently translators successfully bridge the gap between low-level features on one hand and words and sentences on the other.

In areas like images, non-speech audio, and video deriving concepts from low-level features is in general not possible. Focusing on a special application domain fosters progress. For instance, consider videos of football matches. Observing a loud sound coming from the crowd and a round object passing a white line, followed by a sharp whistle, often indicates a semantically interesting concept: a goal. A combination of low-level features may imply a high-level feature (see also Chapters 9 and 10).

## 1.5 Schematic Overview of MIRS

We deal with a system that stores and retrieves multimedia objects. In this book we concentrate on the retrieval part, which is the reason that we call such a system a multimedia information retrieval system (MIRS). In Figure 1.2 we give a schematic overview of a MIRS. It shows that arriving multimedia objects are archived while metadata are extracted and stored in a so-called metadata server or index. A user poses queries in a certain way and with the help of metadata from the index an answer set is composed. But, things are not always that simple: querying has *vague* aspects. Sometimes, the user knows what she is looking for but is not able to formulate it. It may happen that a user does not know exactly what she is looking for, but she will know when she sees the right result. The user operates more or less like a woman looking for a dress in a shop. This kind of querying multimedia data is supported by a blend of browsing and searching steps. Searching and browsing result in a list of multimedia objects that are sent to the user where it can be viewed or played.

Below we treat the parts of a MIRS in more detail.

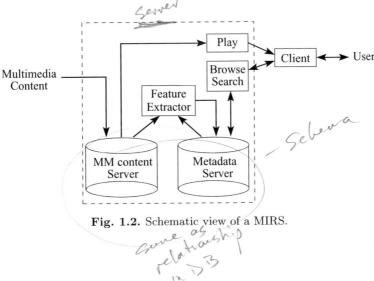

**Fig. 1.2.** Schematic view of a MIRS.

### 1.5.1 Archiving

The main characteristics of multimedia data that influence the architecture of a MIRS are that they are voluminous and that visible or audible delays in their playback are unacceptable. Hence, accessing multimedia content poses fundamentally different requirements in comparison to ordinary data. Therefore, there often is a strict separation between the "raw" multimedia content, be it audio, video, or other documents, and the metadata describing it. The multimedia content is managed separately in a special multimedia content server. At storage time a multimedia object gets an identification that can be used in other parts of the MIRS. Topics like compression and protection have to be dealt with. In this book almost no attention will be paid to compression.

### 1.5.2 Feature Extraction (Indexing)

Metadata are extracted from an incoming multimedia object. Metadata contain annotations and descriptions of the multimedia content, and features extracted from content.

The extraction process is also sometimes called *indexing*. Metadata play a dominant role in retrieval of multimedia objects, so it is important that retrieval of metadata is efficient. Moreover, as the metadata can be voluminous by itself, compact storage is also required. For example, the content of text documents may be indexed by a sorted list of keywords. These keywords together may require a lot of space.

**Extraction Dependencies**

Metadata, especially features, not only depend on the raw data of a multimedia object, but also on each other. Consider for example a content-based video search system that allows the user to search for net playing or shortest/longest rallies in tennis matches [2]. One can imagine the following steps to be taken for the required annotation of the video objects with start and end times of net playing and games:

- The video object is segmented and for each segment a key frame is chosen.
- Dominant color and other low-level features are extracted for the key frames.
- Based on the low-level features of the key frames, the segments are classified into shots of the playing field, audience and close-ups.
- From the playing field shots, the position of the player is detected in each frame.
- Another detector then extracts body-related features for the player like eccentricity, orientation, positions of the arms relative to the body, etc.
- It is then determined where rallies and net playing starts and ends.

In this example, each step presupposes the results of one or more previous steps to be available. The subsystem which controls the automatic feature extraction has to take care of these dependencies and use them to call algorithms and evaluate rules in the right order.

**Incremental Maintenance**

Complicating the task of the feature extraction subsystem further, the metadata stored in the database may reflect only the current status in an evolving environment. There are several possible sources of change.

- Multimedia objects may be modified. Upon modification of a multimedia object, features previously extracted from this object need to be invalidated and re-extracted. Note that this is a recursive process, because features that depend on other invalidated features, need to be invalidated and re-extracted as well.
- Detectors (feature extractors) may be modified. If an algorithm is improved (or a bug fixed), features generated by the previous version need to be invalidated and re-extracted (again recursively).
- The output/input dependencies between features may be modified. Any feature that is generated based on dependencies that have changed, needs to be invalidated and re-extracted.

Since feature extraction is an expensive process and the number of multimedia objects and features handled may be huge, it is often not feasible to simply do the feature extraction all over again when a number of such changes have occurred. A feature extraction architecture like ACOI [22] as shown in Figure 1.3 analyzes the dependencies and reruns only those extractions which

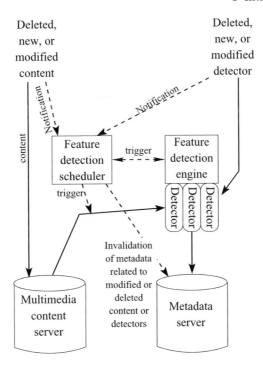

**Fig. 1.3.** ACOI feature extraction architecture.

are affected by the change. Any insert, delete, or modification of multimedia content or detector results in a notification to the feature detector scheduler. It invalidates the appropriate metadata and triggers the various detectors to (re-)extract features for multimedia objects in the right order. In this way, a complete rerun, including unnecessary reruns of expensive algorithms, is prevented and the database is maintained incrementally.

### 1.5.3 Searching

An SQL query on a relational DBMS precisely describes the information need of a user. The result of processing the query exactly satisfies the description. In other words, there is an *exact match* between specification by the user and result issued by the SQL system. In a multimedia environment this is normally not the case. How to describe a multimedia object, e.g., a photo, in a search condition? We are unable to specify the bits defining the photo. Maybe we can use low or high level features or some annotation that is added to the photo? Multimedia queries are *diverse*: the user can specify queries in many different ways. In Figure 1.2 the arrow from the client into the system indicates the issued query.

We distinguish two cases of specifying an information need, a direct and an indirect case. In the direct case the user specifies the information need by herself. In the indirect case she relies on other users. These cases are sometimes called pull and push respectively. See Figure 1.4 for an overview. Below we discuss the possible querying scenarios.

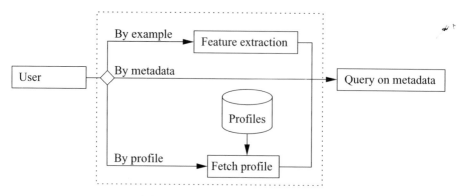

**Fig. 1.4.** Composition of query.

**Queries Based on Profile**
Let us start with the *push case*, which is also called collaborative searching. In the push case users expose their preferences in one way or another. These preferences are stored in the MIRS as a *user profile*. Suppose a user wants to buy a New Age CD, but is not certain about her taste. She trusts, however, the taste of a friend. Using the profile of the friend, the MIRS searches for CDs and returns results to the user who makes her choice.

In the *pull case* the user may exploit each of the four kinds of metadata described before, and also combinations of these. Indexes allow the MIRS to find corresponding multimedia objects. Below we describe briefly the four query types including the so-called query by example.

**Queries Based on Descriptive Data**
Queries can be based on format and factual information about a multimedia object. As an example consider a query about all movies with DIRECTOR = "Steven Spielberg".

**Queries Based on Annotations**

As shown before, annotations can be text based, but also based on concepts. Let us address text based annotations. Queries can be a set of keywords or a text in natural language. An example query can be: "Show me the movie in which Tom Cruise marries Jennifer Lopez". In this case a set of keywords is derived from the query. The set of keywords is compared with the keywords occurring in text annotations of movies and similarity is computed according to information retrieval techniques (see later on).

**Queries Based on Features**

These queries are also called content based queries as the features are derived
(semi-)automatically from the content of the multimedia object. Low and high
level features can be used. We are all familiar with querying text documents by
issuing a few keywords which characterizes the documents we are looking for.
Another example query might be: "Give all photos with a color distribution
like THIS" (THIS indicates a given photo!). Or "Give me all football videos
in which a goal occurs between the $75^{th}$ and $90^{th}$ minute". In the latter query
the high-level feature "goal" must be known to the MIRS.

**Query by Example (Search)**

Suppose you want to see photos of beach scenes. A way to indicate that is
showing an example photo of a beach scene hoping that the MIRS is able to
find other ones. The MIRS extracts all kinds of features from the example
object. In fact, the resulting query is a query based on features.

**Similarity**

In multimedia retrieval the concept of similarity is important. *Similarity* describes the degree to which a query and a multimedia object of the MIRS are
similar. Similarity is calculated by the MIRS and is based on metadata of the
multimedia object and the query. Similarity tries to approximate the value or
relevance of a multimedia object for the user. In Figure 1.5 we briefly describe
the retrieval process.

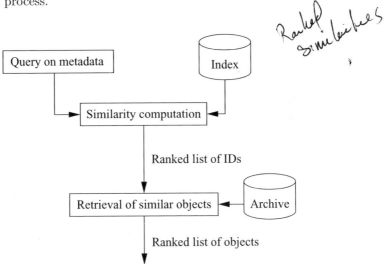

**Fig. 1.5.** General retrieval model.

The output is a list of multimedia objects. Normally it is a *descending ordered
list*, the ordering criterion being the similarity value computed by the MIRS.

The list can be very long. As users normally do not have much patience it is very important that the most relevant objects are high on the output list. Otherwise the users might miss them. The final judgment (relevant or not) belongs always to the user. A problem is, however, that human judgment is subjective and even context dependent. So, it may happen that the computed similarity is high, while the user does not consider the object relevant.

**Relevance Feedback**
Users often do not know exactly what they are looking for, which causes a problem with respect to query formulation. An interactive approach can help to alleviate this problem. By specification or by issuing an example, the user formulates a starting query. The MIRS composes a result set and the user judges the output by saying relevant/not relevant to objects. The MIRS uses this *relevance feedback* to improve the retrieval process. In Figure 1.6 relevance feedback is pictured.

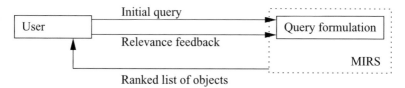

**Fig. 1.6.** Relevance feedback.

In a query you can of course combine the types mentioned here. If videos have text annotations, then queries based on text annotation and video features can be formulated.

**1.5.4 Browsing**
As stated before users often may not be able to precisely specify what they want. They can, however, recognize what they want when they see it. This phenomenon underlies relevance feedback, but also allows a process called browsing. Browsing multimedia objects means scanning through those objects. Browsing often exploits hyperlinks which lead the user from one object to the other. As soon as the MIRS shows an object, the user can judge its relevance and proceed accordingly. As objects tend to be huge often small representative "icons" are displayed in browsing mode. See also the next subsection.

There are several ways to obtain a starting point for browsing. One way is to start with a query that describes the information need as good as possible. Another way is to ask the system for a starting point. When browsing does not end up in a satisfying result, the user asks for another starting point, and so on. Finally, a third way is to classify objects in one way or another, e.g., on topic. Topics may have subtopics, and so on. This classification can be exploited by the user to obtain a sensible starting point.

### 1.5.5 Play: Output Presentation

A MIRS returns an (ordered) list of multimedia objects. First, the system has to determine whether the user has the right to see the objects. Now we enter the realm of digital rights management DRM (see also Chapter 12). Let us assume that the user has the necessary rights, so presentation may start. In general, the objects are huge. Moreover, the number of objects in a result set is often large. So the question arises how to service the user as good as possible.

Of course, the user interface should be able to present all kinds of multimedia data. Besides text, this means also audio, video, and images. To deal with the size of objects, the MIRS has to take measures. Presenting the whole object is out of the question, but the user still has to get a perception of the content of the object. The problem is to extract and present essential information for users in order to continue browsing and selecting objects. The familiar way for text documents is to give a title of the document with some additional information about the content: a kind of summary, or the places in the document where the query keywords occur. Summarizing audio is not that easy. From a song you can select a tune or the start. For images this means that the MIRS constructs and presents small summaries of images (called thumbnails). But how to summarize a video? We can cut a video into scenes and we can choose from each scene a prime image. Together these images give an impression of the video. Other techniques are available as well.

In many settings, multimedia content is accessed by many users through a network. Especially for audio and video, there are special requirements regarding smooth real-time playing. It is not acceptable when parts of the screen do not correspond with the rest, and that audio and video do not synchronize or that the screen is blank for short periods. Furthermore, it is usually not acceptable that a user has to wait for an audio or video file to be completely downloaded before it can be played. Therefore, a multimedia content server is often equipped with support for *streaming*. The content is sent to the client at a specific rate and, except for buffering, played directly. With current network technology, glitch-free streaming data is hard to deliver, because:

- An audio or video stream is in fact a stream of packets. This stream cannot, however, be delivered as a continuous stream of packets, but only as many individual packets that compete equally with other applications for network resources.
- The large number of packets needed to deliver audio or video consumes a huge amount of disk, bus and network resources.
- A shared Ethernet network card can drop packets due to transmission timeouts in heavy network traffic.

Measures to deal with such problems are:

- Using switched Ethernet instead of shared Ethernet establishes a dedicated link to each client.

- Disk and bus problems in the content server itself can be dealt with by using striping. An audio or video object is stored on multiple disks in a fragmented way such that reading consecutive fragment means accessing many disks at the same time.
- For glitch-free enjoyment of audio or video, it is necessary that all available frames are actually played. Skipping frames during play-back is a common technique for graceful degradation in quality when resources become scarce like insufficient network bandwidth or temporary congestion.

When the amount of multimedia content and/or number of client requests grows larger than can be handled by one server system, scalability problems come into play. The multimedia content can be fragmented over several content servers. A logical component in between client and server is needed to divert client requests to the corresponding server. To deal with the problem of too many clients, video content can be replicated over different servers. A similar intermediary component is needed for load balancing.

Sometimes presentation of multimedia objects is accompanied by advertisements, banners, and the like. A user may specify that she is not interested in those data. Of course, these wishes have to be met. Chapter 11 concentrates on user interaction meaning querying, browsing, and output presentation.

## 1.6 Quality of an MIRS

To compare relational database management systems, efficiency is often taken as a criterion. How fast are certain important queries answered? The underlying assumption is that correct results are obtained by all competing systems. Matters are more complicated for MIRSs as in general the results to a certain query are not equal. In other words, different MIRSs compute different result sets. The users have to decide how relevant these results are. Remember, the user determines the relevance and not the system! So, how to compare MIRSs?

The effectiveness of a system is mostly expressed in *recall* and *precision*. Let $r$ be the number of relevant documents retrieved by the system, $n$ the number of documents retrieved, and $R$ the number of relevant documents in the considered collection. Then recall is defined as the fraction of the relevant objects that is actually retrieved, which is $r/R$. Precision is the fraction of the objects retrieved that appear to be relevant, which is $r/n$.

The concepts of recall and precision come from the information retrieval society. Based on these concepts, this society defined an approach to evaluate Information Retrieval systems (IR systems). The Text REtrieval Conference (TREC) [15] is a conference where IR systems are evaluated. First of all, a set of text objects is selected. Then a set of queries is defined that has to be applied to the object set. All IR systems are requested to process the queries. Often, each IR system also indicates the degree to which this object is similar to the user request. The collective results are judged by humans whether they are relevant for the queries or not. Finally, TREC determines a measure to which the IR systems are compared and a judgment of the IR systems is computed.

In the meantime TREC has tracks involved in evaluating MIRSs [16, 17]. So now queries involving audio, video, and other media types are defined, a collection of multimedia objects is obtained, and so on. Chapter 13 addresses the problem of evaluating MIRSs.

## 1.7 Role of DBMSs

Multimedia data strongly differ from structured alphanumeric data. We have proposed an MIRS to deal with multimedia objects. As is known, (relational) DBMSs have been defined to handle large amounts of structured, alphanumeric data. Can a DBMS be helpful to implement an MIRS? Before answering that question we first summarize some differences between multimedia objects and structured, alphanumeric objects:

- Multimedia objects are in general huge in size.
- Continuous, multimedia objects have a temporal dimension.
- The meaning of multimedia objects is often unclear and at least subjective.
- Multimedia objects lack obvious semantic structure.
- To capture the meaning of multimedia objects, metadata have to be derived.

A DBMS has a schema that gives the structure to which the data in the database have to conform. For collections of multimedia objects it is mostly impossible to define such a schema. Moreover, a DBMS is based on the exact match paradigm, which does not apply to an MIRS. So, query formulation and query processing is essentially different. To make things worse, a DBMS is suitable to present structured, alphanumeric results, but not to present multimedia data with continuous aspects. So, a MIRS cannot be mapped simply onto a DBMS.

A DBMS can, however, be useful to manage a part of a MIRS, namely the metadata that play an important part in capturing the meaning of multimedia objects. Brief textual annotations, a color histogram, the average pitch level of an audio signal, all these data can be described by structured, alphanumeric data. So a DBMS could be used to manage metadata. This does not go, however, without problems: current DBMSs have to be extended. For example, to store and access color histograms efficiently, a DBMS must offer access and storage structures for multidimensional data. Today, many DBMSs do not offer those structures.

## 1.8 Role of Information Retrieval Systems

Information retrieval systems have a long history. These systems have been designed and used to allow storage and retrieval of text documents. Text documents form an important information source in most organizations. Think of libraries containing books, letters, manuals, and so on. IR techniques can be used to query such libraries. Text can, however, also be used to annotate multimedia objects like images and videos. Therefore the same IR techniques can be used to retrieve multimedia objects. Text also results when a speech recognizer processes speech. Consider a video in which speech is transformed to text. These videos can be searched for later on using conditions applied to spoken text. So, IR techniques can be useful to support multimedia retrieval. Think, e.g., of query formulation, similarity computations, and evaluation of systems.

## 1.9 Organization of the Book

The book consists of 13 chapters.

In this introductory chapter, we have given a schematic description of an MIRS. In Chapter 2 we sketch languages to describe various types of metadata, namely Dublin Core, RDF, and MPEG-7/MPEG-21 [21]. The descriptions will be a starting point for mapping of metadata on database structures. During indexing metadata are stored in a DBMS. At query time a MIRS exploits these metadata to compose the result set.

Low-level features are not suitable for searching directly. Pattern recognition tries to derive a high-level description of the multimedia data. Chapter 3 introduces various methods of pattern recognition and shows what role these methods play in multimedia content analysis. As such this chapter plays a central place in the book. For example, hidden Markov models, unsupervised learning and pattern clustering, and dimension reduction are nicely described.

Chapter 4 deals with retrieval of text documents. The indexing process is described briefly. Mathematical formulas to compute similarity between a text document and a query are explained and formulas are compared.

Chapter 5 concentrates on analysis of static images. This results in a description of the content of the image. A hierarchy of data representation (pixels, points, line segments, and so on until objects) is used as a guideline. Not only image analysis, but also the other way around is covered: find images based on a description which may be abstract or based on an example. We also cover some underlying mathematics.

Chapter 6 provides generative probabilistic models for text and image retrievals. Such kinds of models offer a concise description of the (visual) characteristics of the document, which is useful in a retrieval setting.

Speech indexing is the topic of Chapter 7. Speech recognition is a pattern matching problem and the solution heavily rests on training. An architecture of speech recognizers will be given. The mathematics behind a recognition process get significant attention.

Chapter 8 proposes a generic approach for semantic video indexing. It combines some successful methods into a semantic value chain. The approach is based on the video production process covering notions of content (e.g., words in audio modality), style (e.g., camera distance), and context (e.g., news setting).

High-level features of video play an important part in Chapter 9. The chapter deals with a tennis case and shows how low-level features are used to automatically derive high-level features like smash, service, etc. A spatial-temporal and a probabilistic approach are described and even combined. Also, some experiments give an indication of retrieval effectiveness.

A common way to add semantics to multimedia data is to annotate with text. Chapter 10 discusses, again, an automatic approach for high-level feature derivation. High-level concepts (e.g., start of race, passing) which occur in Formula-1 car races are introduced. Low-level features are derived from videos and fed into a (dynamic) Bayesian Network to derive concepts. Parameters, i.e., conditional probabilities, of the network are obtained by a training process. Various networks are used in experiments and results are given.

Chapter 11 focuses on interaction. How to input a query and how to issue relevance feedback? How does a user keep control during browsing? Which techniques can a MIRS use to implement collaborative searching? These and other questions are covered together with issues regarding the presentation of output results.

Users may not freely retrieve all kinds of multimedia objects. Most objects are protected against unauthorized access. This is the area of digital rights management (DRM). When a user accesses a certain object, however, her privacy must be guaranteed as well. In Chapter 12 various techniques regarding protection of content and privacy are described. Attention is paid to the balance between protection of content and privacy of user.

Finally, Chapter 13 elaborates on the important topic of evaluating multimedia retrieval systems. Efficiency is of minor importance in this chapter. Most attention is devoted to effectiveness. As an MIRS deals with many media types, evaluation becomes much more complicated than in the context of traditional text documents. Questions to be answered are: which media to include, which queries to be selected, which collections of multimedia objects to choose. Notice that a query may address many media. The TREC conferences, well-known in the information retrieval community play an important part. TREC has extended its task to include also multimedia data.

# References

1. ISO/IEC JTC 1/SC34. JTC 1/SC 34 – Document Description and Processing Languages. http://www.jtc1sc34.org/.
2. Henk Ernst Blok, Menzo Windhouwer, Roelof van Zwol, Milan Petkovic, Peter M. G. Apers, Martin L. Kersten, and Willem Jonker. Flexible and scalable digital library search. In *Proceedings of 27th International Conference on Very Large Data Bases (VLDB), September 11–14, 2001, Roma, Italy*, pages 705–706. Morgan Kaufmann, September 2001.
3. L. Chiariglione. Short MPEG-1 description. http://www.chiariglione.org/mpeg/, June 1996. ISO/IECJTC1/SC29/WG11 N MPEG96, Final.

4. L. Chiariglione. Short MPEG-2 description. http://www.chiariglione.org/mpeg/, October 2000. ISO/IECJTC1/SC29/WG11 N MPEG00, Final.

5. R.J. Clarke. *Transform Coding of Image.* Academic Press, 1984.

6. J. Farreres. *The DSSSL Book: An XML/SGML Programming Language.* Springer, September 2003.

7. Myron Flickner, Harpreet Sawhney, Wayne Niblack, Janathan Ashley, Qian Huang, Byron Dom, Monika Gorkani, Jim Hafner, Denis Lee, Dragutin Petkovic, David Steele, and Peter Yanker. Query by Image and Video Content: The QBIC System. *IEEE Computer*, 28(9):23–32, September 1995.

8. Dublin Core Metadata Initiative. Dublin core metadata element set, version 1.1: Reference description. http://www.dublincore.org/documents/desc/, 1997.

9. R. Koenen. MPEG-4 overview. http://www.chiariglione.org/mpeg/, March 2002. ISO/IECJTC1/SC29/WG11 N4668, Jeju meeting.

10. G. Lu. Fractal Image Compression. *Signal Processing: Image Communication*, 4(4):327–343, October 1993.

11. G. Lu. *Multimedia Database Management Systems.* Artech House, Inc., 1999.

12. M. Markkula and E. Sormunen. Searching for photos – journalists'practices in pictorial IR. In *The challenge of image retrieval*, Newcastle upon Tyne, UK, 1998. University of Northumbria.

13. J.M. Martinez. Overview of the MPEG-7 standard. http://www.chiariglione.org/mpeg/, July 2002. ISO/IEC JTC1/SC29/WG11 N4980, Klagenfurt meeting.

14. S. Newcomb, N. Kipp, and V. Newcomb. The HYTIME, Hypermedia Time based Document Structuring Language. *Communications of the ACM*, 34(11):67–83, 1991.

15. National Institute of Standards and Technology (NIST). TREC Overview. http://trec.nist.gov/overview.html.

16. National Institute of Standards and Technology (NIST). TREC Tracks. http://trec.nist.gov/tracks.html.

17. National Institute of Standards and Technology (NIST). TREC Video Retrieval Evaluation. http://www.itl.nist.gov/iaui/894.02/projects/trecvid.

18. D. Pan. A tutorial on MPEG/Audio Compression. *IEEE Multimedia*, 2(2):60–74, 1995.

19. W3C. Extensible Markup Language (XML). http://www.w3.org/XML/.

20. W3C. HyperText Markup Language (HTML). http://www.w3.org/MarkUp/.

21. W3C. Resource Description Framework (RDF). http://www.w3.org/RDF/.

22. M.A. Windhouwer. *Feature Grammar Systems – Incremental Maintenance of Indexes to Digital Media Warehouses.* PhD thesis, Universiteit van Amsterdam, Amsterdam, The Netherlands, November 2003.

23. I.H. Witten, A. Moffat, and T.C. Bell. *Managing Gigabytes: Compressing and Indexing Documents and Images.* Morgan Kaufmann Publishing, San Francisco, 2nd edition, May 1999. ISBN 1-55860-570-3.

24. R. van Zwol. *Modelling and searching web-based document collections.* Ph.D. thesis, University of Twente, Enschede, The Netherlands, April 2002.

# 2

# Languages for Metadata

Ling Feng[1], Rogier Brussee[2], Henk Blanken[1], and Mettina Veenstra[2]

[1] University of Twente
[2] Telematica Instituut

## 2.1 Introduction

### 2.1.1 What is Metadata?

The term *meta* origins from the Greek word $\mu\epsilon\tau\alpha$, meaning *after*. The word *Metaphysics* is the title of Aristotle's book coming after his book on nature called *Physics*. This has given *meta* the modern connotation of a nature of a higher order or of a more fundamental kind [1]. Literally, *metadata* is "data about data". It can be any descriptive information about other data sources that is used to aid the organization, identification, representation, localization, interoperability, management, and use of the data [1, 14, 17].

Well-known examples of metadata are data such as title, author and year of publication that libraries use to organize their books and to make them retrievable. Disk space on personal computers is ever growing in size and is used to store entertainment data. As a consequence of the popularity of digital photography and gadgets such as MP3 players and iPods many people have become librarians (of files) themselves. Every owner of a substantial collection of digital music finds out the importance of good metadata. At first, the collection is restricted and it is easy to find songs on the basis of their filename only. When, however, the collection expands good metadata become indispensable. The problem is to keep the metadata on the personal computer up-to-date: CDs do not electronically contain metadata like title, genre, and so on. Therefore, software for ripping CDs such as Windows Media Player and iTunes use music databases on the Internet to store metadata of songs on the personal computer. The software recognizes the album by its unique fingerprint consisting of the duration of all the songs on the album in sequence or of each separate song based on its unique acoustic properties [11]. Once recognized, the appropriate metadata of songs and albums can be retrieved from the Internet databases. These music databases are never perfect, no matter whether they are maintained by professionals or by communities of volunteers. Spelling mistakes are made, the choice of genre is disputable or wrong etc., resulting in inconveniences for the owners of digital music collections. For instance, suppose someone wants to select all the songs from the artist Pink from a collection of music. Unfortunately, for one of Pink's albums her name is spelled as "P!nk" while for the others it is spelled as "Pink". In this case a query "Pink" might not retrieve all of Pink's songs. Still, for owners of large collections of digital music, partly incorrect metadata are much better than nothing.

In a multimedia context, metadata is used to deal with the complexity of describing, managing, and using multimedia data. Some of this complexity comes from the following facts:

- Multimedia objects are very large in size, making them expensive to transmit and process, and difficult to scan and search for specific contents.
- Multimedia objects are usually stored in compressed formats, making the extraction of subsets of information difficult.
- Multimedia is content-rich but in a way that is not easy to summarize in textual, or structured forms.
- There are emergent properties of multimedia data that require significant amounts of processing and expertise before they are accessible, but which, once extracted can easily be put in a structured format. For example, it requires a serious amount of processing to segment a video in shots but once done it is easy to store the first and last frame number.
- Multimedia can have a complex creation process both from a technical and an economical or rights perspective.
- Multimedia can have many different components for which the mutual relation is important.

The complexity of multimedia itself is reflected in its metadata, demanding various kinds of metadata description and presentation methods [3]. However, metadata still helps to overcome the complexity of multimedia by providing structure [3]. Data is often unusable without knowing its structure. In particular for multimedia it is often better to consider the whole package, media data together with its metadata, as one media object. This means that there is a certain amount of arbitrariness in where the data ends and the metadata begins: what is metadata for one application may be data for another. For example, the metadata of a music collection can be put in a database by an application to organize music collections. When a media player queries for this metadata it will look to the database system like any other query for data.

The subject of this chapter is languages, extra structure, to handle the metadata themselves. This means that in this chapter it will sometimes *seem* as if the metadata are the "real" data. The relation with the content lies in the semantics of the metadata, and that semantics is only very partially encoded in the data itself.

## 2.1.2 Why Do We Need Metadata?

To better understand the relation between data and metadata we have to understand what metadata is used for [14, 3, 15, 17]. We can summarize the key functions as follows [1]:

- Description – to describe and identify data sources. Such descriptions allow to create indexes and catalogs, etc., thereby improving access to them.
- Querying – to formulate queries. While people are very good at recognizing pictures or sounds, it is hard to formulate queries as sounds or images. Even though research has been in query by humming or drawing, widely used systems allow users to use titles, descriptions, authors, composers, tag labels, etc. to formulate a query. In fact querying for author or subject is also useful for texts even though they can be searched full text.
- Administration – to provide information to help manage and administrate a data source, such as when and how it was created, and who can legally access it.
- Preservation – to facilitate data archival and preservation like data refreshing and migration, etc.
- Technical – to indicate how a system functions or metadata behaves, such as data formats, compression ratios, scaling routines, encryption key, and security, etc.
- Use – to indicate the level and type of use of data sources like multiversion, user tracking, etc.

In Chapter 1 we mention some scenarios of multimedia usage: journalism, media selection for radio and TV channels, and searching the Web. The list of applications can be easily extended, for instance e-commerce with personalized advertising, control of traffic by surveillance cameras, and Internet shopping while searching for clothes that one likes. All these applications have in common that querying and updating metadata play a major part.

## 2.1.3 Semantics of Metadata and Metadata Languages

Since metadata serves as an interface to the content proper, it is important that different parties have a shared understanding of the meaning of the metadata. This is the reason that metadata languages exist. By using a metadata language with a standardized semantics, we can make applications interoperable with content from different sources. In this context the word 'semantics' has a computer technical and a conventional layer. For example, if we have an author as a metadata element for books, then on a technical level this might be standardized as a null terminated string of ASCII characters. Technically this allows the publisher of this book to fill the author metadata element with any string of ASCII characters he likes, for example with his own name. If an application is conforming to the standard it will have no problems displaying the author. Both the publisher and the application held to the technical part of the standard. However, on the convention level the publisher clearly breached the rule that the author element is supposed to be used for the author of the book.[3] Metadata describes the relation between the media content and the outside world and a metadata language must enable this.

### 2.1.4 Relation to Other Chapters

The Description function mentioned in Section 2.1.2 is important for retrieval purposes. Metadata as explained in Chapter 1 concentrates on this function. The current chapter introduces the reader to some of the languages that people use to give metadata descriptions of content. It describes three representative languages for metadata, which can facilitate the specification and management of multimedia contents including text, image, video, and audio to be addressed in subsequent chapters of the book.

### 2.1.5 Outline

First, we give a brief discussion of metadata in the life cycle of multimedia objects in Section 2.2.1 We present three prominent metadata schemas, namely Dublin Core, Resource Description Framework (RDF), and MPEG Multimedia Metadata Standard. These languages are described in Section 2.3, 2.4, and 2.5, respectively. Dublin Core has been designed to deal with what has been called descriptive metadata in Chapter 1. RDF offers facilities to describe the semantics of Web resources. MPEG-7 and MPEG-21 are geared towards multimedia objects of type text, audio, image, and video. The last two sections summarize the chapter and give some hints for further reading.

## 2.2 Metadata in Multimedia Retrieval Systems

### 2.2.1 Metadata in the Life Cycle of Multimedia Objects

A multimedia object undergoes a life cycle consisting of production, organization, searching, utilization, preservation, and disposition. Metadata passes through similar stages as an integral part of these multimedia objects [1, 10]:

- Creation. Objects of different media types are created often generating data of how they were produced (e.g., the EXIF files produced by digital cameras) and stored in an information retrieval system. Associated metadata is generated accordingly for administrating and describing the objects.
- Organization. Multimedia objects may be composed of several components. Metadata is created to specify how these compound objects are put together.

---

[3] This example is not as far fetched as it might seem. Many Word documents have metadata that names the author of the template style file as author of the document, and publishers routinely distribute such style files!

- Searching and retrieval. Created and stored multimedia objects are subject to search and retrieval by users. Metadata provides aids through catalog and index to enable efficient query formulation and resource localization.
- Utilization. Retrieved multimedia objects can be further utilized, reproduced, and modified. Metadata related to digital rights management and version control, etc. may be created.
- Preservation and disposition. Multimedia objects may undergo modification, refreshing, and migration to ensure their availability. Objects that are out-of-date or corrupted may be discarded. Such preservation and disposition activities can be documented by the associated metadata.

### 2.2.2 Classification of Metadata

Metadata directly affects the way in which objects of different media types are used. Classifying metadata can facilitate the handling of different media types in a multimedia information retrieval system. Based on its (in)dependence on media contents, metadata can be classified into two kinds, namely *content-independent* and *content-dependent* metadata [15, 16]:

- Content-independent metadata provides information which is derived independently from the content of the original data. Examples of content-independent metadata are date of creation and location of a text document, type-of-camera used to record a video fragment, and so on. These metadata are called descriptive data in Chapter 1.
- Content-dependent metadata depends on the content of the original data. A special case of content-dependent metadata is *content-dependent descriptive metadata*, which cannot be extracted automatically from the content but is created manually: annotation is a well-known example. In contrast, *content-dependent non-descriptive metadata* is based directly on the contents of data (see the next paragraph for examples).

Some authors divide content-dependent non-descriptive metadata into two categories [15, 16]:

- Domain-independent metadata. This type of metadata captures information presented in the data without using domain specific concepts. For example, the color histogram of an image. We call these metadata low-level features in Chapter 1.
- Domain-dependent metadata. This type of metadata uses domain specific concepts, like land cover [9], the GIS domain or fly outs in a Formula 1 car race. We call these metadata high level features in Chapter 1.

## 2.3 Dublin Core (DC)

The Dublin Core Metadata Element Set arose from the first OCLC/NCSA Metadata workshop in 1995 held in Dublin, Ohio (USA).

The continuing development of the Dublin Core and related specifications are managed by the Dublin Core Metadata Initiative (DCMI), an organization dedicated to prompting the widespread adoption of interoperable metadata standards and developing specialized metadata vocabularies for describing resources that enable more intelligent information discovery systems [8].

### 2.3.1 Dublin Core Elements

*Formalization of how to categor unstructured data.* (handwritten annotation)

The Dublin Core is a framework for descriptive metadata. It standardizes the way bibliographical information that you can find in the colophon of many books such as title, author and date of publication, is structured and described. It was developed to be simple, concise, extensible, and semantically interoperable for cross-domain information resource description. An information resource can be anything, but the primary application domain is books, pictures, articles, videos, Web pages etc, for which there are human consumers and producers. The Dublin Core element set has achieved significant acceptance within diverse sectors including libraries, universities, healthcare, governmental agencies, museums, and commercial organizations. The set and its supporting documentation have been translated into at least 24 languages to date. It is widely used in applications such as word processors, video editors or content management systems. Since the title and author of a resource is rather obviously useful information, there are many examples of other metadata schemes where (a subset) of the metadata can be translated to and from (a subset of) the Dublin Core set.

The Dublin Core metadata element set has 15 core elements [7]:

- **Contributor** – an entity (person, organization) responsible for making contributions to the content of the resource
- **Coverage** – The extent or scope of the content of the resource, for example the jurisdiction under which a legal text is relevant
- **Creator** – An entity primarily responsible for creating the content of the resource
- **Description** – A textual description of the content of the resource
- **Date** – A date of an event in the life cycle of the resource, typically its date of publication. Recommended practice is to use an encoding scheme, such as the W3CDTF profile of ISO 8601
- **Format** – The physical or digital manifestation of the resource. Recommended best practice is to use a controlled vocabulary such as mime-type.
- **Identifier** – An unambiguous reference to the resource within a given context. Recommended best practice is to use a formal identification system, for example an url or the ISBN number of a book
- **Language** – A language of the intellectual content of the resource. Recommended practice is to use the two-letter code[4] of RFC 3066 (ISO 639)

---

[4] Some very small languages have three-letter codes.

- **Publisher** – An entity responsible for making the resource available, typically the publisher
- **Relation** – A reference to a related resource. Recommended best practice is to use an identifier in a formal identification system
- **Right** – Information about rights held in and over the resource, typically statements about copyrights and other intellectual copyrights
- **Source** – A reference to a resource from which the present resource is derived. Recommended practice is to use a formal identification system
- **Subject** – A topic of the content of the resource. Typically, the topic will be represented using keywords, key phrases, or classification codes. Recommended practice is to use a controlled vocabulary
- **Title** – A name given to the resource
- **Type** – The nature or genre of the content of the resource described. Recommended best practice is to use a controlled vocabulary such as the DCMI type vocabulary that contains terms such as Text (books, articles, newspapers, etc.), InteractiveResource (Webpage, applets, etc.), MovingImage (films, videos, etc.), PhysicalObject, Event, etc.

Here is a small example of a Dublin Core record for a Web resource:

```
Identifier = "http://dublincore.org/"
Title = "Dublin Core Metadata Initiative -- Home Page"
Description = "The Dublin Core Metadata Initiative Web site"
Date = "2006-12-18"
Format = "text/html"
Language = "en"
Creator = "The Dublin Core Metadata Initiative (DCMI)"
Contributor = "The Dublin Core Usage Board"
Type = "InteractiveResource"
```

The example shows a particular encoding of the information model described above. Other encodings exist. For example the <meta> XHTML tag is commonly used to embed Dublin Core data in Web pages.

The simplicity of the Dublin Core framework makes it easy to mix with existing practices and applications and this has been a very important factor in its success. On the other hand the standard is not very precise. For example, the date field may refer to the date of "some event" in the content creation process. Moreover, the standard is standardizing the attributes, but the values are just strings for which at best a recommended practice exists. This means that the attributes can be full text searched or presented for human consumption (two *very* important applications) but that interoperability in a cross organizational or cross domain setting may be restricted to using common conventions.

The Dublin Core standard has been extended in several directions. There are several standards that incorporate (part of) the Dublin Core as a baseline standard for the description of media objects often after some minor syntactic change. For example the MPEG-7 standard, which we will discuss in Section 2.5, and the IEEE-LOM, which is used in educational environments, use Dublin Core this way.

There are also the so-called Dublin Core qualifiers [6] that allow us to be more precise about the attributes of the core set. For example, the broadly defined "date" attribute can be qualified to a "date.created", "date.modified" to express the creation, respectively the modification date of a document. The DCMI has defined some controlled vocabularies that are recommended to be used for the value strings of the attributes.

Finally, there has been push to do something about the lack of formal meaning of the value fields. For example, the Dublin Core author field is commonly filled with the name of the author. However, there are many different ways to write a persons name, with or without their first name, with initials before or after their name, etc. This would be solved if the value of the author attribute would be a typed "Person" data structures that can themselves have different attributes both of value types like strings and integers and dates and other data structure objects. This point of view is useful not just for media objects, but for many other things that benefit from being described. A popular language for expressing this in an open environment like the Web is the so-called resource description framework (RDF), which we will describe in Section 2.4. The Dublin Core and its qualifications therefore have been given a binding to RDF that allows to describe more of the intended semantics of the standard, of both attributes and values, in a more precise and formal way.

## 2.4 Resource Description Framework (RDF/RDFS)

RDF is a family of World-Wide Web Consortium (W3C) specifications which for our purposes includes the RDF schema language RDFS. As stated in the W3C documents [20, 22], RDF is originally based on the syntax format XML and intended to represent metadata about Web resources, such as the title, author, copyright, and modification date of a Web document. However, it was later realized that RDF is in fact a language for expressing metadata statements about "things" called resources having "attributes" called properties. Once this became clear, it also became clear that XML only provides one among several possible notations. Many RDF applications will therefore use the RDF language and a concrete RDF schema, which is itself expressed in RDF. The schema and the RDF language are used together to annotate concrete resources like Web pages with concrete properties like their author. For example the Dublin Core framework discussed in Section 2.3 can be expressed in an RDFS schema that defines the Dublin Core attributes as RDF properties, one for each attribute. This combo is then used to denote Dublin Core metadata statements about concrete Web pages, documents or video's with an RDF syntax. Thus, the RDF language is one level of abstraction above that of Dublin Core.

Below we describe the most important elements of RDF. It will become clear that RDF has similarities to the binary relational and the object oriented data model.

### 2.4.1 Basic Information Model

The basic concept of RDF is a statement which we can think of as a binary predicate. Figure 2.1 shows a graph model for an RDF statement, consisting of a node for the subject, a node for the object, and an arc for the predicate, directed from the subject node to the object node.

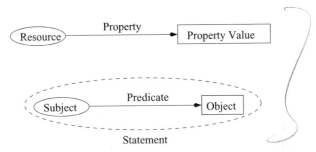

**Fig. 2.1.** Graph model for an RDF statement.

A collection of such statements builds up an directed labeled graph, by identifying nodes with the same labels. RDF is nothing more than a syntax to define such labeled directed graphs, and any semantics that RDF statements have is defined in terms of this graph. Conversely by cutting a graph in elementary edges we can denote any labeled graph with RDF. The one caveat here is that RDF has special syntax for compactly describing class hierarchies which means that some RDF statements will actually generate several edges in the graph. We will see this when we discuss classes and subclasses.

In the following, we exemplify the basic ideas behind the RDF model using the turtle syntax [2]. This is an RDF/XML equivalent large subset of the N3 language specified by Dave Beckett. The N3 language [12] was designed by Berners Lee to express RDF in a human friendly and compact syntax and is therefore well suited for a book like this. Unlike the XML syntax it is mostly self explanatory. More detailed descriptions of RDF/XML syntax can be found at the W3C Website [20, 22].

We introduce the following terminology:

- A *Resource* is anything that exists in RDF.
- A *Property* is a specific attribute, property or a relation used to describe a resource.
- A *Property Value* is the value of a property for a certain resource. There are two types of property values: literals of type integer, string, XML string, date, url, etc., and resources.

32      Ling Feng, Rogier Brussee, Henk Blanken, and Mettina Veenstra

- A *Statement* or *triple* is the assertion that a resource (called the *subject*) has an attribute or property (called the *predicate*) with a certain value resource (called the *object*). A triple is itself a resource.

The RDF language specifies that resources and properties (nodes and edges) are labeled by URI's. URI's are used as Web wide unique identifiers where uniqueness is helped by the fact that it is considered impolite to choose a URI in a domain that you do not control.

**Example 1**

Assume a simple English expression:
*"http://www.example.org/index.html has as creation-date August 16, 1999"*.
The RDF graph for this expression, after assigning a URI to the creation-date property, is shown in Figure 2.2.

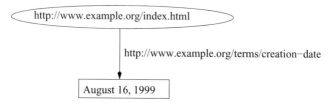

**Fig. 2.2.** An RDF graph for the example statement (Example 1).

The same information can also be put in Table 2.1. We observe that the subject as well as the property happens to be a resource, while the object is a literal of type date.

**Table 2.1.** An RDF statement example (Example 1).

| | |
|---|---|
| Subject (Resource) | http://www.example.org/index.html (resource) |
| Predicate (Property) | http://www.example.org/terms/creation-date (resource) |
| Object (Property Value) | 1999-09-16 (date value) |

The corresponding RDF/Turtle statement is the following *triple*:

```
<http://www.example.org/index.html>
<http://www.example.org/terms/creation-date>
"1999-08-16"^^<http://www.w3.org/2001/XMLSchema#date>.
```

The subject, predicate, and object are thus simply listed with as much whitespace as we want, ending the triple with a dot. A resource or property can be denoted by putting angle brackets around its URI label. A string is put between quotes, a non-negative integer is written in decimal form without quotes, and for more uncommon data types such as a date, we borrow simpletypes

2 Languages for Metadata

from XML schema [23] and denote it with a string in the XML schema defined format followed by two carets and the data type. Because it is annoying to read and write long URI's we can abbreviate this by declaring and using some namespaces and write exactly the same triple as:

```
@prefix exterms: <http://www.example.org/terms/>.
@prefix xs: <http://www.w3.org/2001/XMLSchema#>.

<http://www.example.org/index.html>
            exterms:creation-date "1999-08-16"^^xs:date.
```

**Example 2**

An RDF graph consisting of multiple statements (i.e., one resource with several properties and corresponding values at the same time) can be represented through multiple RDF triples. For example, consider Figure 2.3.

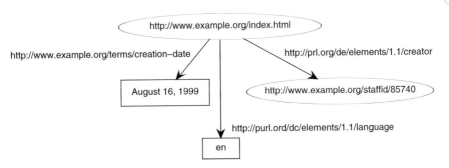

**Fig. 2.3.** An RDF graph containing multiple statements (Example 2).

We recognize that the graph is a group of statements about the same resource `http://www.example.org/index.html`. We can use the following turtle code to denote the RDF graph:

```
@prefix dc: <http://purl.org/dc/elements/1.1/>.
@prefix exterms: <http://www.example.org/terms/>.
@prefix xs: <http://www.w3.org/2001/XMLSchema#>.

<http://www.example.org/index.html>
        exterms:creation-date "1999-08-16"^^xs:date.
<http://www.example.org/index.html> dc:language "en".
<http://www.example.org/index.html>
        dc:creator <http://www.example.org/staffid/85740>.
```

Because it is common that the subject is repeated, the three triples may be abbreviated to:

```
<http://www.example.org/index.html>
        exterms:creation-date "1999-08-16"^^xs:date;
        dc:language "en";
        dc:creator <http://www.example.org/staffid/85740>.
```

This example also shows how Dublin Core metadata is expressed using RDF
*together* with the RDF encoded Dublin Core metadata vocabulary. In Section 2.4.3 we will see how to define such a vocabulary as a predefined metadata
schema

For this simple example we will also give the RDF/XML notation corresponding to the graph in Figure 2.3. This can be skipped at first reading, but
is useful for understanding RDF/XML files. We should warn that there are
several ways of expressing an RDF graph in XML.

```
1.  <?xml version="1.0">
2.  <rdf:RDF
        xmlns:rdf="http://www.w3.org/1999/02/22-rdf-syntax-ns#"
3.      xmlns:dc="http://purl.org/dc/elements/1.1/"
4.      xmlns:exterms="http://www.example.org/terms/">
5.      <rdf:Description
            rdf:about="http://www.example.org/index.html">
6.          <exterms:creation-date
             rdf:datatype =
                 "http://www.w3.org/2001/XMLSchema#date"
            >1999-08-16</exterms:creation-date>
7.          <dc:language>en</dc:language>
8.          <dc:creator
             rdf:resource =
                 "http://www.example.org/staffid/85740"/>
9.      </rdf:Description>
10. </rdf:RDF>
```

Lines 1–4 are general "housekeeping" necessary to indicate that these lines
contain RDF/XML content. Line 1 states that the following code can be
parsed by an XML parser and specifies what XML version is used. This parser
understands angle brackets and namespaces but as far as its concerned RDF
is just like any other XML file. Line 2 and line 10 indicate that we deal
with RDF text. The terms the syntax of the RDF/XML are made available
by declaring the XML namespace http://www.w3.org/1999/02/22-rdf-syntax-
ns#. All tags prefixed with rdf: are part of this namespace. Likewise in line 3
we associate the prefix exterms: with the namespace identified by the URI
http://www.example.org/terms/. Lines 5–9 specify the statement in Figure 2.3.
In line 5, the rdf:Description element defines the subject resource whose label is
the value of the *about* attribute. Elements inside the rdf:Description element are
interpreted as properties. Line 5 provides a *property* element exterms:creation-
date. The content of this property element is the object (i.e., the property

value) of the statement, the literal 1999-08-16. Because we have added the
rdf:datatype = "http://www.w3.org/2001/XMLSchema#date" as an attribute
the value is interpreted as a date rather than the plain string. In line 8 the
object of the dc:creator property is itself a resource whose URI has to be
spelled out including its long namespace.

### 2.4.2 Structured Property Values: Blank Nodes

Sometimes the property value is structured. For example we may want to
describe the author of a document as a person which has a first and a last
name, an email address, telephone number, homepage etc. However, people
do not have a natural URI that identifies them in a globally unique way. RDF
uses the concept of a blank node to solve this problem.

### Example 3

Figure 2.4 shows an RDF graph saying that *"The document* http://www.w3.
org/TR/rdf-syntax-grammar *has a title* 'RDF/XML Syntax Specification'
*and has an editor. The editor has a name* 'Dave Beckettt' *and a home page*
http://purl.org/net/dajobe/".

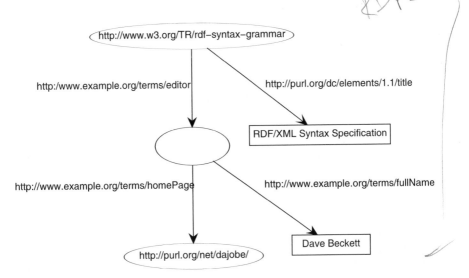

**Fig. 2.4.** An RDF graph containing a blank node (Example 3).

Leaving out the namespace declarations (which are as in Examples 1 and 2)
we can express this in RDF/turtle as follows:

```
<http://www.w3.org/TR/rdf-syntax-grammar>
        dc:title "RDF/XML Syntax Specification";
        exterms:editor [ exterms:fullName "Dave Beckettt";
                        exterms:homePage
                            <http://purl.org/net/dajobe/>].
```

Alternatively we can give the Dave Beckett node a name which has scope in the RDF file in which it is defined. The blank node is given a name in the pseudo namespace _:

```
<http://www.w3.org/TR/rdf-syntax-grammar>
        dc:title "RDF/XML Syntax Specification";
        exterms:editor _:dave.

  _:dave exterms:fullName "Dave Beckettt";
         exterms:homePage <http://purl.org/net/dajobe/>.
```

The advantage of the latter construction is that the _:dave node can be used in several other triples just like a node with a URI label. For example, Dave Beckett has also written the turtle specification. We can express this fact by adding the triples:

```
<http://www.dajobe.org/2004/01/turtle>
        dc:title "Turtle - Terse RDF Triple Language";
        exterms:author _:dave.
```

Note that the corresponding RDF graph is not a tree, since it has two root nodes. Many metadata descriptions start out as trees. This is an efficient data representation but the world is simply not always organized as a tree.

There are several ways to represent graphs containing blank nodes in RDF/XML [22]. The simplest way to create a blank node is to create an <rdf:Description> element without an rdf:about attribute.

### 2.4.3 RDF Schema

RDF provides a way to express simple statements about resources via named properties and values. However, it provides no means for defining application-specific classes and properties associated with these classes. RDF Schema is an extension of RDF, which provides facilities needed to describe such classes and properties, and to indicate which classes and properties are expected to be used together. Note that RDF Schema itself does not provide application-specific classes and properties either. It merely provides the mechanism to describe such application-specific classes and properties [21].

### Class in RDF Schema

Class in RDF Schema is superficially like a class in an object-oriented programming languages such as Java. We can state that a resource belongs to one or more classes, and classes can be organized in a hierarchical fashion via subclass relationship [20, 21]. If we look more closely we see that a class in RDF is more like a classification mechanism for instances. No assumption is made about the structure of the instance because the instance does not have an underlying data structure.

By definition, a resource x is a member of a class C if there is a triple:

```
x rdf:type C.
```

Because rdf:type is common idiom, turtle uses the special suggestive notation:

```
x a C.
```

Classes in RDFS are themselves resources. A resource C is a class if and only if there is a triple C rdf:type rdfs:Class. Using the turtle abbreviation this becomes:

```
C a rdfs:Class.
```

The special-general relationship between two classes is described using the predefined rdfs:subClassOf property. Thus, C is a subclass of D if and only if there is a triple:

```
C rdfs:subClassOf D.
```

So far there is nothing special about rdfs:subClassOf and rdf:type. However the special-general relation is transitive. Therefore it is part of the semantics of the RDFS language that:

```
C rdfs:subClassOf D.
D rdfs:subClassOf E.
```

implies

```
C rdfs:subClassOf E.
```

Likewise, if an instance is member of a class it is a member of all its super-classes. Therefore it is also part of the semantics of RDFS that:

```
x rdf:type C.
C rdfs:subClassOf D.
```

implies

```
x rdf:type D.
```

As a consequence, the labeled directed RDF graph defined by the triples involving rdf:type and rdfs:subClassOf is the transitive closure of the labeled directed graph defined by the triples themselves.

**Property in RDF Schema**

In addition to describing the specific classes of things, RDF Schema also provides a vocabulary for describing specific properties that instances may have. In addition one can express how these properties and classes are intended to be used together. A property p is itself a resource and a resource is a property if it has rdf:type of rdf:Property (note, not rdfs:Property). Thus a property is declared by:

```
p a rdf:Property.
```

Since properties are used in triples to relate instances, the most important information about a property is the class of instances that can occur as subject and the class of instances that can occur as object. This can be stated using the RDF Schema properties rdfs:range and rdfs:domain [20, 21] respectively. More precisely it is part of the semantics of the RDFS language that:

```
p a rdf:Property;
     rdfs:domain D;
     rdfs:range R.
x p y.
```
implies
```
x a D.
y a R.
```

However, many tools to create RDF enforce that the type of x and y is already known before you can "apply" p.

Just like classes can be hierarchically organized, properties in an RDF Schema can be organized in more and less specialized properties using the predefined rdfs:subPropertyOf property. A property may be a subproperty of zero, one, or more properties. The semantics of subproperty is that:

```
p rdfs:subPropertyOf q;
x p y.
```
implies
```
x q y.
```

RDF Schema rdfs:range and rdfs:domain properties that apply to an RDF property also apply to each of its subproperties.

**Example 4**

As we have seen in Section 2.3 the Dublin Core defines the contributor attribute of a media object whose value is anybody who contributed in the life cycle of a media object. We have earlier defined an editor property that is supposed to indicate the editor role. Suppose we mean that the editor role is that of a human editor of a journal. We can express (more of) the intended semantics of the properties as follows:

```
@prefix dc: <http://purl.org/dc/elements/1.1/>.
@prefix exterms: <http://www.example.org/terms/>.

exterms:Journal a rdfs:Class;
     rdf:comment "the class of journals".
exterms:Person a rdfs:Class;
     rdf:comment "the class of persons".
exterms:editor a rdf:Property;
     rdfs:domain exterms:Journal;
     rdfs:range exterms:Person;
```

```
rdf:comment "the person who edits the journal";
rdfs:subPropertyOf dc:contributor.
```

This mechanism has been proposed for standardization in the RDF binding of Dublin Core Qualifiers (see the end of Section 2.3.1) .

### A Vehicle RDF Schema Example

As an example outside of the metadata world consider a more elaborate conceptual schema of a *Vehicle* class hierarchy. It contains among other things classes *MotorVehicle, PassengerVehicle, Van* and *MiniVan. PassengerVehicle* and *Van* are subclasses of *MotorVehicle*, and *MiniVan* is a subclass of *Van* and *PassengerVehicle*. Property *registeredTo* applies to any *MotorVehicle* and its value belongs to the *LegalPerson* class. Property *rearSeatLegRoom_cm* applies only to instances of class *PassengerVehicle*. Its value is an integer giving the number of centimeters of rear seat legroom. The RDF Schema representation for this kind of vehicle class hierarchy and associated properties is as follows:

```
@prefix veh: <http://example.org/schemas/vehicles#>.
@prefix law: <http://example.org/schemas/law#>.
@prefix rdf: <http://www.w3.org/1999/02/22-rdf-syntax-ns#>.
@prefix rdfs: <http://www.w3.org/2000/01/rdf-schema#>.
@prefix xs: <http://www.w3.org/2001/XMLSchema#>.

xs:integer a rdfs:Datatype.
xs:string a rdfs:Datatype.

law:LegalPerson a rdfs:Class.
law:Person a rdfs:Class;
        rdfs:subClassOf law:LegalPerson.

law:name a rdf:Property;
        rdfs:domain law:LegalPerson;
        rdfs:range xs:string.

veh:MotorVehicle a rdfs:Class.
veh:PassengerVehicle a rdfs:Class;
        rdfs:subClassOf veh:Motorvehicle.
veh:Van a rdfs:Class;
        rdfs:subClassOf veh:MotorVehicle.
veh:MiniVan a rdfs:Class;
        rdfs:subClassOf veh:Van, veh:PassengerVehicle.
veh:RenaultEspace a rdfs:Class;
        rdfs:subClassOf veh:MiniVan.

veh:registeredTo a rdf:Property;
```

```
        rdfs:domain veh:MotorVehicle;
        rdfs:range  law:LegalPerson.
veh:registration a rdf:Property;
        rdfs:domain veh:MotorVehicle;
        rdfs:range  xs:string.

veh:rearSeatLegRoom_cm a rdf:Property;
        rdfs:domain veh:PassengerVehicle;
        rdfs:range  xs:integer.

veh:driver a rdf:Property;
        rdfs:domain veh:MotorVehicle;
rdfs:range  law:Person.
veh:primaryDriver a rdf:Property;
        rdfs:subPropertyOf veh:driver.
```

Note that Renault Espace is considered to be a class. After all there are many Renault Espaces driving around! Also note that it might have been useful to borrow the notion of person from another schema.

A schema like this can be used to denote that a Renault Espace owned by Lease Boys Inc. is driven by John and Mary with Mary as preferred driver. Leaving out namespaces this would become:

```
lb:leaseBoys a law:LegalPerson;
        law:name "Lease Boys inc.".
lbcar:12AB34 a veh:RenaultEspace;
        veh:registration "12-AB-34";
        veh:registeredTo lb:leaseBoys;
        veh:rearSeatLegRoom_cm 75.
lbcust:john a law:Person;
        law:name "John Doe".
lbcust:mary a law:Person;
        law:name "Mary Doe".

lbcar:12AB34 veh:driver lbcust:john, lbcust:mary;
        veh:preferedDriver lbcust:mary.
```

Note that this bit of RDF mentions instances and that the schema is effectively the language to describe them.

It is problematic to say that the Renault Espace has a legroom of 75 cm, because writing

```
veh:RenaultEspace veh:legRoom_cm 75.
```

would imply that the Renault Espace (a class of vehicles) is itself a passenger vehicle. In fact, the legroom of different Renault Espace members varies. However treating a class as an individual is common practice (or according to some, abuse). More elaborate schema languages like OWL [19] allow one, and force one, to be more precise in such matters.

### 2.4.4 Other RDF features
### Containers and Collections

Property values that are set valued can be described by RDF containers and collections. The contained resources are called *members* which may be resources (including blank nodes) or literals.

An RDF *container* is a resource that contains other resources. RDF defines three types of containers, namely, rdf:Bag a group of resources or literals possibly containing duplicates, rdf:Seq a sequence of resources possibly with duplicates where order is important, and rdf:Alt a group of resources that are alternatives [20]. A typical use of an RDF container is to express that a property value is a group of things. Note however that properties in RDF are effectively multivalued because triples with the same subject and predicate but different objects are allowed. Therefore container classes are not needed as often as one might think.

An RDF *collection*, is a resource of type rdf:List. A resource x is a member of a rdf:List L if either L rdf:first x or L rdf:rest M and x is a member of M. The predefined list rdf:Nil has no members.

### Example 5

The sentence "*The players in the tournament are Jeroen, Johann, and Maria*" can be represented using the RDF graph in Figure 2.5.

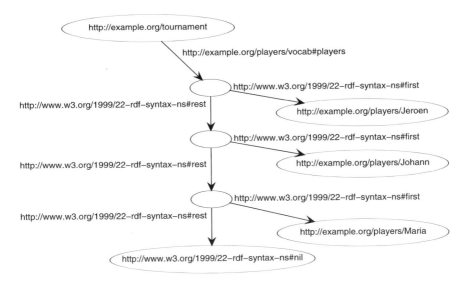

**Fig. 2.5.** An RDF collection example (Example 5).

In turtle this would be:

```
ex:tournament
    ex:players [ a rdf:List;
                 rdf:first ex:jeroen;
                 rdf:rest [ a rdf:List;
                            rdf:first ex:johann;
                            rdf:rest [ a rdf:List;
                                       rdf:first ex:maria;
                                       rdf:rest rdf:Nil]]].
```

Since this quickly becomes unreadable this can be abbreviated to:

```
ex:tournament ex:players (ex:jeroen ex:johann ex:maria).
```

### 2.4.5 Statements about Statements: Reification

RDF statements (triples) are themselves resources of type rdf:Statement The statement itself is encoded using the properties rdf:subject, rdf:predicate, and rdf:object. This is useful because for a reified statement we can state what the source is, where and when it was made etc. For example the statement:

```
ex:john ex:loves ex:mary.
```

can be reified to:

```
_:lovedeclaration a rdf:Statement;
rdf:subject ex:john;
rdf:predicate ex:loves;
rdf:object ex:mary.
```

and we can now state that this declaration of love was made on Valentine in 2000:

```
_:lovedeclaration dc:date "2000-02-14"^^xs:date.
```

John may or may not love Mary happily ever after, but a love declaration is not the same as an eternal fact.

## 2.5 Moving Picture Experts Group (MPEG)

The ISO/IEC Moving Picture Experts Group (MPEG) has developed a suite of standards for digitally coded representation of audio and video. One of these standards, MPEG-7 (Multimedia Content Description Interface, ISO/IEC 15938 [13]), addresses languages and technology for multimedia content description. MPEG-7 is a large and complex standard that includes several sub-languages and specific vocabulary for media like audio and video and the way they are segmented. Moreover, it tries to cover a wide field with vocabulary for such different aspects as rights management and image, audio, video and speech analysis.

For some parts of the standard the semantics of the standard is highly non-trivial. For example MPEG7 allows descriptions of texture of image elements by a few numerical values. These numbers will represent the coefficient in a wavelet transforms[5] of that image element. These numbers can therefore not be properly used by an application without software implementing a wavelet transform texture classification or texture generation algorithm. Writing such software requires a description of the precise model used to represent texture through wavelets. Such non-trivial semantics account for a great deal of the complexity of MPEG-7. A separate standard, MPEG-21 (Multimedia Framework, ISO/IEC 21000) [5] defines how the whole MPEG architecture including MPEG-7 and media formats such as MPEG-4 are related to each other. The sheer size and complexity of the standard has been a significant impediment to its wide adoption even though it has never been the intention that applications implement all the parts meant for specialized areas.

MPEG-7 defines the metadata elements that are used to describe audiovisual objects including still pictures, graphics, 3D models, music, audio, speech, video, and multimedia collections. Some of the main elements describe the structure of the media objects and the relationships between different components. The main elements of the MPEG-7 standard are:

- A **Description Definition Language**(DDL). The language to define the syntax of the Descriptors and Description Schemes. It is a version of XML schema [24] with some extensions to represent things like large arrays of real numbers. The DDL allows the creation of new, and the extension and modification of existing Description Schemes.
- **Descriptors** (Ds) A descriptor is a predefined vocabulary to describe an aspect of a media object. A descriptor can be used in different schemas. Hundreds of predefined DDL classes for descriptors are defined.
- **Description Schemes** (DSs) A descriptor scheme is a schema in DDL that specifies the syntactic structure for composing descriptors. A description scheme consists of other description schemes and descriptors.
- **A binary format** (BiM) A format to encode the verbose XML in a binary format which is more efficient for streaming and storage while leaving the tree structure of the XML intact.
- **System Tools** The software needed to support storage and transmission, synchronization of descriptions with contents, and management and protection of intellectual property.

Figure 2.6 shows the relationships among different MPEG-7 elements. The DDL is used to define descriptors and description schemes. Predefined descriptors are used to define more specialized description schemes in DDL. User defined schemes can also reuse other description schemes. DDL can also be used for defining completely new descriptors, effectively extending the MPEG7

---

[5] Wavelet decompositions are a clever mathematical trick to zoom into details of a pattern. They are somewhat similar to Fourier transforms.

universe. A particular media object can be annotated with metadata in an
MPEG7 document that conforms to a particular descriptor scheme. If necessary such instantiation of the descriptor scheme can then be further encoded,
packaged and transmitted by an MPEG7 aware system tool.

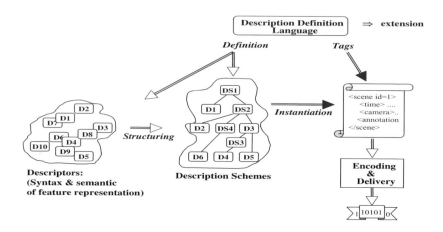

**Fig. 2.6.** MPEG-7 main elements [13].

As we can see there is a similarity between the MPEG-7 and RDF frameworks. MPEG-7's DDL provides the mechanism to create new descriptors
and descriptors scheme similar to RDFS. Metadata for a particular media
object is denoted with such a descriptor scheme and the facilities provided
by DDL. Likewise, we can have to metadata for a particular media object in an RDFS defined schema and the facilities of RDF. However unlike
RDF/RDFS, MPEG-7 provides predefined vocabulary in the form of descriptors, for concrete multimedia related domains. Indeed, RDF has strongly influenced MPEG-7, in particular the DDL. However, it was decided to base DDL
on XML schema rather than RDF because RDF was not finished when MPEG-
7 was standardized and XML tools were (and are) much wider available. Work
is being done to encode MPEG-7 in OWL, an extension of RDF [18].

Figure 2.7 shows an instantiation of a hypothetical Descriptor Scheme for
a video clip As we can see there are different Descriptors for different aspects
of the media, and for the way that the media can be decomposed in smaller
parts. Each of the parts can be annotated separately. Some of the descriptors
reuse Dublin Core for descriptive metadata. Descriptors for visual and audio
objects are defined separately using a hierarchy of elements and subelements.

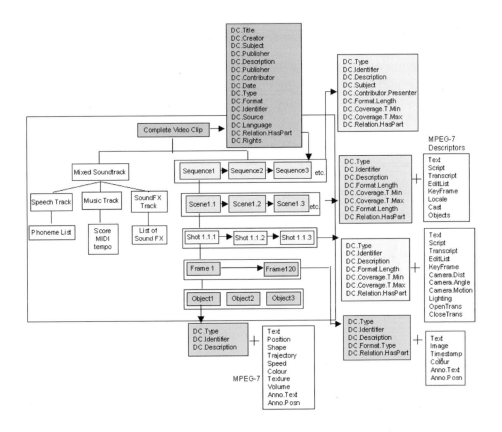

**Fig. 2.7.** Example MPEG-7 descriptor scheme.

### 2.5.1 Structure of MPEG-7 Documents

In the following (adapted from Kosch [9]), we show the flavor of MPEG-7 documents using the XML Schema based Descriptor Description Language (DDL). Note that the following description is by nature sketchy since the complete DDL defines several hundreds of types [13].

The main parts of an MPEG-7 document are a header, a root element, top level elements, and segments. The header information declares an MPEG-7 document as an XML document. In the root element <Mpeg7> the MPEG-7 namespace urn:mpeg:mpeg7:schema:2001 and the XML schema-instance and XML namespace are declared. The MPEG-7 top level element can be either a description unit or a complete description. The description of a part of the media object uses the former, that of the whole uses the latter. For example, the description of an image uses a complete description if the image is the whole media object and that of description unit if it is the illustration of a book. Complete descriptions or description units can themselves be built up out of description units that describe different aspects, e.g., the shape or color of an image.

Figure 2.8 shows the hierarchy of classes that can occur as top level description units. The term abstract means that only more specific subclasses with subelements that detail more parts can be instantiated in a concrete MPEG-7 metadata file.

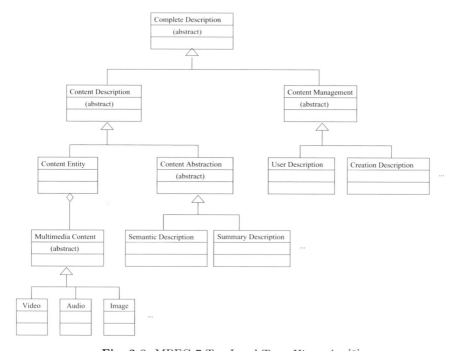

**Fig. 2.8.** MPEG-7 Top-Level Type Hierarchy [9].

Here is an example definition of a ContentEntityType in DDL:

```
<! - Definition of ContentEntity Top-level Type ->
<complexType name="ContentEntityType">
  <complexContent>
    <extension base="mpeg7:ContentDescriptionType">
      <sequence>
        <element name= "MultimediaContent"
                 type="mpeg7:MultimediaContentType"
                 minOccurs="1"  maxOccurs="unbounded"/>
```

```
        </sequence>
      </extension>
    </complexContent>
  </complexType>
```

*Segment elements* are used to describe the decomposition of a multimedia object in smaller parts. Each segment may be separately annotated, which can lead to a hierarchical description of content, where a global overview can coexist with detailed descriptions of smaller subobjects. The definition of segment depends on the medium. For streaming media we can describe the structure of the content object in temporally defined segments such as shots or songs. For visual objects, including video, there are descriptors for the visual segmentation. Each segment can be further annotated with, e.g., textual descriptions, color, texture, shape, motion or basic structure relationships and localization.

The SegmentType is the root descriptor type for describing the characteristics (e.g., creation, media, usage, semantics, text annotation, and matching hints, etc.) of segments. For more specific descriptions, types derived from SegmentType such as VideoSegmentType are used. The VideoSegmentType is a subtype of SegmentType, so it inherits all the elements of SegmentType. In addition, it has elements specific to video. Likewise the StillRegionType is used for describing an image or a two-dimensional spatial region of an image or a video frame. It extends the SegmentType in a similar fashion as VideoSegment-Type. In Figure 2.9 the segment type class hierarchy is given and in Figure 2.10 a list is given of the elements of some of these types.

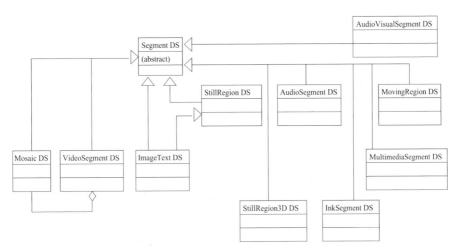

**Fig. 2.9.** MEPG-7 subclasses of the segment description schemes [9].

Some specialized visual objects such as faces have their own descriptors. Many of the descriptors only make sense as parameter input for specialized algo-

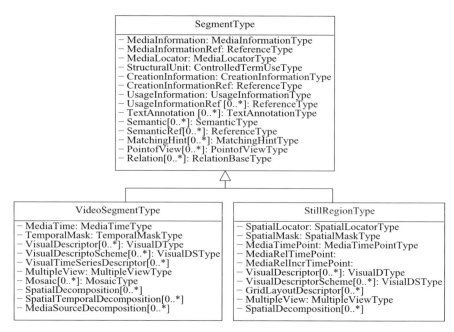

**Fig. 2.10.** MPEG-7 SegmentType and its subtypes [9].

rithms which means that their semantics is standardized together with that
of the descriptors themselves.

Audio descriptors are divided into low-level descriptors that are common
to audio objects across most applications, and high-level descriptors that are
specific to particular applications of audio. The cross-application low-level
descriptors cover *structures* and *temporal and spectral features* The domain-
specific high-level descriptors are meant to describe special types of sounds.
For example for music, musical instrument timbre, and melody may be described. Likewise, for speech there is a complete spoken content description
scheme that is meant to be output by an automatic speech recognition engine.

**Example 6**

Below is an example taken from Kosch [9] of an MPEG-7 document for a
video containing one shot, the Leaning Tower of Pisa. For clarity, white space
has been added in the body of the elements. The video is located at a certain
URL and has a title in English: "Pisa video". Moreover, some administrative
and timing information is given. We hope that the text is self explanatory:

```
<Mpeg7>
  <Description xsi:type="ContentEntityeType">
    <MultimediaContent xsi:type="videoType">
      <Video>
        <MediaLocator>
```

```
      <MediaUri>file://pisa.mpeg</MediaUri>
  </MediaLocator>
  <CreationInformation>
    <Creation>
      <Title xml:lang="en"> Pisa Video </Title>
      <Abstract>
        <FreeTextAnnotation>
          This video shows the Pisa Leaning Tower
        </FreeTextAnnotation>
      </Abstract>
      <Creator>
        <Role href=
    "urn:mpeg:mpeg7:cs:RoleCS:2001:PRODUCER">
            <Name xml:lang="en"> Anchorman </Name>
        </Role>
        <Agent xsi:type="PersonType">
          <Name>
            <GivenName> Stephan </GivenName>
            <FamilyName> Herrmann </FamilyName>
          </Name>
        </Agent>
      </Creator>
    </Creation>
    <Classification>
      <ParentalGuidance>
        <ParentRating href=
    "urn:mpeg:mpeg7:cs:FSKParentalRatingCS:2003:1"/>
        <Region>de</Region>
      </ParentGuidance>
    </Classification>
  </CreationInformation>

  <TemporalDecomposition>

    <VideoSegment id="VS1">
      <MediaTime>
       <MediaTimePoint>T00:00:00:0F25</MediaTimePoint>
       <MediaIncrDuration mediaTimeUnit="PT1N25F">218
       </MediaIncrDuration>
      </MediaTime>
      <SpatialTemporalDecomposition>
        <StillRegion>
          <MediaRelIncrTimePoint
           mediaTimeUnit="PT1N25F"> 23
          </MediarelIncrTimePoint>
```

```
            <SpatialDecomposition/>
          </StillRegion>
        </SpatialTemporalDecomposition>
      </VideoSegment>

      </TemporalDecomposition>
    </Video>
  </MultimediaContent>
</Description>
</Mpeg7>
```

## 2.6 Summary

Metadata is indispensable for effective management and use of multimedia information. In this chapter, we review three prominent metadata schemas for managing multimedia objects, namely, Dublin Core, Resource Description Framework (RDF), and MPEG multimedia metadata. The characteristics of these standards and their applications are also presented. Dublin Core concentrates on descriptive data and is widely used. RDF is in fact a general data model, so can also be used to describe metadata. MPEG-7 offers facilities detail metadata for audio-visual data. The standard is extensive and complicated. The prospective success is, however, therefore doubtful.

## 2.7 Further Reading

Some general introduction to metadata and its usage in the multimedia environment can be found at various places [1, 3, 10, 15]. Dublin Core is completely described at several Websites [4, 8, 7]. Documents related to the RDF from the W3C can be found in W3C publications [20, 22, 21]. The OWL extension of RDF is described in another W3C document [19]. For detailed description of MPEG-7 and its usage in the multimedia domain, please refer to [9, 13].

## References

1. M. Baca. Introduction to metadata – pathways to digital information. `http://www.getty.edu/research/conducting\_research/standards/intrometad%ata/index.html`, 2000.
2. D. Becket. Turtle – terse rdf triple language. `http://www.dajobe.org/2004/01/turtle`, 2004.
3. Industry Canada. Metadata searching in a multimedia database environment. `http://dopey.hil.unb.ca/Imaging\_docs/IC/index.html`, 2000.
4. S. Haigh. The Dublin Core Metadata Initiative. `http://www.collectionscanada.ca/9/1/p1-262-e.html`, December 1999.
5. K. Hill and J. Bormans. Overview of the MPEG-21 Standard. ISO/IECJTC1/SC29/WG11N4041. `http://www.chiariglione.org/mpeg/`, October 2002.

6. Dublin Core Metadata Initiative. Dublin core qualifiers. `http://dublincore.org/documents/2000/07/11/dcmes-qualifiers/`, JULY 2000.
7. Dublin Core Metadata Initiative. DCMI metadata terms. `http://dublincore.org/documents/dcmi-terms/\#H2`, 2005.
8. Dublin Core Metadata Initiative. Dublin Core Metadata Initiative – making it easy to find information. `http://dublincore.org/`, 2005.
9. H. Kosch. *Distributed Multimedia Database Technologies – Supported by MPEG-7 and MPEG-21.* CRC Press LLC, USA, 2004.
10. H. Kosch, L. Boszormenyi, M. Doller, M. Libsie, P. Schojer, and A. Kofler. The life cycle of multimedia metedata. *IEEE Multimedia*, 12(1):80–86, January/March 2005.
11. D. Lebel. Audio fingerprinting summary. *Music Information Acquisition, Preservation, and Retrieval*, 611, 2006.
12. T. Berners Lee. Notation 3 (n3). `http://www.w3.org/DesignIssues/Notation3`, 1998.
13. J.M. Martínez. MPEG-7 overview (version 9). `http://www.chiariglione.org/mpeg/standards/mpeg-7/mpeg-7.htm`, March 2003.
14. National Information Standards Organization. Understanding metadata. `http://www.niso.org/standards/resources/UnderstandingMetadata.pdf`, 2004.
15. A. Sheth and W. Klas. *Multimedia Data Management – Using Metadata to Integrate and Apply Digital Media.* McGraw-Hill, 1997.
16. V.S. Subrahmanian and S. Jajodia, editors. *Multimedia Database Systems: Issues and Research Directions*, chapter Metadata forBuilding the MultiMedia Patch Quilt (V. Kashyap, K. Shah, and A. Sheth). Springer, Germany, 1996.
17. C. Taylor. An introduction to metadata. `http://dopey.library.uq.edu.au/iad/ctmeta4.html`, 2003.
18. R. Troncy, W. Bailer, M. Hausenblas, P. Hofmair2, and R. Schlatte. Enabling Multimedia Metadata Interoperability by Defining Formal Semantics of MPEG-7 Profiles. In Y. Avrithis et al., editor, *SAMT 2006, LNCS 4306*, pages 41–55. Springer-Verlag Berlin Heidelberg, 2006.
19. W3C. Owl web ontology language overview. `http://www.w3.org/TR/owl-features/`, February 2004.
20. W3C. RDF primer. `http://www.w3.org/TR/rdf-primer/`, February 2004.
21. W3C. RDF vocabulary description language 1.0: RDF Schema. `http://www.w3.org/TR/rdf-schema/`, February 2004.
22. W3C. Resource Description Framework (RDF): Concepts and abstract syntax. `http://www.w3.org/TR/rdf-concepts/`, February 2004.
23. W3C. Xml schema part 0. `http://www.w3.org/TR/xmlschema-0/`, October 2004.
24. W3C. XML Schema part 0: Primer second edition. `http://www.w3.org/TR/xmlschema-0/`, October 2004.

Mangement of complex imagry
(Video, Audio, Imagry)

Downloading multi-Media at once allows for
sophistacked apps to run in web environment.
⮑ molti-media running in browsers.

*[handwritten: think of from perspective of merging data where do we head in DB technology.]*

# 3

# Pattern Recognition for Multimedia Content Analysis

Elena Ranguelova[1] and Mark Huiskes[2]

[1] Centrum voor Wiskunde en Informatica (CWI)
[2] Universiteit Leiden, LIACS

## 3.1 Introduction

### 3.1.1 Recognizing Patterns in Multimedia Content

This chapter looks at the basics of recognizing patterns in multimedia content. Our aim is twofold: first, to give an introduction to some of the general principles behind the various methods of pattern recognition, and second, to show what role these methods play in multimedia content analysis.

We start by diving right in by exploring two examples that give a first flavor of how pattern recognition can contribute to a better understanding and description of multimedia content.

*[handwritten: Cant handle volume till semi-automate or automate]*

**Example 1: Semi-automatic Annotation of Multimedia Content**

*[handwritten: This is where DB tech can help]*

One of the foremost uses of pattern recognition is in fulfilling the need for high-quality *metadata*, a key ingredient of successful multimedia retrieval systems. Low-level multimedia bitstreams are not suitable for searching directly, and pattern recognition is needed to obtain more meaningful and useful descriptions of the data.

Traditionally, multimedia retrieval systems have been based on manual annotations of the content. Given the typical quantities of material produced, such annotation is generally a labor-intensive, and thus also expensive, task. One may think, for example, of the BBC broadcasting company which, on a daily basis, needs to archive material of four television stations as well as a large number of radio stations. Additionally, for some programs, a single hour of broadcasting may require an archivist more than 7 hours of cataloging.

For many applications such manual annotation is not very practical, and thus we have a natural need to automate this process. And although it is currently not yet possible to design systems that annotate with the same level of detail as that of well-trained human annotator, there is nevertheless great scope for systems that provide some basic annotations automatically.

A promising approach to tackle this automatization problem is by means of a combination of pattern classification methods and carefully designed concept

*[handwritten: Creating annotation in a somewhat automatic way.]*

hierarchies. The latter serve to provide a standard for the multimedia content descriptions. One example is the large scale concept ontology for multimedia initiative, or LSCOM [23], defining about 1000 concepts divided into categories such as Activities (e.g., `walking`), Scene (e.g., `indoor`), People (e.g., `soldier`, `Pope`), Objects (e.g., `car`) and Events (e.g., `crash`).

Given such a well-defined set of concepts, the pattern classification approach to automated annotation is to design classifiers for each of the concepts in the set. In practice, this means that a small part of the multimedia collection is still annotated by hand in order to obtain a set of annotated examples to train the classifiers. Once the classifiers are trained, the bulk of the collection is then annotated automatically.

## Example 2: Surveillance and Automatic Interpretation of Multimedia Streams

Another very promising field of study is automatic activity recognition in videos. Currently, a commercially interesting example is the automatic interpretation of data from surveillance cameras, with applications such as:

- monitoring customer behavior in shops, both for security purposes, and data mining for marketing;
- smart home applications, e.g., to keep the elderly and children out of danger, or to automatically put on the lights or heating;
- various security applications, e.g., detecting suspicious behavior in parking garages or on the street, monitoring high-risk objects like nuclear power plants, airports and stations;
- detection of emotions and moods for more natural human computer interaction.

Here various pattern recognition approaches can be used. Again, detection of activities may be based on classification and supervised learning. However, more explicit *modeling* of the situation also has proven to be very useful, and has given excellent results in a number of applications.

For example, an often used approach is to model what is going on in the data stream by means of finite state descriptions. Each state corresponds to a dominant activity in the data stream. For example, the default state may be that nothing happens, e.g., somebody is walking normally. Other states correspond to less likely or unexpected events, such as an elderly person falling down, or a burglar breaking into a car. Detailed scenarios can be modeled by means of hidden Markov models and Bayesian networks. These models describe the dependencies between the states using different parameters, e.g., the state transition probabilities, the state emission probabilities etc. As before, the model parameters can be learned from a *training* set of, possibly multimodal, video sequences for example by labeling shots as "normal" and "falling".

Yet another approach would be to analyze the multimedia streams by methods of *unsupervised learning* to discover patterns without first explicitly modeling them. For example in the application of customer behavior monitoring in shops, we could observe the order in which different shelves are visited. Then analyzing the many sequences collected for all the customers, recurring spatial patterns can be clustered. This in turn may result in suggestions for improving the spatial layout of the shop.

### 3.1.2 The Pattern Recognition Process

Pattern recognition is a well-developed subject of study which has close ties to the field of machine learning. It is the study of how machines can "observe" the environment and learn to discover and distinguish interesting patterns from a possibly cluttered background. Based on these patterns some reasonable assumptions and decisions about the environment can be made.

Pattern recognition (PR) aims to classify the data (patterns) based on either a priori knowledge or on statistical information extracted from them. Roughly, a PR system consists of a sensor that gathers the data to be described; a feature extractor that computes numeric or symbolic representations (features) from the data; and a classifier which uses the extracted features to classify the patterns to suitable categories.

The sensor provides the measurements, or "raw data", from the environment, e.g., the pixels of an image provided by a digital camera. Preprocessing and feature extraction may include some signal processing such as smoothing and noise filtering. Next, while it is possible to handcraft a classifier, benchmark results have proven that better recognition accuracy is often obtained with systems that have tunable parameters that can be adjusted to correctly classify a set of given training examples. In multimedia information retrieval a wide variety of learning machines have been used, ranging from simple classical methods such as "nearest neighbors" to, for instance, the more sophisticated support vector machines. For some recognition tasks, the classifier/learner can be complemented by systems that take contextual information into account. For example, in handwriting or speech recognition applications, language models or grammars are often incorporated in the postprocessing stage.

More formally, PR systems may be subdivided by their relations between the inputs and output of the system:

- **Pattern classification/supervised learning**
  Pattern classification is based on a collection of example patterns for which the desired system output has been specified. The output is usually a class or category assigned to the patterns. Based on the collection of input–output pairs, the *training set*, the system learns a *prediction function* which can then be used to obtain the class of newly supplied (input) patterns.
  The aim of pattern classification is to provide good generalization performance from the set of example patterns. Ideally a classification method captures the true structure in the example patterns, while not overfitting

to peculiarities and coincidences. Pattern classification will be discussed in detail in Section 3.2.

- **Reinforcement learning**
  In this case no correct input-output pairs are presented; instead, the system responds to a given input pattern by generating its own output. This output is then rewarded (or punished) according to a given reward function. This allows the system to assess the appropriateness of the generated output. Reinforcement learning is usually used in a context where the inputs are perceived states, and the outputs are actions of the system. Since the system is not explicitly corrected for sub-optimal actions, an important issue is the balance between exploring new actions and the exploitation of already acquired knowledge of actions that provide a good reward.
- **Pattern clustering/unsupervised learning**
  With unsupervised learning, no feedback is given at all and the system is expected to discover natural structure in unlabeled patterns by itself, for instance by grouping the patterns into clusters. Various methods used for clustering patterns occurring in multimedia content are discussed in Section 3.4.

Recently there has also been a lot of interest in methods for semi-supervised learning. For these labeled and unlabeled examples are combined to obtain better classifiers. This is illustrated in Figure 3.1.

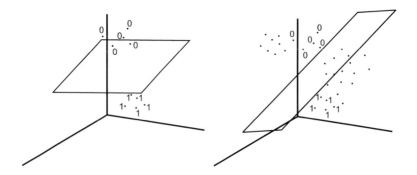

**Fig. 3.1.** Semi-supervised learning. The use of unlabeled examples (right) may improve classifier performance.

Focusing mainly on pattern classification and pattern clustering, we can subdivide the pattern recognition process in the following main stages:

1. **Pattern representation**: feature extraction and feature selection.
   In this stage the data is collected, and a feature representation for the patterns is chosen. Features for multimedia content may vary widely in type.

Feature selection may already occur at this stage and is generally desirable: the features should be as relevant as possible for the task at hand. Insights from later stages may further contribute to feature selection. Feature extraction can also take the form of transforming the features to obtain new features that are better adapted to the data.

2. **Modeling**

   Next, a learning method needs to be decided upon. This means that, explicitly or implicitly, we need to choose a model to explain the system output in terms of the available pattern features. After that, learning amounts to figuring out the best parameters of the model in order to obtain a prediction function explicitly relating the inputs to the outputs. In some applications, very elaborate models are devised to describe this relationship. An important class of models, often used in multimedia pattern analysis, are hidden Markov models. These are introduced in detail in Section 3.3. Also, very commonly, models for the prediction function are defined implicitly by the choice for a particular machine learning technique. For example, if a support vector machine method is chosen, this implies a model consisting of a certain kernel function together with a high-dimensional separating hyperplane; similarly, boosting is often used in combination with decision tree models. A number of models underlying learning methods are discussed in Section 3.2.

3. **Learning**: classification or clustering

   This is the training stage where the collected data is used in conjunction with the model to determine the prediction function or clustering. For explicit models this may take the form of Bayesian parameter estimation. The training stage often involves further dimension reduction, e.g., in the case of decision trees.

   For classification, training usually proceeds by minimizing the error on the training set, possibly regulated by a complexity penalty. This is discussed in more detail in Section 3.2. Unsupervised clustering is discussed in Section 3.4.

4. **Evaluation**

   To assess the performance of a PR system it is desirable to test the system using an independent test set. In case no such independent test set is available cross-validation may offer a good alternative. This is also discussed further in Section 3.2.2.

These stages do not always proceed independently; they may, and generally should, interact to get good performance. Two examples of such interactions are: (i) The evaluation stage may offer feedback on the training stage, e.g., straightforward training may lead to overfitting; evaluation through for instance cross-validation may regulate this tendency. (ii) The learning stage often provides new insight into which features are useful for class discrimination. This may lead to further feature selection and dimension reduction. This is discussed in more detail in Section 3.5.

### 3.1.3 Relation to Other Chapters

Many methods for object recognition (e.g., template matching, statistical shape models, image features and feature extraction) in the area of image processing are presented in Chapter 5, Image Processing. Parameter estimation (more specifically the EM algorithm) is discussed in Chapter 6, Generative Probabilistic Models. In Chapter 7, Speech Indexing, hidden Markov models are used for speech recognition. Chapter 8, Semantic Video Indexing, deals with the semantic indexing as pattern recognition problem and uses support vector machines. Chapter 9, Detection of Object and Events in a Tennis Video, uses hidden Markov models for stochastic event recognition as well as Bayesian networks. Chapter 10, Fusion of Evidence for Video Events, uses Bayesian networks for detection of excited speech.

### 3.1.4 Outline

The basics of pattern classification are presented in Section 3.2. Explicit modeling of multimedia content via hidden Markov models is the topic of Section 3.3. Unsupervised learning and pattern clustering are introduced in Section 3.4. Finally, methods for dimension reduction are discussed in Section 3.5.

## 3.2 Pattern Classification

### 3.2.1 Introduction

The main aim of pattern classification is to generalize from the class structure of a set of labeled example patterns. What this usually means is that for a set of example patterns (i) we know what class they have, and (ii) we have their feature representations, i.e., each pattern can be considered as a point (or vector) in a feature space. From this information we would like to be able to decide the class of new input patterns, also represented as features. This immediately gives rise to a host of issues that need to be taken into account, for example:

- **Residual uncertainty**. Even though most pattern classification procedures lead to a *prediction function*, i.e., a deterministic function mapping pattern features to pattern classes, the true relationship between features and pattern classes is generally not deterministic. Rather, it is *probabilistic* in the sense that given a pattern feature vector, the pattern class is not fully determined and the remaining uncertainty can be quantified by means of a probability distribution over the different classes. Conceptually, we can thus represent the true relationship between pattern features $x$ and pattern class $k$ as a joint probability function $p(x, k)$. However, note that we generally do not know this function.
- **Limited availability of data**. When classifying a new pattern feature, we would like, ideally, to have a number of samples at that particular feature point. We could then estimate which class has the highest probability and then assign the new pattern to that class. In fact, this is precisely

the topic of statistical decision theory. This field studies the definition of optimal classifiers given a certain joint probability function and given a penalty function describing the cost of misclassification. One famous result describes the optimal classifier for the so-called zero–one loss penalty function. This standard penalty function assigns unity cost to each misclassification. The optimal prediction function in this case is the *Bayes' classifier*, which is defined as:

$$f(x) = \operatorname*{argmax}_{k \in \mathcal{K}} p(k|X = x). \tag{3.1}$$

This equation states that the best we can do to minimize expected loss is to assign each pattern feature $x$ to that class $k \in \mathcal{K}$ that has the highest probability given the feature. In practice, of course, we often do not have a number of samples at every feature point, so our methods should be designed to still do a decent job also with limited data.

- **Need for prior assumptions**. Not having sufficient data usually takes quite extreme forms: not only do we not have several samples at a feature point, most of the time we have none at all. It is clear that it is ill-advised to decide the class for a pattern if it is not somehow sufficiently represented by the example data. When we are confident that the data do give sufficient information on a new pattern feature, we can use the available data to interpolate or extrapolate the observed class structure to the desired point. An immediate consequence is that we must make prior assumptions about the form of our classifier, thereby implicitly or explicitly stating how the true relationship is expected to behave. The so-called no-free-lunch theorems [44] state that there is no reason to favor any assumptions on purely theoretical grounds. This means that the assumptions must ideally be decided based on the problem and the data at hand. Assumptions often take the form that the behavior of the prediction function is to some extent regularized, i.e., limited in its complexity. This means that we assume, unless we have information to the contrary, that the prediction function changes gradually between data points.

- **Noise and error**. The available data may be affected by noise and there may be measurement errors. This may be the case for both feature and class measurements. Ideally, the mentioned assumptions on the regularity of the prediction function can also deal to some extent with false and misleading measurements, i.e., lead to a method that is robust in the sense that it is not too strongly affected by mistakes and outliers in the sample set.

- **Under- and overfitting** This brings us to a key issue in learning: on the one hand we do not want to make our assumptions so restrictive that we cannot sufficiently capture the class variation through the feature space (a phenomenon called *underfitting*), and on the other hand we do not want the prediction function to react to every single peculiarity of the data (*overfitting*) such as to the errors mentioned early, but also to, for instance, variations in density of representation through the feature space. Finding the balance in how much variation to allow in our prediction function, based on our data and knowledge of a problem, is one of the main challenges in designing classification systems.

- **Irrelevant feature variables**. A final issue we mention is that in many classification problems we are working with a feature space where some of the feature variables are irrelevant to the classification task. Such variables just serve as more noise to deal with and can seriously hamper the performance of the classifier. Selecting those variables really relevant to the task is another main challenge in designing the classification system.

After introducing some more general terminology in the next section, we briefly visit a number of popular classification methods. Our goal is not to explain these methods in great detail, but rather to take a tour along some of the exciting ideas important to modern classification.

We start out with two approaches, $N$-nearest neighbors and discriminant analysis, that directly implement the insight contained in the Bayes' classifier: estimate the class probabilities at a given feature point, and then assign to the most likely class. Next, we discuss support vector machines (SVMs) as an example of margin-maximizing approaches. Finally, we introduce boosting as an example of an ensemble method.

### 3.2.2 Measuring Classifier Performance: Training and Test Error

The result of a classification procedure is a classifier, or prediction function, that maps feature values to classes. All the points which map to a certain class form a subset of the feature space. The prediction function thus partitions the feature space into disjoint regions, each corresponding to a certain class; note that the region belonging to a certain class does not have to consist of single connected component.

The subset of points where the regions belonging to different classes meet, is called the *decision boundary*. Depending on the classification method this boundary is defined in different ways. For the Bayes' classifier it consists of those feature values for which the two most likely classes have equal probability.

One obvious method to assess the performance of a classifier is to consider how well the prediction function maps the training samples to their provided labels. This can be measured using the *training error* for the prediction function $\hat{f}(x)$. If the training set is given by $\mathcal{X} = \{(x_1, y_1), \ldots, (x_n, y_n)\}$ for feature vectors $x_i$ and class labels $y_i$, then the training error is defined as:

$$\bar{e}(\mathcal{X}, \hat{f}) = \frac{1}{n} \sum_{i=1}^{n} L(y_i, \hat{f}(x_i)),$$

where $L$ is a loss function describing the cost of misclassification for a single sample. A commonly used loss function is the already mentioned zero-one loss, defined by:

$$L(y_i, \hat{f}(x_i)) = \begin{cases} 0 & \text{if } y_i = \hat{f}(x_i) \\ 1 & \text{if } y_i \neq \hat{f}(x_i) , \end{cases}$$

i.e., a misclassification is given a penalty of 1 and a correct classification gets no penalty. With this loss function the training error is simply the fraction of training samples that do not get mapped to their labeled class.

Many classification approaches guarantee that zero training error can be achieved. However, in the previous we have already seen that we must beware of overfitting to the data, and that zero or small training error does not mean that we have a good classifier: a less complex classifier that misclassifies some of the training examples may have a better performance on new data. Generally, the best way to establish the performance of a classifier is to measure the performance on a set of new, independently obtained, patterns that have not been used to train the classifier. Loss measurement on a previously unseen data set provides an estimate to the ultimate measure of classifier performance: the *test error*. It is defined as:

$$e(\hat{f}) = E_{p(x,y)}[L(Y, \hat{f}(X)],$$

i.e., as the expectation of the loss if both $Y$ and $X$ are drawn from their (true) joint distribution $p(x, y)$.

In practice we often do not have too many annotated samples, and we would like to use them all for training, rather than keep a subset apart for testing only. In this case we can still get a (more biased) estimate of classifier performance on new data by means of so-called ($K$-fold) *cross-validation*. The idea there is to split the sample set into $K$ (often $K = 10$ is used) subsets. Then $K$ tests are performed where at each test one of the sets is taken to be the test set and the other $K - 1$ sets are used to train the classifier. The $K$ errors of these tests are averaged to give an estimate for the test error.

### 3.2.3 Nearest Neighbor and Discriminant Methods

The Bayes' classifier tells us that if we want to minimize the number of classification errors, we should classify patterns with feature vector $x$ to the class with the highest probability given that feature vector. As mentioned already, ideally we would have several sample patterns with feature $x$ such that we can estimate these class probabilities. Unfortunately, usually this is not the case. However, a natural approach to find the most probable class is to compare class frequencies *in a neighborhood of* $x$. This leads to the $N$-nearest neighbor method of classification which classifies patterns $x$ to the most dominant class in the set of the $N$ training sample patterns closest to $x$.

For satisfactory performance, two key requirements must be met: (i) we need enough patterns sufficiently close to $x$ to be representative for patterns in $x$, and (ii) we need a sensible distance metric between the patterns. Both requirements are generally hard to fulfill in high-dimensional feature spaces. In particular performance tends to deteriorate rapidly with an increasing number of feature dimensions that are not strictly relevant to the task at hand, and that influence the distance metric. To prevent such performance degradation calls for a careful feature selection process.

Another issue with nearest neighbor methods is that they do not have a training stage. The prediction function follows directly from an interpolation of example features. This has the disadvantage that the entire data set must be kept, and that all work has to be done at run-time.

Despite these characteristics, nearest neighbor methods are often used in multimedia retrieval applications. Since multimedia applications typically deal with very large data sets, it is particularly pressing to make sure that for each classification we do not have to visit all samples of the data set to determine the nearest neighbors. Many indexing structures have been developed to prevent this; Böhm et al. [8] provide an overview of such methods particularly geared to the requirements of multimedia databases.

Discriminant methods also implement the insight contained in the Bayes' classifier. However, unlike the nearest neighbor methods, they do not estimate class probabilities directly. Instead they first estimate the probability density of feature values given a certain class, and next use Bayes' law to obtain estimates for the class probabilities given a feature value $x$:

$$p(Y = k|X = x) = \frac{p(X = x|Y = k)P(Y = k)}{p(X = x)} = \frac{p_k(x)\pi_k}{P(X = x)}, \qquad (3.2)$$

where the $\pi_k$ are the prior probabilities for class $k$, and $p_k(x)$ the probability density functions of the features $x$ given class $k$. For classification we are only interested in the relative magnitudes of the class probabilities, so we may use:

$$\delta_k(x) = p_k(x)\pi_k \qquad (3.3)$$

as discriminant functions to obtain a discriminant classifier given by:

$$\underset{k\in\mathcal{K}}{\operatorname{argmax}}\, \delta_k(x). \qquad (3.4)$$

Discriminant methods thus require us to estimate the feature value densities for each class. Different choices of how to do this lead to different discriminant methods. Assuming a multivariate Gaussian density for each of the classes leads to the well-known method of linear discriminant analysis if we also assume that the class densities share a common covariance matrix. If we relax this assumption such that each class may have its own covariance matrix, this leads to quadratic discriminant analysis. Also mixtures of Gaussians can be used in case we require multimodal density models; we refer to the book by Hastie et al. [22] for further details.

Despite the fact that the assumptions in discriminant analysis are often not fully warranted, discriminant methods have shown to provide competitive performance for many classification problems. A likely reason is that their usually simple assumptions prevent overfitting to the data.

### 3.2.4 Support Vector Machines

Support vector machines (SVMs) derive their, generally excellent, performance from a number of interesting ideas and insights. First, the training examples are mapped nonlinearly into a, usually, high-dimensional space. There, in order to obtain the support vector classifier, a linear decision boundary between the classes is determined by constructing an optimal separating hyperplane. To obtain good generalization performance despite the high dimension of the space, this hyperplane is chosen in such a way that the training examples are as far away from the decision boundary as possible. The linear decision boundary obtained from this process of *margin-optimization* corresponds to a nonlinear decision boundary in the original space.

Another crucial feature of support vector machines is that the map from the original space into the new space is usually not constructed explicitly. Instead, it is implicitly defined by the choice of a *kernel* function $k(x, x')$. It turns out that evaluating a kernel function is equivalent to first mapping its arguments by a certain map $\Phi$ into an inner product space and then taking the inner product of the resulting vectors, i.e., $k(x, x') = \langle \Phi(x), \Phi(x') \rangle$. If we have an algorithm formulated in terms of inner products and replace the inner products by the kernel function, the result is that we are still using the same algorithm but now in the mapped space instead of the original space. This, currently very popular, method of using kernels in inner product-based algorithms is known as the *kernel trick*.

In the following, we first discuss margin optimization and the construction of separating hyperplanes, and then show how we can apply the kernel trick to the resulting algorithm.

Following the book by Schölkopf [39], we first assume that our training examples have already been mapped into an inner product space $\mathcal{H}$. We consider a two-class problem and, for convenience, assume that the training examples $(x_i, y_i), i = 1, \ldots, n$ are labeled by $y_i = 1$ or $y_i = -1$.

The margin of a correctly classified training example is defined as its distance to the decision boundary. Our aim is to construct a hyperplane that: (i) separates the two classes as well as possible, and (ii) makes the margins as large as possible. For standard support vector classifiers the latter goal is implemented by maximizing the minimum margin, which is known as the *geometrical* margin of the training set.

A general hyperplane can be defined by:

$$\langle w, x \rangle + b = 0, \tag{3.5}$$

where $w$ determines the orientation of the plane, and $b$ its offset from the origin. The hyperplane can be used as linear decision boundary for a classifier by taking $f(x) = \text{sign}(\langle w, b \rangle + b)$. Input values on one side of the hyperplane are classified as 1 and values on the other side as $-1$. Note that we have a choice in how we scale the vector $w$. The equations above are understood most easily by taking the vector $w$ to be of unit size and interpreting $\langle w, x \rangle$

as a projection on $w$. However, for the purpose of working with margins, it turns out to be more convenient to scale $w$ differently: we assume that the length of $w$ is such that the distance of the hyperplane to the labeled examples with smallest margins is equal to $1/||w||$, in other words: we assume that the geometrical margin is $1/||w||$. If we define the hyperplane in this way, the hyperplane is in *canonical form*. It is an easy exercise to check that for a hyperplane in canonical form the dashed hyperplanes in Figure 3.2 are defined by $\langle w, x \rangle + b = \pm 1$.

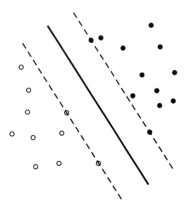

**Fig. 3.2.** Separating hyperplane.

Thanks to this canonical form we can formulate the construction of a separating hyperplane as a simple constrained minimization problem:

$$\min_{w \in \mathcal{H}, b \in \mathbb{R}} \frac{1}{2}||w||^2 \qquad (3.6)$$

$$\text{subject to} \quad y_i(\langle w, x_i \rangle + b) \geq 1, \quad \text{for } i = 1, \ldots, n. \qquad (3.7)$$

The constraints make sure that the training examples are correctly classified, and minimizing $||w||$ corresponds to maximizing the geometrical margin $(1/||w||)$. A solution to this problem will exist only if the training examples can indeed be separated by a linear hyperplane. As this is not always the case and it is important to build in robustness to outliers, usually a *soft margin* formulation based on "slack" variables $\xi_i$ $(i = 1, \ldots, n)$ is used:

$$\min_{w \in \mathcal{H}, b \in \mathbb{R}} \frac{1}{2}||w||^2 + C \sum_{i=1}^{n} \xi_i \qquad (3.8)$$

$$\text{subject to} \quad y_i(\langle w, x_i \rangle + b) \geq 1 - \xi_i, \quad \xi_i \geq 0, \quad \text{for } i = 1, \ldots, n. \qquad (3.9)$$

Positive values $\xi_i > 0$ of the slack variables correspond to violations of the constraints, i.e., to training examples that are either misclassified, or are still correctly classified but are within the geometrical margin. The parameter $C$ controls the trade-off between margin maximization and training error minimization.

The classic method to characterize the solutions of constrained optimization problems is as a saddle points of the *Lagrangian* function:

$$L(w, b, \xi, \alpha) = \frac{1}{2}||w||^2 + C\sum_{i=1}^{n}\xi_i - \sum_{i=1}^{n}(\alpha_i(y_i(\langle w, x_i\rangle + b) - 1 + \xi_i) + \beta_i\xi_i). \quad (3.10)$$

To obtain solutions to (3.8), the Lagrangian should be minimized with respect to the primal variables $w$, $b$, and $\xi$, and maximized with respect to the Lagrange multipliers, or dual variables, $\alpha_i$ and $\beta_i$. The Lagrange multipliers $\alpha_i$ are zero for inactive constraints, and non-zero for active constraints, i.e., only for training examples that are either on the geometric margin, or for examples with positive slack variables. Such examples are known as the support vectors of the problem, and it can be shown that:

$$w = \sum_{i=1}^{n}\alpha_i y_i x_i, \quad (3.11)$$

giving:

$$f(x) = \text{sign}\left(\sum_{i=1}^{n}\alpha_i y_i\langle x, x_i\rangle + b\right) \quad (3.12)$$

as the support vector classifier. Note that this means that the outcome of the classifier is determined only by the support vectors; the examples with higher margins could be left from the training data without changing the resulting classifier. To determine the Lagrange multipliers, one has to solve the *dual* problem:

$$\max_{\alpha \in I\!R^n} \sum_{i=1}^{n}\alpha_i - \frac{1}{2}\sum_{i,j=1}^{n}\alpha_i\alpha_j y_i y_j\langle x_i, x_j\rangle \quad (3.13)$$

$$\text{subject to} \quad 0 \leq \alpha_i \leq C, \quad \text{for } i = 1, \ldots, n \text{ and } \sum_{i=1}^{n}\alpha_i y_i = 0. \quad (3.14)$$

For a detailed discussion on how to derive the dual problem as well as to gain a better grasp of the geometry of the setting, we recommend the textbooks by Schölkopf et al. [39] and Bazaraa et al. [4].

One advantage of the dual formulation is that the constraints are simplified considerably. The most important advantage, however, is that the training examples enter the problem exclusively through their inner products. This is exactly what is needed to be able to use the kernel trick.

To apply the kernel trick, we replace the inner products by a kernel function $k$, giving:

$$\max_{\alpha \in I\!\!R^n} \sum_{i=1}^{n} \alpha_i - \frac{1}{2} \sum_{i,j=1}^{n} \alpha_i \alpha_j y_i y_j k(x_i, x_j) \tag{3.15}$$

under the same conditions as before; the classifier is now given by:

$$f(x) = \text{sign} \left( \sum_{i=1}^{n} \alpha_i y_i k(x, x_i) + b \right). \tag{3.16}$$

As mentioned above, replacing the inner product by a kernel in this manner, implicitly corresponds to mapping into an inner product space followed by taking the inner product in that space. Given a kernel, there are different ways to construct the inner product space. One insightful way to do this is by means of reproducing kernel Hilbert spaces which allow the kernel to be interpreted, to some extent, as a similarity measure. Unfortunately, this theory is beyond the scope of the current chapter, and we must refer to Chapter 2 of the book by Schölkopf et al. [39] for more details; Chapter 13 of the same text provides further detail on how to design kernel functions for specific problems. For general purpose problems the most commonly used kernels are the Gaussian kernel:

$$k(x, x') = \exp \left( -\frac{||x - x'||^2}{2\sigma^2} \right), \tag{3.17}$$

and the, homogeneous and inhomogeneous, polynomial kernels:

$$k(x, x') = \langle x, x \rangle^d, \text{ and } k(x, x') = (\langle x, x \rangle + c)^d. \tag{3.18}$$

Performance of these kernels often turns out to be quite similar in practice. The parameters are usually determined by cross-validation, see Section 3.2.2. Finally we mention that an excellent resource for SVM software is available at http://www.kernel-machines.org.

### 3.2.5 Ensemble Methods and Boosting

Ensemble methods construct a set of classifiers and then combine these to obtain a new classifier by taking a (weighted) vote of their predictions. Classic ensemble methods are *Bayesian averaging* and *bagging*. The latter method uses the original set of samples to bootstrap new training data sets and then simply takes a majority vote of the classifiers resulting from these sets. Here we will focus on *boosting* which in particular in combination with decision tree classifiers often provides excellent off-the-shelf performance.

Boosting has its origins in PAC learning (Kearns [28] gives an introduction; "PAC" stands for *probably approximately correct*). Schapire [38] has shown that using boosting a so-called weak learner (a classifier that performs at least slightly better than random) can be transformed into a strong learner (a classifier that is PAC in a well-defined mathematical sense) by combining a weighted sum of the weak learners.

With boosting we start with a base (weak) classifier. Theoretically this should be a learner that can obtain better than random performance on any sample from the true data distribution. In practice, one usually takes a decision tree classifier, often even a tree stump, i.e., a classifier that partitions the feature space into two classes by splitting along a single dimension. The base classifier is trained and then the performance on the training set is evaluated. The main idea of boosting is now to train the next classifier by giving more weight to the samples that were misclassified in the previous stage. This can be done in two ways: if the method to train the base classifier allows it, we can work with weighted examples; if this is not the case, we may also resample from the original data set using sampling probabilities that reflect the weights given to the samples. This is repeated a number of iterations and then the final classifier is obtained by taking a weighted vote of the individual classifiers. The classifier weights depend on the performance of the classifier on the training data.

The most well-known scheme that implements these ideas is AdaBoost ("Adaptive Boosting"), introduced by Freund and Schapire [17]. The Ada-Boost procedure consists of the steps listed in the box on the next page [16]. Note that again we have assumed two classes that are labeled as 1 and −1.

The AdaBoost procedure can be motivated in a number of interesting ways. One is that it implements an iterative process where at each step a new classifier is added such that a loss function in terms of the example margins is minimized. This means that, just as SVMs, boosting can be understood to increase the margins of the training samples in a specific feature space. For example Hastie et al. [22] show that if an exponential loss function is used, the classifier weights that minimize the loss are those of (3.19) below.

An interesting effect that is sometimes observed with boosting is that even after the training error has reached zero, further iterations still lead to better generalization performance, as witnessed by a decreasing test error. This can, partially, be explained by the fact that even when examples are already correctly classified their margins can still be increased. For a more detailed introduction to AdaBoost and its various variants we refer to Freund and Schapire [16].

**AdaBoost algorithm**

1. Initialize the sample weights, or sample probability distribution:

$$m_i(1) = \frac{1}{n}, \ i = 1, \dots, n.$$

2. For iteration $t = 1$ to $T$:
   - Train base learner $f_t(x)$ according to example distribution $m_i(t)$.
   - Compute the weighted training error:

   $$\varepsilon_t = \sum_{i=1}^{n} m_i(t) I(y_i \neq f_t(x_i)) = \sum_{i:f_t(x_i) \neq y_i} m_i(t).$$

   - Compute the classifier weight:

   $$\alpha_t = \frac{1}{2} \log((1 - \varepsilon_t)/\varepsilon_t). \tag{3.19}$$

   - Update the example distribution:

   $$m_i(t+1) = m_i(t) \frac{\exp(\alpha_t \cdot I(y_i \neq f_t(x_i)))}{Z_t},$$

   where $Z_t$ is a normalization factor such that the distribution sums to one.

3. The resulting classifier is $f(x) = \text{sign} \left( \sum_{t=1}^{T} \alpha_t f_t(x) \right).$

## 3.3 Modeling

Hidden Markov Models (HMMs) are a very popular choice for modeling in multimedia applications. HMMs are stochastic automata consisting of connected states with transition probabilities, as well as probabilities describing the possible outputs of the states. Only the outputs of the states can be observed, not the states themselves, hence the name *hidden* Markov models. HMMs are widely used in speech recognition to describe acoustic model probabilities, see Chapter 7, Speech Indexing. Rabiner [37] presents a classic tutorial on HMMs and applications in speech recognition. HMMs are also widely used in other fields, such as image processing and computer vision, text recognition, control theory, communications, the biosciences, and meteorology to mention just a few. To get some hands-on experience with hidden Markov models, we recommend the Matlab HMM toolbox which is available at: `http://www.cs.ubc.ca/~murphyk/Software/HMM/hmm.html`.

## Markov Models and the Markov Property

Consider a simple example: we want to predict the weather in our city based on the weather in the past few days. Let us assume the weather can be in any of three *states*: Sunny ($S$), Rainy ($R$) or Foggy($F$) and is constant for one day. In this case the conditional probability for the weather $q_n$, expressing the dependence of the weather on day $n$ on the weather of the preceding $n - 1$ days, seems like a reasonable statistical model for our predictions. The larger $n$, the more accurate the prediction, but also the larger the amount of weather observations we must collect. Therefore often a first-order Markov assumption is used, i.e., we assume the probability of a certain observation at time $n$ depends only on the observation at time $n - 1$:

$$P(q_n|q_{n-1}, q_{n-2}, \ldots, q_1) = P(q_n|q_{n-1}). \tag{3.20}$$

This is also known as a *Markov property*. Suppose that the *transition* probabilities for our weather example are given in Table 3.1.

**Table 3.1.** Transition probabilities from today's to tomorrow's weather.

| Today \ Tomorrow | $S$ | $R$ | $F$ |
|---|---|---|---|
| $S$ | 0.8 | 0.05 | 0.15 |
| $R$ | 0.2 | 0.6 | 0.2 |
| $F$ | 0.2 | 0.3 | 0.5 |

These first-order Markov model transition probabilities can also be depicted as the finite state automaton shown in Figure 3.3.

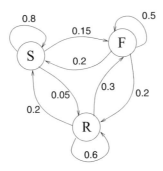

**Fig. 3.3.** Markov model for the weather with transition probabilities as in Table 3.1.

Using the transition probabilities, we can answer questions like: "Given that today is sunny, what is the probability that tomorrow will also be sunny and the day after tomorrow rainy?":

$$P(q_2 = S, q_3 = R|q_1 = S) = P(q_3 = R|q_2 = S, q_1 = S) \cdot P(q_2 = S|q_1 = S)$$
$$\text{(Markov assumption} \rightarrow) = P(q_3 = R|q_2 = S) \cdot P(q_2 = S|q_1 = S)$$
$$= 0.05 \cdot 0.8 = 0.04. \tag{3.21}$$

We can arrive at the same result by moving along the corresponding finite state automaton path.

## Hidden Markov Models

HMMs are tools for representing probability distributions over sequences of observations. Two main characteristics of HMMs are: (i) the observation at time $n$ is generated by a process whose state is *hidden* from the observer, and (ii) the state of the process satisfies the Markov property.

In the context of the weather example, we can get a hidden Markov model if we assume that the weather outside cannot be directly observed but we can observe, for example, if a person carries an umbrella into the house: $(U)$ or not $(\bar{U})$. Then for day $i$, we denote the observation for weather state $q_i$ by $o_i$. Let's assume that the probabilities relating the outside weather and the person's umbrella are given in Table 3.2.

**Table 3.2.** Probability of carrying an umbrella based on the weather.

| Weather | Probability of umbrella $U$ |
|:---:|:---:|
| $S$ | 0.1 |
| $R$ | 0.8 |
| $F$ | 0.3 |

To calculate the probability of the weather given "umbrella" or "no umbrella", we use Bayes' rule:

$$P(q_i|o_i) = \frac{P(o_i|q_i)P(q_i)}{P(o_i)}. \tag{3.22}$$

This equation can be generalized for a sequence of weather states $Q = \{q_1, q_2, \ldots, q_n\}$ and umbrella observations $O = \{o_1, o_2, \ldots, o_n\}$. To draw conclusions about the weather outside, given our umbrella observations, we use the *likelihood* $L$ given the Markov assumption:

$$P(Q|O) \propto L(Q|O) = P(O|Q) \cdot P(Q)$$
$$= \prod_{i=1}^{n} P(o_i|q_i) \cdot \prod_{i=1}^{n} P(q_i|q_{i-1}). \tag{3.23}$$

**Example**: Consider a case where the initial weather states are assumed to be equiprobable (so for instance $P(q_1 = S) = 1/3$), and we don't observe any umbrellas for 3 days. We would like to calculate the likelihood that the weather over these three days has been $Q = \{q_1 = S, q_2 = F, q_3 = S\}$:

$$L(q_1 = S, q_2 = F, q_3 = S | o_1 = \bar{U}, o_2 = \bar{U}, o_3 = \bar{U}) =$$
$$P(o_1 = \bar{U} | q_1 = S) \cdot P(o_2 = \bar{U} | q_2 = F) \cdot P(o_3 = \bar{U} | q_3 = S) \cdot$$
$$P(q_1 = S) \cdot P(q_2 = F | q_1 = S) \cdot P(q_3 = S | q_2 = F) =$$
$$0.9 \cdot 0.7 \cdot 0.9 \cdot 1/3 \cdot 0.15 \cdot 0.2 = 0.0057. \tag{3.24}$$

**HMM variables and parameters**:

- States: $S = \{s_1, s_2, \ldots, s_{N_S}\}$. In the weather example context, there are $N_S = 3$ weather states: $\{S, R, F\}$.
- Initial state distribution (prior probabilities) $\pi$: $\pi_i = P(q_1 = s_i)$, i.e., the probability that $s_i$ is the first state of the sequence. If the states are equiprobable $\pi_i = \frac{1}{N_S}$.
- Transition probabilities: $A = (a_{i,j})$, where $a_{i,j} = P(q_{n+1} = s_j | q_n = s_i)$ is the probability that the HMM goes from state $s_i$ to state $s_j$.
- Emission probabilities $B$:
  - for *discrete* HMMs $o_n \in \{v_1, \ldots, v_K\}$, $B$ is a matrix of emission probabilities $b_{i,k} = P(o_n = v_k | q_n = s_i)$, i.e., the probability of observing $v_k$ given that the current state is $s_i$. For the weather example $K = 2$: $v_1 = U, v_2 = \bar{U}$.
  - for *continuous* HMMs $o_n \in \mathbb{R}^D$, we can similarly define conditional probability density functions for the outputs given the state.

**Trellis Diagram**

A Trellis diagram is used to visualize likelihood calculations of HMMs. Figure 3.4 (on the left) shows such a diagram for a HMM with 3 states.

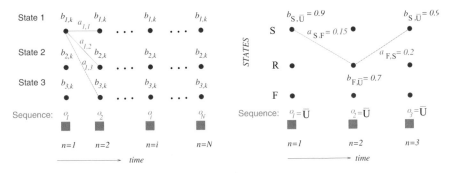

**Fig. 3.4.** Trellis diagram: *left*: general three-states HMM; *right*: weather example.

Each column of the diagram shows the possible states at time $n$. Each state in one column is connected to each state in the adjacent columns by the transition probability $a_{i,j}$; $b_{i,k}$ is the probability of an observation $o_n = \nu_k$ in state $q_n = s_i$. The observation sequence $O$ is at the bottom of the diagram.

A Trellis diagram for the weather example is shown in Figure 3.4 (on the right). The likelihood of the state sequence given the observed sequence can be found easily by following the path in the Trellis diagram and multiplying the transition and observation probabilities:

$$L = \pi_S \cdot b_{S,\bar{U}} \cdot a_{S,R} \cdot b_{R,\bar{U}} \cdot a_{R,S} \cdot b_{S,\bar{U}}$$
$$= 1/3 \cdot 0.9 \cdot 0.15 \cdot 0.7 \cdot 0.2 \cdot 0.9 = 0.0057. \qquad (3.25)$$

### Pattern Recognition with HMMs

There are three basic HMM problems:

- **Evaluation.** Computing the probability of an observation sequence $O$ given an HMM model $\lambda = (A, B, \pi)$. For the evaluation of an HMM the *forward algorithm* is used. Rabiner [37] gives further details of the algorithm. This problem appears in classification tasks.
- **Decoding.** Given the observation $O$ and the model $\lambda$, how do we find the *optimal state sequence*, i.e., the one which explains the observations best? The *Viterbi algorithm* is used in recognition tasks.
- **Learning.** How to adjust the model parameters to maximize the probability of the observation given the model $P(O|\lambda)$. The *Baum–Welch (or forward–backward) algorithm* is used to solve this problem.

The learning algorithm is an *Expectation-Maximization* (EM) algorithm; Lance Pérez [1] gives more details. The evaluation algorithm consists of the E-step only.

The likelihood of an observation sequence $O$ given the model $\lambda$ can be written as:

$$p(O|\lambda) = \sum_{\text{every possible } Q} p(O, Q|\lambda), \qquad (3.26)$$

i.e., as the sum of the joint likelihood of the sequence over all possible state sequences (see the Trellis diagram in Figure 3.4). The naïve solution to the evaluation problem is computationally very expensive as there are $N_S^N$ possible state sequences (even for small HMMs, e.g., with $N_S = 10$ states and $N = 10$ observations, there are 10 billion different paths). A better approach to the solution of the evaluation and decoding problems is the use of *dynamic programming*.

In speech recognition (see Section 7.2.2, Acoustic modeling, in Chapter 7, Speech Indexing) and other PR applications, it is useful to associate an "optimal" state sequence to an observation sequence given the parameters of the model: $Q^* = \text{argmax}_Q P(Q|O, \lambda)$. The main idea of the *Viterbi algorithm* is to keep the best state sequences to reach a certain state at a certain step. We define two variables:

1. $\delta_n(i)$: the *maximum* likelihood of a single path among all paths ending in state $s_i$ at time $n$:

$$\delta_n(i) = \max_{q_1,q_2,\ldots,q_{n-1}} p(q_1, q_2, \ldots, q_{n-1}, q_n = s_i, o_1, o_2, \ldots, o_n|\lambda), \quad (3.27)$$

2. $\psi_n(i)$: the best path ending in state $s_i$ at time $n$:

$$\psi_n(i) = \operatorname*{argmax}_{q_1,q_2,\ldots,q_{n-1}} p(q_1, q_2, \ldots, q_{n-1}, q_n = s_i, o_1, o_2, \ldots, o_n|\lambda). \quad (3.28)$$

The algorithm inductively finds the most probable path at each intermediate step up to the terminating state:

---

**Viterbi algorithm**

1. Initialization:

$$\delta_1(i) = \pi_i b_{i,o_1}, \quad i = 1, \ldots, N_S$$
$$\psi_1(i) = 0.$$

2. Recursion:

$$\delta_n(j) = \left[\max_{1 \le i \le N_S} \delta_{n-1}(i)a_{i,j}\right] \cdot b_{j,o_n}, \quad 2 \le n \le N, 1 \le j \le N_S.$$
$$\psi_n(i) = [\operatorname*{argmax}_{1 \le i \le N_S} \delta_{n-1}(i)a_{i,j}], \quad 2 \le n \le N, 1 \le j \le N_S$$

3. Termination:

$$p^*(O|\lambda) = \max_{1 \le i \le N_S} \delta_N(i)$$
$$q_N^* = \operatorname*{argmax}_{1 \le i \le N_S} \delta_N(i).$$

4. Backtracking:

$$Q^* = \{q_1^*, q_2^*, \ldots, q_N^*\}$$
$$q_n^* = \psi_{n+1}(q_{n+1}^*), \quad n = N-1, N-2, \ldots, 1.$$

---

**Example**: For a simple illustration of the Viterbi algorithm consider again our weather model. Assume that the initial true weather is not known and that we observe $\{\bar{U}, \bar{U}, U\}$. We want to find the most probable weather sequence for these three days using the Viterbi algorithm:

1. **Initialization**
   $n = 1$:

$$\delta_1(S) = \pi_S b_{S,\bar{U}} = 1/3 \cdot 0.9 = 0.3, \quad \psi_1(S) = 0$$
$$\delta_1(R) = \pi_R b_{R,\bar{U}} = 1/3 \cdot 0.2 = 0.0667, \quad \psi_1(R) = 0$$
$$\delta_1(F) = \pi_F b_{F,\bar{U}} = 1/3 \cdot 0.7 = 0.233, \quad \psi_1(F) = 0.$$

2. **Recursion**

   $n = 2$:

   We calculate the likelihood of getting to state '$S$' from all states in $S$, choosing the most likely one:

   $$\delta_2(S) = \max(\delta_1(S) \cdot a_{S,S}, \ \delta_1(R) \cdot a_{R,S}, \ \delta_1(F) \cdot a_{F,S}) \cdot b_{S,\bar{U}}$$
   $$= \max(0.3 \cdot 0.8, \ 0.0667 \cdot 0.2, \ 0.233 \cdot 0.2) \cdot 0.9 = 0.216$$
   $$\psi_2(S) = S.$$

   The same is repeated for states: '$R$' and '$F$':

   $$\delta_2(R) = \max(\delta_1(S) \cdot a_{S,R}, \ \delta_1(R) \cdot a_{R,R}, \ \delta_1(F) \cdot a_{F,R}) \cdot b_{R,\bar{U}}$$
   $$= \max(0.3 \cdot 0.05, \ 0.0667 \cdot 0.6, \ 0.233 \cdot 0.3) \cdot 0.2 = 0.01398$$
   $$\psi_2(R) = F$$

   $$\delta_2(F) = \max(\delta_1(S) \cdot a_{S,F}, \ \delta_1(R) \cdot a_{R,F}, \ \delta_1(F) \cdot a_{F,F}) \cdot b_{F,\bar{U}}$$
   $$= \max(0.3 \cdot 0.15, \ 0.0667 \cdot 0.2, \ 0.233 \cdot 0.5) \cdot 0.7 = 0.08155$$
   $$\psi_2(F) = F$$

   $n = 3$:

   $$\delta_3(S) = \max(\delta_2(S) \cdot a_{S,S}, \ \delta_2(R) \cdot a_{R,S}, \ \delta_2(F) \cdot a_{F,S}) \cdot b_{S,U}$$
   $$= \max(0.216 \cdot 0.8, \ 0.01398 \cdot 0.2, \ 0.08155 \cdot 0.2) \cdot 0.1 = 0.017$$
   $$\psi_3(S) = S$$

   $$\delta_3(R) = \max(\delta_2(S) \cdot a_{S,R}, \ \delta_2(R) \cdot a_{R,R}, \ \delta_2(F) \cdot a_{F,R}) \cdot b_{R,U}$$
   $$= \max(0.216 \cdot 0.05, \ 0.01398 \cdot 0.6, \ 0.08155 \cdot 0.3) \cdot 0.8 = 0.0196$$
   $$\psi_3(R) = F$$

   $$\delta_3(F) = \max(\delta_2(S) \cdot a_{S,F}, \ \delta_2(R) \cdot a_{R,F}, \ \delta_2(F) \cdot a_{F,F}) \cdot b_{F,U}$$
   $$= \max(0.216 \cdot 0.15, \ 0.01398 \cdot 0.2, \ 0.08155 \cdot 0.5) \cdot 0.3 = 0.012$$
   $$\psi_3(F) = F.$$

3. **Termination**

   The globally most likely path is determined by looking at the last state of the most likely sequence:

   $$p^*(O|\lambda) = \max(\delta_3(i)) = \delta_3(R) = 0.0196$$
   $$q_3^* = \operatorname{argmax}(\delta_3(i)) = R.$$

4. **Backtracking**
The optimal sequence can be obtained backtracking the values of $\psi$ (see Figure 3.5):
$n = N - 1 = 2$:

$$q_2^* = \psi_3(q_3^*) = \psi_3(R) = F$$

$n = N - 2 = 1$:

$$q_1^* = \psi_2(q_2^*) = \psi_2(F) = F.$$

Therefore, the optimal (most likely) weather sequence given the observations and the model is: $Q^* = \{q_1^*, q_2^*, q_3^*\} = \{F, F, R\}$.

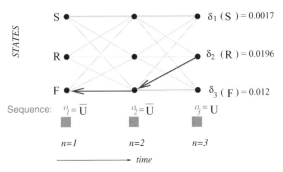

**Fig. 3.5.** Trellis diagram for the most likely weather sequence found via the Viterbi algorithm.

The HMMs can be considered as a simple type of Bayesian network. We do not treat such networks here; a thorough presentation of the theory and a good example of using Bayesian Networks can be found in Section 4.3.4 in the context of ranked retrieval of text documents. Also in Chapter 10, Fusion of Evidence for Video Events, Section 10.3 presents an example of using Bayesian networks for detection of excited speech.

## 3.4 Unsupervised Learning and Clustering

Jain et al. [26] define clustering as "the unsupervised classification of patterns (observations, data items, or feature vectors) into groups (clusters)". Clustering methods may differ in how they form such groups, yet most use similarity or proximity measures to group patterns that are sufficiently *similar* to each other. Other methods more explicitly aim to discover the sparse and, in particular, the dense regions in a data set. Pavel Berkhin [5] gives an excellent overview.

Clustering methods can be roughly divided in hierarchical methods, and iterative optimization methods. The former simply group items/clusters that are closest to each other in the order of their proximity (or split the far-thest pair by increasing distance). The latter optimize a certain criterion that measures the quality of the obtained clustering. These are typically iterative, where at each iteration patterns are relocated from one cluster to another to further optimize the clustering criterion.

In almost all methods a prominent role is played by the function defining the distance between two patterns. The quality of the resulting clusters de-pends to a large extent on how meaningful this distance measure is for the task at hand. Also, we often require a distance measure between clusters (i.e., groups of patterns), and as a special case, between clusters and individual patterns. Depending on how we define such measures, we may place more emphasis on the similarity between patterns in a cluster, or on the connec-tivity between the patterns in a cluster. In the first case, we aim for compact clusters where all cluster members are similar to each other; in the second case, we allow individual cluster members to be far apart as long as they are connected through other cluster members.

### 3.4.1 Hierarchical Clustering

Hierarchical clustering does not explicitly aim for optimal clusters; rather it keeps merging the closest pair of patterns/clusters until a threshold distance is reached and no further merging is possible within that distance. This results in clusters that themselves consist of subclusters, which have been formed earlier: hence the name "hierarchical".

The general form of (agglomerative) hierarchical clustering methods, given a threshold $\varepsilon$, is:

1. Compute the distance, or *connectivity*, matrix containing the distance between each pair of patterns. Treat each pattern as a cluster.
2. Find the most similar pair of clusters using the connectivity matrix (i.e., find the pair with the smallest distance). If this distance is smaller than $\varepsilon$, merge these two clusters into one cluster. Otherwise, stop.
3. Update the connectivity matrix to reflect this merge operation. If we do not already have one large cluster, return to step 2.

Methods differ in the way they characterize the similarity between a pair of clusters. Two commonly used varieties are single link and complete link clustering. In the single link method, two clusters are within distance $\varepsilon$ of each other, already if even a single link between the clusters is smaller than $\varepsilon$. The distance between two clusters is defined as the minimum of the distances between all pairs of patterns in the two clusters, where one element is from the first cluster, and the other from the second.

In the complete link algorithm, two clusters are within distance $\varepsilon$ of each other, only if *all* links between the clusters are smaller than $\varepsilon$. The distance between two clusters is defined as the maximum of all pairwise distances between patterns in the two clusters.

Figure 3.7 (together with 3.6) demonstrates the difference between these two methods for an example in which we cluster the colors in an image. The figure shows two boxes; one box has a very gradual color gradient going from white to black; the other box has a white region on the left and a black region on the right, with in between a small region with a strong gradient of shades going from white to black.

We are clustering the colors (or gray levels) only and do not take into account the spatial layout of the pixels. With single link clustering we obtain one large cluster, as, due to the gradient, all colors are connected by in-between colors. For the top box with a small spatial gradient this is indeed what is desired, but in other "applications" this may not be appropriate behavior: in the bottom box such clustering is not desirable. Complete link clustering has the opposite behavior. The spectrum of colors is split into clusters of similar colors. Now the white and black of the bottom box are nicely separated, but the top box is over-segmented.

The figure also shows the hierarchical nesting structure of the clusters by means of a *dendrogram*. The level of the horizontal lines connecting different clusters indicates the distance between the respective clusters. If the value of the threshold is higher than this value these clusters are merged. As can be seen from these dendrograms, single link clustering leads to large clusters more easily.

Many varieties with different link measures have been devised, e.g., average link (distance between clusters is the average link distance), methods based on cluster representations by a single point (e.g., centroid, and minimum variance links), and methods based on cluster representations based on a subset of points (e.g., CURE [18]). This latter method also takes special care of outliers.

The outcome of hierarchical clustering depends only on the distances (dissimilarities) between the sample points. However, keeping the entire connectivity matrix of these distances needs in memory is generally not feasible for larger data sets. One solution to this issue, other than the general strategies for dealing with large databases (see Section 3.4.3), is to keep only the distances to the nearest neighbors (see, e.g., CHAMELEON [27]).

For categorical data, two hierarchical methods are ROCK [19] and COB-WEB [13].

### 3.4.2 Partitioning Relocation Methods

The second family of clustering methods creates clusters that optimize a quality criterion. Usually the result is a single partitioning of the data set. A simple, yet useful, representative is the $K$-means clustering method, which is also, arguably, the most well-known and popular of all clustering methods.

$K$-means clustering is an iterative method that aims to minimize the squared error cluster quality criterion. Given a pattern set $\mathcal{X} = \{x_1, \ldots, x_n\}$, the goal is to assign each pattern to one of $K$ clusters, such that the summed squared distances to the centers $c_k$ of the clusters are minimized. The number of clusters $K$ is fixed beforehand: determining a proper value of $K$ is treated

Original image

**Fig. 3.6.** Hierarchical clustering. See companion Figure 3.7 for explanation.

as a separate problem. Formally, the aim is to find a labeling $\mathcal{L} = [l_1, \ldots, l_n]$ with $l_i \in \{1, \ldots, K\}$ such that the squared error criterion:

$$e^2(\mathcal{X}, \mathcal{L}) = \sum_{k=1}^{K} \sum_{i \in \mathcal{C}_k} ||x_i - c_k||^2$$

is minimized. The "prototypes" $c_k$, $k = 1, \ldots, K$, are the centroids of the clusters of patterns with label $k$, defined by:

$$c_k = \frac{1}{n_k} \sum_{i \in \mathcal{C}_k} x_i,$$

with $n_k$ the number of items in cluster $k$.

Figure 3.8 together with 3.9 gives an illustration of the iterative process to minimize this criterion. We start out with $K$ initial cluster prototypes. Given a set of prototypes, we can assign each data set item to its closest prototype. This is known as the *assignment* stage and creates $K$ clusters. Next, in the *update* stage, new prototypes are determined by computing the centroids of the items now belonging to the different clusters. This can be repeated until a certain level of convergence is reached. Two possible termination criteria are, for instance, detecting that no reassignment of items has occurred, or detecting insufficient decrease in the optimization criterion.

Many other iterative relocation methods follow a similar strategy for assignment and update as in $K$-means clustering. This leads for instance to the following variations:

- Instead of computing the centroid, the prototype can be computed in a different way, e.g., as a medoid (or, "the point at the center of the cluster", similar to the one-dimensional median). Such alternate cluster

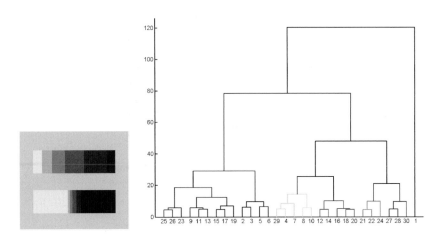

Complete link color clustering and dendrogram

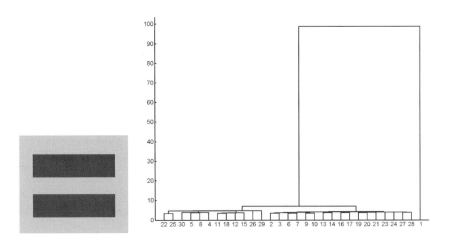

Single link color clustering and dendrogram

**Fig. 3.7.** Hierarchical clustering. Observe the effect of the linkage measure on the resulting clustering. The complete link measure leads to compact clusters. The single link measure puts more emphasis on color connectivity leading, in this case, to one cluster consisting of all the gray scales. Also shown are the dendrograms of the two methods (see text).

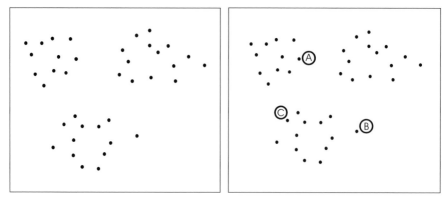

Original data set to be clustered, and initial prototype seeds

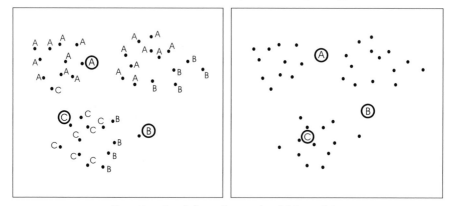

Iteration 1 – *left*: assignment; *right*: update

**Fig. 3.8.** Iterative clustering. See companion Figure 3.9 for explanation.

representatives are usually designed to be more robust to outliers; on the other hand such methods may be less amenable to statistical analysis.

- Instead of hard assignment of each pattern to a single cluster, one may also opt for soft, or fuzzy, assignment. In this case the method assigns each pattern with degrees, or probabilities, of membership to belong to the clusters. A straightforward "fuzzification" of the $K$-means method leads to the prominent fuzzy c-means algorithm, see the book *Fuzzy Cluster Analysis* [24].

- Still more generally we can use probabilistic models to describe pattern clusters. The assignment/update process is then usually based on the EM-procedure [32]. In the "E"-, or expectation-stage, the class probabilities for the different training patterns are estimated, corresponding to a soft assignment of the patterns to the various classes. In the "M", or maximization-stage these soft assignments are assumed to be given in

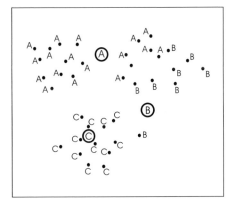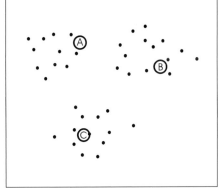

Iteration 2 – *left*: assignment; *right*: update

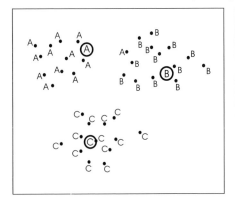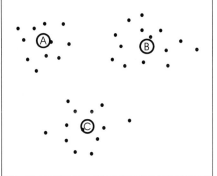

Iteration 3 – *left*: assignment; *right*: update

**Fig. 3.9.** Iterative clustering.

order to be able to obtain the maximum likelihood estimates of the parameters of the probability density functions describing the clusters in the feature space. The case where mixtures of Gaussians are used to model the pattern clusters is discussed in detail in Chapter 6, Generative Probabilistic Models. Regular $K$-means clustering can be interpreted as a special case of the mixture of Gaussians model where all Gaussians have isotropic variances.

All of these methods struggle with their dependence on the initial choice of prototypes: different initial choices may converge to different local optima of the clustering criterion; there are no guarantees that a global optimum will be found. One common strategy to deal with this problem to some extent is to try out many sets of initial prototypes. Another strategy is to start with random prototypes and run the clustering method on a subset of the original data set; next, the resulting prototypes are used as initial seeds to cluster the entire set.

### 3.4.3 Clustering for Large Databases

When clustering patterns for multimedia databases, simple implementations of the previously discussed methods are generally not feasible: the number of patterns will be simply too large. In particular, pattern sets are often so large that the required data for the cluster computations does not fit into main memory. If no special measures are taken, runtimes will then be dominated by disk paging of the data back and forth into main memory. In this section we will discuss a number of strategies to deal with this issue. Note that it may also be the case that databases are large in the sense that the patterns are represented by high-dimensional features; this problem is addressed separately in Section 3.5 on dimension reduction.

In case we are working with prototype methods such as $K$-means clustering, one obvious strategy to deal with space complexity is to split the original data set into smaller sets. First, each of these sets are clustered independently. Next, the resulting prototypes are combined into a new set which can, in turn, also be clustered. Additional stages can be used if this is required to keep the sets sufficiently small. This so-called divide and conquer approach [26] is discussed by Murty [34].

Another way to deal with space limitations are the *incremental* approaches. Here patterns are visited one at a time and then discarded. They are either added to the already existing clusters, or a new cluster is formed. A disadvantage of these methods is that they are order-dependent: the resulting clustering depends on the order in which the patterns are visited. The BIRCH method [45] deserves a special mention. In the first scan, it creates a height-balanced tree of nodes that summarize the data by accumulating its zero, first, and second moments. Additional passes through the data can be used to improve the tree.

Finally, clustering approaches can be speeded up by parallel processing, e.g., Dhillon [11] discusses a parallel implementation for the $K$-means clustering algorithm; Olson [35] discusses parallel hierarchical clustering.

## 3.5 Dimension Reduction

Dimension reduction is the process of reducing the number of features for pattern representation. As already mentioned in Section 3.2, features irrelevant to the problem can seriously hamper classification accuracy and selecting a set of relevant features is often crucial for effective classification. Generally, a limited set of salient features simplifies the representation and also requires fewer memory and time resources. On the other hand, reduction of the number of features can affect the classifier's performance due to loss of discriminant power. The importance of a careful choice of suitable features is further supported by Watanabe's *ugly duckling theorem* [12] according to which any two patterns are similar if encoded by a sufficiently large number of redundant features.

Dimension reduction can be divided into *feature extraction* and *feature selection*. Feature extraction methods aim to construct an appropriate subspace of a lower dimension than the original feature space by using transformations of the original features. Feature selection methods select a subset of the original feature set in order to reduce classification error.

Fodor [14] gives a good survey on dimension reduction techniques.

### 3.5.1 Feature Extraction

Feature extraction methods create new features by combination and transformation of the original features. Principal Component Analysis (PCA) and Linear Discriminant Analysis (LDA) are two commonly used methods to reduce dimension by obtaining transformed features.

**Principal Component Analysis (PCA)**

PCA, also known as the discrete Karhunen–Loève transform (KLT), is a linear technique for dimension reduction. The idea is to retain only those characteristics of the data set that contribute most to its variance. To this end, first the directions in the data of maximum variance are identified. Next, the data is projected into the lower-dimensional space formed by these directions of highest variance. As a result we obtain the principal components, i.e., the new coordinates after transformation of the data. The first principal component accounts for as much of the variability in the data as possible, the second component accounts for as much of the remaining variability as possible, and so on.

The derivation of the PCA transformation proceeds by finding linear projections that maximize the variance in the data after projection. We start with a data set of $n$ vectors $\{x_1, x_2, \ldots, x_n\}$, all of dimension $m$, i.e., consisting of $m$ components. The sample covariance matrix of such set is given by:

$$\hat{\Sigma} = \sum_{i=1}^{n} \frac{(x_i - \bar{x})(x_i - \bar{x})^T}{n}, \tag{3.29}$$

where $\bar{x}$ is the sample mean $\bar{x} = \sum_{i=1}^{n} x_i/n$. Given a vector $w$ of unit length, the variance in the data after projection on $w$ is given by $\sigma^2(w) = w^T \hat{\Sigma} w$. This means (see for instance the article by Hotelling [25]) that the $k$ principal axes $\{w_1, w_2, \ldots, w_k\}$ that maximize variance after projection are given by the (normalized) eigenvectors corresponding to the $k$ largest eigenvalues of the sample covariance matrix. We thus have:

$$\hat{\Sigma} w_j = \lambda_j w_j, \quad j = 1, \ldots, k, \tag{3.30}$$

where the $\lambda_j$ are the $k$ largest eigenvalues of $\hat{\Sigma}$. To obtain the transformed coordinates $y_i$ for the data vector $x_i$, we first subtract the sample mean and then project the data on these orthonormal eigenvectors, i.e.:

$$y_i = W^T(x_i - \bar{x}),  \tag{3.31}$$

where $W = (w_1; w_2; \ldots; w_k)$. The new coordinates are uncorrelated: it is easy to check that the new sample covariance matrix $\sum_{i=1}^{n} y_i y_i^T / n$ is diagonal with elements $\lambda_i$. It is also common to "sphere" the data, i.e., to transform the data using $\tilde{y} = \Lambda^{-\frac{1}{2}} W^T (x - \bar{x})$. In that case the resulting transformed data is uncorrelated and has unit variance for each component.

Another property of PCA is that of all orthogonal linear projections, as (3.31), the principal component projection minimizes the squared reconstruction error $\sum_{i=1}^{n} ||x_i - \hat{x}_i||^2$, where the optimal linear reconstruction $\hat{x}$ is given by:

$$\hat{x} = Wy + \bar{x}.  \tag{3.32}$$

We will illustrate how PCA works with a simple example.

**Example**: The input is the simple 2D data illustrated in Figure 3.10.

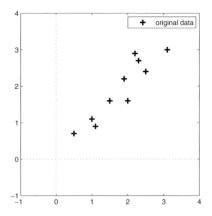

**Fig. 3.10.** Original PCA data plot.

1. **Subtracting the sample mean**
   The first step is to "center the data" by subtracting the sample mean in each dimension.
2. **Covariance matrix**
   The sample covariance matrix is computed using (3.29). For example:

$$\hat{\Sigma} = \begin{pmatrix} 0.61656 & 0.61544 \\ 0.61544 & 0.71656 \end{pmatrix}.$$

The positive non-diagonal elements of $\hat{\Sigma}$ confirm the positive correlation between the first and second components of the data vectors.

3. **Eigenvectors and eigenvalues of the covariance matrix**

The eigenvalues of $\hat{\Sigma}$ are $\lambda_1 = 0.049083$ and $\lambda_2 = 1.284$. The matrix with the eigenvectors is:

$$\begin{pmatrix} -0.73518 & -0.67787 \\ 0.67787 & -0.73518 \end{pmatrix}.$$

Figure 3.11 illustrates the normalized data and the eigenvectors. It can be seen that the eigenvectors are indeed orthogonal to each other. The direction of the solid line is the direction with the largest variance in the data.

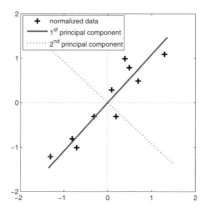

**Fig. 3.11.** Normalized PCA data and the principal components.

4. **Selecting principal components**

The eigenvector $w_1$ of the largest eigenvalue (in our example $\lambda_2$) corresponds to the first principal component of the data set (again the solid line in Figure 3.11).

In general, once the eigenvectors have been computed the next step is to order them in decreasing order of the corresponding eigenvalues. This gives the components in order of decreasing variance. Ignoring components with small variance leads to loss of information, but that loss is small if the eigenvalues are small, i.e., dimension reduction may be achieved at little cost. The original data set had data of dimension $m$; by choosing the $k$ most significant components, we reduce the dimension to $k$. In our example we have only two components, so there are two options: (i) to keep both components as features and (ii) ignore the smaller component. In the former case the linear transform is defined via:

$$W = (w_1; w_2) = \begin{pmatrix} -0.67787 & -0.73518 \\ -0.73518 & 0.67787 \end{pmatrix},$$

while in the latter via:

$$W = (w_1) = \begin{pmatrix} -0.67787 \\ -0.73518 \end{pmatrix}.$$

5. **Transformation of the data set**
   The new data set is obtained by projecting the original data set to the new basis $W$ by applying (3.31). In the first case of keeping both components the transformed data values are shown on the left in Figure 3.12.

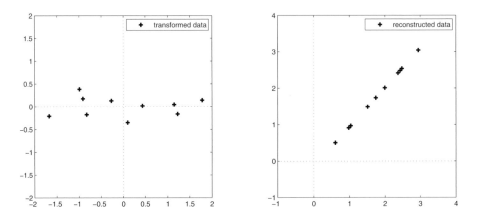

**Fig. 3.12.** *Left*: transformed PCA data plot; *right*: reconstructed data transformed using a single principal component.

This plot is a rotated (and translated) version of the original data plot; we have no loss of information as we did not reduce the dimension. For case (ii), the transformed data is one-dimensional, corresponding to the first coordinate in the left graph of Figure 3.12.

The reconstruction of the original data set can be obtained using (3.32). The loss of information when only one principal component has been kept as feature is illustrated in the right graph of Figure 3.12. Comparing with the original data set (Figure 3.10), we observe that while the variation along the principal eigenvector has been kept, the variation along the other component has been removed.

In the context of multimedia analysis, PCA is often applied in face recognition (see the book *Computer Vision and Pattern Recognition* [43]). The face images are first decomposed into a set of characteristic feature images. These images, which are the principal components of the original training set of face images, are called *eigenfaces*. Recognition is performed by projecting new face images onto the subspace spanned by the eigenfaces, followed by a classification. The eigenface approach has certain advantages over other face recognition methods such as speed, simplicity, learning capability and robustness to small changes.

In the information retrieval community, PCA is used in Latent Semantic Indexing (LSI [10]). The covariance matrix of the data in PCA corresponds to the *document-term matrix* multiplied by its transpose. Entries in the covariance matrix represent co-occurring terms in the documents. The eigenvectors of this matrix corresponding to the dominant eigenvalues are related to dominant combinations of terms (*topics, semantic concepts*) occurring in the corpus. A transformation matrix constructed from these eigenvectors projects a document onto these *latent semantic concepts*, and a new lower dimensional representation is achieved. The eigen-analysis can be performed efficiently using a sparse variant of the singular value decomposition (SVD) of the document-term matrix.

**Linear Discriminant Analysis (LDA)**
PCA deals with the data in its entirety; it does not take into account any underlying class structure. Dimension reduction based on Linear Discriminant Analysis (LDA) on the other hand, explicitly aims to find those directions in the data that best separate the classes. If the dimension reduction is required for a classification, i.e., supervised, problem this can be a distinct advantage compared to the unsupervised approach in PCA.

As already mentioned in Section 3.2.3, discriminant methods construct a classifier by picking the class with maximum posterior probability:

$$\operatorname*{argmax}_{k \in \mathcal{K}} p_k(x)\pi_k, \tag{3.33}$$

where $p_k(x)$ is the feature probability density given class $k$, and $\pi_k$ is the prior probability for class $k$. Assuming a multivariate Gaussian density:

$$p_k(x) = \frac{1}{(2\pi)^{m/2}|\Sigma_k|^{1/2}} \exp\left(x - \mu_k\right)^T \Sigma_k^{-1}(x - \mu_k), \tag{3.34}$$

for each class, where $\mu_k$ are the class means, leads to a linear discriminant if we assume a common covariance matrix, i.e., $\Sigma_k = \Sigma$, $\forall k$. After substituting (3.34) in (3.33) and some derivation we obtain:

$$\delta_k(x) = x^T \Sigma^{-1} \mu_k - \frac{1}{2}\mu_k^T \Sigma^{-1}\mu_k + \log(\pi_k). \tag{3.35}$$

The decision boundary between two classes $k$ and $l$ is $x : \delta_k(x) = \delta_l(x)$, or:

$$\log\left(\frac{\pi_k}{\pi_l}\right) - \frac{1}{2}(\mu_k + \mu_l)^T \Sigma^{-1}(\mu_k - \mu_l) + x^T \Sigma^{-1}(\mu_k - \mu_l) = 0. \tag{3.36}$$

**Example**: Let's consider a simple binary 2D classification example. We assume that the classes are equiprobable, i.e., $\pi_1 = \pi_2 = 0.5$. The parameters of the bivariate Gaussian distributions are $\mu_1 = (0,0)^T$, $\mu_2 = (2,-2)^T$ and:

$$\Sigma = \begin{pmatrix} 1 & 0 \\ 0 & 0.5625 \end{pmatrix}.$$

The probability distribution of the mixture is illustrated on the left in Figure 3.13. The decision boundary obtained via (3.36) is then $5.56 - x_1 + 3.56x_2 = 0$. The class separation is illustrated on the right in Figure 3.13.

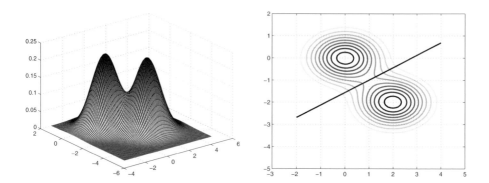

**Fig. 3.13.** Two class problem. *Left*: mixture distribution; *right*: 2D contour plot of the distributions and the LDA decision boundary.

Based on the linear discriminants we can reduce the dimension of the problem by leaving out directions that are not relevant to class separation. Basically the idea is that after transforming the data based on the within-class covariance, using a transformation as in PCA, the data can be summarized by their distances to the class means. Distances perpendicular to the plane of class means are not relevant for classification. In the book *Elements of Statistical Learning* [22] it is shown that we can achieve further dimension reduction by applying a PCA on the transformed class means, such that we obtain directions that optimally separate the classes. This turns out to be equivalent to the direct approach of Fisher linear discriminants (FLD) where coordinates are chosen corresponding to directions that maximize the ratio of the between-class variance to the within-class variance. The criterion to be maximized in the Fisher-LDA is:

$$J(w) = \frac{w^T S_B w}{w^T S_W w}, \tag{3.37}$$

where $S_B$ and $S_W$ are the between-class and within-class scatter matrices (which are proportional to the covariance matrices). The scatter matrices are defined as follows:

$$S_B = \sum_{k \in \mathcal{K}} n_k (\mu_k - \bar{x})(\mu_k - \bar{x})^T \tag{3.38}$$

and

$$S_W = \sum_{k \in \mathcal{K}} \sum_{i \in \mathcal{C}_k} (x_i - \mu_k)(x_i - \mu_k)^T, \tag{3.39}$$

where $\mu_k = \frac{1}{n_k} \sum_{i \in \mathcal{C}_k} x_i$ is the mean vector for class $k$, and $n_k$ is the number of data items belonging to class $k$.

Martinez and Kak [31] compare PCA and LDA for face recognition applications, and Torkkola [41] discusses an application of LDA in document classification.

### 3.5.2 Feature Selection

The problem of feature selection can be characterized as follows: given a set of $n$ features, select a subset of *relevant* features of size $k < n$ which are *useful* for building a good classifier. For a discussion about "relevance" and "usefulness" see the overview paper by Blum and Langley [7].

Guyon and Elisseeff [20] give a good overview of up-to date feature selection methods. They also present a heuristic checklist for choosing an appropriate feature selection algorithm. We follow their three main types of feature selection methods: *filters*, *wrappers* and *embedded* methods.

- **Filter Methods**.

   These are methods which aim to *filter out* the irrelevant features prior to the learning stage (Figure 3.14).

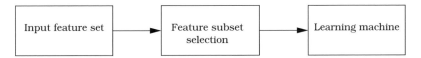

**Fig. 3.14.** The filter approach to feature selection.

Many filter methods have *variable ranking* as the main feature selection mechanism. The ranking is done by ordering the variables in decreasing order of the value of a given scoring function. It is a preprocessing step and is independent of the learning algorithm. Under some assumptions, however, the ranking can be optimal in respect to a given predictor. For example using the FLD (3.37) as a ranking criterion can be optimal for Fisher's linear discriminant classifier [12].

Let $\{(x_i, y_i)\}$, $i = 1, \ldots, n$ be a set of labeled examples with $m$ input variables $x_{i,j}$, $j = 1, \ldots, m$, and $y_i$ a scalar output variable. A widely used scoring function is based on the estimate of the correlation coefficient:

$$R(j) = \frac{\sum_{i=1}^{n} (x_{i,j} - \bar{x}_j)(y_i - \bar{y})}{\sqrt{\sum_{i=1}^{n} (x_{i,j} - \bar{x}_j)^2 \sum_{i=1}^{n} (y_i - \bar{y})^2}}. \tag{3.40}$$

Another approach is to select variables based on their predictive power when used in single variable classifier. The predictive power of the variable

can be measured in terms of the error rate. George Forman [15] gives
an extensive study on a number of feature selection metrics for binary
variables in text classification.

Another important criterion for variable selection is the *mutual infor-mation* (MI) between each variable and the class variable (target). For
discrete variables it is defined as:

$$\text{MI}(j) = \sum_{x_j} \sum_{y} P(X = x_j, Y = k) \log \frac{P(X = x_j, Y = k)}{P(X = x_j) P(Y = k)}, \quad (3.41)$$

where $P(Y = k)$ are the class prior probabilities, $P(X = x_j)$ is the distri-bution of the input variable and $P(X = x_j, Y = k)$ is the joint probability.
For the continuous case it is harder to estimate these probabilities; a dis-cretization of the variables is considered by Torkkola [42]. For using MI
between images and their associated text for the purpose of data mining,
see the article by Barnard and Yanai [3].

Taking one variable at a time obviously has some limitations: presumably
redundant variables can help each other, and similarly, a variable that is
useless by itself, can be useful with others.

- **Wrapper Methods**.
  Where the filter methods are essentially a preprocessing step, *wrapper*
  methods treat the learning machine as a black box, calling it as a subrou-tine to evaluate the usefulness of a given subset of variables (Figure 3.15).

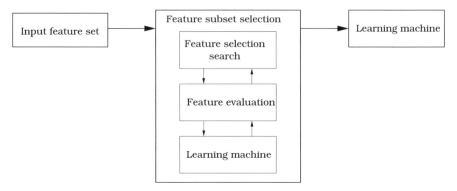

**Fig. 3.15.** The wrapper approach to feature selection.

The general argument for the wrapper methodology is that the learner
used on a subset of the features will give a better estimate of the perfor-mance accuracy than a separate measure. Four main issues when consid-ering a feature selection method as a *heuristic search* [7] are: (i) selecting
a starting point in the feature space, (ii) organization of the search, i.e.,
how to go through all of the possible variable subsets, (iii) evaluation of

the prediction performance of a learning machine and (iv) how to halt the search.

Considering the starting point, there are two main approaches: *forward selection* and *backward elimination*. Forward selection refers to starting with an empty set of features and progressively incorporating new features into larger and larger subsets, while backward elimination starts with the full set of features progressively eliminating the least promising ones. The former approach is preferred due to computational reasons of building fast classifiers with just a few features, while the latter, which may be better at capturing feature interactions, is computationally more expensive.

The feature space can be explored using exhaustive search only for a small number of variables. The problem is NP-hard and the search quickly becomes computationally intractable. A wide range of search strategies can be used, such as greedy search, simulated annealing or genetic algorithms; Kohavi [29] gives an overview.

Performance evaluation is usually done using a validation set or by cross-validation (see Section 3.2.2). Another issue is the choice of predictor. Popular choices are decision trees, naïve Bayes, least-squares linear predictors and SVMs.

Considering the learning machine as a black box (i.e., the method is not important, but only the interface) makes the wrapper methods universal. A disadvantage of the wrappers is their computational cost, because they invoke the learner at each step of the feature selection search; efficient search strategies can alleviate this problem to some extent.

- **Embedded Methods**.
  These methods *embed* the feature selection within the learning process and thus are dependent on the particular algorithm. They use the same criteria for the usefulness of features and performance validation measurement as the wrappers, but the search is guided by the learning process. As a result, the embedded methods tend to be less computationally expensive and less prone to overfitting than the wrappers. Also they do not need to split the data into training and validation sets.

  The embedded methods can be further divided in three main groups: into *forward* and *backward* selection methods (as already explained above) and into *nested* methods. Whereas in the forward selection methods new features are added and in the backward selection methods- removed, in the nested approaches features may be either added or deleted at each iteration.

  Methods in the first group include those based on least squares forward selection and decision trees. Forward selection using Gram–Schmidt diagonalization is introduced by Stoppiglia [40]. The main idea there is as follows: select a first feature $x$ with maximum cosine with the target $\cos(x,y) = \langle x,y \rangle / \|x\| \|y\|$. For each remaining feature $x_j$ project it and the target $y$ on the null space of the features already selected and compute the cosine of $x_j$ with the target in the projection. Select the feature $x_j$ with maximum cosine with the target in the projection. This can be considered as an embedded method for the linear least square predictor. Embedded methods using decision trees include the classical CART method [9] and C.4.5 [36] which have built-in mechanisms to perform variable selection. Decision trees are built iteratively by splitting the data depending on the value of a specific feature. The "splitting" feature (node) is chosen according to its importance for the classification task.

An important method in the group of the backward elimination methods is Recursive Feature Elimination (RFE [21]). The main idea is as follows: start with the set of all features and train a learning machine $l$ on the current subset of features by minimizing some risk functional $J(l)$. For each (remaining) feature $x_j$ estimate, without retraining $l$, the change in $J(l)$ resulting from the removal of $x_j$. Remove the feature $x_j$ that results in improving (or least degrading) $J$. RFE is an embedded method for SVMs, kernel methods and neural networks.

Embedded methods are relatively new methods for feature selection. Lal et al. [30] give a good overview as well as a unified theoretical framework.

## 3.6 Summary

This chapter gives an introduction to the main pattern recognition tools used in multimedia content analysis. The fields of pattern recognition and more generally of machine learning are very broad, therefore it is difficult to make a complete overview. We have opted for presenting representative methods used in the main stages of the recognition process and to illustrate them with simple examples. The chapter presents the main issues in pattern classification such as uncertainty, limited and noisy data, over- and underfitting and measuring classifier performance. The Bayes classification paradigm is presented together with classical approaches such as nearest neighbors and discriminant functions and the topical support vector machines and boosting. Hidden Markov models are presented because of their suitability for explicit modeling of the patterns in multimedia data. The large area of unsupervised learning and clustering is also introduced outlining both the main concepts and methods as well as the specific issues of clustering in large databases. Finally, we have given an overview of the main methods for dimension reduction.

In conclusion, it is clear that the quality of our "computational under-standing" of multimedia is directly related to the quality of the metadata we can acquire. As pattern recognition is exactly aiming at the effective acquisi-tion of such metadata, the importance of the area to automatic multimedia analysis can hardly be overemphasized.

## 3.7 Further Reading

A classic for the field is *Pattern Classification* by Duda, Hart and Stork [12]. Another good book is Bishop's *Neural Networks for Pattern Recognition* [6] which covers material, in particular on classification using neural networks, not presented in this chapter. A very good introduction to statistical learning is provided by Hastie, Tibshirani and Friedman in *Elements of Statistical Learning* [22]. Schölkopf [39] gives an excellent introduction to kernel-based methods and support vector machines; good introductions to boosting are provided by Meir and Rätsch [33] and Freund and Schapire [16]. A good starting point into the clustering literature, focused on large databases, is offered by Pavel Berkhin [5]. A number of interesting articles on feature selection methods have been published in the special issue on *Variable and Feature Selection* of the *Journal of Machine Learning Research* [2].

## References

1. Hidden Markov Models and the Baum–Welch Algorithm. In Lance Pérez, editor, *IEEE Information Theory Newsletter*, volume 53, December 2003.
2. Special Issue on Variable and Feature Selection, JMLR, 2003. `http://jmlr.csail.mit.edu/papers/special/feature03.html`.
3. Kobus Barnard and Keiji Yanai. Mutual information of words and pictures, 2006. Information Theory and Applications Inaugural Workshop, `http://kobus.ca/research/publications/ita-2006.pdf`.
4. M.S. Bazaraa, H.D. Sherali, and C.M. Shetty. *Nonlinear Programming – Theory and Algorithms*. Wiley, 1979, 3rd ed. 2006.
5. Pavel Berkhin. Survey of clustering data mining techniques. Technical report, Accrue Software, San Jose, CA, 2002. `http://www.accrue.com/products/rp_cluster_review.pdf`.
6. Christopher M. Bishop. *Neural Networks for Pattern Recognition*. Oxford University Press, November 1995.
7. Avrim L. Blum and Pat Langley. Selection of relevant features and examples in machine learning. *Artif. Intell.*, 97(1–2):245–271, 1997.
8. Christian Böhm, Stefan Berchtold, and Daniel A. Keim. Searching in high-dimensional spaces: Index structures for improving the performance of multimedia databases. *ACM Comput. Surv.*, 33(3):322–373, 2001.
9. L. Breiman, J. Friedman, R. Olshen, and C. Stone. *Classification and Regression Trees*. Wadsworth and Brooks/Cole, 1984.
10. Scott C. Deerwester, Susan T. Dumais, Thomas K. Landauer, George W. Furnas, and Richard A. Harshman. Indexing by latent semantic analysis. *Journal of the American Society of Information Science*, 41(6):391–407, 1990.
11. I. Dhillon and D. Modha. Cactus–clustering categorical data using summaries. In *Proceedings of Largescale Parallel KDD Systems Workshop, ACM SIGKDD*, pages 245–260. ACM Press, 1999.
12. R. Duda, P. Hart, and Stork D. *Pattern Classification*. Wiley, 2001.
13. D. Fisher. Knowledge acquisition via incremental conceptual clustering. *Machine Learning*, (2):139–175, 1987.
14. Imola Fodor. A survey of dimension reduction techniques, 2002.

15. George Forman. An extensive empirical study of feature selection metrics for text classification. *Journal of Machiche Learning Research*, 3:1289–1305, 2003.
16. Y. Freund and R. Schapire. A short introduction to boosting, 1999. J. Japan. Soc. for Artif. Intel. 14(5) (1999), 771–780. 11, citeseer.ist.psu.edu/freund99short.html.
17. Yoav Freund and Robert E. Schapire. A decision-theoretic generalization of on-line learning and an application to boosting. *J. Comput. Syst. Sci.*, 55(1):119–139, 1997.
18. Sudipto Guha, Rajeev Rastogi, and Kyuseok Shim. Cure: an efficient clustering algorithm for large databases. *SIGMOD Rec.*, 27(2):73–84, 1998.
19. Sudipto Guha, Rajeev Rastogi, and Kyuseok Shim. ROCK: A robust clustering algorithm for categorical attributes. *Information Systems*, 25(5):345–366, 2000.
20. Isabelle Guyon and Andrè Elisseeff. An introduction to variable and feature selection. *J. Mach. Learn. Res.*, 3:1157–1182, 2003.
21. Isabelle Guyon, Jason Weston, Stephen Barnhill, and Vladimir Vapnik. Gene selection for cancer classification using support vector machines. *Machine Learning*, 46(1–3):389–422, 2002.
22. Y. Hastie, R. Tibshirani, and J. Friedman. *Elements of Statistical Learning – Datamining, Inference, and Prediction*. Springer, 2001, 3rd ed. 2003.
23. A.G. Hauptmann. Towards a large scale concept ontology for broadcast video. In *Proceedings of the International Conference on Image and Video Retrieval (CIVR 2004), Dublin, Ireland*, pages 674–675, 2004.
24. F. Höppner, F. Klawonn, R. Kruse, and T. Runkler. *Fuzzy Cluster Analysis*. Wiley, 1999.
25. H. Hotelling. Analysis of a complex of statistical variables into principal components. *Journal of Educational Psychology*, 24(8):417–441, 1933.
26. A. K. Jain, M. N. Murty, and P. J. Flynn. Data clustering: a review. *ACM Comput. Surv.*, 31(3):264–323, 1999.
27. George Karypis, Eui-Hong (Sam) Han, and Vipin Kumar NEWS. Chameleon: Hierarchical clustering using dynamic modeling. *Computer*, 32(8):68–75, 1999.
28. M.J. Kearns and U.V. Vazirani. *An Introduction to Computational Learning Theory*. MIT Press, 1994.
29. Ron Kohavi and George H. John. Wrappers for feature subset selection. *Artificial Intelligence*, 97(1–2):273–324, 1997.
30. O. Chapelle J. Weston Lal, T. N. and A. Elisseeff. *Embedded Methods. Feature Extraction, Foundations and Applications*, pages 137–165. Springer-Verlag, Berlin, Heidelberg, Germany, 2006.
31. Aleix M. Martinez and Avinash C. Kak. PCA versus LDA. *IEEE Transactions on Pattern Analysis and Machine Intelligence*, 23(2):228–233, 2001.
32. G. McLachlan and T. Krishnan. *The EM Algorithm and Extensions*. Marcel Dekker, 1997.
33. Ron Meir and Gunnar Rätsch. *An introduction to boosting and leveraging*, pages 118–183. Springer-Verlag New York, Inc., New York, NY, USA, 2003.
34. M.N. Murty and G. Krishna. A computationally efficient technique for data clustering. *Pattern Recognition*, 12:153–158, 1980.
35. C.F. Olson. Parallel Algorithms for Hierarchical Clustering. *Parallel Computing*, 21(28):1313–1325, 1995.
36. Ross J. Quinlan. *C4.5: Programs for Machine Learning*. Morgan Kaufmann Publishers Inc., 1993.

37. L. Rabiner. A tutorial on Hidden Markov Models and Selected Applications in Speech Recognition. In *Proceedings of the IEEE*, volume 77, pages 257–286, February 1989.
38. Robert E. Schapire. The strength of weak learnability. *Mach. Learn.*, 5(2):197–227, 1990.
39. B. Schölkopf and A. J. Smola. *Learning with Kernels: Support Vector Machines, Regularization, Optimization, and Beyond*. MIT Press, Cambridge, MA, 2002.
40. Hervé Stoppiglia, Gérard Dreyfus, Rémi Dubois, and Yacine Oussar. Ranking a random feature for variable and feature selection. *Journal of Machine Learning Research*, 3:1399–1414, 2003.
41. K. Torkkola. Linear discriminant analysis in document classification, 2001. In: *IEEE ICDM-2001 Workshop on Text Mining* (TextDM'2001), San Jose, CA (2001), `citeseer.ist.psu.edu/torkkola01linear.html`.
42. Kari Torkkola. Feature extraction by non parametric mutual information maximization. *Journal of Machine Learning Research*, 3:1415–1438, 2003.
43. M. A. Turk and A. P. Pentland. Face recognition using eigenfaces. In *Computer Vision and Pattern Recognition, 1991. Proceedings CVPR '91., IEEE Computer Society Conference on*, pages 586–591, 1991.
44. David H. Wolpert. The lack of A priori distinctions between learning algorithms. *Neural Computation*, 8(7):1341–1390, 1996.
45. Tian Zhang, Raghu Ramakrishnan, and Miron Livny. Birch: an efficient data clustering method for very large databases. *SIGMOD Rec.*, 25(2):103–114, 1996.

# 4

# Searching for Text Documents

Henk Blanken and Djoerd Hiemstra

University of Twente

## 4.1 Introduction

Many documents contain, besides text, also images, tables, and so on. This chapter concentrates on the text part only. Traditionally, systems handling text documents are called information storage and retrieval systems. Before the World-Wide Web emerged, such systems were almost exclusively used by professional users, so-called indexers and searchers, e.g., for medical research, in libraries, by governmental organizations and archives. Typically, professional users act as "search intermediaries" for end users. They try to figure out in an interactive dialogue with the system and the end user what it is the end user needs, and how this information should be used in a successful search. Professionals know the collection, they know how documents in the collection are represented in the system, and they know how to use Boolean search operators to control the number of retrieved documents.

Many modern information retrieval systems, like Internet search engines, are specifically designed for end users who are not familiar with the collection, the representation of the documents, and the use of Boolean operators. The main requirements for these systems are the following. Firstly, users should  be able to enter any natural language word(s), phrase(s) or sentence(s) to the system without the need to enter operators. Secondly, the system should rank the retrieved documents by their estimated degree or probability of usefulness for the user.

In this introduction we will reconsider some concepts from previous chapters and describe what these concepts mean in the information retrieval realm.

### 4.1.1 Text Documents

A (text) document has an identification and can be considered to be a list of words. So, a book is a document, but so is a paper in the proceedings of a conference or a Web page. The identification may be an ISBN number for a book, the title of the paper together with the ISBN of the conference proceedings or a URL for a Web page.

Retrieval of text documents does normally not imply the presentation of the whole document (this is too space and time consuming). Instead the system presents the identifications of the selected documents possibly together with brief descriptions and/or their rankings.

### 4.1.2 Indexing

Indexing is the process of deriving metadata from documents and storage of the metadata in an index. The index describes in one way or another the content of the documents; for text documents the content is described by *terms* like `social` or `political`. During retrieval, the system uses the index to determine the output.

There are two ways to fill the index, namely manually and automatically. Professional users like librarians may add so-called *assigned terms* to documents as a kind of annotation. Sometimes these terms are selected from a prescribed set of terms, the *catalog*. A catalog is composed by specialists and describes a certain (scientific) field. An advantage of this approach is that the professional users know the allowed terms to be used in query formulation. A clear disadvantage is the amount of work needed to perform the manual indexing process.

Describing the content of documents can also be done automatically resulting in so-called *derived terms*. Several steps are required, for instance a step in which an algorithm identifies words in an English text and puts them to lower case. Other steps use basic tools like *stop word removal* and *stemming*. Stop words are words in the document with little meaning, mostly function words like "the" and "it". These words are removed. Stemming conflates the words in the document to their stem. For instance, the stemmer introduced by Porter [23] conflates the words "computer", "compute" and "computation" to the stem `comput`.

### 4.1.3 Query Formulation

The process of representing the information need is often referred to as the *query formulation* process. The resulting formal representation is the query. In a broad sense, query formulation might denote the complete interactive dialogue between system and user, leading not only to a suitable query but possibly also to a better understanding by the user of his/her information need. Here, however, query formulation denotes the formulation of the query when there are no previously retrieved documents to guide the search, that is, the formulation of the initial query.

Again we must distinguish between the professional searcher and the casual end user. The first one knows the document collection and the assigned terms. The professional will use Boolean operators to compose the query and will be able to adequately rephrase the query depending on the output of the system. If the result set is too small, the professional must broaden the query, if too large the professional must make the query more restrictive. See Section 4.2.

The end user likes to communicate the need for information to the system in natural language. Such a natural language statement of the information need is called a request. Automatic query formulation includes receiving the request and generating an initial query by applying the same algorithms as used for the derivation of terms. The query consists in general of a list of query terms. The system accepts this list and composes in one way or another a result set. The end user may indicate the documents that are considered to be relevant. This *relevance feedback* allows the system to formulate a successive query.

### 4.1.4 Matching

Probably the most important part of an information retrieval system is the matching algorithm. The algorithm compares the query against the document representations in the index. We distinguish *exact matching* and *inexact matching* algorithms. To start with the first kind: a Boolean query formulated by a professional searcher defines exactly the set of documents that satisfy the query. For each document the system generates a yes/no decision.

If a system uses inexact matching, it delivers a ranked list of documents. Users will walk down this document list in search of the information they need. Ranked retrieval will hopefully put the relevant documents somewhere in the top of the ranked list, minimizing the time the user has to invest on reading the documents. Simple but effective ranking algorithms use the frequency distribution of terms over documents. For instance, the words "family" and "entertainment" mentioned in a small part of a book, may occur relatively infrequent in the rest of the book, which indicates that the book should not receive a top ranking for the request "family entertainment". Ranking algorithms based on statistical approaches easily halve the time the user has to spend on reading documents. The description of ranking algorithms is a major theme of this chapter.

### 4.1.5 Relation to Other Chapters

If a document contains text and for instance images, then an algorithm needs to separate those parts. In Chapter 3 approaches are described to deal with this problem.

In Section 4.3.6 we deal with the PageRank algorithm used in the Google Web search engine. The algorithm takes into account the hyperlink structure on the Web and has some similarities with collaborative filtering that is explained in Chapter 11. In this technique the opinion of users regarding documents influences the selection process.

### 4.1.6 Outline

In the traditional information retrieval systems, which are usually operated by professional searchers, only the matching process is automated; indexing and query formulation are manual processes. These information retrieval systems use the Boolean model of information retrieval. The Boolean model is an *exact matching model*, that is, it either retrieves documents or not without ranking them. The model also supports the use of structured queries, which do not only contain query terms, but also relations between the terms defined by the query operators AND, OR and NOT. In Section 4.2 we explain the Boolean model.

In modern information retrieval systems, which are commonly used by non-professional users, query formulation is also automated. Mathematical models are used to model the matching process. There are many candidate models for the matching process of ranked retrieval systems. These models are so-called *inexact matching models*, that is, they compute a ranking for each document retrieved even if the document only partly satisfies the query. Each of these models has its own advantages and disadvantages. However, there are two classical candidate models for approximate matching: the vector space model and the probabilistic model. In Section 4.3 we explain these models as well as other ranking models like the p-norm extended Boolean model, and the Bayesian network model.

So-called language models were first used in telecommunications and some time later in speech recognition. Language models build a mathematical model of a language. This model can be used for instance to determine the probability that a certain word follows a recognized word. Recently the models got much attention in the IR community. Language models are treated in Section 4.3.5.

Web search engines are a rather new phenomenon and the most successful engine is probably Google. Besides some content oriented ranking techniques, Google also exploits the so-called PageRank algorithm. The idea is that the opinion of the user community with respect to a document, that is Web page, influences the ranking of the page. The opinion is modeled by considering the reference pattern which can be derived from the Web. Section 4.3.6 discusses Google's ranking mechanism.

Until now terms are treated equally in a query and in the document as represented in the index. Much attention in IR research has been paid, however, to so-called term weighting algorithms. A *term weight* is a value of the term's importance in a query or a document. Term weighting is described in Section 4.4.

## 4.2 Boolean Model

The Boolean model is the first model of information retrieval and probably also the most criticized model. The model is based on set theory and can be explained by thinking of a query term as an unambiguous definition of a set of documents. For instance, the query term economic simply defines the set of all documents that are indexed with the term economic. Using the operators of George Boole's mathematical logic, query terms and their corresponding sets of documents can be combined to form new sets of documents. Boole defined three basic operators: AND, OR, and NOT [4]. Combining terms with the

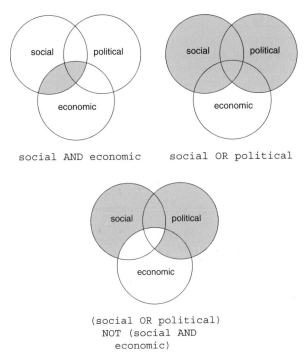

social AND economic      social OR political

(social OR political)
NOT (social AND
economic)

**Fig. 4.1.** Three Boolean combinations of sets visualized as Venn diagrams.

AND operator will define a document set that is smaller than or equal to the document sets of any of the single terms. For instance, the query `social AND economic` will produce the set of documents that are indexed both with `social` and `economic`. Combining terms with the OR operator will define a document set that is bigger than or equal to the document sets of any of the single terms. So, the query `social OR political` will produce the set of documents that are indexed with either `social` or `political`, or both.

This is visualized in the Venn diagrams of Figure 4.1[1] in which each set of documents is visualized by a disk. The intersections of these disks and their complements divide the document collection into eight non-overlapping regions, the unions of which give 256 different Boolean combinations of social, political and economic documents. In Figure 4.1, the retrieved sets are visualized by the shaded areas.

## 4.2.1 Proximity Searching: ADJ, NEAR

With the emergence of *automatic full text indexing* (meaning that every word of the document is indexed), commercial retrieval systems added new Boolean operators to the standard Boolean operators. These operators use positions

---

[1] Often, the NOT-operator is implemented as a logical difference instead of a set complement, requiring the use of **A NOT B** instead of **A AND NOT B**

of words in text. The ADJ operator allows for the search of exact phrases by looking for documents that contain two adjacent terms in the specified order. For instance, `environmental ADJ damage` selects only documents containing the exact phrase "environmental damage". The NEAR operator allows for the search of two terms that are near to each other without any requirements on the order of the words. Table 4.1 list some examples.

**Table 4.1.** Proximity operators.

| Query | Interpretation |
|---|---|
| `waste ADJ management` | select documents containing the exact phrase "`waste management`" |
| `waste NEAR management` | select documents containing, e.g., "`waste management`", "`manage-ment of waste`" or "`waste of valuable management talent`" |
| `(hazardous OR toxic) ADJ wastes` | select documents containing either "`hazardous wastes`" or "`toxic wastes`" |
| `(hazardous AND waste) ADJ management` | ill-defined because "`management`" could not be adjacent to both "hazardous" and "waste" |

The last example of Table 4.1 requires some explanation. Some systems produce an error if such a query is entered as these systems claim that it is impossible that a term `management` is adjacent to two other terms `hazardous` and `waste`. But `management` may occur many times in a document and usually system designers decide to process the last example as (`hazardous ADJ management`) `AND` (`waste ADJ management`).

### 4.2.2 Wildcards
Wildcards are used to mask a part of a query term with a special character, allowing it to match any term that maps to the unmasked portion of the query term. Table 4.2 shows some examples of the use of wildcards, taken from Kowalski [14].

From the options in Table 4.2, suffix searches are the most common. In some systems suffix searches are the default without the user having to specify this. Suffix truncation is also the easiest of the options above to implement.

### 4.2.3 Discussion
We give two advantages of Boolean retrieval. Firstly, the model gives (expert) users a sense of control over the system. It is immediately clear why a

**Table 4.2.** Wildcards.

| Query | Interpretation |
|-------|----------------|
| dog* | suffix truncation selects documents containing, e.g., "dog", "dogs" or "doggy", but also "dogma" and "dogger" |
| *computer | prefix truncation: selects documents containing, e.g., "minicomputer", "microcomputer" or "computer" |
| colo*r | infix truncation: selects documents containing, e.g., "colour", "color", but also "colorimeter" or "colourbearer" |
| multi$national | single position truncation: selects documents containing "multi-national" or "multinational", but no "multi national" as it contains two processing tokens |

document has been retrieved given a query. If the resulting document set is either too small or too big, it is directly clear which operators will produce respectively a bigger or smaller set. Secondly, the model can be extended with proximity operators and wildcard operators in a mathematically sound way, which makes it a powerful candidate for full text retrieval systems as well.

We also give two disadvantages of the Boolean model starting with its inability to rank documents. For this reason, the model does not fit the needs of modern full text retrieval systems like for instance Web search engines. On the Web, and for many other full text retrieval systems, ranking is of utmost importance.

A second disadvantage is that the rigid difference between the Boolean AND and OR operators does not exist between the natural language words "and" and "or". For instance, someone interested in "social" *and* "political" documents, should enter the query social OR political to retrieve all possibly interesting documents. In fact, the Boolean model is more complex than the real needs of users would justify. Expert users of Boolean retrieval systems tend to use faceted queries. A *faceted query* is a query that uses disjuncts of quasi-synonyms: the facets, conjoined with the AND operator. The following query for instance has two facets: (economic OR financial OR monetary) AND (internet OR www OR portal).

## 4.3 Models for Ranked Retrieval

The Boolean model's inability to rank documents is addressed by the models presented in this section. A key issue of models of ranked retrieval is automatic query formulation. Non-expert users should be able to enter a request in natural language, or possibly just a couple of terms, without the use of operators. Both ranking and the fact that operators are not mandatory is shared by the approaches presented in this section. Pros and cons are identified for each model.

### 4.3.1 The Vector Space Model

Luhn [16] was the first to suggest a statistical approach to search for information. He suggested that in order to search in a document collection, the user should first prepare a document that is similar to the needed documents. The *degree of similarity* between the representation of the prepared document and the representations of the documents in the collection are used to search the collection.

Salton [30] found a nice theoretical underpinning of Luhn's similarity criterion. They considered the representations of the documents in the index and the query as vectors embedded in a high-dimensional Euclidean space, where each term is assigned a separate dimension. The document's index representation is a vector $\mathbf{d} = (d_1, d_2, \cdots, d_m)$ of which each component $d_k$ ($1 \le k \le m$) is associated with an index term, while the query is a similar vector $\mathbf{q} = (q_1, q_2, \cdots, q_m)$ of which the components are associated with the same terms.

The similarity measure is usually the cosine of the angle that separates the two vectors $\mathbf{d}$ and $\mathbf{q}$. The cosine of an angle is 0 if the vectors are orthogonal in the multidimensional space and 1 if the angle is 0 degrees:

$$\text{score}(\mathbf{d}, \mathbf{q}) \quad = \quad \frac{\sum_{k=1}^{m} d_k \cdot q_k}{\sqrt{\sum_{k=1}^{m}(d_k)^2} \cdot \sqrt{\sum_{k=1}^{m}(q_k)^2}}. \tag{4.1}$$

The metaphor of angles between vectors in a multidimensional space makes it easy to explain the implications of the model to non-experts. Up to three dimensions, one can easily visualize the document and query vectors. Figure 4.2 visualizes an example document vector and an example query vector in the space that is spanned by the three terms `social`, `economic` and `political`.

### Relevance Feedback

Measuring the cosine of the angle between vectors is equivalent with normalizing the vectors to unit length and taking the vector inner product:

$$\text{score}(\mathbf{d}, \mathbf{q}) \quad = \quad \sum_{k=1}^{m} n(d_k) \cdot n(q_k) \quad \text{where } n(v_k) = \frac{v_k}{\sqrt{\sum_{k=1}^{m}(v_k)^2}}. \tag{4.2}$$

Some rather *ad hoc*, but quite successful retrieval algorithms are nicely grounded in the vector space model if the vector lengths are normalized. An example is the relevance feedback algorithm by Rocchio [26]. He suggested the following algorithm for relevance feedback, where $\mathbf{q}_{old}$ is the original query, $\mathbf{q}_{new}$ is the revised query, $\mathbf{d}_{rel}^{(i)}$ ($1 \le i \le r$) is one of the $r$ documents the user

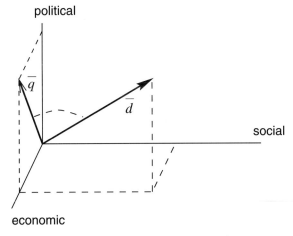

**Fig. 4.2.** A query and document representation in the vector space model.

selected as relevant, and $\mathbf{d}_{nonrel}^{(i)}$ $(1 \le i \le n)$ is one of the $n$ documents the user selected as non-relevant:

$$\mathbf{q}_{new} = \mathbf{q}_{old} + \frac{1}{r} \sum_{i=1}^{r} \mathbf{d}_{rel}^{(i)} - \frac{1}{n} \sum_{i=1}^{n} \mathbf{d}_{nonrel}^{(i)}. \qquad (4.3)$$

The normalized vectors of documents and queries can be viewed at as points on a hypersphere at unit length from the origin. In (4.3), the first sum calculates the centroid of the points of the known relevant documents on the hypersphere. In the centroid, the angle with the known relevant documents is minimized. The second sum calculates the centroid of the points of the known non-relevant documents. Moving the query towards the centroid of the known relevant documents and away from the centroid of the known non-relevant documents is guaranteed to improve retrieval performance. The sphere is visualized for two dimensions in Figure 4.3. The figure is taken from Savino [32].

### Discussion

A strong point of the vector model is the ease of explaining it to non-expert users. The main disadvantage of the vector space model is that it does not in any way subscribe what the values of the vector components should be. Now we touch the problem of term weighting which is addressed in Section 4.4. Early experiments [27] already suggested that term weighting is not a trivial problem at all. A second disadvantage of the vector space model is that it is not possible to include term dependencies into the model, for instance for modeling of phrases or adjacent terms. It is however possible to give a geometric interpretation of Boolean-structured queries, which is described in Section 4.3.3. A third problem with the vector space model is its implemen-

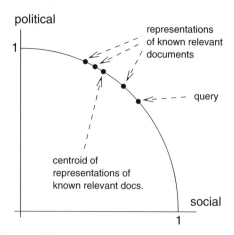

**Fig. 4.3.** Rocchio's relevance feedback method.

tation. The calculation of the cosine measure needs the values of all vector components, which may be difficult to provide in practice [41].

### 4.3.2 The Probabilistic Model

Sometimes it is argued that a retrieval system should rank the documents in the collection in order of their *probability of relevance*. This seems a rather trivial requirement indeed, since the objective of information retrieval systems is defined in Chapter 1 as "to help the user to find relevant documents". However, Robertson showed that optimality of ranking by the probability of relevance can only be guaranteed if the following conditions are met. Firstly, relevance should be a dichotomous variable, either yes or no. Secondly, relevance of a document to a request should not depend on the other documents in the collection.

### The Probability of Relevance

Whereas Luhn's intuitive similarity criterion raises the question "What exactly makes two representations similar?", Robertson's probability ranking principle raises the question "How, and on the basis of what data, should the probability of relevance be estimated?"

Relevance is ultimately determined by the end user. So, the probabilistic model that is based on relevance, is only useful if the system has information about relevance of documents. This information may be given by the end user as a result of relevance feedback.

It is possible that the similarity criterion and the relevance criterion do not coincide as the following reasoning shows. First let us make the notion "probability of relevance" explicit. Robertson adopted the Boolean model's viewpoint by looking at a term as a definition of a set of documents. Suppose a user enters a query containing a single term, for instance the term social. If all documents that fulfill the user's need were known, it would be possible to divide the document collection into four non-overlapping subsets as visualized in the Venn diagram of Figure 4.4. The figure contains additional information about the size of each of the non-overlapping subsets. The collection in question has 10,000 documents, of which 1000 contain the word "social"; only 11 documents are relevant to the query of which 1 contains the word "social". If a document is taken at random from the set of documents that are indexed with `social`, then the probability of picking a relevant document is $1/1000 = 0.0010$. If a document is taken at random from the set of documents that are *not* indexed with `social`, then the probability of relevance is bigger: $10/9000 = 0.0011$. Since the user entered only one index term, the system has only two options: either the documents indexed with the term are presented first in the ranking, or the documents that are not indexed with the term are presented first. In the example of Figure 4.4, it is wise to present the user first with documents that are not indexed with the query term `social`, that is, to present first the documents that are "dissimilar" to the query. Clearly, such a strategy violates Luhn's similarity criterion.

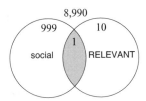

**Fig. 4.4.** Venn diagram of the collection given the query term `social`.

**Notation**
Let $L$ be the random variable "document is relevant" with a binary sample space $\{0, 1\}$, 1 indicating relevance and 0 non-relevance. Let a query contain $n$ terms. To each document $n$ random variables are assigned and let $D_k$ ($1 \leq k \leq n$) be a random variable indicating "the document belongs to the subset indexed with the $k$th query term" with a binary sample space $\{0, 1\}$. We concentrate on the $k$th query term and assume it to be `social`. We compute the four conditional probabilities $P(D_k|L)$ by the sizes of non overlapping subsets caused by the term `social`. Figure 4.5 shows the formulas for the documents indexed with `social`. The sizes are defined by: $R$ = the number of relevant documents, $n_k$ = the number of documents indexed with `social`, $r_k$ = the number of *relevant* documents that is indexed with `social`, and $N$ = the total number of documents in the collection.

**The Binary Independence Assumption**
If the user enters two terms, for instance the terms `social` and `political`, then there are four sets that must find their place in the final ranking:

$$P(D_k{=}1|L{=}1) \quad = \quad \text{``\#(social} \cap \text{RELEVANT)}/R\text{''} \qquad\qquad = \quad r_k/R$$

$$P(D_k{=}1|L{=}0) \quad = \quad \text{``\#(social} \setminus \text{RELEVANT)}/(N-R)\text{''} \qquad = \quad \frac{n_k - r_k}{N - R}$$

$$P(D_k{=}0|L{=}1) \quad = \quad \text{``\#(RELEVANT} \setminus \text{social)}/R\text{''} \qquad\qquad = \quad \frac{R - r_k}{R}$$

$$P(D_k{=}0|L{=}0) \quad = \quad \text{``\#(all} \setminus (\text{RELEVANT} \cup \text{social}))/(N-R)\text{''} \quad = \quad \frac{N - n_k - R + r_k}{N - R}$$

**Fig. 4.5.** Definition of probabilities, see Figure 4.4. The sizes of the sets `social` and `RELEVANT` are defined by: $R$ = the number of relevant documents, $n_k$ = the number of documents indexed with `social`, $r_k$ = the number of *relevant* documents that is indexed with `social`, and $N$ = the total number of documents in the collection.

`social AND political`, `social NOT political`, `political NOT social` and `NOT(social OR political)`. Each of these Boolean subsets can be represented by a pair of binary values, the first value indicating whether the subset includes documents indexed with `social`, the second value indicating whether the subset includes documents indexed with `political`. The four Boolean subsets are represented by respectively $(1,1)$, $(1,0)$, $(0,1)$ and $(0,0)$. Below we detail the probability computations; first we consider increasing the number of query terms.

The number of non-overlapping subsets increases exponentially with the number of query terms. To make the computation of the probability of relevance possible in reasonable time, the binary independence assumption is introduced:

*In documents terms occur independently from each other.*

In our example this means that the probability that a relevant document contains both `social` and `political` is equal to the product of the probabilities of the terms alone:

$$\text{P(social, political} \,|\, L{=}1) = P(\text{social} \,|\, L{=}1) \, P(\text{political} \,|\, L{=}1).$$

We would like to compute the probability that a document is relevant given values for the random variables $D_1, D_2, \cdots, D_n$. We will show that in that computation the independence assumption will be used. First we remark that the computation may involve many multiplications of sometimes small probabilities. To prevent computational problems often a logistic transformation of probabilities is used. Equation (4.4) is a variation of Bayes' rule that uses a logistic transformation of probabilities, which is defined by $\text{logit } P(L) = \log(P(L)/(1-P(L)))$. The transformation is strictly monotonic, so ranking documents by (4.4) will in fact rank them by the probability of relevance. Let $L$ and $D_k$ ($1 \leq k \leq n$) be defined as before. Given a query of length $n$ documents will be assigned the value defined by (4.5). Documents with the same values for $D_1, D_2, \cdots, D_n$ should be ranked equally [25, 39].

Note that duplicate query terms retrieve the same subset of documents and should be ignored in the formulas:

$$\text{logit } P(L{=}1|D_1,\cdots,D_n) = \log \frac{P(L{=}1|D_1,\cdots,D_n)}{P(L{=}0|D_1,\cdots,D_n)} \quad (4.4)$$

$$= \log \frac{P(L{=}1)P(D_1,\cdots,D_n|L{=}1) \,/\, P(D_1,\cdots,D_n)}{P(L{=}0)P(D_1,\cdots,D_n|L{=}0) \,/\, P(D_1,\cdots,D_n)}$$

$$= \log \frac{P(D_1,\cdots,D_n|L{=}1)}{P(D_1,\cdots,D_n|L{=}0)} + \text{logit } P(L{=}1)$$

$$= \sum_{k=1}^{n} \log \frac{P(D_k|L{=}1)}{P(D_k|L{=}0)} + \text{logit } P(L{=}1), \quad (4.5)$$

and, regarding the latter term,

$$\text{logit } P(L{=}1) = \log \frac{P(L{=}1)}{1 - P(L{=}1)} = \log \frac{P(L{=}1)}{P(L{=}0)}.$$

The binary independence assumption is used to derive 4.5 from 4.4.

**Implementation**
Equation (4.5) needs some computation for subsets for which $D_k = 0$, that is for non-matching query terms. In the vector space model non-matching terms are assigned zero weight, which is usually convenient for implementation reasons. Therefore, $\sum_{k=1}^{n} \log(P(D_k{=}0|L{=}1) \,/\, P(D_k{=}0|L{=}0))$ is subtracted from the score of each document subset. This does not affect the ranking of the documents and assigns a score of zero to documents with no matching terms:

$$P(L{=}1|D_1,\cdots,D_n) \propto \sum_{\substack{k \,\in\, \text{match-} \\ \text{ing terms}}} \log \frac{P(D_k{=}1|L{=}1)\,P(D_k{=}0|L{=}0)}{P(D_k{=}1|L{=}0)\,P(D_k{=}0|L{=}1)}. \quad (4.6)$$

**Relevance Computation**
The values of $n_k$ and $N$ are available to the system, but the values of $r_k$ and $R$ are only available if the user provides those to the system, typically by marking some previously retrieved documents as relevant. If $r_k$ and $R$ are not available to the system, it is necessary to make some assumptions about them. Robertson et al. [25] simply add 0.5 to each non-overlapping subset and Croft et al. [5] assume a constant value for $P(D_k|L{=}1)$. If the additional assumption is made that the number of relevant documents is much smaller than the size of the collection, more specifically: $R, r_k \ll N, n_k$, then documents might be ranked by a idf-like measure: $\log((N{-}n_k) \,/\, n_k)$ (see Section 4.4).

## Discussion

The probabilistic model is one of the few retrieval models that do not need an additional term weighting algorithm to be implemented (see Section 4.4). Ranking algorithms are completely derived from theory. The probabilistic model has been one of the most influential retrieval models for this very reason. Unfortunately, in many applications the distribution of terms over relevant and non-relevant documents will not be available. In these situations probability of relevance estimation is of theoretical interest only.

The main disadvantage of the probabilistic model is that it only defines a partial ranking of the documents. For short queries, the number of different subsets will be relatively low. By looking at a term as a definition of a set of documents, the probabilistic model ignores the distribution of terms within documents. In fact, one might argue that the probabilistic model suffers partially from the same defect as the Boolean model. It does not allow the user to really control the retrieved set of documents. For short queries it will sometimes assign the same rank to, for instance, the first 100 documents retrieved.

### 4.3.3 The $p$-norm Extended Boolean Model

The $p$-norm extended Boolean model was developed by [29], following the vector space model's metaphor of documents in a multi-dimensional Euclidean space. If the two terms social and political are again considered, the vector space spanned by the terms can be easily visualized. If document vectors are normalized to unit length, then the point (1,1) in the space represents the situation that both terms are present with weight 1 (which implies a length greater than one!). This is the desirable location for a document matching the query social AND political. For the query social OR political on the other hand, the point (0,0) representing the situation that both terms are absent, is the undesirable location for a document.

Therefore, AND-queries should rank documents in order of increasing distance from the point (1,1) and OR-queries in order of decreasing distance from the point (0,0). If the distances are properly normalized to fall between 0 and 1, then the following formulas apply. In the formula $d_a$ denotes the weight of the term $a$ in a document with index representation $\mathbf{d}$:

$$\text{score}(\mathbf{d}, a \text{ OR } b) = \sqrt{\frac{(d_a - 0)^2 + (d_b - 0)^2}{2}}$$

$$\text{score}(\mathbf{d}, a \text{ AND } b) = 1 - \sqrt{\frac{(1 - d_a)^2 + (1 - d_b)^2}{2}}. \tag{4.7}$$

Salton [29] suggested two generalizations of the basic idea. First of all, query term weights were included to reflect the importance of individual terms. Secondly, the Euclidean distance measures were generalized by introducing a parameter $p$ for each set operator. The resulting $p$-norm model uses the following formulas:

$$\text{score}(\mathbf{d}, \mathbf{q}\,\text{OR}_{(p)}) = \left(\frac{\sum_{k=1}^{m}(q_k)^p(d_k)^p}{\sum_{k=1}^{m}(q_k)^p}\right)^{1/p}$$

$$\text{score}(\mathbf{d}, \mathbf{q}\,\text{AND}_{(p)}) = 1 - \left(\frac{\sum_{k=1}^{m}(q_k)^p(1-d_k)^p}{\sum_{k=1}^{m}(q_k)^p}\right)^{1/p}. \tag{4.8}$$

For $p = 2$ the formulas will use the Euclidean distance measures as in (4.7). For $p = 1$ the OR-operator and the AND-operator produce the exact same results and the model behaves like the vector space model. If $p \rightarrow \infty$ then the ranking is evaluated according to the standard fuzzy set operators [44].

The $p$-norm model belongs to the best performing extended Boolean models. Based on recent publications about such models, the $p$-norm model is probably more popular for extended Boolean retrieval than other well-performing algorithms. Greiff et al. [8] copied the behavior of the $p$-norm model in their inference network architecture and Losada and Barreiro [15] propose a belief revision operator that is equivalent to a $p$-norm case.

A disadvantage of the $p$-norm model is that it needs an additional term weighting algorithm to be implemented.

### 4.3.4 Bayesian Network Models

A Bayesian network is an acyclic directed graph that encodes probabilistic dependency relationships between random variables. A directed graph is acyclic if there is no directed path $A \rightarrow \cdots \rightarrow Z$ such that $A = Z$. Probability theory ensures that the system as a whole is consistent. Some alternative names for Bayesian networks are belief networks, probabilistic independence networks, influence diagrams and causal nets [21]. This is further explained by the following simple model suggested by Turtle [37, 38], and Ribeiro [24].

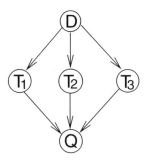

**Fig. 4.6.** Simple Bayesian network.

The nodes in the Bayesian network of Figure 4.6 represent binary random variables with values $\{0, 1\}$. Arrows indicate probabilistic dependency relationships, e.g., the arrow from node $D$ to node $T_1$ indicates that the value for $D$ influences the probability distribution of $T_1$. A missing arrow indicates probabilistic independence. So, $T_1$ and $T_2$ are independent. The random variables $T_1$, $T_2$, and $T_3$ stand for query terms, in our case social, political, and economic. If the document is relevant ($D = 1$), then the probability will be high that some of the terms will be present in the document. The information need of the user is indicated by $Q$. Expression $Q = 1$ indicates that the need is satisfied. The occurrence of (some of) the terms in the document will increase the probability that the information need is satisfied.

We now consider the joint probability distribution of the random variables of the Bayesian network. By the chain rule of probability, the joint probability is:

$$P(D, T_1, T_2, T_3, Q) =$$
$$P(D)P(T_1|D)P(T_2|D, T_1)P(T_3|D, T_1, T_2)P(Q|D, T_1, T_2, T_3). \quad (4.9)$$

Independence relationships in the Bayesian network are used to simplify the joint probability distribution as follows. The second, third and fourth term in (4.10) are simplified because $T_1$, $T_2$ and $T_3$ are independent given their parent $D$. The last term is simplified because $Q$ is independent of $D$ given its parents $T_1$, $T_2$ and $T_3$:

$$P(D, T_1, T_2, T_3, Q) = P(D) P(T_1|D) P(T_2|D) P(T_3|D) P(Q|T_1, T_2, T_3). \quad (4.10)$$

We proceed using the network. If it is hypothesized that the document is relevant ($D = 1$), the probability of query fulfillment $P(Q=1|D=1)$ can be used as a score to rank the documents:

$$P(Q=1|D=1) = \frac{P(Q=1, D=1)}{P(D=1)} \quad (4.11)$$

$$= \frac{\sum_{t_1, t_2, t_3} P(D=1, T_1=t_1, T_2=t_2, T_3=t_3, Q=1)}{P(D=1)}. \quad (4.12)$$

The joint probability distribution defined by (4.10) can be used to calculate the score. The only thing that is still missing is the specification of the probabilities. These are shown in the form of tables in Fig. 4.7. For example, the conditional probability $P(Q|T_1, T_2, T_3)$ is given in the lower left table. With help of these tables, $P(Q=1|D=1)$ can be computed for each document. The table of $P(Q|T_1, T_2, T_3)$, however, shows a potential difficulty of this approach. The number of probabilities that have to be specified for a node grows exponentially with its number of parents, so a query of $n$ non-equal terms requires the specification of $2^{n+1}$ possible values of $P(Q|T_1, T_2, \cdots, T_n)$. Despite the simplifying assumptions made by the conditional independencies, the model has to make additional simplifying assumptions to make it possible

| $P(D=0)$ | $P(D=1)$ |
|---|---|
| 0.999 | 0.001 |

| $D$ | $P(T_1 = 0)$ | $P(T_1 = 1)$ |
|---|---|---|
| 0 | 0.60 | 0.40 |
| 1 | 0.05 | 0.95 |

| $T_1$ $T_2$ $T_3$ | $P(Q=0)$ | $P(Q=1)$ |
|---|---|---|
| 0  0  0 | 1.000 | 0.000 |
| 0  0  1 | 0.901 | 0.099 |
| 0  1  0 | 0.887 | 0.113 |
| 0  1  1 | 0.992 | 0.008 |
| 1  0  0 | 0.547 | 0.453 |
| 1  1  0 | 0.332 | 0.664 |
| 1  0  1 | 0.271 | 0.729 |
| 1  1  1 | 0.220 | 0.780 |

| $D$ | $P(T_2 = 0)$ | $P(T_2 = 1)$ |
|---|---|---|
| 0 | 0.88 | 0.12 |
| 1 | 1.00 | 0.00 |

| $D$ | $P(T_3 = 0)$ | $P(T_3 = 1)$ |
|---|---|---|
| 0 | 0.97 | 0.03 |
| 1 | 0.02 | 0.98 |

**Fig. 4.7.** Example specification of the model's parameters.

to calculate the probability in reasonable time. Turtle [37, page 53] therefore suggests the use of four canonical forms of $P(Q|T_1, T_2, \cdots, T_n)$ which can be computed on the fly in linear time. The four canonical forms which are called "and", "or", "sum" and "weighted sum" ("wsum" for short), are displayed in Figure 4.8. The weights $w_1$, $w_2$ and $w_3$ in the last columns are restricted to positive values and should sum up to one.[2]

| $T_1$ $T_2$ $T_3$ | $P_{and}(Q)$ | | $P_{or}(Q)$ | | $P_{sum}(Q)$ | | $P_{wsum}(Q)$ | |
|---|---|---|---|---|---|---|---|---|
| | 0 | 1 | 0 | 1 | 0 | 1 | 0 | 1 |
| 0  0  0 | 1 | 0 | 1 | 0 | 1 | 0 | 1 | 0 |
| 0  0  1 | 1 | 0 | 0 | 1 | $\frac{2}{3}$ | $\frac{1}{3}$ | $1-w_3$ | $w_3$ |
| 0  1  0 | 1 | 0 | 0 | 1 | $\frac{2}{3}$ | $\frac{1}{3}$ | $1-w_2$ | $w_2$ |
| 0  1  1 | 1 | 0 | 0 | 1 | $\frac{1}{3}$ | $\frac{2}{3}$ | $1-w_2-w_3$ | $w_2+w_3$ |
| 1  0  0 | 1 | 0 | 0 | 1 | $\frac{2}{3}$ | $\frac{1}{3}$ | $1-w_1$ | $w_1$ |
| 1  0  1 | 1 | 0 | 0 | 1 | $\frac{1}{3}$ | $\frac{2}{3}$ | $1-w_1-w_3$ | $w_1+w_3$ |
| 1  1  0 | 1 | 0 | 0 | 1 | $\frac{1}{3}$ | $\frac{2}{3}$ | $1-w_1-w_2$ | $w_1+w_2$ |
| 1  1  1 | 0 | 1 | 0 | 1 | 0 | 1 | 0 | 1 |

**Fig. 4.8.** Canonical forms of $P(Q|T_1, T_2, T_3)$.

Suppose for now that the values of $P(T_1|D)$, $P(T_2|D)$ and $P(T_3|D)$ are known and given by $p_1$, $p_2$ and $p_3$. The calculation of $P(Q=1|D=1)$ by the canonical forms of Figure 4.8 will give the same results as the following calculations, which only require linear time:

---

[2] The definition of "wsum" by Turtle [37] is more general.

$$P_{\text{and}}(Q{=}1|D{=}1) = p_1\,p_2\,p_3$$
$$P_{\text{or}}(Q{=}1|D{=}1) = 1 - (1{-}p_1)(1{-}p_2)(1{-}p_3)$$
$$P_{\text{sum}}(Q{=}1|D{=}1) = (p_1 + p_2 + p_3)\,/\,3$$
$$P_{\text{wsum}}(Q{=}1|D{=}1) = w_1\,p_1 + w_2\,p_2 + w_3\,p_3.$$

$$(4.13)$$

The main advantage of the Bayesian network models [38] is that the network topology can be used to combine evidence in a complex way. Many other recent approaches to information retrieval seek for new ways of combining evidence from multiple sources [7, 33, 40, 43].

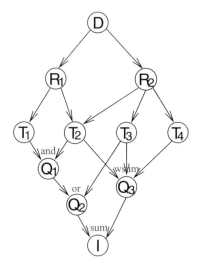

**Fig. 4.9.** Complex Bayesian network.

Figure 4.9 shows such a complex Bayesian network. In the network $R_1$ and $R_2$ define different representations of the document, for instance one might represent the document's title words, whereas the other might represent words from the abstract. The model's probabilities might indicate that title words are more important than words from the abstract. The nodes $Q_1$, $Q_2$ and $Q_3$ represent different queries for the same information need, which is represented by the node $I$. The query represented by $Q_2$ is evaluated as $\mathtt{or}(\mathtt{and}(T_1\ T_2)$ $T_3))$, whereas the query $Q_3$ is evaluated as $\mathtt{wsum}(T_2\ T_3\ T_4)$.

There are two disadvantages of the Bayesian network models presented in this section. Firstly, the approaches do not suggest how the probability measures $P(T_i|D)$, $(1 \leq i \leq n)$ should be estimated. Instead, the approaches suggest the use of Bayesian probabilities. In a nutshell, the Bayesian probability of an event is a person's degree of belief in that event, which does not have to refer to a physical mechanism or experiment. In contrast, the classical probability always implies such an experiment and therefore can always be interpreted as a relative frequency. Considering probabilities as a person's degree of belief is quite practical if a medical expert system is built [9]. For full text information retrieval systems however, experts are by definition not available for specifying the probabilities of the network because it implies manual indexing of the collection. The models therefore use one of the term weighting algorithms that use term frequencies and document frequencies as presented in Section 4.4. The joint probability distribution defined by (4.10) can be used as follows to calculate the score.

A second disadvantage of the Bayesian network models presented in this section is that the calculation of the probabilities generally takes exponential time in the number $n$ of non-equal query terms. The introduction of the four canonical forms solves this problem, but it could have been solved by the network topology. For instance the definition of $P_{\text{and}}$ in (4.13) actually suggests (conditional) independence between the probabilities $p_1$, $p_2$ and $p_3$ and, for instance the definition of $P_{\text{wsum}}$ suggests the use of a mixture model topology [13]. By using the four canonical forms, the network is tractable if it is used for inference, but it is still intractable if used for updating the probabilities. Updating the probabilities might be an effective approach to relevance feedback. Although the Bayesian network formalism comes with efficient learning algorithms, these algorithms can in practice not be applied in reasonable time on the network model presented in this section [36].

### 4.3.5 Language Model

A language model is a mathematical model of a language. Such a model can be very simple, for instance a list with the words of a language together with the frequency with which the word occurs in sentences. Language models have been around for quite a long time. They were first applied by Andrei Markov at the beginning of the 20th century to model letter sequences in works of Russian literature [17]. Later on language models were also used to model word sequences [34]. At the end of the 1970s language models were first successfully used for automatic speech recognition. Recently, statistical language models are very popular in the area of information retrieval. In this case one builds a simple language model for each document in the collection and given a query, documents are ranked by the probability that the language model of each document generated the query. It may be instructive to describe the process of generating the query from the model as if it were a physical process.

### An Informal Description: the Urn Model Metaphor

The metaphor of "urn models" [19] might give more insight. Instead of drawing balls at random with replacement from an urn, we will consider the process of drawing words at random with replacement from a document. Suppose someone selects one document in the document collection; draws at random, one at a time, with replacement, ten words from this document and hands those ten words (the query terms) over to the system. The system can now make an educated guess as from which document the words came from, by calculating for each document the probability that the ten words were sampled from it and by ranking the documents accordingly. The intuition behind it is that users have a reasonable idea of which terms are likely to occur in documents of interest and will choose query terms accordingly [22]. In practice, some query terms do not occur in any of the relevant documents. This can be modeled by a slightly more complicated urn model. In this case the person that draws at random the ten words, first decides for each draw if he will draw randomly from a relevant document or randomly from the entire collection. The yes/no decision of drawing from a relevant document or not, will also be assigned a probability. This probability will be called the relevance weight of a term, because it defines the distribution of the term over relevant and non-relevant documents. For *ad hoc* retrieval all non-stop-words in the query will be assigned the same relevance weight. The user's feedback might be used to re-estimate the relevance weight for each query term.

### Definition of the Corresponding Probability Measures

Based on the ideas mentioned above, probability measures can be defined to rank the documents given a query. The probability that a query $T_1, T_2, \cdots, T_n$ of length $n$ is sampled from a document with document identifier $D$ is defined by:

$$P(T_1, T_2, \cdots, T_n | D) = \prod_{i=1}^{n} ((1-\lambda_i) P(T_i) + \lambda_i P(T_i | D)). \qquad (4.14)$$

In the formula, $P(T)$ is the probability of drawing a term randomly from the collection, $P(T|D)$ is the probability of drawing a term randomly from a document and $\lambda_i$ is the relevance weight of the term. If a query term is assigned a relevance weight of $\lambda_i = 1$, then the term is treated as in exact matching: the system will assign zero probability to documents in which the term does *not* occur. If a query term is assigned a relevance weight of 0, then the term is treated like a stop word: the term does not have any influence on the final ranking. It can be shown that this probability measure can be rewritten to a *tf.idf* term weighting algorithm.

### Parameter Estimation

It is good practice in information retrieval to use the term frequency and document frequency as the main components of term weighting algorithms. The term frequency $\mathrm{tf}(t, d)$ is defined by the number of times the term $t$ occurs in the document $d$. The document frequency $df(t)$ is defined by the number of documents in which the term $t$ occurs. Estimation of $P(T)$ and $P(T|D)$ in (4.14) might therefore be done as follows [10, 12]:

$$P(T_i = t_i | D = d) = \frac{\text{tf}(t_i, d)}{\sum_t \text{tf}(t, d)} \qquad (4.15)$$

$$P(T_i = t_i) = \frac{df(t_i)}{\sum_t df(t)}. \qquad (4.16)$$

From the viewpoint of using language models for retrieval and from the viewpoint of the urn model metaphor, (4.16) would not be the obvious method for the estimation of $P(T)$. One might even argue that it violates the axioms of probability theory, because $P(T_i{=}t_{i1} \cup T_i{=}t_{i2}) \neq P(T_i{=}t_{i1}) + P(T_i{=}t_{i2})$ if $t_{i1}$ and $t_{i2}$ co-occur in some documents. Therefore the following equation, (4.16$b$), would be the preferred method for the estimation of $P(T)$, where the collection frequency cf$(t)$ is defined by the number of times the term $t$ occurs in the entire collection:

$$P(T_i = t_i) \quad = \quad \frac{\text{cf}(t_i)}{\sum_t \text{cf}(t)} \quad = \quad \frac{\sum_d \text{tf}(t_i, d)}{\sum_d \sum_t \text{tf}(t, d)}. \qquad (4.16b)$$

The latter method was used by various authors [1, 18, 20, 22]. We try to relate the language modeling approach to the traditional approaches, so we will use former method. By using (4.16), the language modeling approach to information retrieval gives a strong theoretical backup for using *tf.idf* term weighting algorithms: a backup that is not provided by the traditional retrieval models. The prior probability $P(D{=}d)$ that a document $d$ is relevant, might assumed to be uniformly distributed, in which case the formulas above suffice. Alternatively, it might be assumed that the prior probability of a document being relevant is proportional to the length of the document as in:

$$P(D = d) = \frac{\sum_t \text{tf}(t, d)}{\sum_t \sum_d \text{tf}(t, d)} \qquad (4.17)$$

It can be included in the final ranking algorithm by adding the logarithm of (4.17) to the document scores as a final step.

### 4.3.6 Ranking in Google

The World-Wide Web has become increasingly important. A Web page may contain all kinds of information: text, images, and so on. We consider a Web page to be a hypertext document, which means that besides text also the HTML referencing mechanism (=link) is available. Many search engines have been developed to address the huge document collection offered by the Web; the dominant search engine is without doubt Google. This engine offers high performance and ease of use. Ease of use is achieved by allowing the user to issue natural language search terms that are subsequently processed as if they were separated by ANDs. In the meantime other Boolean operators (OR, NOT) are allowed via an advanced search interface. Actually, Google uses a Boolean matching model.

The decisive factor, however, in the success of Google is probably its ranking mechanism. An important part in this mechanism is the so-called PageRank algorithm [3]. The algorithm is based on the citation index, which is generally accepted in the academic world: the importance of a paper can be judged by the number of references to it. In Web terms: the number of links referring to a Web page.

Within the past few years many adjustments and modifications regarding Google's ranking mechanism have occurred. PageRank is only part of the mechanism determining what results get displayed high up in a Google output. For example, there is some evidence to suggest that Google is paying a lot of attention these days to the text in a link's anchor when deciding the relevance of a target page. PageRank remains, however, an interesting algorithm. Below we will describe one of the first versions of the algorithm.

## PageRank
The original PageRank algorithm as described by Brin and Page is given by:

$$PR(A) = (1 - d) + d\left(\frac{PR(T_1)}{C(T_1)} + \cdots + \frac{PR(T_n)}{C(T_n)}\right), \qquad (4.18)$$

where $PR(A)$ is the PageRank of page $A$, $PR(T_i)$ is the PageRank of a page $T_i$, $C(T_i)$ is the number of outgoing links (=references) from the page $T_i$, and $d$ is a damping factor in the range $0 < d < 1$, usually $d = 0.85$.

So, the PageRank of a Web page is the sum of the PageRanks of all pages referring to the page (its incoming links), divided by the number of links on each of those pages (its outgoing links). This means that the influence of a referring page is positively related to its PageRank and negatively by the number of references it makes.

$PR$ is a recursive function: To compute $PR(A)$, we must know $PR(T_i)$ of all pages referring to $A$. But to compute these $PR$'s we need to know the $PR$ of referring pages (may be from page $A$), and so on. An iterative algorithm solves this problem after assigning a starting PageRank value of 1 to each page on the web.

## Example
Consider a small Web consisting of three pages $A$, $B$, and $C$. Page $A$ refers to $B$ and $C$; page $B$ to $A$ and $C$, and page $C$ to $B$. Let us assume that the damping factor $d = 0.5$. Actually, the damping factor appears to have a significant influence on the convergence characteristics of the algorithm, but for explanation purposes it is not relevant. Now we get:

$$PR(A) = 0.5 + 0.5 \left( \frac{PR(B)}{2} \right)$$

$$PR(B) = 0.5 + 0.5 \left( \frac{PR(A)}{2} + PR(C) \right)$$

$$PR(C) = 0.5 + 0.5 \left( \frac{PR(A)}{2} + \frac{PR(B)}{2} \right).$$

Solving these equations results in the following PageRank values for the pages:

$$PR(A) = \frac{4}{5}; \quad PR(B) = \frac{6}{5}; \quad PR(C) = 1.$$

The sum of all $PR$'s equals the total number of Web pages ($= 3$).

Page and Brin published a second version of the algorithm to compute $PR$. In that version the term $1-d$ is divided by $N$, the total number of pages on the web. It can be shown that the PageRanks now form a probability distribution over the web pages, so they sum up to one.

### Random Surfer Model
In their publications, Page and Brin describe the random server model which is a justification for the PageRank formula. The random server visits a Web page with a probability which is derived from the $PR$ of the page. Now the surfer randomly selects one link on the page and follows that link. However, from time to time (probability $(1-d)/N$) the surfer gets bored, does not follow a selected link, but jumps to another random page instead. In this way an intuitive reasoning for the computation of PR results.

### Remark
It may be commercially interesting for a Web page to get a high ranking. So Google pays a lot of attention to obstruct efforts of Webmasters to elude the system. For instance, Google introduced the concept of the "importance" of the page. This may help to minimize the effect of artificially generated Web pages which refer to a certain page in order to increase its ranking.

## 4.4 Term Weighting
Of the models presented in Section 4.3, the vector space model, the $p$-norm model and the Bayesian network models all need an additional term weighting algorithm before they can be implemented. Weighting of search terms is the single most important factor in the performance of information retrieval systems. The development of term weighting approaches is as much an art as it is a science: Literally thousands of term weighting algorithms were used experimentally during the last 25 years, especially within the Smart projects.

These algorithms often imply the use of some statistics on the terms, that is, they somehow take into account the number of occurrences of terms in the documents or in the index to compute rankings.

In this section we give an example of term weighting and choose the tf.idf weights of the original Smart retrieval system. This system was developed at Harvard University in the early 1960s and later developed at Cornell University. Salton [31] experimented with weighting algorithms that use the so-called *inverse document frequency*. They suggested to combine it with the frequency of a term within a document, the *term frequency*, tf for short. The assumption is that if a term occurs frequently, it is likely to be characteristic for a document.

The document frequency df of a term is defined by the number of documents a term occurs in. A term with a low document frequency is more specific than a term with a high document frequency. Sparck et al. [35] suggested that therefore, the system should treat matches on non-frequent terms as more valuable than ones on frequent terms. An intuitive way to relate the matching value of a term to its document frequency is suggested by a Zipf-like distribution of words in a vocabulary [17]. If $f(df) = m$ such that $2^{m-1} < df \leq 2^m$, and $N$ is the number of documents in the collection, then the weight of a term that occurs $df$ times is $f(N) - f(df)$.[3] A continuous approximation of $f$ is the logarithm to the base 2. The ranking algorithm is displayed in Figure 4.10. The weight $\log(N/df)$ will be called the "inverse document frequency": *idf* for short.

$$\text{cosine:} \qquad \text{score}(\mathbf{d}, \mathbf{q}) = \frac{\sum_{k=1}^{m} d_k \cdot q_k}{\sqrt{\sum_{k=1}^{m} (d_k)^2} \cdot \sqrt{\sum_{k=1}^{m} (q_k)^2}}$$

$$\text{term weights:} \qquad d_k = q_k = \text{tf} \cdot \log \frac{N}{df}$$

**Fig. 4.10.** Original *tf.idf* with cosine normalization (tfc.tfc).

The introduction of the so-called tf.idf weights is one of the major breakthroughs of term weighting in information retrieval. Most modern weighting algorithms are versions of the family of tf.idf weighting algorithms. Salton's original tf.idf weights perform relatively poor, in some cases even poorer than simple idf weighting.

Salton [28] summarizes the results of 20 years of research into term weighting with the Smart system. A total of 1800 different combinations of term weight assignments were used experimentally, of which 287 were found to be

---

[3] The adding of 1 used by Sparck–Jones [35] was ignored because it is no longer used in later papers.

distinct. Experimental results of these term weighting algorithms on six document collections were reported. Term weighting algorithms were named by
three letter combinations. The first letter indicated the tf component, the
second component indicates the idf component and the third component indicates the normalization component. For instance, the three letter code tfc is
the code for the original tf.idf weights with cosine normalization introduced
above. They concluded that the best performing algorithm is one that maps
the document vectors differently in the vector space than the query vectors.
Figure 4.11 displays the tfc.nfc formula which uses a normalized tf factor for
the query term weights.

$$\text{cosine:} \qquad \text{score}(\mathbf{d}, \mathbf{q}) \quad = \quad \frac{\sum_{k=1}^{m} d_k \cdot q_k}{\sqrt{\sum_{k=1}^{m}(d_k)^2} \cdot \sqrt{\sum_{k=1}^{m}(q_k)^2}}$$

$$\text{document term weight:} \qquad d_k \quad = \quad \text{tf} \cdot \log \frac{N}{df}$$

$$\text{query term weight:} \qquad q_k \quad = \quad \left( 0.5 + \frac{0.5\,\text{tf}}{\text{max tf}} \right) \cdot \log \frac{N}{df}$$

**Fig. 4.11.** tfc.nfc term weighting algorithm.

## 4.5 Summary

A brief description of thirty years of IR research has been given. Two classes
of users are identified, namely professional indexers and searchers on one hand
and casual end users on the other. The formulation of queries for these two
groups is described and the process of deriving a query from a natural language
request is briefly sketched. Most attention has been paid to matching problems. The Boolean approach resulted in exact matching; other approaches
included ranking of resulting documents (which means inexact matching).
Several approaches to ranking are given. The vector space approach maps
documents and queries in a $n$-dimensional vector space. Relevance feedback
nicely fits into this approach. The probabilistic approach tries to estimate
the probability that a document is relevant for the user. If users are able to
characterize relevant (or irrelevant) documents this approach may be useful.
An example may be email documents where users are able to specify terms to
characterize spam. The Bayesian approach is useful when evidence from many
different sources have to be integrated. Think of evidence coming from an audio, and image channel in a video. A language model is originally a (simple)
mathematical model of a language. In the meantime these models are heavily
used in IR. Systems built on these models are very competitive and perform as

well as, or better than, today's top-performing algorithms. The World-Wide Web is a collection of interconnected Web pages. Google searches the Web and its ranking algorithm (PageRank) takes these connections (=hyperlinks) into account. Some retrieval models perform dramatically better if query terms that occur in documents get a weight. Some variants have been discussed, but term frequency (how often does the term occur in a document) and document frequency (in how many documents does the term occur) play an important part.

## 4.6 Further Reading

This chapter briefly introduces probabilistic retrieval models. Fuhr [6] elaborates on this topic.

IR deals with documents containing free text. For presentation purposes free text is more and more embedded in a language like HTML. More recent is the development to use XML to structure documents. This poses new challenges to IR systems. For instance, how to deal with queries that contain conditions related to both structure and content? Blanken et al. [2] give more information on IR and structured data.

Retrieval models deal with structured queries, relevance feedback, ranking, term weighting, and so on. There have been attempts to model these phenomena into one framework [38]. Section 4.3.5 introduces the language model. An extension of the model integrates structured queries and relevance feedback into one mathematical framework [11].

Implementation aspects did not get much attention. Consider queries like: how to store terms in an index, and how to access indexes? Efficiency is of course an important topic. Witten et al. deal with indexing in Chapter 3 of their book [42].

In this chapter, architectural aspects are totally neglected. Brin and Page [3] give more information about architectural aspects of Google.

## References

1. A. Berger and J. Lafferty. Information retrieval as statistical translation. In *Proceedings of the 22nd ACM Conference on Research and Development in Information Retrieval (SIGIR'99)*, pages 222–229, 1999.
2. H.M. Blanken, T. Grabs, H.-J. Schek, and G. Weikum, editors. *Intelligent Search on XML data: Applications, Languages, Models, Implementations, and Benchmarks*, volume 2818. Springer: LNCS series, 2003.
3. S. Brin and L. Page. The anatomy of a large-scale hypertextual web search engine. *Computer Networks and ISDN Systems*, 30:107–117, 1998.
4. G.G. Chowdhury. *Introduction to modern information retrieval.* Wiley, 1998.
5. W.B. Croft and D.J. Harper. Using probabilistic models of document retrieval without relevance information. *Journal of Documentation*, 35(4):285–295, 1979.
6. N. Fuhr. Probabilistic models in information retrieval. *The Computer Journal*, 35(3):243–255, 1992.

7. N. Fuhr. Probabilistic datalog: A logic for powerful retrieval methods. In *Proceedings of the 18th ACM Conference on Research and Development in Information Retrieval (SIGIR'95)*, pages 282–290, 1995.

8. W.R. Greiff, W.B. Croft, and H.R. Turtle. Computationally tractable probabilistic modeling of boolean operators. In *Proceedings of the 20th ACM Conference on Research and Development in Information Retrieval (SIGIR'97)*, pages 119–128, 1997.

9. D.E. Heckerman. *Probabilistic Similarity Networks*. MIT Press, 1991.

10. D. Hiemstra. A linguistically motivated probabilistic model of information retrieval. In *Proceedings of the Second European Conference on Research and Advanced Technology for Digital Libraries (ECDL)*, pages 569–584, 1998.

11. D. Hiemstra and A.P. de Vries. Relating the new language models of information retrieval to the traditional retrieval models. Technical Report TR-CTIT-00-09, Centre for Telematics and Information Technology, 2000. `http://www.ub.utwente.nl/webdocs/ctit/1/00000022.pdf`.

12. D. Hiemstra and W. Kraaij. Twenty-One at TREC-7: Ad-hoc and cross-language track. In *Proceedings of the seventh Text Retrieval Conference TREC-7*, pages 227–238. NIST Special Publication 500-242, 1999.

13. M.I. Jordan, editor. *Learning in Graphical Models*. Kluwer Academic Press, 1998.

14. G. Kowalski. *Information Retrieval Systems: Theory and Implementation*. Kluwer Academic Publishers, 1997.

15. D.E. Losada and A. Barreiro. Using a belief revision operator for document ranking in extended boolean models. In *Proceedings of the 22nd ACM Conference on Research and Development in Information Retrieval (SIGIR'99)*, pages 66–73, 1999.

16. H.P. Luhn. A statistical approach to mechanised encoding and searching of litary information. *IBM Journal of Research and Development*, 1(4):309–317, 1957.

17. C. Manning and H. Schütze. *Foundations of Statistical Natural Language Processing*. MIT Press, 1999.

18. D.R.H. Miller, T. Leek, and R.M. Schwartz. A hidden Markov model information retrieval system. In *Proceedings of the 22nd ACM Conference on Research and Development in Information Retrieval (SIGIR'99)*, pages 214–221, 1999.

19. A.M. Mood and F.A. Graybill. *Introduction to the Theory of Statistics, Second edition*. McGraw-Hill, 1963.

20. K. Ng. A maximum likelihood ratio information retrieval model. In *Proceedings of the eighth Text Retrieval Conference, TREC-8*. NIST Special Publications, to appear.

21. J. Pearl. *Probabilistic Reasoning in Intelligent Systems: Networks of Plausible Inference*. Morgan Kaufmann, 1988.

22. J.M. Ponte and W.B. Croft. A language modeling approach to information retrieval. In *Proceedings of the 21st ACM Conference on Research and Development in Information Retrieval (SIGIR'98)*, pages 275–281, 1998.

23. M.F. Porter. An algorithm for suffix stripping. *Program*, 14:130–137, 1980.

24. B.A.N. Ribeiro and R. Muntz. A belief network model for ir. In *Proceedings of the 19th ACM Conference on Research and Development in Information Retrieval (SIGIR'96)*, pages 252–260, 1996.

25. S.E. Robertson and K. Sparck-Jones. Relevance weighting of search terms. *Journal of the American Society for Information Science*, 27:129–146, 1976.

26. J.J. Rocchio. Relevance feedback in information retrieval. In G. Salton, editor, *The Smart Retrieval System: Experiments in Automatic Document Processing*, pages 313–323. Prentice Hall, 1971.

27. G. Salton. *The SMART retrieval system: Experiments in automatic document processing*. Prentice-Hall, 1971.

28. G. Salton and C. Buckley. Term-weighting approaches in automatic text retrieval. *Information Processing & Management*, 24(5):513–523, 1988.

29. G. Salton, E.A. Fox, and H. Wu. Extended boolean information retrieval. *Communications of the ACM*, 26(11):1022–1036, 1983.

30. G. Salton and M.J. McGill. *Introduction to Modern Information Retrieval*. McGraw-Hill, 1983.

31. G. Salton and C.S. Yang. On the specification of term values in automatic indexing. *Jounral of Documentation*, 29(4):351–372, 1973.

32. P. Savino and F. Sebastiani. Essential bibliography on multimedia information retrieval, categorisation and filtering. In *Slides of the 2nd European Digital Libraries Conference Tutorial on Multimedia Information Retrieval*, 1998.

33. F. Sebastiani. A probabilistic terminological logic for modelling information retrieval. In *Proceedings of the 17th ACM Conference on Research and Development in Information Retrieval (SIGIR'94)*, pages 122–130, 1994.

34. C.E. Shannon. A mathematical theory of communication. *Bell System Technical Journal*, 27:379–423, 623–656, 1948.

35. K. Sparck-Jones. A statistical interpretation of term specifity and its application in retrieval. *Journal of Documentation*, 28(1):11–20, 1972.

36. H. Turtle and W.B. Croft. Evaluation of an inference network-based retrieval model. *ACM Transactions on Information Systems*, 9(3):187–222, 1991.

37. H.R. Turtle. *Inference Networks for Document Retrieval*. PhD thesis, Centre for Intelligent Information Retrieval, University of Massachusetts Amherst, 1991.

38. H.R. Turtle and W.B. Croft. A comparison of text retrieval models. *The Computer Journal*, 35(3):279–290, 1992.

39. C.J. van Rijsbergen. *Information Retrieval, second edition*. Butterworths, 1979. http://www.dcs.gla.ac.uk/Keith/Preface.html.

40. C.J. van Rijsbergen. A non-classical logic for information retrieval. *The Computer Journal*, 29(6):481–485, 1986.

41. I.H. Witten, A. Moffat, and T.C. Bell. *Managing Gigabytes: Compressing and Indexing Documents and Images*. Van Nostrand Reinhold, 1994.

42. I.H. Witten, A. Moffat, and T.C. Bell. *Managing Gigabytes: Indexing*. Morgan Kaufmann, 1999.

43. S.K.M. Wong and Y.Y. Yao. On modeling information retrieval with probabilistic inference. *ACM Transactions on Information Systems*, 13:38–68, 1995.

44. L.A. Zadeh. Fuzzy sets. *Information and Control*, 8:338–353, 1965.

# 5

## Image Processing

Ferdi van der Heijden and Luuk Spreeuwers

University of Twente

### 5.1 Introduction

The field of image processing addresses handling and analysis of images for many purposes using a large number of techniques and methods. The applications of image processing range from enhancement of the visibility of certain organs in medical images to object recognition for handling by industrial robots and face recognition for identification at airports, but also searching for images in image databases. The methods applied range from low-level approaches like boundary detection and color based segmentation to advanced object detection using statistical geometric models. Often several techniques must be combined to obtain a desired result, e.g., first low-level feature extraction, next clustering into regions, extraction of shape parameters and finally object recognition.

Whereas image processing basically includes all thinkable operations on images, its subfield image analysis addresses the extraction of certain information from images and aims to generate a description of (part of) the image or objects present in the image. In this chapter the emphasis will be on image analysis rather than on image processing in general and on static images rather than on image sequences. Examples of generating descriptions of images are recognition of a face in an image, counting the number of a certain type of cell in an image and labeling the different organs in a CT image of the chest (heart, lungs, ribs). Thus, given an image, image analysis aims to generate a description. On the other hand, the common task of image processing in multimedia database applications is to find images based on a description, where the description can range from an abstract description to an example of an object in the form of another image. Of course, both viewpoints are closely related, because in order to find an image based on a description, one must also be able to generate a description from an image.

### 5.1.1 Relation to Other Chapters

Images form one of the main types of data used in multimedia retrieval systems. The other types of data are covered in Chapter 4 (text), Chapter 7 (speech) and Chapters 9 and 10 (video). In Chapter 1 querying and retrieval were introduced. In the case of image data, formulating queries refers to properties and/or contents of the images. This chapter gives an overview of which features and descriptions can be extracted from images and how they can be extracted and does this from an image analysis point of view. Forming queries and retrieval themselves are not addressed here. For details on querying and retrieval, please refer to Chapters 6 and 11. Of course there is a close relation between image and video data. Often, more accurate and robust image analysis is possible and a more complete description of the scene can be generated if a sequence of images of the same object or scene is available instead of a single image. In this chapter, however, only static imagery is considered. Chapters 9 and 10 deal with video data.

### 5.1.2 Outline

This chapter gives an overview of the main applications for and methods used in image processing, where the emphasis is on techniques for image analysis. In Section 5.2 a brief overview of the different types of image processing and the main application fields of image processing is given. The subsequent sections are devoted to image analyses and techniques used in image analysis. In Section 5.3 an overview is given of the types of data that can be distinguished and the methods used in image analysis. Furthermore, a model-based framework for image analysis is introduced and low-level versus high-level and bottom-up versus top-down approaches will be discussed. Often, an important first step in any image analysis approach is the extraction of basic features, like color, edges, lines, shapes etc. from the raw image. Section 5.4 addresses the types of features used in image analysis and the extraction of the features from images. In Section 5.5 several important image analysis methods are presented, both illustrating the operation of the model-based approach as well as how and what kind of descriptions are generated from images.

## 5.2 Types of Image Processing and Applications

### 5.2.1 Types of Image Processing

Image processing in principle incorporates all operations on images that can be imagined. Here, an overview is given of some of the most important types of image processing.

*Image Acquisition*

Image acquisition is the process that creates images from a real world scene. The best known and most widespread method of image acquisition is of course using a color or black-and-white camera for visible light. The image is projected on the image sensor using a system of lenses. Nowadays, mostly CCD or CMOS image sensors are used that consist of a grid of image elements (pixels). Each image element produces a signal that has a direct relation with the intensity of the incoming light. This signal is in its turn quantized using an analog to digital converter (ADC). For many applications, e.g., in industrial vision, not only the camera itself, but also the illumination and a carefully planned setup are of great importance for the acquisition of images that can be used for reliable image analysis. In order to perform accurate measurements with cameras, they must be calibrated, i.e., the position and orientation of the camera relative to a world coordinate system must be determined and the parameters of the optical system (focal distance and lens distortions) and the image sensor (position and measures of the image elements) must be determined. The position and the orientation of the camera are called the extrinsic parameters, while the properties of the camera itself (focal distance, lens distortion, sensor characteristics, like area of the sensor) are called in intrinsic camera parameters. Apart from this geometric calibration, radiometric calibration might be required as well in order to allow precise measurements using intensity and color. The camera and its extrinsic geometric parameters are shown in Figure 5.1. Except for single images, sequences of images may be recorded and multiple imagers can be used, like, e.g., a set of cameras to obtain stereo images.

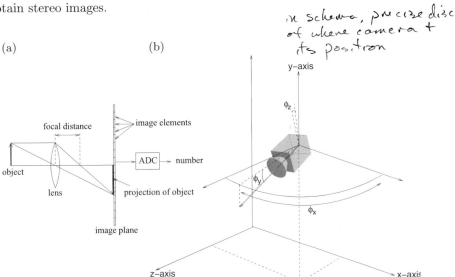

**Fig. 5.1.** The standard CCD/CMOS camera. (a) projection of an object on the image plane, the incident light is integrated over the area of each image element and over time and converted to a digital representation; (b) extrinsic geometric camera parameters: three position and three orientation parameters.

Apart from these regular cameras many other imaging devices exist, like document scanners (flat bed scanners), finger print scanners, and in the medical world X-ray imagers, CT (computer tomography) and MR (magnetic resonance) scanners and US (ultra sound) devices. The latter do not use direct projection on an image plane, but rather reconstruct images from measuring the spatial distribution of other entities. For example, in CT (Computer Tomography), absorption of X-rays by the different tissues of the body is measured. By projecting the X-rays under different angles, the absorption as a function of position can be reconstructed, resulting in a 2- or 3-dimensional X-ray absorption image. In MRI (magnetic resonance imaging), the resonance properties of certain molecules in a strong magnetic field are exploited. The resonance frequency of these molecules depends on the strength of the magnetic field and the molecules can be brought into resonance by applying a rapidly changing magnetic field with the same frequency. When the changing magnetic field is removed again, the density of the resonating molecules can be measured using the induction currents caused in a receiver coil. By a carefully designed place and time dependent coding of the magnetic field, the density of the molecules can be measured as a function of position, resulting again in a 2- or 3-dimensional image. In ultrasound, the reflection of high frequency sound at the interface between different tissues is exploited and positional information is obtained by using the speed of sound as well as using multiple sensors.

In the end all image acquisition methods generate images in the form of a matrix of numbers. The indices of the matrix define the position on the image plane (or the imaged volume) and the corresponding value represents the measured entity.

## Image Restoration

Often recorded images suffer from distortions, like geometric distortions caused by imperfect lens systems, noise caused by, e.g., low light conditions, unsharpness (blur) as a result of incorrect focusing, motion etc. Image restoration attempts to find out how the image would have been without these distortions. In the case of geometric distortions, this means a geometric warping of the image. In the case of the presence of noise, different techniques for noise suppression can be applied. The sharpness of blurred images can be improved by, e.g., deconvolution. Some examples of image distortions are shown in Figure 5.2.

## Image Reconstruction

The aim of image reconstruction is to construct an image using models, e.g., a model of the acquisition system. Examples were already mentioned in the paragraph on image acquisition above. Another example is reconstruction of an image as if it were generated from another viewpoint or using another imaging device.

For example, one can generate from a stereo pair of images an image from a new viewpoint where actually no camera is present. In image analysis, sometimes it is possible to reconstruct an image using a previously generated de-

(a)    (b)

(c)    (d)

**Fig. 5.2.** Image distortions. (a) original image; (b) lens distortion; (c) noisy image; (d) unsharp image.

scription. In Section 5.5.2 it is shown how a facial image can be reconstructed using a weighted sum of so-called eigenfaces.

*Image Enhancement*

If image processing is used to improve the visibility of certain objects or properties in the image, we are speaking of image enhancement. Image enhancement is mainly used for visualization for human observers to allow them to better interpret the images. Classical examples are contrast enhancement, histogram normalizations and edge enhancement.

*Image Registration*

In many applications images must be either registered or aligned to each other or to a fixed coordinate system. In medical applications images from different modalities like CT and MR may have to be aligned or images of the same modalities but recorded at a different time, in order to measure the progression of a disease. In cartography a scanned map may have to be aligned with an aerial photograph or satellite image. A third example of image registration is the alignment of facial images for face recognition to a coordinate system based on the positions of the eyes, nose and mouth. Image registration can be divided into rigid registration (translation, rotation and scaling) and non-rigid registration where the actual shape is changed.

*Image Compression, Storage and Transmission*

Images and especially video image sequences and 3D volume images represent large amounts of data. In order to be able to handle, store and transmit these images, compression is often required. Two ways of compression can be distinguished: lossless and lossy. An image compressed with a lossless compression method can be exactly reconstructed. Lossy compression methods on the other hand only allow an approximate reconstruction. An example of lossless compression is run-length encoding. The best-known lossy compression methods are JPEG for static images and MPEG for image sequences.

*Image Analysis*

Of all the types of image processing, probably the one that appeals most to our imagination is image analysis, because it resembles human vision and because it poses the largest challenge. Ultimately, image analysis aims to interpret the image, recognizing imaged objects, the relations between the objects and the properties of the imaged objects. Such a complete analysis of an imaged scene may be required for guiding autonomous moving robots. For many applications however, a partial description of the image suffices, e.g., detection of and measurements on a single object in the image (measuring the diameter of an ink-droplet for inspection of inkjet printer cartridges). Thus we can define image analysis as follows: Image analysis aims to generate a description of (part of) the image or of objects present in the image.

## 5.2.2 Application Areas

Image processing has applications in many areas. Some examples for the most important application areas are described here.

*Medical Imaging*

A large application area for image processing including 3D image processing is medical imaging. Many of the image processing problems are typical for the types of images and imaging devices (MR, CT and US). Much of the medical image processing is tailored towards visualization and storage in so-called PACS (Picture Archiving and Communication System). Two of the main areas of research in medical imaging are segmentation of images into segments representing the different tissues and organs and registration of images acquired with different scanners and at different times.

*Geo Information Systems, Satellite and Aerial photography and Cartography*

Processing aerial and satellite images and using them to produce and update maps is an important and extensive application area for image processing. Different types of image restoration, image enhancement and image reconstruction are used to obtain images with the required properties and from the correct perspective. In order to compare photographs with maps for updating the maps or with other photographs to determine changes, they must be aligned using a registration technique. Geographical Information Systems

(GIS) can be regarded as the high tech equivalent of the map in which different sets of information from a map (roads, settlements, vegetation, etc.) are stored and can be used as required. This provides flexibility far beyond the traditional paper map. Because the data are stored on a computer, analysis and modeling become possible, e.g., optimal path planning for a heavy transport between buildings in a city. Of course, creating and keeping a GIS up to date requires extensive processing of the available photographic material.

*Biometry*

Image processing for biometric purposes is mainly concentrated on face recognition and fingerprint recognition. Other, smaller subjects are hand-palm recognition and tracking people. For face recognition, there are so-called feature-based approaches and holistic approaches. The feature-based approaches try to detect significant features like the eyes, nose and mouth, and based on the characteristics of these features and their relations attempt to identify a face. In the holistic approaches the appearance of the whole face is used as the input of a classifier. An example of the holistic approach is the eigenface based method described in Section 5.5.2.

*Optical Character Recognition*

One of the first large scale successes for image processing was optical character and hand writing recognition especially for cheques, document processing and automatic handling of post. A more recent application is license plate recognition for vehicles.

*Industrial Vision* — Next Ex

One of the largest application areas of image processing is industrial vision. Industrial vision ranges from relatively simple applications like measuring the volume of an ink droplet to vision systems for programmable autonomously moving and operating robots. Other examples are the inspection of weldings and sorting fruit. For industrial vision often careful planning of the camera setup and illumination is necessary to obtain reliable results. Careful conditioning of the environment can make a large difference in the reliability and cost effectiveness of a system. For example, recognition of nuts and bolts that lie separated on a homogeneous background is much easier than when they lie on a pile on top of each other, see Figure 5.3.

*Multimedia and Image Databases* The next level

A relatively new application area of image processing is that of multimedia image databases. The main objectives in this area are to be able to retrieve images based on a description of their content (e.g., find all pictures with red cars of a certain brand or in medical databases all MRI recordings of hearts with a certain disease) or, e.g., based on similar images (e.g., a picture or a drawing of a fish). Another example is to be able to find a point in a video stream based on certain image properties, like the appearance of a certain person or object.

Starker, Sharper border twee obj, easier for sware to recognize

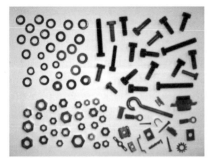

**Fig. 5.3.** In industrial vision, conditioning of the setup is of great importance: recognition of separated objects is much easier than of a pile of objects.

## 5.3 Image Analysis

### 5.3.1 The Type of Output of Image Analysis Systems

The goal of image analysis is to extract information from an image. The objective of computer vision, for instance, is to obtain a meaningful description of the objects in a scene being imaged. In other areas, such as in the "query-by-image" paradigm, there is no strict need for such a semantic description of an image. Here, it suffices to describe the image in terms of, for instance, the shapes, the colors, or the textures. In any case, we may distinguish the various image analysis systems according to the type of their output. The different types vary from simple output (i.e., one bit information) to complex, e.g., hierarchically structured data. Table 5.1 presents an overview. In all examples presented in this table there is a direct relation between the output and the imaged object(s). As such they are typical computer vision applications. However, the issues mentioned in the table also apply to non-semantic descriptions of the image. For instance, in a "query-by-image" application a relevant question could be "are there textured regions in the image", i.e., a detection problem.

Low level question.

**Table 5.1.** Different types of output.

| issue | output range | example |
|---|---|---|
| detection | boolean | burglar alarm (yes/no) |
| classification | finite set of classes | classification of different types of fruits ("apples", "pears", "oranges") |
| parameter estimation | vectors | geometrical parameters (position, orientation, size, shape) |
| structural analysis | structured data | document analysis (sender + address, logo, body text, date, signature, etc.) |

Some of the issues occur in different versions. For instance, in biometrical applications, *verification* is the task of authorizing a person based on his/her biometrical signature (e.g., a fingerprint). It boils down to a detection problem where it is decided whether the person is found in a database, or not. Combinations of different types of problems also occur. *Identification* is the process of finding out whether an object (or person) is in a database (a verification problem), and if so, to what entry in the database this object corresponds. Thus, here we have a combined detection and classification problem. The task of a vision system of a pick-and-place robot is to detect the objects in an image, to classify each object, and finally, to estimate their positions and orientations. Here we have combined detection/classification/estimation problems. These kinds of combinations are typical in structural analysis.

### 5.3.2 Methodology for Image Analysis

Early research in digital image analysis and computer vision stems from the 1960's. Since then, an impressive amount of literature has been produced and published in the many periodicals, conference proceedings, and textbooks devoted to this field of science. The yearly flow of new publications is still increasing. This overwhelming research effort has lead to a diversity of techniques and methods. Therefore, it is difficult to present a unifying framework in which each method fits. Nevertheless, the overview shown in Figure 5.4 is an attempt in that direction. The figure shows a computational structure which we call "an elementary data processing step" because in most image analysis applications it reoccurs at different levels of the data representation, see below.

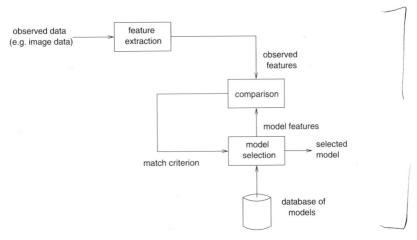

**Fig. 5.4.** An elementary data processing step in image analysis and computer vision.

All approaches lean strongly on models that embody prior knowledge that we have concerning the image and the objects therein. Prior knowledge is the information that we have about objects (or other entities in the image) before actually having acquired the image. For instance, in a pure classification problem the prior knowledge of a given application is the classes of objects that can occur (e.g., "apple", "pear", and "orange"), along with their probability of occurrence, and a list of discriminating features of the objects (e.g., the colors and shapes that are typical for the various classes). The model of an apple is that its contour is approximately round with two small indentations at opposite sides. Its color varies between green, yellow and red.

In Figure 5.4, the prior knowledge is represented in the block "database". The word "database" suggests that the knowledge is stored in a systematic way, and that transparent facilities are available for managing it. However, the word is loosely used here, because in practice, much of the prior knowledge is implicitly hidden in the code that implements the image analysis. Because models take a central position in the framework of Figure 5.4, this is often called the *model-based image processing framework*.

The features stored in the database are called "model features" in order to discriminate them from the "observed features". The latter are features that are extracted from the observed image. The purpose of feature extraction is twofold. The first goal is to achieve data reduction, i.e., to remove the non-relevant aspects in the image data in order to obtain a more concise data representation of the information. The second goal is to transform the data to a data representation that carries the information in a more explicit way. For example, the image data can be transformed into shape features (describing the contours of the imaged objects). These shape features are much more concise (usually about ten shape features are sufficient to grossly typify a contour), but it depends on the application whether the shape features are really informative. For example, shape features are usable to discriminate apples from bananas, but not usable if one would like to distinguish apples from oranges.

The obtained observed features and model features should be at the same level. If this is the case, then we are able to compare observed features with model features. This allows us to select the model whose model features best match the observed features. The image analysis task basically boils down to the application of a selection strategy which consults the database to find the model whose features fits with the observed features.

When implementing this generic framework many choices still have to be made. These choices relate to:

1. the selection of the features that will be used;
2. the representation of the models;
3. the matching criterion;
4. the selection strategy.

Conceptually, numerous types of features could be extracted from the observed data. These features can be found at different levels of a hierarchy (see below): pixel features, regions, regional properties, and so on. In some applications and techniques it is immediately clear which features should be used. But in other applications, it is not. In that case, a learning process might be needed in which a number of proposed features are empirically evaluated.

The representation of prior knowledge is another design issue. We may distinguish procedural knowledge (knowing how) from declarative knowledge (knowing that). As an example, consider the following statement: "in a Gaussian classification problem, the optimal classifier implements quadratic decision functions". This statement represents procedural knowledge. An example of declarative knowledge is "the shape of an apple is approximately round with some indentations". Procedural knowledge is often hard coded in the computer program. Declarative knowledge can be represented in different ways. For instance, we can represent the knowledge in parameters of probabilistic models, e.g., the shape of an apple can be represented by means of an expectation vector of a shape feature vector together with a covariance matrix (that represents the uncertainty around the expectation). Alternatively, we can represent the knowledge by storing many examples (e.g., the contours of many different apples previously seen).

In order to evaluate a selected model we have to compare the associated model features with the observed features. The result of this evaluation is a matching score that quantifies how well the proposed model fits the observed data. Many different matching criteria exist. Criteria that express a probabilistic measure include risk, a posterior probability, likelihood, and, mean square error. These criteria have a probabilistic view on the set of allowable models. Alternatively, in the data fitting approach, the criterion is based on a metric in the feature domain, that is, on the differences between model features and observed features. Criteria in this category include the least squared error (sum of squared differences) and robust error norms (such as Geman–McClure) for real valued feature vectors, the Hamming distance for binary feature vectors, and the Tanimoto metric for comparing sets.

The task of the model selector is to find the best model. With the adoption of a quantitative matching criterion, selection of the best model boils down to an optimization problem (either a maximization or a minimization; this depends on the criterion). A first dichotomy is between bottom-up and top-down strategies. The bottom-up strategy is data-driven. The data (features) are processed in a first layer (or iteration) yielding intermediate results. These intermediate results are processed in a second layer (iteration), and so on. This continues until the final result is obtained. An example is a feed-forward neural network (often trained to minimize the sum of squared errors). Another category of bottom-up strategies are the iterative function minimization procedures (e.g., the Gauss–Newton optimizer). Top-down strategies use the hypothesis generation/refinement/verification paradigm. Hypothesis generation comes down to proposing a solution (either generated randomly, or generated using prior knowledge). If necessary, a proposed solution can be refined using the data. The next step is to verify the solution. If the solution fits the data, we can accept it. If not, we have to reject it, and we must generate a new hypothesis. Possibly, this procedure is repeated to achieve more robust and accurate solutions.

*Hierarchies*

Image analysis seldom occurs in one single processing step. Usually, the data is regarded at different levels of abstraction. These levels form a hierarchy. Figure 5.5 provides an example. The original image data (pixels representing intensities (gray levels), or RGB color components) form the lowest level. At the top, we have the objects and their attributes. Various intermediate levels exist in-between. Just above the lowest level, we have point features, i.e., pixels that are marked as special: edge elements, line elements, corner points, and so on. Edge and line elements that are grouped together as a chain form line segments. Line segments, grouped together, may form a closed contour, thus defining a region in the image plane. Such a region may also be defined directly by grouping pixels that share a common property (e.g., color). Regions are characterized by their properties in the geometric domain (shape, position, orientation, size) and in the radiometric domain (color, texture). Relations between regions (e.g., "adjacent-to", "surrounds", "larger-than") are often represented as an attributed graph similar to a semantic network.

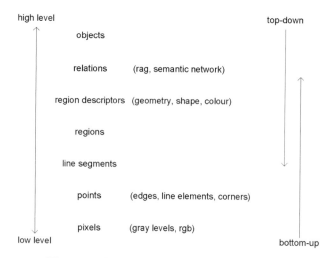

**Fig. 5.5.** A hierarchy of data representations.

The elementary data processing step in Figure 5.4 is often applicable at different levels of the hierarchy. For instance, the detection and localization of edge elements is generally referred to as "edge detection", but in fact, it can be phrased as a combined detection/estimation problem. The features are the gray levels of the pixels in a neighborhood. Usually, the model of an edge is a 2-dimensional step function with parameters "position" and "orientation".

Segmentation (the determination of regions) can be phrased as a pixel classification problem using color or texture as features. Regional description is often in essence a parameter estimation problem. In simple applications, object recognition can be regarded as a classification problem (with regional descriptors as features). In more involved applications, object recognition comes down to matching structures (e.g., attributed graphs). Note that the transformation of the data from one level to the next level can be done either bottom-up (data driven) or top-down (hypothesis generation/verification) as outlined above.

*Coping with Disturbing Factors*

A complicating factor in all these techniques is the presence of nuisance parameters. These are unknown parameters that affect the data, but do not provide information about the entity of interest. For instance, in image based object recognition, the viewpoint of the camera strongly affects how the object appears in the image (perspective projection). An object can have many different views (appearances), but still all those views must lead to the same solution.

There are many techniques to undo the influence of the nuisance parameters, e.g.:

- Normalizing the features with respect to the nuisance parameters.
  For example, in order to describe the shape of a region, we may first want to resize the region such that its area is normalized. This prevents that the size of the region influences the shape description.
- Transforming the features to a domain which is not affected by the nuisance parameters.
  As an example, consider the ratio between the area and the squared perimeter of a region. This feature is not influenced by the position, size and orientation of the region, and, therefore, only describes the shape.
- Storing all possible appearances as model features in the database.
- Robust estimation.
  The strategy here is to use only the part of the data that seems to be reliable.

## 5.4 Features and Feature Extraction

This section presents an overview of different features that are used in computer vision and image analysis techniques. The section is organized in four subsections which correspond to four levels in the hierarchy of data representation. Several techniques to compute features from images are introduced.

To understand how features can be calculated from images, it is important to realism that an image is actually a 2-dimensional signal. An image is represented by a matrix of values of $N$ rows and $M$ columns. A pixel is addressed by the row index $n$ and the column index $m$ and the pixel value (generally the intensity or brightness of the pixel) is denoted by $f(n, m)$. So, the intensity can be regarded as a function of the position $(n, m)$ in the image. This means all kinds of mathematical operations on images are possible, e.g., a derivative in the row or column direction: $\partial f(n, m)/\partial n$ and $\partial f(n, m)/\partial m$. Of course, since $n$ and $m$ are discrete, we need discrete mathematical operators. For $\partial f(n, m)/\partial n$ a possible discrete implementation is:

$$\frac{\partial f(n, m)}{\partial n} = \frac{f(n + 1) - f(n)}{\Delta}, \tag{5.1}$$

where $\Delta$ is the distance between two pixels and is usually set to 1. Figure 5.6 shows an image of a chess board and the derivatives to the row and column indices.

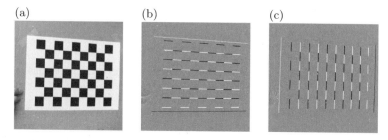

**Fig. 5.6.** Result of taking the derivative of an image: (**a**) original image $f(n, m)$; (**b**) $\partial f(n, m)/\partial n$; (**c**) $\partial f(n, m)/\partial m$; "gray" in the derivative images means "0".

An operation used in this section that may need some introduction, is the Fourier transform. It transforms a signal $f(x)$ into the frequency domain using:

$$F(k) = \int_{-\infty}^{\infty} f(x)e^{-2\pi jkx} dx. \tag{5.2}$$

Here $k$ are the frequencies present in the signal $f(x)$ and $F(k)$ indicates the strength of the frequency $k$. $F(k)$ consists of a real and an imaginary part. Often the magnitude $\|F(k)\|$ is used, resulting in a power density spectrum. For example, a constant signal results in a single spike ($\delta$ function) at frequency 0, a sine results in a single spike at the frequency of the sine, and a block signal results in spikes at the base frequency and all its higher harmonics. In image processing, Fourier transforms can be used to analyze repetitive structures in images, like textures (Section 5.4.4). For discrete signals, like images, a discrete Fourier transform is used. For further details on the Fourier transform, see the book by Bracewell [2].

### 5.4.1 Pixel Features

The original image data form the features at the lowest level. The image is represented by a matrix $\mathbf{F}$ of pixels consisting of $N$ rows and $M$ columns. A pixel $f(n, m)$ of the image is either an intensity (in case of achromatic imagery), or a vector consisting of 3 RGB components (in case of a color image). Other representations also exist, but are used less frequently.

*Neighborhood and Image Filtering*

In some applications, it suffices to regard each separate pixel as an individual feature. In that case, a feature is either 1-dimensional (an intensity), or 3-dimensional (the RGB components). In other applications, the context between neighboring pixels is an important clue. Here, pixels should be grouped together. The image plane is divided then into rectangular blocks of size $K \times L$. In some algorithms non-overlapping blocks may suffice. This is, for instance, the case in algorithms for image compression. But in image analysis, the blocks are usually overlapping. In fact, each pixel in the input image can be associated with its own block. Such a block is called the *neighborhood* of the pixel. The neighborhood is a $K \times L$ sub-image $\mathbf{F}(n, m)$ centered on the concerning pixel $(n, m)$. Sometimes, it is convenient to represent the data in the neighborhood as a vector $\mathbf{f}(n, m)$ of dimension $KL$ (intensity images) or $3KL$ (color images).

Neighborhood processing is used to obtain higher level features (point features, regions). Usually, the first stage of the operation is a linear operation. That is:

$$g(n, m) = \mathbf{h}^T \mathbf{f}(n, m), \tag{5.3}$$

where $\mathbf{h}$ is a $KL$-dimensional vector (or $3KL$-dimensional in case of color). The results $g(n, m)$ can be arranged in a $N \times M$ dimensional matrix $\mathbf{G}$ which can be regarded as an output image. The operation in (5.3) essentially implements a linear image filter. For intensity images, the operation is mathematically equivalent to:

$$g(n, m) = \sum_k \sum_\ell h(k, \ell) f(n - k, m - \ell), \tag{5.4}$$

where $h(k, \ell)$ is a $K \times L$ array called the kernel of the operator. The operation itself is called (discrete) *convolution*, and is often denoted by the symbol $*$. That is, $g(n, m) = h(n, m) * f(n, m)$. The elements $h(k, \ell)$ of the kernels are found back as the coefficients in the vector $\mathbf{h}$.

The linear operation of (5.3) can easily be extended to:

$$\mathbf{g}(n, m) = \mathbf{H} \mathbf{f}(n, m), \tag{5.5}$$

where $\mathbf{H}$ is a $P \times KL$ matrix. The resulting pixel features are now $P$-dimensional. Equation (5.5) can also be regarded as a parallel bank of $P$

image filters. The kernels of the filters correspond to the rows of $\mathbf{H}$. The concept can also easily be extended to color images. In that case, $\mathbf{H}$ is $P \times 3KL$ dimensional. Often, the three components of the color image are filtered individually by using a parallel bank of $3P$ filters.

*Scale Space and Derivatives*

The scale at which objects are seen in an image depends on the distance between object and camera. Variations of the distance not only cause proportional zooming of the imaged objects, but also influence the fineness of detail that can be resolved. Scale space theory [17] is a theory for handling image structures at different scales. The original image corresponds to the finest scale. This image is linearly filtered and possibly zoomed out to get images at a courser scale. The so-called *scale parameter* $\sigma$ is a parameter that controls the level of fineness. The original image is associated with $\sigma = 0$. An image at scale $\sigma$ is obtained by filtering the original image with a Gaussian kernel (Figure 5.7a):

$$h(k, \ell) = \frac{1}{2\pi\sigma^2} \exp\left(\frac{-(k^2 + \ell^2)}{2\sigma^2}\right). \tag{5.6}$$

Application of the filter with a range of values of $\sigma$ produces a stack of images. In fact, the 2-dimensional structure of an image is extended to a 3-dimensional space. Figure 5.7 provides an example. Here, the scale range is sampled at five points logarithmically distributed between 0 and 2. Thus, each input pixel is transformed into a 5-dimensional feature vector. Note that, since images of a larger scale contain less detail, the size of the image can also be reduced without losing information. Smaller images take up less storage and also operations on the images are sped up significantly (often linear with the number of pixels). If one would create a stack of all images with increasing scale with the largest scale at the top and appropriate image size reduction, a pyramid results. Such a stack is sometimes called a resolution pyramid.

   Scale space theory is a sound basis for the definition of the derivatives of a digital image, and for their numerical calculation. The derivatives are features that are important for edge detection, point feature detection, and so on. The derivatives of a digital image are numerical approximations of the derivatives of continuous images, i.e., $f(x, y)$ with $(x, y) \in \mathbb{R}^2$. Since continuous images are always smooth, the definition of derivatives is clear: $f_x(x, y) = \partial f(x, y)/\partial x$, $f_{xy}(x, y) = \partial^2 f(x, y)/\partial x \partial y$, and so on. For convolution and differentiation the following theorem holds true:

$$\frac{\partial}{\partial x}(f(x, y) * h(x, y)) = f(x, y) * \frac{\partial}{\partial x}h(x, y). \tag{5.7}$$

The numerical approximation of the derivatives is obtained with the (discrete) convolution:

$$f_x(n, m) = f(n, m) * h_x(n, m), \tag{5.8}$$

(a)

(b)

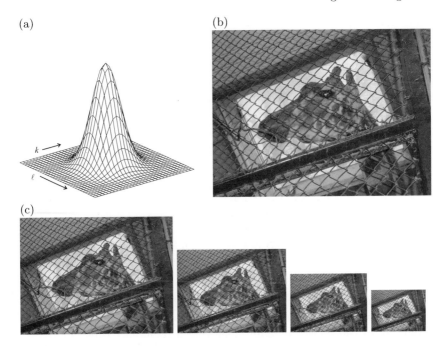

(c)

**Fig. 5.7.** The scale space. (a) Gaussian kernel; (b) original image; (c) images at scales 0.7, 1, 1.4, 2, respectively.

where $h_x(n, m)$ is the first derivative of the Gaussian with respect to $n$. The spatial support (which is always needed in numerical differentiation) is fully controlled by the scale parameter $\sigma$. As a rule of thumb, $K = L \approx 7\sigma$. The smallest scale that can be applied is $\sigma \approx 0.7$. Figure 5.8 shows an example of a derivative of a Gaussian, and the application of this kernel to the giraffe image in Figure 5.7. Other derivatives, $f_y(n, m), f_{xy}(n, m)$ and so on, are computed in likewise manner.

*Texture*
Many surfaces of objects are made up of a small elementary pattern that is repeated periodically or quasi-periodically along the surface. The origin of the patterns are either geometrical (e.g., a rough surface) or radiometric (e.g., wallpaper), or both (the bricks in a wall). Textured surfaces in the scene will create textured regions in the image. Therefore, textures in the image are important clues for segmenting the image plane into meaningful regions. In order to find these textured regions, each pixel in the rough image should be transformed to texture features.

The transformation should be such that different textures are mapped to non-overlapping areas in the feature space. Since textures are repetitions of an elementary pattern, a texture is typified by the following properties:

- the distance over which the pattern is repeated;

(a)                                                    (b)

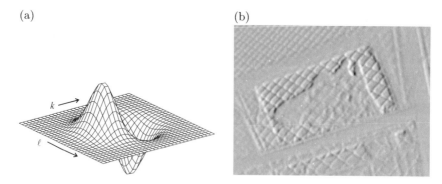

**Fig. 5.8.** Differentiation using the scale space. (a) First derivative of a Gaussian kernel; (b) Application to the giraffe image; $\sigma = 2$.

- the direction in which the pattern is repeated;
- the properties of the elementary pattern.

As the repetitions occur more or less randomly, it is not easy (or perhaps even impossible) to catch these properties with a few descriptors. In addition, the repetitions can be isotropic implying that a preference direction does not exist. Anyway, the strategy is to find an operator that takes into account pairs of pixels that hold a specific spatial relation. The spatial relation is defined by a separation distance $\rho$ and an orientation $\theta$. Consider the pair of pixels $(\mathbf{n}_1, \mathbf{n}_2)$ (with $\mathbf{n}_1 = (n_1, m_1)$ and $\mathbf{n}_2 = (n_2, m_2)$), then the separation distance $\rho$ and the orientation $\theta$ are:

$$\begin{aligned}
\rho &= \|\mathbf{n}_2 - \mathbf{n}_1\| \\
\theta &= \angle(\mathbf{n}_2 - \mathbf{n}_1).
\end{aligned} \tag{5.9}$$

For each neighborhood, and for each value of $(\theta, \rho)$, a finite set of pixel pairs with this spatial relation exists. The purpose of the operator is to measure the concurrence of intensities of the pairs within such a set.

A possible measure is provided by the so-called *co-occurrence* matrices [10]. Such a matrix is a 2-dimensional histogram: the intensity scale is divided into a number of bins. An element $C_{\theta,\rho}(i, j)$ of the co-occurrence matrix $\mathbf{C}_{\theta,\rho}$ equals the count of pairs $(\mathbf{n}_1, \mathbf{n}_2)$ within the set for which $f(\mathbf{n}_1)$ falls in the $i$-th bin and $f(\mathbf{n}_2)$ in the $j$-th bin. Since many separation distances and orientations are possible, there are as many co-occurrence matrices. The calculation of all possible co-occurrence matrices in a neighborhood is unwieldy. Some sort of data reduction is needed. The data reduction can be obtained by using a property of the 2D histogram instead of the whole histogram. An example of such a property is the covariance between $f(\mathbf{n}_1)$ and $f(\mathbf{n}_2)$. The covariance is a measure for how much $f(\mathbf{n}_1)$ and $f(\mathbf{n}_2)$ covariate. This, and some other properties are discussed in Section 5.4.4.

Another possibility for extracting texture features is to project the neighborhood on a number of templates. Let $h_p(k, \ell)$ be a $K \times L$ image containing the $p$-th template. Arrange the elements of $h_p(k, \ell)$ in a $KL$-dimensional vector $\mathbf{h}_p$, then the projection on a neighborhood equals $\mathbf{h}_p^T \mathbf{f}(n, m)$. Thus, the projection on $P$ different templates is equivalent to (5.5), and can be implemented as a parallel bank of $P$ image filters. A template should match a translated version of the elementary pattern. Since the orientation and distance of the repetition is unknown, a number of templates should be applied with different orientations and distances of the translation.

A popular choice of the templates is the so-called Gabor filters [18]:

$$h_p(k, \ell) = \frac{1}{2\pi\sigma_p^2} \exp\left(\frac{-(k^2 + \ell^2)}{2\sigma_p^2}\right) \exp\left(j2\pi\left(u_p k + v_p \ell\right)\right). \qquad (5.10)$$

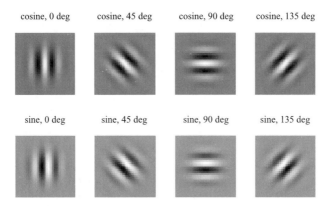

**Fig. 5.9.** Gabor filters.

Figure 5.9 provides some examples of these templates. Each filter consists of a real part (the cosine) and an imaginary part (the sine). These can easily be derived from (5.10) using: $e^{j\theta} = \cos\theta + j\sin\theta$, where $j = \sqrt{-1}$. The templates are parameterized by the spatial frequency $(u_p, v_p)$ and the scale $\sigma_p$. The two frequency parameters define the orientation and separation distance to which the template is sensitive. The templates in Figure 5.9 have a separation distance of about 8 pixels, orientations of $0°$, $45°$, $90°$, and $135°$, and a scale of 5. The idea behind these filters is that any elementary pattern can be decomposed into a weighed sum of these templates (conform Fourier transforms).

Figure 5.10 shows an example of the application of the four texture filters. The original image has two types of textured regions which are hatched in two different orientations. The spatial frequencies in Figure 5.9 are selected such that they more or less match these repetitive patterns.

(a)  (b)

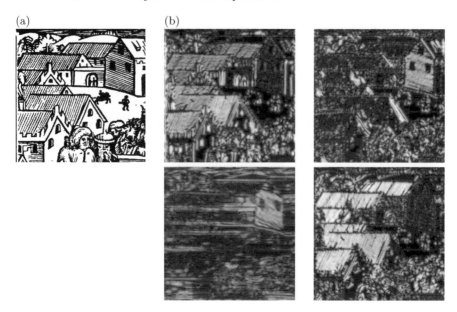

**Fig. 5.10.** Texture features using Gabor filtering. (**a**) Original; (**b**) the results from the filters shown in Figure 5.9.

### 5.4.2 Point Features

Some pixels in the image are special because they mark a distinctive position in the image plane. Some of these points are inherently isolated (e.g., corner points). Others are inherently linked together because they should form a curve in the image plane (e.g., line elements that form a line segment).

*Interest Points*

Interest points are pixels in the image that are distinctive from their immediate surroundings. Examples are corner points and spots. The detection of these points is of interest in a number of applications, including video tracking, stereo matching, and object recognition. Many techniques have been proposed to find interest points. Here, we discuss briefly the Harris corner detector [11] (Figure 5.11a) and the SIFT keypoints detector [13](Figure 5.11b).

Harris considers an image $f(n,m)$ and a shifted version of this image $f(n+x, m+y)$. Suppose that we want to test whether a point $(n,m)$ is distinctive. What we need to do is to check whether all pixel intensities surrounding $(n,m)$ are distinctive from $f(n,m)$, that is, whether $f(n+x, m+y)$ is distinctive from $f(n,m)$ for all small values of $(x,y)$. A suitable specification of the problem is as follows:

$$E(x,y) \stackrel{def}{=} \sum_{k,\ell} h(k,\ell)\left(f(n-k, m-\ell) - f(n+x-k, m+y-\ell)\right)^2. \quad (5.11)$$

(a)    (b)

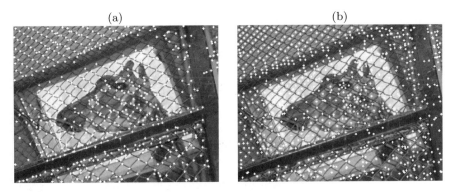

**Fig. 5.11.** Interest points. (**a**) Harris' corners; (**b**) SIFT keypoints (only a subset is shown).

The function $h(k, \ell)$ is a Gaussian window that is used to suppress the influence of noise. The criterion is that $E(x, y)$ should change fast for small shifts $(x, y)$ in any direction. This can be made effective by approximating $E(x, y)$ in a truncated Taylor series expansion:

$$E(x, y) \cong \sum_{k, \ell} h(k, \ell) \left( x f_x(m + k, m + k) + y f_y(n + k, m + k) \right)^2, \quad (5.12)$$

which can be written as:

$$E(x, y) \cong ax^2 + by^2 + 2cxy,$$

$$\text{with}: \begin{cases} a = \sum_{k, \ell} h(k, \ell) f_x^2(n + k, m + k) \\ b = \sum_{k, \ell} h(k, \ell) f_y^2(n + k, m + k) \\ c = \sum_{k, \ell} h(k, \ell) f_x(n + k, m + k) f_y(n + k, m + k), \end{cases} \quad (5.13)$$

where $f_x(n, m)$ and $f_y(n, m)$ are the first derivatives of $f(n, m)$. To find out whether $E(x, y)$ changes rapidly Harris proposes the following test variable:

$$g = ab - c^2 - \alpha (a + b)^2, \quad (5.14)$$

where $\alpha$ is a constant set to 0.04. The test variable is defined such that it is invariant to rotations of the image data. That is, $g$ does not depend on the accidental choice of the orientation of the coordinate system. The term $ab - c^2$ is large only if $E(x, y)$ changes rapidly in all directions. The second term $(a + b)^2$ is large if at least one direction exists for which $E(x, y)$ changes rapidly. The constant $\alpha$ is selected such that $g$ is positive at corners or isolated spots, and negative for edges. Pixel $(n, m)$ is marked as an interest point if $g$ exceeds some predefined threshold.

If (5.13) and (5.14) are executed for all image points, then $a, b, c$ and $g$ can be regarded as images. The operations in (5.13) become convolutions, e.g., $a(n, m) = h(n, m) * f_x^2(n, m)$, and so on. Corners and spots are detected at all positions where $g(n, m)$ is larger than the threshold, and where $g(n, m)$ is a local maximum. The latter requirement guarantees that the found points are isolated.

Another approach for finding a descriptive set of stable points is the so-called SIFT (scale invariant feature transform). Here, the following stack of images is considered:

$$d(n, m, \sigma) \overset{def}{=} \sigma^2 f(n, m) * (h_{xx}(n, m, \sigma) + h_{yy}(n, m, \sigma)), \qquad (5.15)$$

where $h_{xx}$ and $h_{yy}$ are the second derivatives of a Gaussian with scale $\sigma$. SIFT keypoints are points in the 3-dimensional space spanned by $(n, m, \sigma)$ for which $d(n, m, \sigma)$ forms local extrema (Figure 5.11b). Projected on $(n, m)$ these points are scale invariant. SIFT keypoints are usually attributed with descriptors that typify the local structure of the image around the keypoints in terms of local orientations.

*Line Elements*

In mathematical terms, a line segment has length, but possesses no width. Line-like objects in the scene have a width in the image equal to the scale of the image. Consequently, a line-like structure in the image must have a Gaussian shaped profile across the line. Measured along the line, the intensities do not change much. The width of the profile matches the scale of the image. Therefore, it depends on the scale at which the image is considered whether an elongated image structure is seen as a line or not.

If we regard the image as a landscape with the altitude given by the intensities, then line elements are the pixels that are on the ridge or on the valley of the landscape (see Figure 5.12). A cross-section of the image taken in the direction orthogonal to the ridge (or valley) will have a zero crossing of the first derivative, and a local extreme in the second derivative. Therefore, one method for extracting line elements is to calculate the second derivative in the direction orthogonal to the gradient vector. Unfortunately, this feature is not always stable because at the ridge the gradient vector might be zero and the direction is ill-defined.

A more stable result is obtained by approximating the neighborhood of each candidate line element by a quadratic surface: $f(n-k, m-\ell) \cong f(n, m) + ak^2 + b\ell^2 + 2ck\ell$. Here, $(n, m)$ is the position of the candidate line element. Using a truncated Taylor expansion it can be seen that:

$$f(n - k, m - \ell) \cong f(n, m) + \begin{bmatrix} k & \ell \end{bmatrix} \mathbf{H} \begin{bmatrix} k \\ \ell \end{bmatrix} \quad \text{with } \mathbf{H} = \begin{bmatrix} f_{xx} & f_{xy} \\ f_{xy} & f_{yy} \end{bmatrix}. \qquad (5.16)$$

(a)          (b)          (c)          (d)          (e)

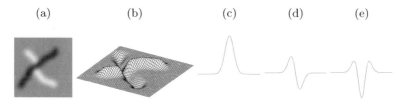

**Fig. 5.12.** Line structures. (a) Gray-level image; (b) viewed as a 3D landscape; (c) cross-section perpendicular to the ridge; (d) first derivative; (e) second derivative.

A brief notation for derivatives is used, e.g., $f_{xx} \equiv f_{xx}(n, m, \sigma)$, and so on. $\mathbf{H}$ is the Hessian matrix. Its eigenvalues $\lambda_1$ and $\lambda_2$, called the principal curvatures, are the second derivatives taken across and along the line, respectively. The direction of the line coincides with the eigenvector associated with the smallest eigenvalue. For a true line element, one eigenvalue should be large, and the other should be small. Thus, if the eigenvalues are ordered, $|\lambda_1| \geq |\lambda_2|$, then $|\lambda_1|$ should be large and $|\lambda_2|$ should be small. The latter requirement is not so important because the case where $|\lambda_1|$ and $|\lambda_2|$ are both large are rare (it corresponds either to an isolated spot or to a saddle).

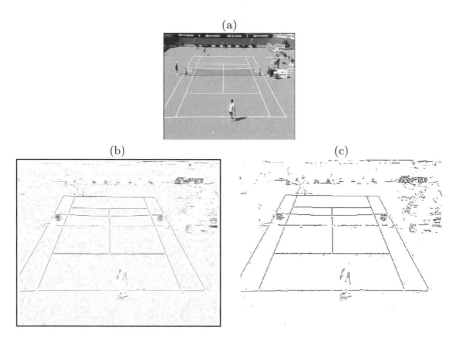

**Fig. 5.13.** Line elements. (a) Original image; (b) line features; (c) detected line elements.

Figure 5.13a shows an example of an image containing a number of lines. The $|\lambda_1|$-image is shown in Figure 5.13b. The detected line elements (Figure 5.13c) are found by the application of a non-local maximum suppression of the $|\lambda_1|$-image in the vertical direction and one in horizontal direction, and next by thresholding the result. Steger [19] discusses more advanced line extractions from images.

*Edge Elements*
The usual model of an edge element is that of an abrupt stepwise transition between two flat plateaus in the intensity landscape. The positions of these transitions are called *edge elements*, or just *edges*. Neighboring edge elements, linked together, form an edge segment. Often, the edge segments are assumed to be a smooth curve. In fact, the step edge model is a bit unrealistic since in any real image transitions never occur abruptly. However, most edge detectors rely on the availability of derivatives. If the scale at which these derivatives are calculated is large enough, then the errors introduced by assuming abrupt transitions is negligible.

At the position of an edge, the gradient vector is large. Therefore, the gradient magnitude $(f_x^2 + f_y^2)^{\frac{1}{2}}$, also called the edgeness, must be large for an edge, and small for a non-edge. Seen in the direction across the edge, the gradient magnitude must have a local maximum located at the position of the edge. The gradient vector itself points in the direction across the edge. Suppose that $w$ is that direction (so that $|f_w| = (f_x^2 + f_y^2)^{\frac{1}{2}}$ is the edgeness). Then, at the position of an edge, the directional second derivative $f_{ww}$ must be zero. $f_{ww}$ can be expressed in $f_x$, $f_{xx}$, etc. using the following relation: $|f_w|^2 f_{ww} = f_x^2 f_{xx} + f_y^2 f_{yy} + 2 f_x f_y f_{xy}$. The proof is beyond the scope of this text. Using the results up to now, we mark a pixel $(n, m)$ as an edge if:

$$\sqrt{f_x^2(n,m) + f_y^2(n,m)} > threshold$$
$$\text{and} \tag{5.17}$$
$$g(n,m) = 0 \quad \text{with} \quad g = f_x^2 f_{xx} + f_y^2 f_{yy} + 2 f_x f_y f_{xy}.$$

This approach is accredited to Canny [3]. In fact, Canny proposed a whole family of edge detectors; the one described above being one of them. A demonstration of the Canny edge detector is provided in Figure 5.14.

For linear edge segments, the procedure can be simplified. For linear edge segments, the second derivative along the edge is also zero. Thus, if $v$ is the direction along the edge, we have $f_{vv} = 0$. From $f_{ww} = 0$ we conclude that $f_{vv} + f_{ww} = 0$. However, $f_{vv} + f_{ww}$ is the Laplacian of the image. Since the Laplacian is rotational invariant, it equals $f_{vv} + f_{ww} = f_{xx} + f_{yy}$. Therefore, the zero crossing criterion can also be expressed as $f_{xx} + f_{yy} = 0$. This criterion was originally proposed by Marr and Hildreth [14].

### 5.4.3 Regions
The purpose of image segmentation is to partition the image plane into a number of disjoint, meaningful regions. The term "meaningful" refers to the

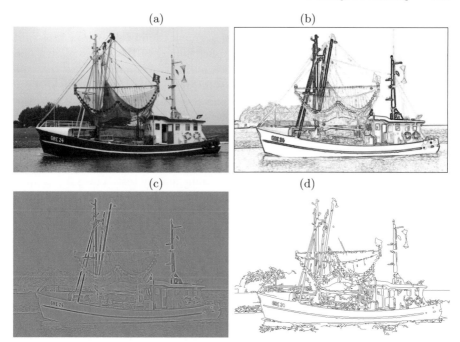

**Fig. 5.14.** Edge elements. (**a**) Original image; (**b**) edginess; (**c**) second directional derivative $f_{ww}$; (**d**) detected edge elements.

property that the regions in the image should have a direct correspondence with (parts of) the objects in the scene.

A first dichotomy for image segmentation techniques is the difference between top-down versus bottom-up approaches (see above). In the top-down approach, the shape, position and/or orientation of the regions are restricted using knowledge from the application domain. For instance, in the application of analyzing a tennis play the image of a tennis court has a given pattern of line segments (Figure 5.13) that can be used to guide the segmentation process. In a pure bottom-up process such restrictions are not used. The segmentation is much more difficult then. Often the result is over-segmented (i.e., a region corresponding to a single part of an object is fragmented into a number of smaller segments), or under-segmented (i.e., two regions from two different neighboring parts of the objects are found as one segment). Only if the application is well-conditioned pure bottom-up approaches are successful.

A second dichotomy can be made on the basis of area-based versus edge-based techniques. Area-based segmentation groups neighboring pixels together in a single region if these pixels share some local homogeneous property (e.g., the color). In contrast, edge-based segmentation strives for finding the boundaries between regions, i.e., locations where the homogeneity of a property breaks down.

*Area-based Segmentation*

A possible implementation of area-based segmentation is the *merge-and-split* approach. Starting point is some initial partitioning of the image plane. The partitioning can, for instance, consist of a number of square regions that together fill the complete image area. The split process involves a check whether some local property within each region passes a homogeneity test. If not, the concerning region is split into two smaller regions. The process is iteratively applied to each region. The iterations continue until all regions have successfully passed the homogeneity test. The next step is merging. We select arbitrarily two neighboring regions and check whether these two regions can be grouped together without violating the homogeneity test. This process also continues iteratively. That is, until no pair of neighboring regions can be found that passes the homogeneity test successful.

Possible homogeneity tests are, for instance:

$$\text{max-min criterion:} \quad \max_{(n,m)\in region} (f_{n,m}) - \min_{(n,m)\in region} (f_{n,m}) < \text{threshold} \tag{5.18}$$

and

$$\text{squared error criterion}: \frac{1}{area_{region}} \sum_{(n,m)\in region} (f_{n,m} - \hat{\mu}_{region})^2 < \text{threshold}. \tag{5.19}$$

Here, $\hat{\mu}_{region}$ is the mean value of the intensities within the region. $area_{region}$ is the number of pixels within the region. These criteria can easily be extended to encompass color and local texture parameters. Also models of shaded regions (with a small gradient in the intensities) can be implemented.

Another approach for area-based segmentation is *pixel classification*. The idea is that each pixel can be assigned a class label. The assignment occurs on the basis of features that are extracted for that pixel. A region is formed by a group of neighboring pixels that carry the same class label.

An obvious choice for the feature in an intensity image is the pixel intensity itself. This finds wide applications in industrial vision if the image acquisition is well-conditioned. A careful design of the illumination enables a division of pixels in a group of background and a group of foreground pixels (Figure 5.15) simply by comparing the pixel intensities against a threshold. Unfortunately, in many other applications this method fails because of the non-uniformity of background and objects.

Pixel classification is largely improved by extending the features. In a color image, we can use the three RGB components for each pixel. If this does not suffice, the feature space can be further enlarged by involving the intensities (or RGB components) in the neighborhood of each pixel. However, this possibility is also limited. Considering a color image and a $3 \times 3$ neighborhood the dimension of the feature space (= number of features per pixel) is already 27. Handling such a dimension not only forms a computational burden. It also

(a)                                    (b)

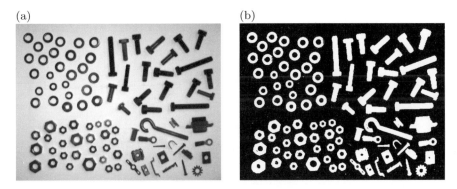

**Fig. 5.15.** Area based segmentation using the intensity. (**a**) Original image; (**b**) segmented by intensity thresholding.

becomes problematic to establish a suitable classification rule. Therefore, the number of features should be limited. A possibility for that is to use the texture features mentioned in Section 5.4.1. As an example, consider the Gabor texture features shown in Figure 5.10. The four filters produce four texture feature images. By stacking these four images each pixel has four texture features thus forming a 4-dimensional feature space. These features are used to classify each pixel using three possible classes: "hatched 1", "hatched 2", and "not hatched". The classification rule is established here by interactively creating a training set consisting of 3000 pixels (1000 pixels from each class). The applied rule is the so-called $K$ nearest-neighbor rule. That is, a new pixel is classified according to the majority of votes coming from the $K$ samples in the training set that are nearest to the feature vector of the new pixel. In this application, $K = 13$ appeared to be a good choice. The result is shown in Figure 5.16a. It can be seen that some pixels are erroneously classified. We may improve the results a little by applying some morphological operations as shown in Figure 5.16b.

*Edge-based Segmentation*

Usually, the first step in bottom-up, edge-based segmentation is the detection of edge elements (or line elements) resulting in an edge (or line) map. Most edge and line detectors not only provide the positions of the elements, but also directions. The second step involves the linking of neighboring elements to a chain. This is not a trivial step because the chain is often fragmented. Consequently, some gaps should be bridged. In addition, most edge and line detectors show some anomalous behavior in the vicinity of corners, T-junctions, and crossings. Furthermore, a textured area may give rise to an area crowded with spurious edge elements. The chains of edge (or line) elements form line segments that should be post-processed to form topologically correct regions.

As an example, consider the line elements shown in Figure 5.13c. From the application domain (scenes of a tennis court), we know that the configuration

(a)                                          (b)

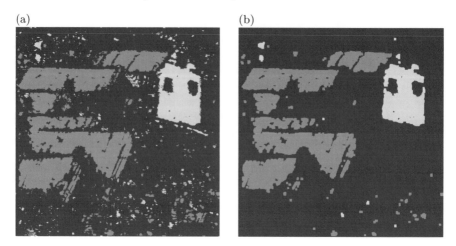

**Fig. 5.16.** Area based segmentation using pixel classification with texture features. (a) Labeled pixels; (b) cleaned.

of line elements form straight line segments. The so-called Hough transform (see, e.g., Jain's book [12]) is a technique to find these straight lines. A straight line is described in the $(x, y)$-domain by an equation $ax+by = 1$. This equation can be rewritten as:

$$\rho = x \sin \theta - y \cos \theta. \tag{5.20}$$

Here, $\theta$ is the angle of the line with the $x$-axis and $\rho$ is a signed distance to the origin. The Hough domain is the space spanned by the $\theta$ and $\rho$ parameters. A straight line in the $(x, y)$-domain corresponds to a single point in the Hough domain. On the other hand, all possible lines through a single point the in $(x, y)$-domain correspond with a curve in the Hough domain ($x$ and $y$ are constants in (5.20) and $\theta$ runs from 0 to $\pi$). If two points lie on a straight line in the $(x, y)$-domain, the $\theta$ and $\rho$ parameters of the line are found by the intersection of the two corresponding curves in the Hough domain.

In order to determine straight lines in an image, a Hough image is created of which each pixel corresponds to a certain $(\theta, \rho)$, i.e., a straight line in $(x, y)$-domain. The value of the pixels is set to the number of curves that pass through the pixel. This is done for each line pixel in the $(x, y)$-domain generating the corresponding curve in the Hough domain and increasing all pixels in the Hough image through which the curve passes. The maxima on the Hough images correspond with the intersections (see Figure 5.17b) and with the straight lines that are supported by most edge pixels in the $(x, y)$-domain (or: received most votes). The Hough image for the line elements from Figure 5.13c is shown in Figure 5.18a.

Detection of these local maxima (indicated by square marks in Figure 5.18a) reveals the parameters of the lines. The corresponding lines are

(a)                                          (b)

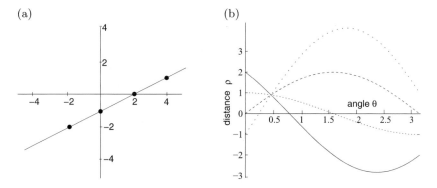

**Fig. 5.17.** The Hough transformation. (**a**) Line in $(x, y)$-domain; (**b**) curves corresponding to the four points; the intersection gives the parameters of the line.

superimposed on the image in Figure 5.18b. Here, the lines are shortened using a mask that is created from the original line elements. The final step is to produce a topologically correct segmentation (Figure 5.18c) by pruning the isolated endpoints of line segments, and to remove isolated line segments.

In this application, top-down segmentation is possible due to the fact that the lines in a tennis court have a pattern. The knowledge of this pattern can be used to get a more stable and robust result. The pattern manifests itself, for instance, in the Hough transform as 6 points in the vicinity of $\theta \approx -90°$ or $\theta \approx +90°$. These points correspond to the 6 horizontal lines of the court. The 5 vertical lines are represented by the 5 points around $\theta = 0°$. The top-down approach boils down to looking for the typical configuration of the 6+5 points in the Hough domain.

### 5.4.4 Regional Description and Relations
The step following after segmentation is the characterization of the regions. The description of the regions includes the following aspects:

- radiometry (mean and variance of intensities or RGB components; texture parameters);
- geometry (position, orientation and shape);
- relations with other regions (adjacencies, relative size, etc.).

*Radiometric Properties*
The regional radiometric properties are derived from the intensities (or RGB components) of the pixels within the region. Perhaps the simplest description is just the mean value of the intensities within the region. For color images, the mean color:

(a)

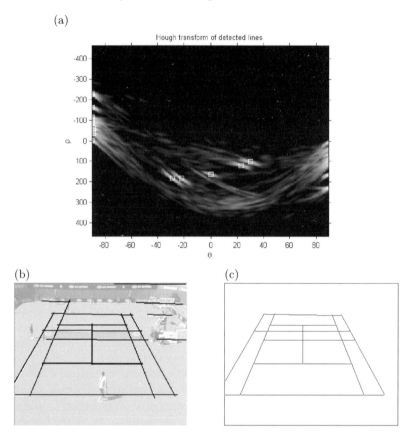

**Fig. 5.18.** Edge based segmentation. (**a**) Hough transform of Figure 5.13c; the squares indicate the parameters of the found lines; (**b**) original image with the found lines superimposed; (**c**) segmented image.

$$\bar{R} = \frac{1}{area_{region}} \sum_{(n,m) \in region} R(n,m)$$

$$\bar{G} = \frac{1}{area_{region}} \sum_{(n,m) \in region} G(n,m) \qquad (5.21)$$

$$\bar{B} = \frac{1}{area_{region}} \sum_{(n,m) \in region} B(n,m)$$

is a good descriptor for objects that are characterized by their color (for instance, some fruits). These descriptions are easily extended by other first-order statistical moments (such as variance, skewness and kurtosis).

For textured regions the second-order statistics is relevant. These follow readily from the co-occurrence matrices $\mathbf{C}_{\theta,\rho}$ (Section 5.4.1) calculated over the whole region. Parameters that can be derived from the co-occurrence matrices are, for instance:

$$\text{contrast} \quad \sum_{i,j} (i - j)^2 \, P_{\theta,\rho}(i,j)$$

$$\text{energy} \quad \sum_{i,j} P_{\theta,\rho}^2(i,j) \tag{5.22}$$

$$\text{correlation} \quad \sum_{i,j} \frac{(i-\mu)(j-\mu)}{\sigma^2} P_{\theta,\rho}(i,j).$$

Here $\mathbf{P}_{\theta,\rho}$ is the normalized co-occurrence matrix derived from $\mathbf{C}_{\theta,\rho}$ (the elements $P_{\theta,\rho}(i,j)$ must sum to one) and $\mu$ and $\sigma$ are the mean and standard deviation of the elements of $P_{\theta,\rho}$.

As an example, consider the regions (background, roof, wall) in Figure 5.16b obtained from the image in Figure 5.10a. Figure 5.19a shows the correlation of the three regions for the following separation distances and orientations:

$$\theta = 0°\,(\text{horizontal}) : \rho = 0, 1, \cdots, 30$$
$$\theta = 90°\,(\text{vertical}) : \rho = 0, 1, \cdots, 30.$$

The periodic nature of the two hatched regions is clearly reflected in these correlations. This is even more explicit in Figure 5.19b where the Fourier transforms of the correlation functions (the power density spectra, i.e., the strength of the pattern as a function of its spatial frequency) are shown. The background region has a maximum at spatial frequency 0, which means, there is no repeating pattern. The roof region has a strong peak at a horizontal frequency of ca. 0.12 [pixel$^{-1}$] and a weaker peak at a vertical frequency of ca. 0.07 [pixel$^{-1}$]. The wall has a strong peak at a vertical frequency of ca. 0.12 [pixel$^{-1}$] and at a horizontal frequency of ca. 0.07 [pixel$^{-1}$].

*Geometric Properties*
The geometry of a region concerns aspects like: position, orientation, size and shape. These features can be extracted using the region seen as an area, but it is also possible to extract them from the contour of the region. First consider an area-based approach. Geometric properties can be extracted using the *moments* of a region. A well-known example is the center of gravity (centroid) defined by:

$$\bar{x} = \frac{1}{area} \sum_{(n,m)\in region} n \qquad \bar{y} = \frac{1}{area} \sum_{(n,m)\in region} m \quad, \tag{5.23}$$

where *area* is the number of pixels within the region. Often, $(\bar{x}, \bar{y})$ is used as the definition for the position of the region.

In fact the center of gravity can be defined in terms of moments. That is, $\bar{x} = M_{10}$ and $\bar{y} = M_{01}$, where the moment of order $pq$ is defined as:

$$M_{pq} = \frac{1}{area} \sum_{(n,m)\in region} n^p m^q. \tag{5.24}$$

(a)

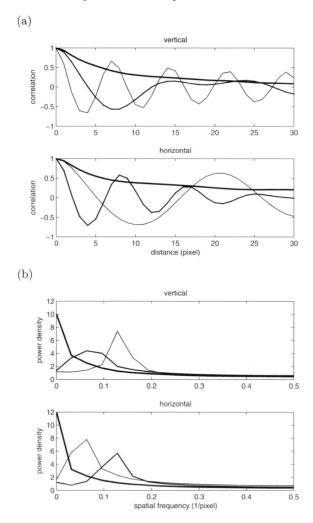

(b)

**Fig. 5.19.** Texture parameters for the three regions in Figure 5.10a. (**a**) Correlation function; (**b**) power density spectrum.

The centralized moments are moments that are made invariant to the position of the region:

$$\mu_{pq} = \frac{1}{area} \sum_{(n,m)\in region} (n - \bar{x})^p (m - \bar{y})^q. \tag{5.25}$$

The second-order moments provide some rough information about the orientation and extension of the region. For that purpose, define the second-order matrix:

$$\begin{bmatrix} \mu_{20} & \mu_{11} \\ \mu_{11} & \mu_{02} \end{bmatrix}. \tag{5.26}$$

The principal axes of the region are spanned by the eigenvectors of this matrix. The corresponding eigenvalues are called principal moments. Their square root is a measure of the extension of the region in the direction of the corresponding principal axes. The direction of the largest principal axis is a measure for the orientation of the region. Figure 5.20 shows the principal axes of the regions obtained in Figure 5.15b. Note that the directions of the rings and nuts are indeterminate due to the rotational symmetry of these objects.

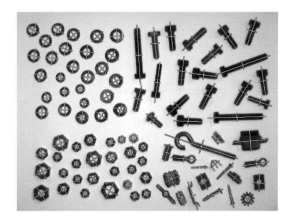

**Fig. 5.20.** Principal axes derived from the second-order moments of the regions.

Another possibility to describe the geometry of a region is by considering the contour of the region. The contour is formed by the set of pixels that belong to the boundary of the region. A contour can be represented by a parametric curve $(x(s), y(s))$ where the parameter $s$ is the running arc length. $(x(0), y(0))$ is some arbitrarily selected starting point of the contour. $s$ is the length of the path along the contour. If $P$ is the perimeter of the region, then the curve is periodic with period $P$, i.e., $x(s+P) = x(s)$ and $y(s+P) = y(s)$. Figure 5.21a illustrates the contour representation of a region.

Since $x(s)$ and $y(s)$ are periodic functions of $s$, their Fourier spectra are discrete. In other words, the functions can be built using a weighed sum of complex harmonic functions:

$$x(s) + jy(s) = \sum_{k=-\infty}^{+\infty} Z_k \exp\left(2\pi j \frac{ks}{P}\right). \tag{5.27}$$

The complex amplitudes $Z_k$, called the Fourier descriptors, are obtained analytically using the Fourier transform:

$$Z_k = \frac{1}{P} \int_{s=0}^{P} (x(s) + jy(s)) \exp\left(-2\pi j \frac{ks}{P}\right) ds. \tag{5.28}$$

In practice, the contours extracted from the regions are discrete (sampled), and the Fourier descriptors are calculated using the FFT-algorithm (Fast Fourier Transform). For the analytic case, the number of Fourier descriptors is infinite, but for the discrete case, the number of usable Fourier descriptors will never exceed the number of points on the contour. So, practically a range from, say, $Z_{-16}$ up to $Z_{16}$ is sufficient.

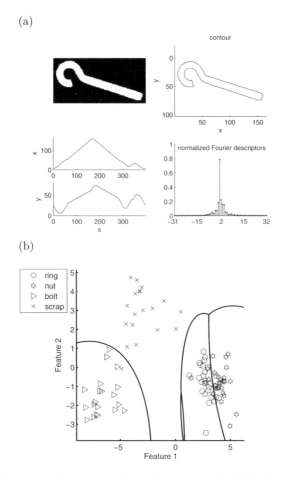

**Fig. 5.21.** Geometrical properties based on normalized Fourier descriptors. (a) Contour representation and NFDs; (b) scatter diagram using Fourier descriptors.

The Fourier descriptors can be used to extract information with respect to position, orientation and size. For instance, the position of the contour is given by $Z_0$ because according to (5.28):

$$Z_0 = \frac{1}{P} \int_{s=0}^{P} (x(s) + \mathrm{j}y(s))\, ds. \tag{5.29}$$

Thus, $Z_0$ is the center of gravity of the contour. The orientation of the region is encoded in the phase of the Fourier descriptors. As said before the starting point of the traced contour is often arbitrarily selected. This starting point is also encoded in the phase. So we need at least two Fourier descriptors to entangle the orientation and the starting point. The size of the objects, i.e., the square root of the area (or optionally the radius of the best fitting circle), is proportional to the magnitude of the descriptors. Therefore, a measure for the size can easily be extracted.

Having the position, orientation, starting point and size of the contour, the descriptors can be made invariant to these aspects by normalizing them, that is, by giving the contour a standard position, orientation, starting point and size. The resulting descriptors are called NFDs (*normalized Fourier descriptors*). Figure 5.21a shows the magnitudes of the NFDs. The range of NFDs shown there are $k = -31, \cdots, -1$ and $2, \cdots, 32$. $Z_0$ and $Z_1$ are excluded since they do not carry any information (they are sacrificed for the normalization: $Z_0 \equiv 0$ and $Z_1 \equiv 1$). The scatter diagram in Figure 5.21b is obtained by, for every object in the image 5.15, first calculating the Fourier descriptors, then from these extracting two features using Fisher's linear discriminant analysis [6] (a linear transformation resulting in a dimension reduction) and plotting the symbol (cross, triangle, box, star) of the objects at the position defined by the found features. The scatter diagram illustrates that the NFDs are usable for shape recognition, because the different objects form clusters that can be separated by e.g., quadratic boundaries.

### Relations

In the preceding section each region was considered individually. In addition to that, relations between regions are also clues for object recognition. As an example, consider the segmented image of a tennis court shown in Figure 5.18c. A proper interpretation of the regions in this image is given in Figure 5.22. It will be difficult to classify these regions without taking into account the context in which they appear. In fact, all regions are rectangles that have been transformed under an (unknown) perspective projection. Therefore, the shape parameters do not provide much information. The eccentricities of the rectangles might be a clue, but this parameter is not invariant to a perspective projection. An additional difficulty rises because the presence of the net cord causes an over-segmentation of the courts.

The context of the regions can be described by relations. A relation is a property between two regions. Relations between three or more regions do

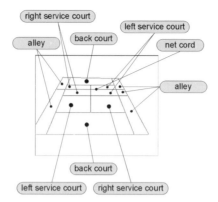

**Fig. 5.22.** Labeled regions of the tennis court image.

exist as well, but these are not discussed here. These relations are either quantifiable attributes of the pair of regions, or propositions that can be true or false. The following is a list of quantities that can be attributed to any two regions $A$ and $B$:

- Relative size: the size of region $A$ relative to the size of region $B$:

$$s(A, B) = \frac{area(A)}{area(B)} \quad \text{or} \quad s(A, B) = \frac{|Z_1(A)|}{|Z_2(A)|}. \quad (5.30)$$

  $|Z_1(A)|$ is the magnitude of the first Fourier descriptor of region $A$, i.e., the radius of the circle that best fits its contour.
- Normalized distance: the distance between two regions relative to their size:

$$d_{relative}(A, B) = \frac{d(A, B)}{\sqrt{|Z_1(A)| |Z_1(B)|}}. \quad (5.31)$$

  $d(A, B)$ is the distance between $A$ and $B$, defined, for instance, using the centers of gravity.
- Similarity: a measure of alikeness of shape. A possibility, using the normalized Fourier descriptors $Z_k$, is:

$$sim(A, B) = \sqrt{\sum_k (Z_k(A) - Z_k(B))^2}. \quad (5.32)$$

- Adjacency: a measure $a(A, B)$ of the extent to what region $A$ is adjacent to region $B$. It can be defined as the fraction of the boundary of $A$ that is adjacent to the region $B$. Thus if $A$ and $B$ do not share a common boundary, then $a(A, B) = 0$. If $A$ is completely surrounded by $B$, and $A$ does not contain holes, then $a(A, B) = 1$.

Examples of propositions are:

- *A* is adjacent to *B*;
- *A* surrounds *B*;
- *A* is left from *B*;
- *A* is above *B*;
- *A* is similar to *B*.

Many of these propositions can be derived simply by thresholding the corresponding quantifiable properties.

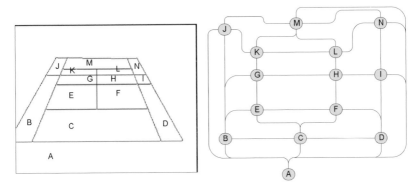

**Fig. 5.23.** Region adjacency graph (RAG) of the tennis court image.

The representation of the regional properties and the relation is often that of an attributed graph. The simplest version is the so-called region adjacency graph (RAG) shown in Figure 5.23. The nodes in the graph represent the regions found in the image. Two nodes are connected by an arc if (and only if) the two corresponding regions are adjacent. The RAG can easily be extended to a directed, attributed graph. Figure 5.24 gives an example (only part of the graph is visualized). Here, labels have been attributed to both the nodes and the arcs. These labels contain the observations that have been made in the image. Labels attached to the nodes are region properties. Labels attached to the arcs are relations. In Figure 5.24 only propositions are given. But, if needed, they can be extended by quantifiable properties.

Instead of an area-based description of regions and relations one can also exploit edge- or line-based descriptions. In fact, the analysis of the tennis court image is easier using relations between the lines that make up the tennis court. Figure 5.25a is an overview of the lines that are defined by the International Tennis Federation. Assuming that the point of view of the camera is always lengthwise with respect to the tennis court (which is usually the case), the baselines, the service lines, and the net are horizontally aligned in the image. Figure 5.25b is a relational model of these lines. The model for the sidelines, i.e., the vertical lines, is likewise. The horizontal lines are subjected to the perspective projection of the camera. Consequently, these lines share a common intersection point, called the vanishing point, see Figure 5.26. Depending on

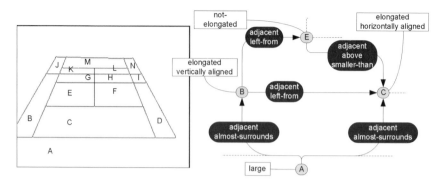

**Fig. 5.24.** Attributed graph describing the regional and relational properties.

the orientation of the camera with respect to the court the vanishing point of the horizontal lines must be either left or right from the image. The vanishing point of the vertical lines must be situated above or below the image. This knowledge is exploited in Figure 5.25b in order to find the set of horizontal lines.

In Figure 5.25b the relations "have-a", "is-a", and "is-a-kind-of" are borrowed from the semantic network representations developed in classic artificial intelligence. The proposition "A is-a B" means that A is an instance of the set B. The proposition "A is-a-kind-of B" means that A is a subset of the set B. The proposition "A has-a B" relates an object B to A. Figure 5.25b shows that horizontal lines are made up by subsets "baselines" and "service lines", and by the instances "net cord" and "center line". The subset "baselines" consists of the instances "lower baseline" and "upper baseline". The subset "service lines" consists of the instances "lower service line" and "upper service line".

The center line is distinguished by the fact that it is positioned midway between the two service lines (and the baselines). However, this predicate only holds true in a metrically correct domain. Due to the perspective projection the image plane does not satisfies this constraint. One way to deal with this problem is to rectify the image using the vanishing points. Figure 5.26 shows an example. A possible additional advantage of this geometric transformation is that the further analysis of the tennis play might be facilitated.

## 5.5 Object recognition

In the previous section mainly bottom-up strategies are described to arrive at regional and relational descriptions of images (see the hierarchy of Figure 5.5). In this section three top-down approaches to object recognition will be presented: template matching, eigenobjects and statistical shape models. Also, it will be shown how these methods fit into the model-based framework to image analysis presented in Figure 5.4.

(a)

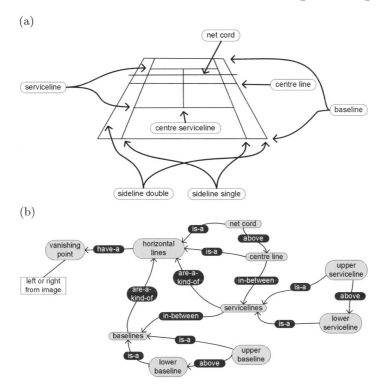

(b)

**Fig. 5.25.** Model of the lines in the tennis court image. (**a**) Definitions of the lines; (**b**) relational model of the horizontal lines.

### 5.5.1 Template Matching

Template matching is a straightforward method for object recognition and localization in images. The objects that must be detected are represented by templates, which often simply are images of the object. To detect an instance of an object in an image, the corresponding template is placed at a certain location on the image and the pixel values of the template and the image under the template are compared to each other. Figure 5.27 shows a scanned document and a template of the letter "a". Template matching would result in low difference values at the positions of a's in the document and high difference values elsewhere.

There are many ways to compare templates to image data. Probably the simplest is the absolute difference measure:

$$d_{T,I}(x,y) = \sum_{u=-m}^{m} \sum_{v=-n}^{n} |T(u,v) - I(x+u, y+v)|, \qquad (5.33)$$

where $T(u,v)$ is the pixel value at coordinates $u,v$ of the template $T$ and $I(x+u, y+v)$ is the pixel value at the corresponding position in the image $I$.

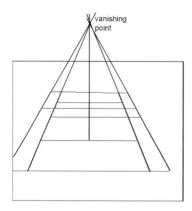
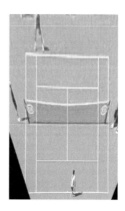

**Fig. 5.26.** Rectification using the vanishing points.

In 1830 there were but twenty-three
miles of railroad in operation in the
United States, and in that year Ken-
tucky took the initial step in the work
west of the Alleghanies.  An Act to
incorporate the Lexington & Ohio
Railway Company was approved by
Gov. Metcalf, January 27, 1830.. It
provided for the construction and re-

**Fig. 5.27.** Template matching by comparing a template (the "a" character on the
right) with the underlying image. If the template of an object is positioned exactly
over the same object in the image, the difference between template and underlying
image will be minimal.

The size of the template is $2m + 1$x$2n + 1$. Generally, the difference measure is
calculated for all positions in the image and an object is located by finding the
maxima in the resulting difference image that are below a certain threshold.
Often, the pixel values of templates and instances of the corresponding objects
in the image differ, because of, e.g., difference in illumination. In this case the
absolute difference is not a good distance measure. A better choice is then to
use cross-correlation:

$$C_{T,I}(x,y) = \sum_{u=-m}^{m} \sum_{v=-n}^{n} T(u,v) \cdot I(u-x, y+v), \qquad (5.34)$$

or normalized cross-correlation:

$$NC_{T,I}(x,y) = \frac{\sum\limits_{u=-m}^{m} \sum\limits_{v=-n}^{n} T(u,v) \cdot I(x+u,y+v)}{\sqrt{\sum\limits_{u=-m}^{m} \sum\limits_{v=-n}^{n} (T(u,v))^2 \sum\limits_{u=-m}^{m} \sum\limits_{v=-n}^{n} (I(x+u,y+v))^2}}. \quad (5.35)$$

These cross-correlation measures are higher if the image under the template differs less from the template.

The normalized cross-correlation of the template in Figure 5.27 with the scanned document is shown in Figure 5.28 on the left. At the positions of an "a" character in the document, a bright spot can be observed. At some positions with characters that have some similarity with the template darker spots can be observed, while the background is completely dark. At the right, the positions of the maxima of the matching results are overlayed on the original document image, showing that all "a" characters were properly detected.

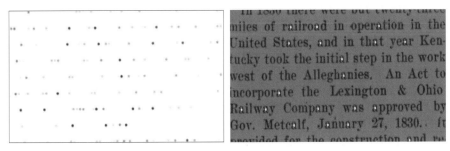

**Fig. 5.28.** Result of the template matching giving maxima for "a"-like characters and the detected characters overlayed on the original scanned document.

The template matching approach fits neatly in the model-based framework as is shown in Figure 5.29.

The model simply consists of the template. The feature consists of a window in the image at a position $x, y$ of the size of the template, the pixels of which are directly compared with the template using the absolute difference or cross-correlation measures. The template matching approach can easily be extended to incorporate multiple templates and to allow rotation and scaling of the templates. Also, instead of comparing image data directly, it is possible to first extract features of the template and the image and perform the comparison between the extracted features.

### 5.5.2 Eigenobjects

Eigenobjects is a method for object recognition that is based on the idea that any object $O$ can be represented by a mean object $\bar{O}$ plus a weighted sum of the eigenobjects $e_i$:

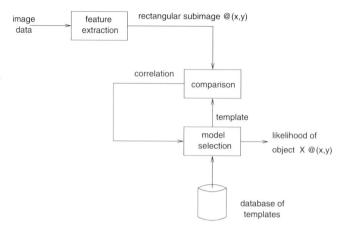

**Fig. 5.29.** Template matching approach cast in the model-based structure.

$$O = \bar{O} + \sum_i w_i e_i. \qquad (5.36)$$

The eigenobjects are determined from a set of example or training objects and a technique called principal component analysis (PCA). An object is recognized by comparing the weights $w_i$ of the object to those of objects in a database of known objects. Details are given by, amongst others, Turk and Pentland [21]; they use the technique for face recognition. An object $O$ is characterized by a vector of features $\mathbf{u}$. The elements of such a feature vector could, e.g., be the intensities of the pixels in an image or other features, like shape, size and color. For an object with index $i$ and $n$ features, this results in the following feature vector:

$$\mathbf{u}^i = \{u_1^i, u_2^i, \ldots, u_n^u\}. \qquad (5.37)$$

If there are $m$ example object feature vectors, the average object feature vector becomes:

$$\bar{\mathbf{u}} = \frac{1}{m} \sum_{k=1}^{m} \mathbf{u}^k. \qquad (5.38)$$

Let us consider the case that the number of features is larger than the number of examples: $n > m$, as is often the case if whole images are used as feature vectors. In this case the eigenobjects $\mathbf{e}^i$ are calculated using:

$$e_l^i = \frac{1}{\sqrt{\lambda_i}} \sum_{k=1}^{m} v_k^i (u_l^k - \bar{u}_l), \qquad (5.39)$$

where $\lambda_i$ and $\mathbf{v}^i = \{v_1^i, v_2^i, \ldots, v_m^i\}$ are the eigen values and eigenvectors of the $m \times m$ matrix:

$$\mathbf{L} = \mathbf{A}^T \mathbf{A}, \tag{5.40}$$

where $\mathbf{A} = [\mathbf{u}^1 - \bar{\mathbf{u}}, \mathbf{u}^2 - \bar{\mathbf{u}}, ..., \mathbf{u}^m - \bar{\mathbf{u}}]$ is an $m \times n$ matrix. If the number of features is less than the number of examples: $n < m$, then the eigenvectors of the $n \times n$ matrix $\mathbf{AA}^T$ are used.

Any input feature vector $u$ of a new object can now be decomposed in the eigenobjects $\mathbf{e}^i$. The coefficients are calculated using:

$$w_i = (\mathbf{e}^i)^T (\mathbf{u} - \bar{\mathbf{u}}). \tag{5.41}$$

The feature vector $u$ of the object can now be reconstructed using the coefficients $w_i$, the eigenobjects $\mathbf{e}^i$ and the mean object feature vector $\bar{\mathbf{u}}$:

$$\hat{\mathbf{u}} = \sum_{k=1}^{m} w_k \mathbf{e}^k + \bar{\mathbf{u}}. \tag{5.42}$$

Identification of the object takes place by determining a distance measure (e.g., the Euclidian distance) between the weights of the object to identify and the weights of objects in a database. Often fewer than $m$ eigenobjects are used for reconstruction and identification. Eigenobjects with corresponding eigenvalues of relatively small magnitude explain only little of the variation of the example set and can, therefore, be discarded without introducing significant reconstruction errors. If the eigenobjects $\mathbf{e}^i$ are ordered according to the magnitude of the corresponding eigenvalues $\lambda_i$, we can simply discard eigenobjects $\mathbf{e}^{m'+1}$ to $\mathbf{e}^m$ and 5.42 reduces to:

$$\hat{\mathbf{u}} = \sum_{k=1}^{m'} w_k \mathbf{e}^k + \bar{\mathbf{u}}, \tag{5.43}$$

where $1 \leq m' \leq m$ and $m'$ is chosen such that most of the variation in the training set is explained by the first $m'$ eigenobjects.

The eigenobjects approach to object recognition can be cast into the model-based framework as displayed in Figure 5.30. Since the weights of the objects are compared, the model must predict the weights of the object in the image. The model, therefore, consists of a database of objects of which features are extracted and the principal components using (5.41). The model contains information of the objects in the training set in the form of the eigenobjects $\mathbf{e}^i$ and the mean object feature vector $\bar{\mathbf{u}}$ as well as of the objects in the database (which may differ from those in the training set). For an input image in which an object must be recognized, first the features vector of the object is extracted and next the weights of the principal components are extracted using (5.41). The parameter to be estimated is the index of the object in the database of objects and the model selection box in the model-based scheme just walks through the complete list of objects and selects the object with the weights closest to the weights $\mathbf{w}$ of the object in the input image.

The resulting "description" of the image is in this case the object index or label. In order to increase recognition speed, the PCA-weights of all objects in the database can be pre-calculated.

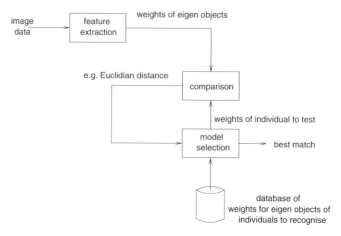

**Fig. 5.30.** Eigenobjects method cast in the model-based structure.

The eigenobject recognition method has been successfully applied to face recognition, in which case it is called eigenface method. The input vectors of features $\mathbf{u}$ consist of the intensities of the pixels of facial images images. This means for facial images of, e.g., $100 \times 100$ pixels that the feature vector $\mathbf{u}$ has 10,000 elements. Generally only the first few hundred elements are used as they explain 95–98% of the variation in training sets. An example of the average face image and the five most significant eigenfaces is shown in Figure 5.31. These images were obtained by training with 1408 images from the so-called FERET facial image database [15].

### 5.5.3 Statistical Shape Models

Statistical shape models and active shape models are described by Cootes et al. [5]. A shape like a contour of the hand or the features of a face can be represented by a set of (connected) landmarks. In Figure 5.32 the shapes of the bolts from Figure 5.3. A set of examples of these shapes can be used to build a statistical shape model, provided that the landmarks are consistent between the shapes.

The first step to build such a statistical model is to align all shape examples by procrustes analysis, i.e., rotate, scale and translate each of them such that the sum of squared difference to the mean of the set is minimized. Each shape can then be represented by a vector with the coordinates of the landmarks. If there are $n$ landmarks on a shape, then a shape $i$ is given by the $2n$-dimensional vector:

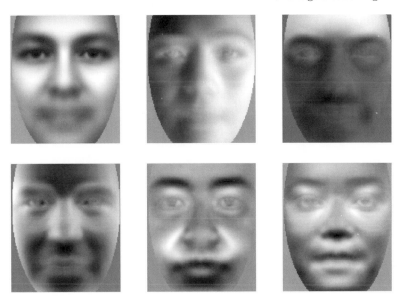

**Fig. 5.31.** Average face and first few eigenfaces of a face recognition system based on PCA. The eigenfaces can be seen as variations on the average face.

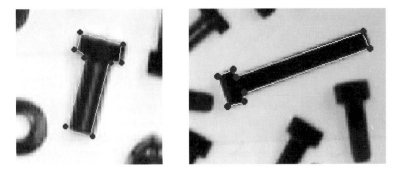

**Fig. 5.32.** Shapes defined by a set of landmarks.

$$\mathbf{x}_i = [x_{i1}, y_{i1}, x_{i2}, y_{i2}, .., x_{in}, y_{in}]^T . \qquad (5.44)$$

Like in the previous section about eigenobjects, the a shape $i$ can be described as the sum of a mean shape and weighted shape variations using principal component analysis:

$$\mathbf{x}_i = \bar{\mathbf{x}} + \mathbf{P}\mathbf{b}_i, \qquad (5.45)$$

where the vector $\bar{\mathbf{x}}$ is the mean of the aligned shapes, the matrix $\mathbf{P}$ describes the modes of variations and the vector $\mathbf{b}$ contains the weights. If there are $N$ shapes in the example set, then:

$$\bar{\mathbf{x}} = \sum_{i=1}^{N} \mathbf{x}_i. \tag{5.46}$$

The $2n \times 2n$ matrix $\mathbf{P}$ consists of the unit eigenvectors $\mathbf{p}_k$ of the covariance matrix:

$$\mathbf{C} = \frac{1}{N} \sum_{i=1}^{N} (\mathbf{x}_i - \bar{\mathbf{x}})(\mathbf{x}_i - \bar{\mathbf{x}})^T. \tag{5.47}$$

Thus $\mathbf{P} = [\mathbf{p}_1, \mathbf{p}_1, ..., \mathbf{p}_{2n}]$ and for each eigenvector $\mathbf{p}_k$ the following holds:

$$\mathbf{C}\mathbf{p}_k = \lambda_k \mathbf{p}_k \qquad \text{and} \qquad \mathbf{p}_k^T \mathbf{p}_k = 1. \tag{5.48}$$

The $\lambda_k$ are the corresponding eigenvalues and the eigenvectors are ordered such that $\lambda_k \geq \lambda_{k+1}$.

Any shape in the example set can be approximated using the mean shape $\bar{\mathbf{x}}$ and a weighted sum of the first $t$ modes of variations:

$$\mathbf{x}_i \approx \bar{\mathbf{x}} + \mathbf{P}_t \mathbf{b}_t, \tag{5.49}$$

where $\mathbf{P}_t = [\mathbf{p}_1, \mathbf{p}_1, ..., \mathbf{p}_t]$ and $\mathbf{b}_t = [b_1, b_2, ..., b_t]^T$. New shapes that are not in the example set can be generated by varying the weights $b_k$. By setting certain limits to the weights, shape constraints can be imposed. Suitable limits are typically in the order of:

$$-3\sqrt{\lambda_k} \leq b_k \leq 3\sqrt{\lambda_k}. \tag{5.50}$$

Figure 5.33 shows variation of the main modes of variation for the active shape models of Figure 5.32. The first mode of variation appears to be the thickness of the bolt relative to the head and the second main mode of variation is the flatness of the head of the bolt. Remember, that the variation in position, orientation and scaling has been eliminated by procrustes analysis.

**Fig. 5.33.** The main modes of variation for the statistical shape models of Figure 5.32 are the thickness of the bolt and the flatness of the head relative to the length of the bolt.

The next step is now to use the statistical shape model to locate similar objects in images. This requires estimation of the position, orientation (rotation) and scale of the object as well as the weights for the modes of variation of the statistical shape model. If the center of a shape $\mathbf{s}$ is given by $X_c, Y_c$ and the scaling $s$ and rotation by $\theta$ are defined by the matrix $\mathbf{M}(s, \theta)$, then an instance of the model can be written as:

$$\mathbf{X} = \mathbf{M}(s, \theta)\mathbf{x} + \mathbf{X}_c, \tag{5.51}$$

where $\mathbf{X}_c = [X_c, Yc, X_c, Y_c, ..., X_c, Y_c]^T$. Now assume that an instance of the model is placed on an image near an object. In order to fit the model, adjustments to the landmarks will have to be found to move them to a better position. If the model points represent the boundaries of the object, this can be realized by moving them to the image edges, e.g., to the maximum gradient near the points. The adjustments of the model points form a vector:

$$d\mathbf{X} = [dX_1, dY_1, ..., dX_n, dY_n]. \tag{5.52}$$

By using procrustes analysis again, a new estimate for the scaling $s'$, the orientation $\theta'$ and the center $\mathbf{X}'_c$ results, such that:

$$\mathbf{M}(s', \theta')(\mathbf{x} + d\mathbf{x}) + \mathbf{X}'_c = \mathbf{X} + d\mathbf{X}, \tag{5.53}$$

where $d\mathbf{x}$ are the residual adjustments that cannot be interpreted by global scaling, rotation and translation of the model. These residual adjustments must be compensated for by adapting the shape of the model, i.e., adjusting $\mathbf{b}$. First, $d\mathbf{x}$ is determined from (5.53):

$$d\mathbf{x} = \mathbf{M}^{-1}(s', \theta')(\mathbf{X} + d\mathbf{X} - \mathbf{X}'_c) - \mathbf{x}. \tag{5.54}$$

In order to find the adjustments for $\mathbf{b}$, the residuals $d\mathbf{x}$ are transformed into the model parameter space. Using (5.49):

$$\mathbf{x} + d\mathbf{x} \approx \bar{\mathbf{x}} + \mathbf{P}_t(\mathbf{b}_t + d\mathbf{b}_t). \tag{5.55}$$

Subtracting (5.49) gives:

$$d\mathbf{x} \approx \mathbf{P}_t d\mathbf{b}_t. \tag{5.56}$$

Now $d\mathbf{b}_t$ can be obtained by inversion of $\mathbf{P}_t$ and since $\mathbf{P}_t$ consists of the unit eigenvectors of a covariance matrix, $\mathbf{P}_t^{-1} = \mathbf{P}_t^T$:

$$d\mathbf{b}_t = \mathbf{P}_t^T d\mathbf{x}. \tag{5.57}$$

In order to ensure that the model only deforms into shapes that are consistent with the shapes in the example set, the weights $\mathbf{b}$ are limited according to (5.50). The whole procedure from (5.52)–(5.57) is repeated until no significant change occurs. Figure 5.34 shows some examples of the bolt model fitted to bolts not present in the example set.

**Fig. 5.34.** Results of fitting the statistical model of a bolt.

This method of fitting statistical shape models to images is often called the Active Shape Model (ASM). There is an extension to the ASM, which not only describes the shape using a statistical model, but for the texture as well. This combined shape and texture model is called Active Appearance Model (AAM) [20]. Numerous applications exist for ASMs and AAMs, ranging from lung detection in X-ray photographs to 2D and 3D segmentation of organs in medical CT and MRI images to face recognition.

In Figure 5.35 the active shape model approach to object recognition is cast into the model-based image processing approach. Since here a number of parameters must be optimized, the model selection approach is more complicated. It handles the steps described in (5.53)–(5.57), i.e., it calculates a new instance of the model (the global position, pose and scale and the shape parameters $\mathbf{b}$) from the displacements $d\mathbf{X}$.

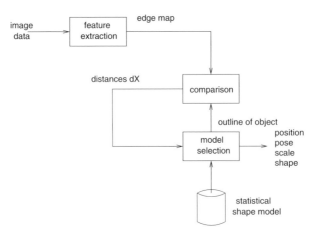

**Fig. 5.35.** Active shape model approach to object detection cast into the model-based framework.

## 5.6 Summary

This chapter gives an overview of the application areas of and techniques used in image processing. Because the field of image processing is very broad, it is impossible to give an exhaustive overview and it was necessary to make a selection of subjects. The emphasis in this overview is on image analysis, where image analysis is defined as the extraction of descriptions of images, imaged scenes or objects in images.

It is explained that these descriptions can contain detections of the presence of objects or features in the image, a classification of objects or features, estimated parameters and structural information. Also, a model-based framework is introduced and the notions of low level, high level and bottom-up and top-down are described. Feature extraction is treated in depth for a range of features from simple pixel based features to high level features describing the shape and appearance of objects.

Finally, examples are given for object recognition in images: character recognition using correlation, face recognition using eigenobjects and recognition of bolts using active shape models.

## 5.7 Further Reading

There exists an overwhelming amount of literature on image processing. Classical publications on the fundamentals of image processing are the books by Pratt [16], Jain [12] and Castleman [4]. An online available book is *Image Processing Fundamentals* [23] by Young, Gerbrands and van Vliet. More in-depth information on object recognition and parameter estimation can be found in [22] by van der Heijden.

Other, more recent books are Gonzalez, Woods and Eddins' book on image processing using MATLAB [8] and the *Handbook on Image and Video Processing* by Bovik [1].

Image processing in multimedia systems has been treated in books by Furht, Smoliar and Zhang [7] and Guan Kung and Larsen [9].

Apart from the many books published on the subject of image processing, many journals and conference proceedings are available, reflecting the ongoing research developments in the field. Some of the most important journals on image processing are the *IEEE Transactions on Image Processing, Computer Vision and Image Understanding* by Elsevier, *IEEE Transactions on Pattern Analysis and Machine Intelligence* and *The International Journal of Computer Vision* by Kluwer. Some important conferences are the *IEEE International Conference on Image Processing (ICIP)* and the *IEEE Conference on Computer Vision and Pattern Recognition (CVPR)*.

Finally, many of the subjects described in this chapter are explained extensively on different Webpages.

For example, `www.wikipedia.org` gives quite extensive explanations and further links on subjects like Hough transform, Fourier transform, cross-correlation, etc.

# References

1. A. Bovik. *Handbook of Image and Video Processing*. Academic Press, 2000.
2. Ron Bracewell. *The Fourier Transform and Its Applications*. McGraw-Hill, New York, 3rd edition, 1999.
3. J. F. Canny. A computational approach to edge detection. *IEEE Trans. Pattern Analysis and Machine Intelligence*, 8(6):679–698, 1986.
4. Kenneth R. Castleman. *Digital Image Processing*. Prentice Hall, 2nd edition, 1996.
5. T. F. Cootes, C. J. Taylor, D. H. Cooper, and J. Graham. Active shape models — their training and application. *Computer Vision and Image Understing*, 61(1):38–59, 1995.
6. J.H. Friedman. Regularized discriminant analysis. *Journal of the American Statistical Association*, 84(405):165–175, 1989.
7. Borko Furht, Stephen W. Smoliar, and Hongjiang Zhang. *Video and image processing in multimedia systems*. Kluwer Academic Publishers, Norwell, MA, USA, 1995.
8. R.C. Gonzalez, R.E. Woods, and S.L. Eddins. *Digital Image Processing Using MATLAB*. Prentice Hall, 2004.
9. L. Guan, S.Y. Kung, and J. Larsen. *Multimedia Image and Video Processing*. CRC press, 2000.
10. Robert M. Haralick, K. Shanmugam, and Its'hak Dinstein. Textural features for image classification. *IEEE Transactions on Systems, Man, and Cybernetics*, 3(6):610–621, 1973.
11. C. Harris and M.J. Stephens. A combined corner and edge detector. In *Alvey Vision Conference*, pages 147–152, 1988.
12. A.K. Jain. *Fundamentals of Digital Image Processing*. Prentice Hall, 1989.
13. D.G. Lowe. Distinctive image features from scale-invariant keypoints. *International Journal of Computer Vision*, 60(2):91–110, 2004.
14. D. Marr and E. Hildreth. Theory of edge detection. *Proc. R. Soc. Lond. B*, 207:187–217, 1980.
15. P. Jonathon Phillips, Hyeonjoon Moon, Syed A. Rizvi, and Patrick J. Rauss. The FERET Evaluation Methodology for Face-Recognition Algorithms. *IEEE Transactions on Pattern Analysis and Machine Intellelligence*, 22(10):1090–1104, 2000.
16. W.K. Pratt. *Digital Image Processing (Second Edition)*. Wiley, 1991.
17. Bart ter Haar Romeny. *Front-End Vision and Multi-Scale Image Analysis*. Kluwer Academic Publishers, 2003.
18. N. Petkov S.E. Grigorescu and P. Kruizinga. Comparison of texture features based on gabor filters. *IEEE Trans. on Image Processing*, 11(10):1160–1167, 2002.
19. C. Steger. An unbiased detector of curvilinear structures. *IEEE Transactions on Pattern Recognition and Machine Intelligence*, 20(2):113–125, 1998.

20. G. J. Edwards T. F. Cootes and C. J. Taylor. Active appearance models. *IEEE Transactions on Pattern Analysis and Machine Intelligence*, 23:681–685, January 2001.
21. M. Turk and A. Pentland. Face Recognition Using Eigenfaces. In *Proceedings of the IEEE Conference on Computer Vision and Pattern Recognition*, pages 586–591, 1991.
22. F. van der Heijden. *Image based measurement systems: Object recognition and parameter estimation*. Wiley, Chichester, England, 1994.
23. I.T. Young, J.J. Gerbrands, and L.J. van Vliet. *Image Processing Fundamentals*. Online Book, 2004. `http://www.ph.tn.tudelft.nl/Courses/FIP/noframes/fip.html`.

# 6

# Generative Probabilistic Models

Thijs Westerveld[1], Arjen de Vries[1], and Franciska de Jong[2]

[1] Centrum voor Wiskunde en Informatica
[2] University of Twente

## 6.1 Introduction

Many content-based multimedia retrieval tasks can be seen as decision theory problems. Clearly, this is the case for classification tasks, like face detection, face recognition, or indoor/outdoor classification. In all these cases a system has to decide whether an image (or video) belongs to one class or another (respectively face or no face; face A, B, or C; and indoor or outdoor). Even the *ad hoc* retrieval tasks, where the goal is to find *relevant* documents given a description of an information need, can be seen as a decision theory problem: documents can be classified into relevant and non-relevant classes, or we can treat each of the documents in the collection as a separate class, and classify a query as belonging to one of these. In all these settings, a probabilistic approach seems natural: an image is assigned to the class with the highest probability.[3]

The generative probabilistic approach to image retrieval described in this chapter is one such approach. To get a feeling for the approach, the following analogy to solving jigsaws is useful. Suppose we have been solving a number of jigsaw puzzles all weekend and put all puzzles in their respective boxes again on Sunday evening. Now it is Monday morning and while cleaning the room, we find a forgotten piece of one of the jigsaws. Of course, in practice, we would keep the piece separate until we solve one of the puzzles again and discover that a piece is missing. But suppose that we have to make an immediate decision and put the piece in one of the boxes. To put it in the proper box, we have to guess to which puzzle this piece belongs. The only clues we have are the appearance of the piece at hand and our memory of the puzzles we solved. A good solution would be to put the piece in the box to which it most likely belongs given these clues. If for example, the piece at hand is mainly

---

[3] If some misclassifications are more severe than others, a decision theoretic approach should be taken, and images should be assigned to the class with lowest risk.

blue with a watery texture, it is most likely to come from a jigsaw with a lot of water.

In the retrieval framework presented here, instead of boxes with jigsaws we have a collection of documents, instead of a forgotten jigsaw piece, we have a query, and instead of our memories of the puzzles we have models of the documents. The goal now, is to find the document that is most likely given the query, similar to choosing the most likely box to put the jigsaw piece in. This generative approach to information retrieval – find the generating source of a piece of information – has proved successful in media specific tasks, like language modeling for text retrieval [2, 8, 16] and Gaussian mixture modeling for image retrieval [7, 14, 21, 23].

### 6.1.1 Relation to Other Chapters

Many chapters in this book discuss techniques for extracting features or knowledge about multimedia content or for generating metadata. This chapter introduces a method for building abstract models from such features. The models described here are independent of the type of features that are used. While the examples in this chapter use different features, the models can easily be adapted to use many of the features discussed in Chapter 5. In addition, the language modeling technique discussed in Chapter 4 is a special case of using generative probabilistic models for information retrieval. Finally, generative models play an important role in speech recognition (cf. Chapter 7).

### 6.1.2 Outline

As generative models can be nicely described without going into the details of parameter estimation, those two aspects are treated separately here. This chapter starts with a basic example of a generative model, followed by detailed descriptions of generative models for visual and textual information in Section 6.2. Such models are concise descriptions of the characteristics of the document, which is useful in a retrieval setting. Section 6.3 explains how the models can be used in a retrieval setting. Section 6.4 continues with a detailed description of the parameter estimation process. Here we explain how the models can be learnt from training data. Finally, Section 6.5 discusses how the two modalities can easily be combined for a truly multimodal search.

## 6.2 Generative Probabilistic Models

Since the goal in information retrieval is to find the best document given a query, one could decide to model the probability of a document given a query directly. In the jigsaw example, this would mean that a direct mapping from the appearance of a piece to a jigsaw box is needed, i.e., we need to calculate the likelihood of the box given the piece, i.e., P(box|piece). This way of modeling the problem is known in the classification literature as *discriminative classification*. In some cases, for example when there are many different boxes, it is hard to learn this direct mapping. In such cases, it is useful to apply Bayesian inversion and estimate for each box the probability that this box produced the piece at hand, i.e., P(piece|box). This approach is known as *generative classification*. In this approach, each box has a model of the type of pieces it generates. The probability of generating the jigsaw piece at hand is computed for each model and that probability is used to find the most likely box.

First, the basic explanation of the generative models is continued. In information retrieval, many possible sources for a query exist; each document in a collection can be a source. Therefore, learning a discriminative classifier is hard and a generative approach is a natural way of modeling the problem. It is important to realism that in such an approach, a separate distribution is estimated for *each* of the documents in the collection. One of the nice things about generative probabilistic models is that they can easily be understood without digging into the details of estimating the models' parameters. Therefore, in the remainder of this section parameter estimation is put aside and only the basics of the models are explained. This section starts with simple examples of generative models (Section 6.2.1). Sections 6.2.2 and 6.2.3 specialize to generative image models and generative text models respectively.

### 6.2.1 Examples

Generative probabilistic models are random sources that can generate (infinite) sequences of samples according to some probability distribution. In the simplest case, the model generates samples independently, thus the probability of a particular sample does not depend on the samples generated previously. These simple models, often called memoryless models, will be the primary focus in this chapter. A good example of a generative source with a memoryless model is an ordinary die. The model describes the process of throwing the die and and observing the outcome. If the die is fair, throwing it generates positive integers between 1 and 6 according to a uniform distribution:[4]

$$P(i) = \frac{1}{6}, \quad \text{for } i \in \{1, 2, 3, 4, 5, 6\}. \tag{6.1}$$

In a memoryless model, the observations or samples are assumed to be independent, so the probability of observing a particular sequence is calculated as the product of the probabilities of the individual observations:

$$P(\{i_1, i_2, \dots, i_n\}) = \prod_{j=1}^{n} P(i_j). \tag{6.2}$$

---

[4] Throughout this chapter, random variables are omitted from the notation of probability functions, unless this causes confusion. Thus, P(i) means the probability that the random variable describing the observed outcome from throwing the die takes value $i$.

Section 6.3 returns to calculating the probabilities of observations. Here, the focus is on the probabilistic models themselves. A probabilistic model is an abstraction from the physical process that generates the data. Instead of specifying that the sequence of positive integers is produced by throwing an ordinary fair die, it suffices to state that there is some source that generates integers between 1 and 6 according to a uniform distribution, (6.1). The underlying physical process can remain unknown. Still, to understand the models it is often useful to think of simple processes like throwing a die, drawing colored balls from an urn, or drawing jigsaw pieces from a box.

Generative models can be more complex and have a hierarchical structure like in the following example. Suppose we have two dice (where we represent a die as a list of faces): Die $A$, with the usual faces 1 through 6, i.e., $A = (1, 2, 3, 4, 5, 6)$, and die $B$, which has ones on all faces, $B = (1, 1, 1, 1, 1, 1)$. Now we can imagine the following random process:

1. pick a die according to a uniform distribution;
2. sample a number by throwing the chosen die.

For this generative process, the probability of observing a single sample $i$ is:

$$P(i) = P(A) \cdot P(i|A) + P(B) \cdot P(i|B) = \begin{cases} \frac{1}{2} \cdot \frac{1}{6} + \frac{1}{2} \cdot 0, & \text{for } i \in \{2, 3, 4, 5, 6\} \\ \frac{1}{2} \cdot \frac{1}{6} + \frac{1}{2} \cdot 1, & \text{for } i = 1. \end{cases}$$

(6.3)

A generative process with a model like this is called a *mixture model*. It is a weighted sum of a number of different probability distributions. As will become clear in Section 6.2.2, mixture models are useful for describing the mixture of aspects that can be present in images.

It is often insightful to represent generative models in a graphical manner. For graphical representations, we follow the standards described in [11], where random variables are represented as nodes and dependencies between them as edges. Observed variables are represented as solid nodes and hidden, or unobserved, variables as open nodes. A box or plate around a part of the graph indicates repetition, i.e., the repeated sampling of variables. As an example, Figure 6.1 represents two variants of drawing a sequence of $N$ numbers from the hierarchical dice. The variant on the left represents the process as described above: for each of the $N$ numbers, we pick a new die. The variant on the right represents the case where we select a die once for the whole process and then repeatedly sample numbers by throwing that die.

The remainder of this section introduces generative models for images and text.

### 6.2.2 Generative Image Models

As stated in the introduction to this chapter, generative image models are like the boxes of jigsaw puzzles, from which one can randomly draw pieces. An important difference though, is the following. Jigsaw boxes contain a finite

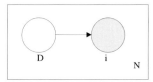 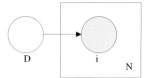

Sampling with repeated choice of dice    Sampling from a single die

**Fig. 6.1.** Graphical representations for dice example variants.

number (say 1000) of discrete pieces; a piece is either in there or not. By
sampling from the box *with replacement*, we can draw infinitely many pieces,
but each piece has to be one of the fixed set of 1000 pieces. The generative
image models described below, however, are probability distributions over a
(high dimensional) *continuous* feature space. The number of different samples
that can be drawn is infinite. The models describe the location in the feature
space where we are most likely to observe samples and what kind of variance
can be expected. The nature of the feature space, i.e., the set of features
used for describing a sample is not discussed in this chapter. The models are
independent of the features. Here we simply assume an image is represented
as a set of samples ($\mathcal{V} = \{v_1, v_2, \ldots, v_S\}$), each described by a $n$-dimensional
feature vector: $v = (v_1, v_2, \ldots, v_n)$, as illustrated in Figure 6.2. The nature of
the samples is independent of the models. The examples used in this chapter
are based on DCT coefficients[5] and position information, but in principle
other features like for example the ones introduced in Chapters 5 and 9 can
be used.

blocks                    feature vectors

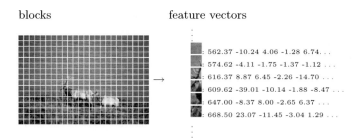

$\rightarrow$

562.37 -10.24 4.06 -1.28 6.74...
574.62 -4.11 -1.75 -1.37 -1.12 ...
616.37 8.87 6.45 -2.26 -14.70 ...
609.62 -39.01 -10.14 -1.88 -8.47 ...
647.00 -8.37 8.00 -2.65 6.37 ...
668.50 23.07 -11.45 -3.04 1.29 ...

**Fig. 6.2.** Illustration of visual document representation.

## Gaussian Mixture Models

The generative image models discussed in this chapter are based on Normal
distributions, or Gaussian distributions as they are often called. These distributions are appropriate models for the situation in which an ideal point in a

---

[5] The Discrete Cosine Transform (DCT) captures both intensity and texture information and is also used in JPEG compression.

feature space exists and where all observations are assumed to be versions of this ideal feature vector that are randomly corrupted by many independent small influences [4]. For simple images this is the case, one can easily imagine a single ideal point in feature space describing for example the perfect water texture. All observations from the water class can be seen as versions of the ideal water texture that have been corrupted by many independent causes (lightning condition, camera angle, etc.). However, most real-life images show more than a single texture or object. Therefore, instead of using a single Gaussian distribution, it makes sense to use a mixture of Gaussian distributions for modeling images with multiple colors and textures [21].

In general, a finite mixture density is a weighted sum of a finite number ($C$) of density functions [20, 4]:

$$p(x) = \sum_{i=1}^{C} P(c_i)p(x|c_i). \tag{6.4}$$

(Notation: in this chapter we consistently use capital $P$ for a probability mass function and lowercase $p$ for a density.)

The mixing weights $P(c_i)$ are the prior probabilities of the components $c_i$ in the mixture. The density functions $p(x|c_i)$ each describe a bit of the total density. These densities are Gaussian distributions in the case of a Gaussian mixture model, but of course other densities can be used in other situations.

Titterington et al. [20] divide the usage of mixture models in two broad classes: *direct application* and *indirect application*. Direct application is used to refer to situations in which it is believed that there exists a number ($C$) of underlying categories or sources such that the observed samples all belong to one of these. Indirect application refers to a situation in which the link between probability distributions and categories is less clear and where a mixture model is merely used as a mathematical way of obtaining a tractable form of analyzing data. Modeling images using finite mixture models is somewhere halfway on the continuum from direct to indirect application. On the one hand, the idea is that an image can contain only a finite number of things; each sample is assumed to be generated by one of the mixture components. For example, one component might describe the grass, another the water and a third the sky in an image. This is the direct application view. On the other hand, we do not explicitly model grass, water and sky. We merely believe that to model the many different facets of an image, a mixture of distributions is needed. This mixture model describes image samples without explicitly separating the components. In that sense, mixture modeling is just a mathematical tool to describe images (indirect application view). Still, the direct application view with separate components for modeling grass, water and sky, is a useful way of thinking about finite mixture models for images, especially for understanding the parameter estimation discussed in Section 6.4.

**Gaussian Mixture Models for Representing Images**

A Gaussian mixture model can describe an image. The idea is that the model captures the main characteristics of the image. The samples in an image are assumed to be generated by a mixture of Gaussian sources, where the number of Gaussian components $C$ is fixed for all images in the collection. A Gaussian mixture model is described by a set of parameters $\boldsymbol{\theta} = (\boldsymbol{\theta}_1, \ldots, \boldsymbol{\theta}_C)$ each defining a single component. Each component $c_i$ is described by its prior probability $P(c_i|\boldsymbol{\theta})$, the mean $\boldsymbol{\mu}_i$ and the variance $\boldsymbol{\Sigma}_i$, thus $\boldsymbol{\theta}_i = (P(c_i|\boldsymbol{\theta}), \boldsymbol{\mu}_i, \boldsymbol{\Sigma}_i)$. Details about estimating these parameters are deferred to Section 6.4.1. The process of generating an image is assumed to be the following (see Figure 6.3):

1. Take the Gaussian mixture model $\boldsymbol{\theta}$ for the image.
2. For each sample $\boldsymbol{v}$ in the document:
   (a) Pick a random component $c_i$ from Gaussian mixture model $\boldsymbol{\theta}$ according to the prior distribution over components $P(c_i|\boldsymbol{\theta})$.
   (b) Draw a random sample from $c_i$ according to the Gaussian distribution $\mathcal{N}(\boldsymbol{\mu}_i, \boldsymbol{\Sigma}_i)$.

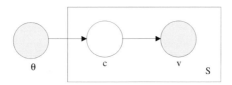

**Fig. 6.3.** Graphical representation of Gaussian mixture model.

Here, $\boldsymbol{\theta}$ is an observed variable, i.e., the mixture model from which the samples for a given image are drawn, is known. For a given sample however, it is unknown which component generated it, thus components are unobserved variables. The probability of drawing a single sample $\boldsymbol{v}$ from a Gaussian mixture model with parameters $\boldsymbol{\theta}$ is thus defined as the marginalization over all possible components:

$$p(\boldsymbol{v}|\boldsymbol{\theta}) = \sum_{i=1}^{C} P(c_i|\boldsymbol{\theta}) p(\boldsymbol{v}|c_i, \boldsymbol{\theta}) \tag{6.5}$$

$$= \sum_{i=1}^{C} P(c_i|\boldsymbol{\theta}) \frac{1}{\sqrt{(2\pi)^n |\boldsymbol{\Sigma}_i|}} e^{-\frac{1}{2}(\boldsymbol{v}-\boldsymbol{\mu}_i)^T \boldsymbol{\Sigma}_i^{-1}(\boldsymbol{v}-\boldsymbol{\mu}_i)}. \tag{6.6}$$

A visualization of the model built from the image in Figure 6.2 is shown in Figure 6.4. For this example, a Gaussian mixture with three components is estimated from the set of feature vectors extracted from the image (cf. Figure 6.2).[6] The resulting model is described by the mean vectors and covariance

---

[6] The process of building a model is described in Section 6.4.1

matrices of the three components in the high-dimensional feature space and by the prior probabilities of the components. The figure shows a projection of the components onto the two-dimensional subspace defined by the position in the image plane (i.e., the space spanned by the $x$ and $y$ coordinates of the feature vectors). The ellipsoids in the image plane show the mean position of the three components along with their variance. The filled areas, are the areas in the image plane, where the standard deviation from the mean position for a given component is below 2. The coloring of the area is a representation of the component's other dimensions: it shows the mean color and mean texture. Variance in color and texture information are not visualized. The bars to the right of each component indicate the component's prior probability.

**Fig. 6.4.** Visualization of a model of the image in Figure 6.2.

In the example, three Gaussian components are used, but that is not necessarily enough to capture all information in an image. Any distribution can be approximated arbitrarily closely by a mixture of Gaussians. The higher the number of components in the mixture, the better the approximation can be. However, keeping in mind that the models will be used for retrieval, a perfect description of an image is not the ultimate goal. The goal is to find images that are similar to a query image. A perfect model would only be able to find exact matches and those are not the most interesting ones. Therefore, it is important to avoid over-fitting. Experiments have shown that eight components are typically enough to capture the most important aspects of an image [22, 24].

### 6.2.3 Generative Language Models

Language models are discussed in Chapter 7, where they are used for speech recognition, and Chapter 4 demonstrates their use for information retrieval. To highlight the generative nature of these models as well as the similarity to the image models discussed above, we look at them again in this chapter.

To repeat what was said before, a language model is a probability distribution over strings of text in a given language. It simply states how likely it is to observe a given string in a given language. For example, a language model for English should capture the fact that the term *the* is more likely to occur than the term *restaurant*. When context is taken into account this might change. For example, after seeing the phrase:

*"They went to an Italian"*,

*restaurant* is a more likely completion than *the*. As discussed in Chapter 7, for speech recognition (but also for example for spelling error correction), this contextual information is important; a limited amount of context is typically taken into account and so called *n-gram models* are used [12]. In *n*-gram models, the probability of observing a given term only depends on the previous $n-1$ terms. If bigram models ($n = 2$) are used, the probability of the next term in the example given above would only depend on *Italian*.

For information retrieval context is of minor importance (cf. Chapter 4). Although language models are generative models, in retrieval they are not used to generate *new* pieces of text. As long as the models capture most of the topicality of a text, they are useful. Therefore, context is typically ignored in information retrieval and terms are assumed to be generated independently. The models are thus memoryless. In language modeling memoryless language models are known as unigram language models. Song and Croft experimented with higher order (*n*-gram) language models for information retrieval and found no significant improvement over unigram models [18].

## Unigram Language Model

In the unigram language modeling approach to information retrieval, documents are assumed to be multinomial sources generating terms. This multinomial basis is not always mentioned explicitly (Chapter 4 ignored it), but, in this chapter, it is useful to take this view because it clearly shows the generative probabilistic nature and it nicely separates the model from the estimation of the model parameters, which is discussed in Section 6.4.1.

Multinomial sources are often introduced using urns with colored balls, but the boxes with jigsaw pieces we used before are equally suitable. Suppose we have a jigsaw puzzle box that contains pieces with grass, pieces with water and pieces with sky. Now, if we draw ten pieces from this box with replacement, what is the probability of observing exactly five grass pieces, two water pieces and three sky pieces? This can be modeled using a multinomial distribution. For unigram language modeling, instead of jigsaw pieces of a particular type (grass, water, sky), we have terms in a given language. A question could now be: If we draw six terms from the English language, what is the probability of observing each of the terms *an, Italian, restaurant, they, to* and *went* exactly once? In the language modeling approach to information retrieval, instead of having a single model for a whole language, each document in a collection is modeled as a separate multinomial source. Each of these models is described by a vector of term probabilities $\phi = (\phi_1, \phi_2, \ldots, \phi_T)$, where $T$ is the size of the vocabulary and $\phi_i$ is the probability of seeing term$_i$ under model $\phi$.

The generative process for textual documents, as visualized in Figure 6.5 is very simple:

1. Pick the language model $\phi$ for the document.
2. For each term:

draw a random term from $\phi$ according to the multinomial distribution $\text{mult}(\phi)$.

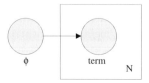

**Fig. 6.5.** Graphical representation of language model.

Like with the Gaussian mixture models for images, the model that generates the samples (terms) is an observed variable; each document has its own, known generative model $\phi$. The probability of observing a particular document $t = (t_1, t_2, \ldots, t_T)$, from this model is defined as:

$$P(t|\phi) = \frac{\left(\sum_{i=1}^{T} t_i\right)!}{\prod_{i=1}^{T} t_i!} \prod_{i=1}^{T} \phi_i^{t_i}. \tag{6.7}$$

The second factor in this equation, $\prod_{i=1}^{T} \phi_i^{t_i}$, is the joint probability of observing the term counts for individual terms, $P(\text{term}_i|\phi) = \phi_i$. The unigram assumption states that all observations are independent, thus the joint probability is simply the product of the probabilities of the individual terms. The normalization factor $\left(\sum_{i=1}^{T} t_i\right)!/(\prod_{i=1}^{T} t_i!)$ implements the *bag-of-words* model, it states that an observation (a query or a document) is a bag, the ordering of the terms is unimportant. A simple example will clarify this. Suppose we have a vocabulary with only four terms: $A,B,C$ and $D$ and observation $ABAC$, then $t = (2, 1, 1, 0)$. Note that in the representation of the observation, the order of the terms is already ignored, it simply says there are two $A$'s, one $B$, one $C$, and no $D$'s. Thus, the probability of observing this $t$ from a given model $\phi$, is in fact the probability of drawing any permutation of the original string $ABAC$: $P(t) = P(ABAC) + P(AABC) + P(ABCA) + P(ACAB) + \ldots$. In total $(2+1+1+0)! / (2!\cdot1!\cdot1!\cdot0!) = \frac{24}{2} = 12$ different possible permutations exist. Thus $P(t) = 12\,\phi_1^2\,\phi_2^1\,\phi_3^1\,\phi_4^0$.

## 6.3 Retrieval Using Generative Models

By drawing enough observations from a single model (or pieces from a box, to take the jigsaw analogy), a random document or a random image can be generated. An example of a random image from the model visualized in Figure 6.4 is shown in Figure 6.6. Different models will produce different random images, just like different boxes can contain different jigsaws. This idea can be used to rank documents.

**Fig. 6.6.** Random sample from image model presented in Figure 6.4.

### 6.3.1 Sample Likelihood

The idea of ranking models based on observations is illustrated by a simple dice example. Suppose we have two dice:

$$\begin{aligned} D_1 &= (1, 2, 3, 4, 5, 6) \\ D_2 &= (1, 1, 3, 4, 5, 6). \end{aligned} \qquad (6.8)$$

Say someone tells us that a sequence of five throws with one of them resulted in the observation: $O = (4, 3, 4, 3, 1)$. We can then easily calculate the likelihood of observing this sequence given each of the models:

$$\begin{aligned} P(O|D_1) &= (\tfrac{1}{6})^5 \\ P(O|D_2) &= (\tfrac{1}{6})^4 \cdot \tfrac{2}{6}. \end{aligned} \qquad (6.9)$$

Since $P(O|D_2) > P(O|D_1)$, the observation is more likely under $D_2$. We call this probability of an observation $O$ given a model $D$ the *Sample Likelihood*: it is the likelihood of observing this sample.

The same principle can be used to rank documents given a query. The assumption is that the query is an observation from one of the generative document models in the collection and the goal is to find the document model under which this query is most likely. For a visual query $\mathcal{V} = \{v_1, v_2, \dots, v_S\}$, assuming memoryless models, we can compute the joint likelihood of observing all samples by taking the product of the likelihoods for the individual samples $v_j$:

$$p(\mathcal{V}) = \prod_{v \in \mathcal{V}} p(v|\boldsymbol{\theta}). \qquad (6.10)$$

For textual queries $\boldsymbol{q} = (q_1, q_2, \dots, q_T)$, we can simply use (6.7).

## 6.4 Estimating Model Parameters

### 6.4.1 Maximum Likelihood Estimates

In the previous sections, the assumption has been that the model parameters $(\boldsymbol{\theta})$ are known. Given the parameters, it is straightforward to use the models for ranking documents (as we have seen in Section 6.3). In general however, the parameters of a specific document model are unknown. Usually, the only available information is the representation of the documents, i.e., the feature vectors. A common way to use this data is to assume that they are observations from the models and use them as training samples to estimate the unknown model parameters. As a first step to estimating these parameters, we will use the *maximum likelihood estimate*. This estimate is defined as the parameter setting which maximizes the likelihood of the observed samples. Thus, for a set of training samples $\mathcal{S} = \{s_1, s_2, \ldots, s_K\}$ and model parameter $\psi$, the maximum likelihood estimate $\psi_{\mathrm{ML}}$ is defined as:

$$\psi_{\mathrm{ML}} = \arg\max_{\psi} \prod_{s \in \mathcal{S}} \mathrm{P}(s|\psi). \tag{6.11}$$

Below this approach is applied to Gaussian mixture models and language models. Techniques for handling unobserved data and for improving generalization capabilities are discussed in Section 6.4.2.

**Estimating Gaussian Mixture Model Parameters**

The maximum likelihood estimate for a Gaussian mixture model from a set of samples $\mathcal{V}$ (an image) is defined as follows:

$$\boldsymbol{\theta}_{\mathrm{ML}} = \arg\max_{\boldsymbol{\theta}} \prod_{\boldsymbol{v} \in \mathcal{V}} \mathrm{P}(v|\boldsymbol{\theta}) \tag{6.12}$$

$$= \prod_{\boldsymbol{v} \in \mathcal{V}} \sum_{i=1}^{C} \mathrm{P}(c_i|\boldsymbol{\theta}) \; \frac{1}{\sqrt{(2\pi)^n |\boldsymbol{\Sigma}_i|}} e^{-\frac{1}{2}(\boldsymbol{v}-\boldsymbol{\mu}_i)^T \boldsymbol{\Sigma}_i^{-1}(\boldsymbol{v}-\boldsymbol{\mu}_i)}.$$

This equation is hard to solve analytically, but we can use the Expectation Maximization (EM) algorithm [3] to find parameters for the model. To understand this iterative procedure, it is useful to assume that an image shows a limited number of different things (such as grass, sky, water), each of which is modeled by a separate Gaussian distribution. Each sample in a document can then be assumed to be generated from one of these Gaussian components.

To accurately describe the different components of a Gaussian mixture model for a given document, it is necessary to decide which of the document's samples are generated by which component. The assignments of samples $\boldsymbol{v}_j$ to components $C_i$ are unknown, but they can be viewed as hidden variables and the EM algorithm can be applied. This algorithm iterates between estimating the a posteriori class probabilities for each sample given the current model settings (the E-step) and re-estimating the components' parameters based on the sample distribution and the current sample assignments (M-step).

The EM algorithm first assigns each sample to a random component. Next, the first M-step computes the parameters ($\boldsymbol{\theta}_i$) for each component, based on the samples assigned to that component. Using maximum likelihood estimates, this comes down to computing the mean and variance of the feature values over all samples assigned to the component.

This assignment of samples to components is a *soft* clustering, a sample does not belong entirely to one component. In fact, we compute means, co-variances and priors on the weighted feature vectors, where the feature vectors are weighted by their proportion of belonging to the class under consideration. In the next E-step, the class assignments are re-estimated, i.e., the posterior probabilities, $P(c_i|v_j)$ are computed. We iterate between estimating class assignments (expectation step) and estimating class parameters (maximization step) until the algorithm converges. Figure 6.7 is a visualization of training a model from the image in Figure 6.2. From top to bottom, it alternates between showing sample assignments (E-step) and visualizations of the intermediate models (M-step). After 10 iterations already, the model accurately distinguishes water, grass and elks.

More formally, to estimate a Gaussian mixture model from a document $V = \{v_1, v_2, \ldots, v_S\}$, the following steps are alternated:

**E-step**

Estimate the hidden assignments $h_{ij}$ of samples to components for each sample $x_j$ and component $c_i$:

$$h_{ij} = P(c_i|v_j) = \frac{p(v_j|c_i)P(c_i)}{\sum_{c=1}^{C} p(v_j|c_c)P(c_c)}. \tag{6.13}$$

**M-step**

Update the component's parameters to maximize the joint distribution of component assignments and samples: $\theta^{\text{new}} = \arg\max_\theta p(V, H|\theta)$, where $H$ is the matrix with all sample assignments $h_{ij}$. More specifically, this means:

$$\mu_i^{\text{new}} = \frac{\sum_j h_{ij} v_j}{\sum_j h_{ij}}, \tag{6.14}$$

$$\Sigma_i^{\text{new}} = \frac{\sum_j h_{ij}(v_j - \mu_i^{\text{new}})(v_j - \mu_i^{\text{new}})^T}{\sum_j h_{ij}}, \tag{6.15}$$

$$P(c_i)^{\text{new}} = \frac{1}{N} \sum_j h_{ij}. \tag{6.16}$$

The algorithm is guaranteed to converge [3]. The error after each iteration is the negative log likelihood of the training data:

$$E = -\log p(V) = -\sum_{v \in V} \log p(v|\theta). \tag{6.17}$$

This error will decrease with each iteration of the algorithm, until a minimum is reached.[7]

---

[7] The found minima are local ones. The effects of this on retrieval quality need thorough investigation.

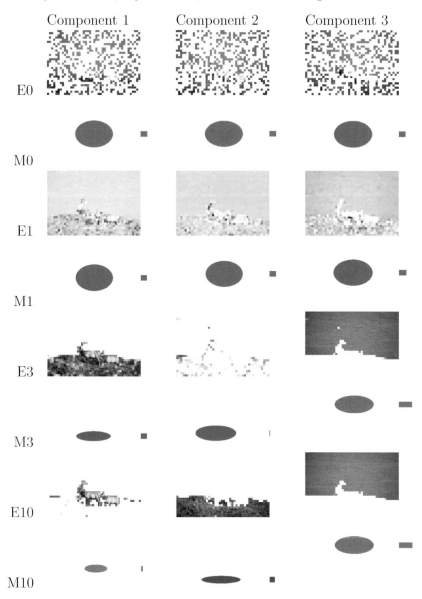

**Fig. 6.7.** Visualization of the estimation of parameters for a Gaussian mixture model built from the image shown in Figure 6.2. E and M steps are shown after initialization and after 1, 3 and 10 iterations. The E-steps show to what degree each sample is assigned to each component (higher transparency indicates a lower degree of assignment). The M-steps show visualizations of the models (cf. Figure 6.4).

**Estimating Language Model Parameters**

The maximum likelihood estimates for the parameters of the multinomial distribution for a given document are straightforward. They are simply the relative frequency of the terms in the document. If a document is represented as a vector of term counts, $\boldsymbol{t} = (t_1, t_2, \ldots, t_T)$, then $\phi_i$, the probability of term $i$ in this document, is estimated by:

$$\phi_{i_{\mathrm{ML}}} = \frac{t_i}{\sum_{j=1}^{T} t_j}. \tag{6.18}$$

### 6.4.2 Smoothing

If maximum likelihood estimates, (6.18), are used to find the language model parameters, we run into the so-called *zero-frequency problem*, a sparse data problem. Terms that did not occur in the training data for a document are assigned zero probability ($\phi_i = 0$ for these terms). This means that a query containing such a term will get zero probability for this document model, no matter how likely the other query terms are.

Consider for example the dice example of Section 6.3, where we introduced the following two dice:

$$\begin{aligned} D_1 &= (1, 2, 3, 4, 5, 6) \\ D_2 &= (1, 1, 3, 4, 5, 6). \end{aligned} \tag{6.19}$$

Now, if we observe the sequence $O = (1, 2, 1, 4, 3)$, we would conclude the observation comes from $D_1$, since $\mathrm{P}(2|D_2) = 0$ and thus $\mathrm{P}(O|D_2) = 0$. If $D_2$ indeed does not have a 2 on one of its faces, this is correct, but if the distribution is estimated from data (as it is in the generative document models) it may not be. Suppose we buy a die in a shop, we roll it six times and we observe the sequence $(1, 1, 3, 4, 5, 6)$, concluding that these six observations correspond to the six faces and that there is no 2 on this die does not seem wise.

**Interpolation**

Smoothing solves the zero-frequency problem by transferring some of the probability mass from the observed samples to the unseen samples. The specific smoothing technique used commonly in the language modeling approach to information retrieval is *interpolation*, also known as Jelinek–Mercer smoothing [10]. For multimedia material, and especially for video data, interpolation is useful, since it allows for easy extension of the language models for describing different levels of a document, like shots, scenes and videos (discussed later in this section). For other smoothing techniques, the interested reader is referred to [12] and [25].

In Jelinek–Mercer smoothing, the maximum likelihood estimates are interpolated with a more general distribution, often called *background model*, or *collection model*; the maximum likelihood estimates are often referred to as *foreground models* or *document models*. The smoothed estimates are calculated as follows:

$$\phi_i = \lambda\phi_{i_{\mathrm{ML}}} + (1-\lambda)\phi_{i_{\mathrm{BG}}}, \tag{6.20}$$

where $\phi_{i_{\mathrm{BG}}} = \mathrm{P}(\mathrm{term}_i)$ is the background probability of observing $\mathrm{term}_i$ and $\lambda$ is a mixing parameter indicating the relative importance of maximum likelihood estimates.[8] The background probability is usually estimated using either collection frequency, the relative frequency of the term in the collection ($\phi_{i_{\mathrm{BG}}} = \sum_d t_{d,i}/\sum_d \sum_j t_{d,j}$), or document frequency the relative fraction of documents that the term occurs in ($\phi_{i_{\mathrm{BG}}} = df(t_i)/\sum_j df(t_j)$). The mixing parameter $\lambda$ can be estimated on a training set with known relevant query-document pairs.

### The *idf* Role of Smoothing

Besides avoiding the zero-frequency problem, smoothing also serves another purpose, namely that of explaining common query terms and reducing their influence [25]. Because common terms have high background probability, the influence of their foreground probability on the ranking will be relatively small. This becomes apparent when we substitute the $\phi$s in the retrieval function, (6.7), for the smoothed estimates, (6.20), and do some formula manipulation:

$$\mathrm{P}(\boldsymbol{q}|\boldsymbol{\phi}) = \frac{\left(\sum_{j=1}^T q_j\right)!}{\prod_{j=1}^T q_j!} \prod_{i=1}^T [\lambda\phi_{i_{\mathrm{ML}}} + (1-\lambda)\phi_{i_{\mathrm{BG}}}]^{q_i} \tag{6.21}$$

$$= \frac{\left(\sum_{j=1}^T q_j\right)!}{\prod_{j=1}^T q_j!} \prod_{i=1}^T \left[\frac{\lambda\phi_{i_{\mathrm{ML}}}}{(1-\lambda)\phi_{i_{\mathrm{BG}}}} + 1\right]^{q_i} \prod_{i=1}^T [(1-\lambda)\phi_{i_{\mathrm{BG}}}]^{q_i}. \tag{6.22}$$

For terms that are not present in the document $\lambda\phi_{i_{\mathrm{ML}}} = 0$ and the corresponding factor reduces to 1. Thus the first product needs only to be considered for query terms that are matched in the document; The latter is document independent and can be ignored for ranking. Also the normalization factor does not affect the ranking. The reduced formula is:

$$\mathrm{P}(\boldsymbol{q}|\boldsymbol{\phi}) \propto \prod_{i\in\{1,...,T\}:t_i>0 \wedge q_i>0} \left[\frac{\lambda\phi_{i_{\mathrm{ML}}}}{(1-\lambda)\phi_{i_{\mathrm{BG}}}} + 1\right]^{q_i}. \tag{6.23}$$

In this last equation, it is clear that the background probability ($\phi_{i_{\mathrm{BG}}}$) plays a normalization role, similar to *idf* in traditional *tf.idf* weighting [17]. Common terms, i.e., terms with high $\phi_{i_{\mathrm{BG}}}$, contribute less to the final ranking; for these terms, the influence of $\phi_{i_{\mathrm{ML}}}$ is reduced.

---

[8] Note that the smoothed distribution is a mixture model (cf. Section 6.2.2), with $\phi_{i_{\mathrm{ML}}}$ and $\phi_{i_{\mathrm{BG}}}$ describing the class densities and where $\lambda$ and $1-\lambda$ are the class priors.

## Interpolated Language Models for Video

Besides smoothing, interpolation can serve other purposes. For example when a document collection contains video material, we would like to exploit the hierarchical data model of video, in which a video is subdivided into scenes, which are subdivided into shots, which are in turn subdivided into frames. Interpolation based smoothing is particularly well-suited for modeling such representations of the data. To include the different levels of the hierarchy, we can simply extend estimation of the mixture of foreground and background model, (6.20), with models for shots and scenes:

$$\phi_i = \lambda_{\text{Shot}}P(\text{term}_i|\text{Shot}) + \lambda_{\text{Scene}}P(\text{term}_i|\text{Scene}) + \lambda_{\text{Coll}}P(\text{term}_i),$$
$$\text{where } \lambda_{\text{Coll}} = 1 - \lambda_{\text{Shot}} - \lambda_{\text{Scene}}. \quad (6.24)$$

The main idea behind this approach is that a good shot contains the query terms and is part of a scene having more occurrences of the query terms. Also, by including scenes in the model, misalignment between audio and video can be handled. Depending on the information need of the user, a similar strategy might be used to rank scenes or complete videos instead of shots, that is, the best scene might be a scene that contains a shot in which the query terms (co-)occur. Finally, interpolated language models are not only suitable for video retrieval, they can be used in any situation where language has a hierarchical structure. For example, it can be used for passage retrieval from (xml) documents, where a document can be a hierarchical structure of chapters, sections and paragraphs [15].

## Interpolated Gaussian Mixture Models

The zero-frequency problem does not exist for images, since they are modeled using Gaussian mixture models and Gaussians have infinite support. However, the *idf* role of smoothing is also useful in image retrieval, since it distinguishes between common and typical features of a document. Suppose we have a query image depicting a clear blue sky over a snowy mountain. Now, if all images in our collection have clear blue skies, than the retrieval results should mainly depend on the snowy and mountainy bits. This means we may want to down-weight the influence of the sky bits. This can, like in the text case, be achieved by interpolating with a more general, background distribution. The new version of the likelihood for a single image sample $\boldsymbol{v}$, cf. (6.5), becomes:

$$\text{p}(\mathcal{V}) = \prod_{\boldsymbol{v} \in \mathcal{V}} \kappa\text{p}(\boldsymbol{v}|\boldsymbol{\theta}) + (1 - \kappa)\text{p}(\boldsymbol{v}), \quad (6.25)$$

where $\kappa$ is used as the mixing parameter. The background density $\text{p}(\boldsymbol{v})$ can be estimated by marginalization over all document models in a reference collection $\boldsymbol{\Theta}$:

$$\text{p}(\boldsymbol{v}) = \sum_{\boldsymbol{\theta} \in \boldsymbol{\Theta}} \text{p}(\boldsymbol{v}|\boldsymbol{\theta})\text{P}(\boldsymbol{\theta}). \quad (6.26)$$

The reference collection $\boldsymbol{\Theta}$ can be either the current collection, a representative sample, or a separate, comparable collection.

This interpolation of foreground and background probabilities has the same effect as in the text case; it will decrease the influence of samples $\boldsymbol{v}$ with a high background probability $\mathrm{p}(\boldsymbol{v})$ on the final ranking. Experiments have shown that, this interpolation with a background collection is crucial for retrieval performance [22, 24].

## 6.5 Combining Visual and Textual Information

Above, we have described models for visual and textural information in isolation, but it makes sense to combine the two. One could imagine textual information setting the context (this shot is about Yasser Arafat), whereas visual information could filter the shots in the video where the person (or his patterned scarf) is actually visible. Vice versa, visual information could set a context (there is an object against a clear blue sky visible), and textual information could help in deciding whether it is a helicopter, an aircraft or a balloon. If both textual and visual information are modeled in a generative framework like discussed in this chapter, combining the modalities is a viable option.

### 6.5.1 Joint Probability

When both visual and textual information are described using generative probabilistic models, we can simply compute the joint probability of observing textual and visual part of a multimedia query, $Q_{MM} = \{\mathcal{V}, \boldsymbol{q}\}$:

$$\mathrm{p}(Q_{MM}|D) = \mathrm{p}(\mathcal{V}|\boldsymbol{\theta_D})\mathrm{P}(\boldsymbol{q}|\boldsymbol{\phi_D}). \qquad (6.27)$$

This requires two independence assumptions:

1. Textual terms and visual samples are generated independently:
   $\mathrm{p}(\mathcal{V}, \boldsymbol{q}|\cdot) = \mathrm{p}(\mathcal{V}|\cdot)\mathrm{P}(\boldsymbol{q}|\cdot)$.
2. The generation of documents in one modality is independent of the model in the other modality. The generation of textual terms only depends on the language model and the generation of visual terms only on the visual model.

Treating textual and visual information independently, contradicts the assumption that textual information is useful for visual multimedia retrieval. If textual information can actually help in retrieving relevant visual images or shots, then documents that have a high likelihood based on textual information should be more likely to be visually relevant than documents with a low textual score. Clearly, textual and visual information are dependent. As soon as a document is likely to be relevant based on the textual information, then the likelihood of observing something visually similar to the query examples should increase. For example, if the name Yasser Arafat is mentioned, the likelihood of observing him increases. Theoretically, this might lead to overly high scores for documents that match on both textual and visual information. In practice this simple multimodal model gives reasonable results, although in many settings textual information is most useful for finding the relevant information [24, 22].

## 6.6 Summary

In this chapter the main principles of generative probabilistic models are introduced. These models provide concise descriptions of the characteristics of a document. The particular instance of generative models described in this chapter, Gaussian mixture models, is well-suited for describing documents with a variety of different characteristics, and therefore useful for modeling heterogeneous images.

In a retrieval setting, the generative properties are used to decide which documents to show to the user. Documents are ranked by decreasing probability of generating the various parts of the query. These query parts can be small descriptions of visual information in a visual setting, query terms in a textual setting, or a combination of both in a multimodal setting.

To train the generative models from data, we start from a maximum likelihood approach. The parameter setting of a model describing a document are those that maximize the likelihood of observing that document. The maximum likelihood estimate however does not distinguish between characteristics that are common for many documents in a collection and characteristics that are typical of a particular document. For retrieval, this distinction is very important. Therefore, we interpolate with a background model, a model describing the main characteristics shared by many documents in the collection. This interpolation decreases the influence of common characteristics and thus improves retrieval results.

Finally, we show how the modeling of textual information in the same generative probabilistic framework can be adapted to describe video documents. The two modalities can then be combined using a simple joint probability. Even though the independence assumption needed for this joint probability is somewhat counter intuitive, in practice this combination of modalities is useful.

## 6.7 Further Reading

A very thorough introduction to generative models can be found in the book by Duda et al. [4]. The book covers many aspects related to this chapter such as maximum likelihood estimation, mixture models and the expectation maximization (EM) algorithm as well as many other pattern classification techniques.

Few examples exist of the application of generative models for multimedia retrieval. The work most closely related to the models presented in this chapter

is that of Vasconcelos et al. [21] and that of Greenspan et al. [7]. Both model
each of the images in the collection using a mixture of Gaussians like discussed
above. Instead of then using the maximum likelihood for ranking, they also
estimate a Gaussian mixture model for the query image and directly compare
the models. Gaussian mixture models that model not only color and texture,
but also the dynamic aspects of those are discussed in [6, 9]. Generative models
are also in computer vision sometimes to classify objects [5] or medical video
clips [14].

A collection of high-quality papers on the application of language modeling techniques is available in the book *Language Modeling for Information
Retrieval*, edited by Croft and Lafferty [2]. A number of papers in this collection are of particular interest. First of all, the paper by Sparck-Jones and
others [19] started some controversy around the idea of using language models
for information retrieval, since the notion of relevance is absent from the framework and the goal is to find *the* document that generated the query terms,
implying there can only be one relevant document. Lavrenko and Croft [13]
solve the problem by estimating *relevance models* rather than *document models*. Finally, Lafferty and Zhai argue that the language modeling framework
and the traditional probabilistic framework are probabilistically equivalent [2].

We briefly discussed the combination of visual and textual information.
Of course they can be more tightly coupled than by their joined probability.
Blei et al. [1] give a fine discussion of a generative approach for representing
images and captions simultaneously.

Finally, the work that lead to this chapter has been published previously
in many places. Elsewhere [22, 23] we give more extensive discussions on the
techniques presented here.

# References

1. David M. Blei and Michael I. Jordan. Modeling annotated data. In Jamie Callan,
   Gordon Cormack, Charles Clarke, David Hawking, and Alan F. Smeaton, editors, *Proceedings of the 26th Annual International ACM SIGIR Conference on
   Research and Development in Information Retrieval*, Toronto Canada, 2003.
   ACM Press.
2. W. Bruce Croft and John Lafferty, editors. volume 13 of *The Kluwer International Series on Information Retrieval*. Kluwer Academic Publishers, 2003.
3. A. P. Dempster, N. M. Laird, and D. B. Rubin. Maximum likelihood from
   incomplete data via the EM algorithm. *Journal of the Royal Statistical Society,
   series B*, 39(1):1–38, 1977.
4. Richard O. Duda, Peter E. Hart, and David G. Stork. *Pattern Classification*.
   Wiley-Interscience, 2nd edition, 2000.
5. R. Fergus, P. Perona, and A. Zisserman. Object class recognition by unsupervised scale-invariant learning. In *Proceedings of the IEEE Conference on
   Computer Vision and Pattern Recognition*, 2003.
6. Hayit Greenspan, Jacob Goldberger, and Arnaldo Mayer. Probabilistic space-
   time video modeling via piecewise GMM. *IEEE Transactions on Pattern Analysis and Machine Intelligence*, 26(3):384–396, 2004.

7. Hayit Greenspan, Jacob Goldberger, and Lenny Ridel. A continuous probabilistic framework for image matching. *Computer Vision and Image Understanding*, 84(3):384–406, 2001.
8. Djoerd Hiemstra. A linguistically motivated probabilistic model of information retrieval. In Christos Nicolaou and Constantine Stephanidis, editors, *Proceedings of the Second European Conference on Research and Advanced Technology for Digital Libraries (ECDL)*, volume 513 of *Lecture Notes in Computer Science*, pages 569–584. Springer-Verlag, 1998.
9. Tzvetanka Ianeva, Arjen P. de Vries, and Thijs Westerveld. A dynamic probabilistic retrieval model. In *IEEE International Conference on Multimedia and Expo (ICME)*, pages 1607–1610, 2004.
10. F. Jelinek and R. L. Mercer. Interpolated estimation of Markov source parameters from sparse data. In E. Gelsema and L. Kanal, editors, *Proceedings of the Workshop on Pattern Recognition in Practice*, pages 381–397, 1980.
11. Michael I. Jordan. Graphical models. *Statistical Science*, 19(1):140–155, 2003. Special Issue on Bayesian Statistics.
12. Daniel Jurafsky and James H. Martin. *Speech and Language Processing – An Introduction to Natural Language Processing, Computational Linguistics and Speech Recognition*. Prentice Hall, 2000.
13. Victor Lavrenko and W. Bruce Croft. Relevance-based language models: Estimation and analysis. In Croft and Lafferty [2].
14. Hangzai Luo, Jianping Fan, Jing Xiao, and Xingquan Zhu. Semantic principal video shot classification via mixture gaussian. In *IEEE International Conference on Multimedia and Expo (ICME)*, 2003.
15. Paul Ogilvie and Jamie Callan. Using language models for flat text queries in XML retrieval. In *Proceedings of the Initiative for the Evaluation of XML Retrieval Workshop (INEX 2003)*, 2003.
16. J. M. Ponte and W. Bruce Croft. A language modeling approach to information retrieval. In W. Bruce Croft, Alistair Moffat, C. J. van Rijsbergen, Ross Wilkinson, and Justin Zobel, editors, *Proceedings of the 21st Annual International ACM SIGIR Conference on Research and Development in Information Retrieval*, pages 275–281. ACM Press, 1998.
17. Gerard Salton and Chris Buckley. Term-weighting approaches in automatic text retrieval. *Information Processing & Management*, 24(5):513–523, 1988.
18. Fei Song and W. Bruce Croft. A general language model for information retrieval. In *Proceedings of the Eighth International Conference on Information and Knowledge Management*, pages 316–321. ACM Press, 1999.
19. Karen Sparck Jones, Stephen Robertson, Djoerd Hiemstra, and Hugo Zaragoza. Language modeling and relevance. In Croft and Lafferty [2].
20. D. M. Titterington, A. F. M. Smith, and U. E. Makov. *Statistical Analysis of Finite Mixture Distributions*. Wiley Series in Probability and Mathematical Statistics. John Wiley and Sons, 1985.
21. Nuno Vasconcelos. *Bayesian Models for Visual Information Retrieval*. PhD thesis, Massachusetts Institut of Technology, 2000.
22. Thijs Westerveld. *Using generative probabilistic models for multimedia retrieval.* PhD thesis, University of Twente, November 2004.
23. Thijs Westerveld and Arjen P. de Vries. Generative probabilistic models for multimedia retrieval: query generation against document generation. *IEE Proceedings – Vision, Image, and Signal Processing*, 152(6):852–858, December 2005.

24. Thijs Westerveld, Arjen P. de Vries, Alex van Ballegooij, Fransiska M. G. de Jong, and Djoerd Hiemstra. A probabilistic multimedia retrieval model and its evaluation. *EURASIP Journal on Applied Signal Processing*, 2003(2):186–198, 2003. Special issue on Unstructured Information Management from Multimedia Data Sources.
25. Chengxiang Zhai and John Lafferty. A study of smoothing methods for language models applied to ad hoc information retrieval. In *Proceedings of the 24th Annual International ACM SIGIR Conference on Research and Development in Information Retrieval*, pages 334–342. ACM Press, 2001.

# 7

# Speech Indexing

Roeland Ordelman[1], Franciska de Jong[1,2], and David van Leeuwen[3]

[1] University of Twente
[2] TNO Information and Communication Technology
[3] TNO Defence, Security and Safety

## 7.1 Introduction

The amount of metadata attached to multimedia collections that can be used for searching is very much dependent on the available resources within the organizations that create or own the collections. Large national audiovisual institutions, such as *Sound&Vision* in The Netherlands,[4] put a lot of effort in archiving their assets and they label collection items with at least titles, dates and short content descriptions (descriptive metadata, see Chapter 2). However, many organizations that create or own multimedia collections lack the resources to apply even the most basic form of archiving. Certain collections may become the stepchild of an archive — minimally managed, poorly preserved, and hardly accessible.

Although the saying "information is in the audio, video is for entertainment[5]" puts it somewhat strongly, it gives an impression of the potential for the deployment of audio and for the application of information extraction techniques to support multimedia information retrieval tasks. Especially the *speech* in audio is an important information source that, once transformed into text and/or enriched with linguistic annotation, can enable the conceptual querying of video content. The basic idea is to use *automatic speech recognition technology* to generate such a linguistic annotation or textual representation (see Figure 7.1) and to use this as (a source for) automatically created metadata that can be used for searching by applying standard text-based information retrieval techniques.

Next to the words spoken, also information about the speaker can be extracted from the speech waveform, referred to as *speaker classification*. Typical examples are the speaker's identity or gender, which can be useful for the detection of document structure (who is speaking when), or even the speaker's background (social, geographic, etc.) or emotional state. Apart from speech,

---

[4] Sound&Vision: `http://www.beeldengeluid.nl/`

[5] Richard Schwartz (BBN Technologies) at the Multimedia Retrieval Video-Conference at the University of Twente in 1999.

often other clues in the audio can have added value, such as background
noise sources, sounds, music, adverts, channel characteristics and bandwidth
of transmission.

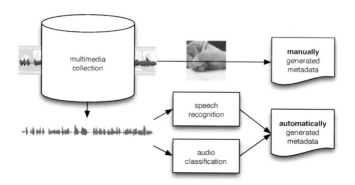

**Fig. 7.1.** Automatic metadata generation using the audio stream.

This chapter will focus on the automatic extraction of information from the
speech in multimedia documents. This approach is often referred to as *speech
indexing* and it can be regarded as a subfield of *audio indexing* that also
incorporates for example the analysis of music and sounds. If the objective
of the recognition of the words spoken is to support retrieval, one commonly
speaks of *spoken document retrieval* (SDR). If the objective is on the coupling
of various media types the term *media mining* or even *cross-media mining*
is used. Most attention in this chapter will go to SDR. The focus is less on
searching (an index of) a multimedia database, but on enabling multiple views
on the data by cross-linking all the available multifaceted information sources
in a multimedia database. In Section 7.6 cross-media mining will be discussed
in more detail.

### 7.1.1 Relation to Other Chapters

Throughout this book, the searching process is generally described as trying to find a match between an information need, formulated in a query and
represented in a *query representation*, and a collection of documents, represented in a *document representation* (often referred to as an index). From a
user's perspective, using natural language to formulate an information need
in a query, is the most evident choice although other modalities are thinkable
(see also "Interaction" in Chapter 11). However, with audiovisual content, the
representation of a natural language query does not match the representation
of the documents (images in pixels, audio in samples). The main focus of this
chapter (and also Chapters 5, 8, and 9) is on solving this representation mis-

match by converting the document collection to the natural language query representation:

> Solving the representation mismatch:
>
> - convert the document collection to the natural language query representation (e.g., speech to text);
> - adjust the query to the document representation (e.g., example image as query);
> - convert both document and query representation to an intermediate representation (e.g., query and speech to sound units).

### 7.1.2 Outline

The remainder of this chapter starts with a brief introduction to speech recognition in general (Section 7.2), and a detailed overview of the application of speech recognition technology in the context of multimedia indexing in a section on spoken document retrieval (Section 7.3). Here, the synchronization or time alignment of collateral data sources, large vocabulary speech recognition, keyword spotting and SDR using subword unit representations will be discussed. In the section on robust speech recognition and retrieval (Section 7.4), we zoom in on the optimization of speech recognition performance in the context of spoken document retrieval, discussing query and document expansion, vocabulary optimization, topic-based language models and acoustic adaptation. The chapter will be finalized by discussing audio segmentation (Section 7.5) and a topic that links speech indexing to other modalities in the multimedia framework: cross-media mining (Section 7.6).

## 7.2 Brief Introduction to Speech Recognition

In the speech recognition process several steps can be distinguished. Recognition systems convert an acoustic signal into a sequence of words via a series of processes that are visualized in a very simplified manner in Figure 7.2.

### 7.2.1 Feature Extraction

First the digitized acoustic signal is converted into a compact representation that captures the characteristics of the speech signal using spectral information. This step is usually referred to as *feature extraction*. A spectrum describes how the different frequency components in a waveform vary in time and this information is represented by vectors of features which are computed for example every 10 ms for a 16 ms overlapping time window. An LPC (Linear Predictive Coding) spectrum is an example of a smoothed spectrum. Often, the spectral features are modified in one way or another in order to make them more consistent with how the human ear works (e.g., Mel-scale), and averaged over spectral bands. A commonly used feature set is based on a derivation of the spectrum, the *cepstrum*, that is computed by taking a Discrete Cosine

Transform of a band-filtered spectrum. When the resulting Cepstral Coefficients are Mel-scaled we end up with the popular MFCC (Mel Frequency Cepstral Coefficients) feature set.

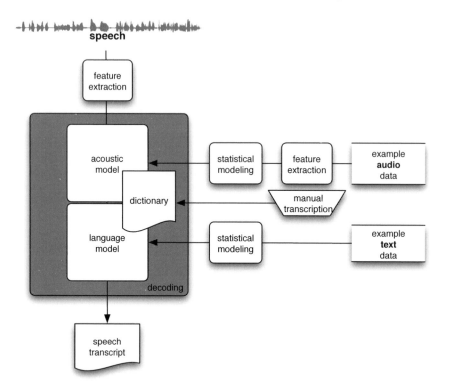

**Fig. 7.2.** Simplified overview of a speech recognition system: on the left the flow from speech to a speech transcription via feature extraction and a decoding stage that includes the acoustic model, the language model and dictionary; on the right the flow of required statistical (audio & text) and manual information.

### 7.2.2 Acoustic Modeling

In the statistical speech recognition framework, the feature vectors are treated as acoustic observations, $O$. The task is formulated as to find the sequence of words $W = \{\omega_1, \omega_2, \ldots, \omega_N\}$ that are most likely to have been spoken on the basis of the the acoustic observations $O$. The probability of a sentence being produced given some acoustic observations is typically expressed as $P(W|O)$. The most likely sentence, $\hat{W}$, is found by computing $P(W|O)$ for all possible sentences and choosing the one with the highest probability:

$$\hat{W} = \arg\max_{W} P(W|O). \tag{7.1}$$

Using Bayes' rule, the conditional probability of a sentence $W$ being spoken, assuming that certain acoustic observations $O$ were made, can be expressed as:

$$P(W|O) = \frac{P(O|W) \cdot P(W)}{P(O)}, \tag{7.2}$$

where $P(O|W)$ is the likelihood that specific acoustic observations are made given a sentence $W$, and $P(W)$ is the prior probability of the sequence of words $W$, which can be estimated using a statistical language model, and finally $P(O)$ is the probability of observing the given speech input. As for the computation of the most probable sentence given a certain speech input, $P(O)$ is the same for all possible $W$, and it may be regarded as a normalization factor that can well be removed from the computation:

$$\hat{W} = \arg\max_{W} P(W|O) = \arg\max_{W} \overbrace{P(O|W)}^{AM} \cdot \overbrace{P(W)}^{LM}. \tag{7.3}$$

The most popular approach in speech recognition is to use hidden Markov models (HMMs) to compute the acoustic model probabilities $P(O|W)$ and language model probabilities $P(W)$. An HMM is a stochastic automaton that consists of a set of connected states, each having a transition probability and an output or emission probability associated with it (probability density functions, see below). The transition probabilities model the transitions from one state to the other. The output probabilities model the observation likelihoods of an observation being generated from a particular state. In HMM speech recognition, the problem of finding $P(O|W)$ can be expressed as finding $P(O|M)$, the likelihood that the observations $O$ were generated by a sequence of word HMM models ($M$) that are associated with a sentence $W$. The word models are in turn composed of subword unit models, typically models based on the smallest unit in speech, the *phone*. In other words, the calculation of $P(O|W)$ involves the computation of the likelihood that the observations $O$ are generated by a particular set of HMM states. The usual HMM training approach is to construct probability density functions (PDFs) that model the likelihood of HMM states emitting a particular observation. These PDFs are typically Gaussians or mixtures of Gaussians. The parameters of the PDFs are typically estimated so as to model the training data. The Viterbi algorithm or alternatively a best-first search algorithm (stack decoding or A*-search), is then used to find the best path through the network of HMMs given the observations.

### 7.2.3 Language Modeling

The prior probability of a sentence $P(W)$ in speech recognition can typically be estimated using statistical $n$-gram models. Using the chain rule of probability, $P(W)$ can be formally expressed as:

$$P(W) = \prod_{i=1}^{n} P(\omega_i | \omega_1, \ldots, \omega_{i-1}), \tag{7.4}$$

where $P(\omega_i | \omega_1, \ldots, \omega_{i-1})$ is the probability that the word $\omega_i$ was spoken, immediately following the preceding word sequence $\omega_1, \ldots, \omega_{i-1}$, that is referred to as the history of the word $\omega_i$. However, computing the probability of a word given a long history of words is not feasible. Theoretically, it depends on the entire past history of a discourse. The $n$-gram language model attempts to provide an adequate approximation of $P(\omega_i)$ by referring to the Markov assumption that the probability of a future event can be predicted by looking at its immediate past. $N$-gram language models therefore use the previous $n-1$ words (typically one or two words) as an approximation of the entire history. That this approximation is reasonably adequate can be derived from the fact that $n$-gram language models were introduced in speech recognition in the 1970's and still remain state-of-the-art. For a two-word history, trigram models can be generated by reformulating (7.4) as:

$$P(\omega) \approx P(\omega_0) \cdot P(\omega_1 | \omega_0) \cdot \prod_{i=2}^{n} P(\omega_i | \omega_{i-2}, \omega_{i-1}). \tag{7.5}$$

Probability estimates for $n$-grams can be computed using the relative frequencies, called maximum likelihood estimates (ML): the normalized counts of $n$-grams in a training corpus. For a trigram model it is:

$$P(\omega_3 | \omega_1, \omega_2) = f(\omega_3 | \omega_1, \omega_2) \doteq \frac{C(\omega_1, \omega_2, \omega_3)}{C(\omega_1, \omega_2)}, \tag{7.6}$$

or in a generalized form:

$$P(\omega_i | \omega_{i-n+1}^{i-1}) = \frac{c(\omega_{i-n+1}^{i-1})}{\sum_{w_i} c(\omega_{i-n+1}^{i-1})}, \tag{7.7}$$

where we used the notation $\omega_i^j$ for the sequence of words $\omega_i, \omega_{i+1}, \ldots, \omega_j$. As even very large training corpora can never cover all possible $n$-grams for a language, it is possible that perfectly acceptable $n$-grams are not encountered in the training corpus. A language model based on (7.6) would assign a zero probability to such "unseen" $n$-grams. So regardless of the evidence provided by the acoustic signal in favor of an $n$-gram not encountered in the training data, the $n$-gram will never be reproduced by the language model. Moreover, it is well-known that using relative frequencies as a way to estimate probabilities, produces poor estimates when the $n$-gram counts are small. To create a more uniform distribution, it is necessary to smooth these zero-probability and low-probability $n$-grams.

### 7.2.4 Dictionary

The speech recognition *vocabulary* is a list of all the words in the language model. It can be considered the model of pronunciation in the recognition system. By presenting for every word in the vocabulary a pronunciation, the *pronunciation dictionary* is the link between the acoustic model and the language model. Word pronunciations can be viewed as rules for the concatenation of phone models to arrive at the words contained in the language model. During decoding, the words in the dictionary are usually compactly represented by networks of phones, e.g., in the form of a *lexical tree*, where each path through the network represents a word. Using this network, a Viterbi based search can be performed to find the most probable path through the network.

To obtain word pronunciations for the large and dynamic speech recognition vocabularies, speech recognition developers usually deploy a large background pronunciation lexicon to enable a flexible generation of word pronunciations. When word pronunciations are not in the background lexicon, word transcripts can be manually generated, or produced by a grapheme-to-phoneme[6] converter (G2P) that uses rules or machine-learning techniques for pronunciation generation. As generating pronunciations manually is time consuming, a G2P converter is often indispensable, especially in the dynamic news domain that has a lot of proper names and names of cities and places that are often not included in background lexicons.

Background lexicons and especially G2P tools usually provide canonical word pronunciations only, according to a normative, "average" pronunciation of words. In practice however, words are pronounced in numerous variations in different degradations from the canonical pronunciation. Among others things this is due to age, gender or dialect (inter-speaker variability) and speaking style, speaking rate, co-articulation or emotional state of the speaker (intra-speaker variability). It has been estimated that in spontaneous speech around 40 % of the words is not pronounced according to the canonical representation. As such mismatches may occur both at acoustic modeling training stage and at the recognition stage, such variations result in a degradation of word accuracy of the speech recognition system. By incorporating pronunciation variations in the lexicon, the number of inaccurate phone-to-word mappings can be reduced.

### 7.2.5 Summary

Speech recognition is based on two important techniques, *modeling* and *search*. The task of *modeling* is to capture the acoustics of speech, the pronunciation of words and the sequence of words in a way that these models are general enough to describe the various sources of variability found in speech (speaker, coarticulation, word choice), whilst being specific enough to extract the linguistic information. The task of the *search* is to find the sequence of models that fit the observed speech data best in an efficient way.

---

[6] Also referred to as text-to-speech or letter-to-phone/sound.

## 7.3 Spoken Document Retrieval

To support spoken document retrieval, the crucial step is to create a textual representation of an audiovisual document by automatically annotating the speech in the data. The resulting representation can be regarded as *automatically generated metadata* that can either be used as a replacement for missing human-generated metadata, or as an additional information source. Especially for smaller organizations that own multimedia collections, resources are often lacking to apply even a basic form of archiving. In such cases, applying spoken document retrieval is the only way to provide means for searching the collections. For larger organizations with audiovisual archives, administrative metadata, such as rights metadata (who is the legal owner of a video item) and technical metadata (such as the format of a video item), is usually available. Often even descriptive human-generated metadata is also preserved with the collection items, such as the title, duration, a short content description and a list of names and places that are mentioned. Although the information density in this type of metadata is usually low, it can nevertheless be very helpful for *locating* specific documents in a collection. This type of information is therefore sometimes referred to as "bibliographic" or "tombstone information" among librarians.[7] However, locating specific parts *within* documents (e.g., the passage where a specific subject is addressed) remains time consuming as it requires manual scrolling through a (possibly large) multimedia document. Although multimedia documents can often be structured using available information sources (such as the occurrence of speaker changes, speech/non-speech boundaries, large silence intervals or shot boundaries) and techniques are being developed to support quick browsing of video documents (e.g., by enabling fast playback of speech), going manually through large video documents can still be cumbersome.

### 7.3.1 Manual versus Automatic Annotation

In theory, instead of using speech recognition technology, the annotation of the speech could as just well be carried out manually. In fact, in the meeting domain, manual annotation of the speech is quite common. Usually meeting *minutes* are generated, either stenographically or not. When the meetings are recorded on video, such annotations can very well be used as a textual representations for indexing and retrieval. Often however, such annotations do not exist and it is usually too expensive to generate them manually. In specific cases though, manual annotation can be a valid option, especially when the collection is relatively small and fixed, and/or the quality of automatic annotations is too low.

The application of automatic speech recognition (ASR) technology for indexing purposes has been made possible thanks to the large improvements

---

[7] Note that besides administrative and descriptive metadata, a third type of metadata is often distinguished: information about the structure and organization of a multipart digital object that can be encoded MPEG-7/21.

in the performance of ASR systems in recent years. This is partly due to the increase in computer power but also to massive speech recognition research efforts especially in the context of benchmark evaluations (often sponsored by DARPA[8]) ranging from evaluations focusing on read speech (*Wall Street Journal*) in the early 1990s, via broadcast news speech in the second half of the 1990s and conversational speech early this decennium to meeting room speech most recently.

### 7.3.2 Requirements for Recognition Performance

IR-oriented benchmarks such as TREC (Text Retrieval Conference) demonstrated that deploying ASR techniques has become more than a theoretical option for the automatic annotation of speech for retrieval purposes. This is especially the case in the broadcast news domain which is very general and makes data collection for training a speech recognition system relatively easy. For the broadcast news domain, speech transcripts approximate the quality of manual transcripts, at least for several languages. Spoken document retrieval in the American-English broadcast news (BN) domain was even declared "solved" with the Spoken Document Retrieval track at TREC in 2000. However, in other domains than broadcast news and for other languages, a similar recognition performance is usually harder to obtain due to a number of factors including the lack of well-balanced speech databases for certain languages, the lack of domain-specific training data for certain domains, and of course due to the large variability in audio quality and speech characteristics. Some of these issues will be discussed in more detail in Section 7.4, but first a number of general techniques used in spoken document retrieval will be outlined.

### 7.3.3 Spoken Document Retrieval Techniques

Below, a number of techniques that can play a role in spoken document retrieval will be described in detail. Which combination of techniques is chosen for the disclosure of a specific multimedia database depends on a number of factors. For each of the techniques these factors will be listed. We will discuss:

- synchronization of available textual resources;
- large vocabulary speech recognition;
- keyword spotting;
- using subword as unit for representation.

The first two are the most frequently used techniques. The last two are sometimes used as the primary annotation strategy, but often in combination with the first two techniques.

---

[8] The Defense Advanced Research Projects Agency (DARPA) is the central research and development organization for the US department of Defense.

## Synchronization of Collateral Data Sources

To allow the conceptual querying of video content without having to set-up a speech recognition system to generate full-text transcriptions, collateral textual resources that are closely related with the collection items can be exploited. A well known example of such a textual resource is subtitling information for the hearing-impaired (e.g., *CEEFAX* pages 888 in the UK) that is available for the majority of contemporary broadcast items, in any case for news programs. Subtitles contain a nearly complete transcription of the words spoken in the video items and provide an excellent information source for indexing. Usually, they can easily be linked to the video by using the time-codes that come with the subtitles. The Dutch news subtitles even provide topic boundaries that can be used for segmenting the news show into subdocuments. Textual sources that can play a similar role are teleprompter files (the texts read from screen by an anchor person, also referred to as auto-cues) and scenarios. Teletext subtitles can relatively easy be obtained using the teletext capturing functionality in most modern television boards. Teleprompter files and scenarios of course have to be provided by the producers of the videos.

The time labels in these sources are crucial for the creation of a textual index into video. In the collateral text sources mentioned above, the available timelabels are not always fully reliable and can even be absent. In that case the text files will have to be synchronized. Examples of such text sources are minutes of meetings or written versions of lectures and speeches. Below, two approaches for the automatic generation of timestamps for minutes will be described using two scenarios: the synchronization of (i) the so-called *Handelingen*, i.e., the meetings of the Dutch Parliament, and (ii) the minutes of Dutch city council meetings to the video recordings of the meetings. Due to the difference in accuracy of the minutes, two different approaches are needed.

The minutes of the meetings of the Dutch Parliament are stenographic minutes that closely follow the discourse of the meeting, only correcting slips of the tongue and ungrammatical sentences. Given the close match with the actual speech, a relatively straightforward so-called forced alignment procedure could be used. Forced alignment is a technique commonly used in acoustic model training in automatic speech recognition (ASR). In order to be able to train phone models, words and phones in pre-segmented sentences are aligned to their exact location in the speech segments using an acoustic model.[9] Given a set of words from a sentence the acoustic model tries to find the most optimal distributions of these words given the audio signal on the basis of the sounds the words are composed of. When using alignment for indexing, pre-segmented sentences are evidently not available but as long as the text follows the speech well enough, the word alignment can be found by using relatively large windows of text.

---

[9] In the first iteration usually an "averaged" bootstrap model is used. The alignment and the model should improve iteratively.

The alignment procedure works well even if some words in the minutes are actually not in the speech signal. However, if the text to be aligned does not match the speech too well, as was the case with city council meetings, and if the text segments are too large, the alignment procedure will fail to find a proper alignment. In order to produce suitable segments, a two-pass strategy can be used, incorporating the following steps as visualized in Figure 7.3:

1. a baseline large vocabulary speech recognition system[10] is used to generate a relatively inaccurate transcript of the speech with word-timing labels, referred to as hypothesis;
2. the hypothesis is aligned on the word level to the minutes using a dynamic programming algorithm;
3. at the positions where the hypothesis and the minutes match (a match may be defined as three words in a row are correctly aligned), so called "anchors" are placed;
4. using the word-timing labels provided by the speech recognition system, the anchors are used to generate suitable segments;
5. individual segments of audio and text are accurately synchronized using forced alignment.

The described methods allow for the synchronization of audiovisual data to available linguistic content that approximates to a certain extent the speech in the source data and they enable the processing of conceptual queries of the audiovisual content. In the second alignment procedure, an initial hypothesis is generated by a large vocabulary speech recognition system. As this hypothesis is only needed for finding useful segments, the performance of the system is not crucial as long as it is able to provide "anchors". However, the relevance of speech recognition performance increases when textual resources suitable for alignment with audiovisual data are *not* available. In the next section, the application of speech recognition technology as the *primary* source for generating a textual representation of audiovisual documents that can be linked to other linguistic content, is described.

**Large Vocabulary Speech Recognition**
Using speech recognition technology to convert spoken audio into text for retrieval purposes, may seem a rather obvious solution. However, in order to obtain reasonable retrieval results, a speech recognition system has to produce reasonably accurate transcription of what was actually spoken. When a system produces lots of errors, successful retrieval will be doubtful. When it produces perfect transcripts, retrieval will resemble the performance of retrieving text documents. How accurate exactly speech recognition should be for acceptable retrieval performance was uncertain at the outset of SDR research, although some experience was gained with the retrieval of corrupted

---

[10] Optionally the speech recognition is somewhat adapted to the task for example by providing it with a vocabulary extracted from the minutes.

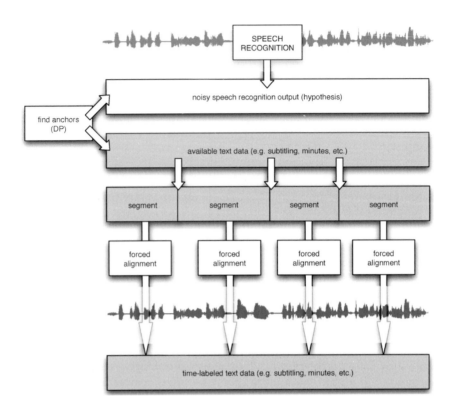

**Fig. 7.3.** Alignment procedure: synchronization of text and audio in a number of steps.

documents (e.g., from OCR) at TREC-5 in 1996. At the first SDR evaluation at TREC-6 on broadcast news data, word error rates fell between 35 % and 40 % which appeared to be good enough for acceptable retrieval results in a known-item retrieval task, simulating a user seeking one particular document. Already at TREC-7, where the known-item retrieval task was replaced by the *ad hoc* retrieval task of searching multiple relevant documents from single topics, speech recognition performance was improved substantially – the University of Cambridge HTK recognition system produced error rates below the 25 % – and almost all retrieval systems performed reasonably well. Also at TREC-7, evidence could be provided for the assumption that better speech recognition performance will also result in better retrieval performance. A speech recognition performance of 50% $WER$ is on the other hand regarded as a minimum for obtaining useful retrieval performance.

In the TREC SDR tracks, retrieval systems that used automatic annotations from a speaker-independent large vocabulary speech recognition systems outperformed other approaches (e.g., phone based approach, see below). Most multimedia retrieval systems that use speech transcripts nowadays use such large vocabulary systems that exists in many flavors and configurations. All systems are speaker-independent and have large vocabularies. The speaker-independence is required in the context of indexing multimedia collections as it is usually not known which speakers appear in the collection. Although speaker adaptation strategies are often applied (for example by clustering audio of single speakers and creating adapted, speaker specific models), speaker-independent models are the basis for LVCSR in the context of multimedia indexing. Speaker-independent models are typically trained using a large amount of example audio data from the task domain to make sure that most of the inter-speaker variabilities are captured. The *large vocabulary* is also a prerequisite, given the variety of words encountered in fluent speech and the fact that it is often very hard to predict which words are going to be used by speakers in a task domain. Typically a vocabulary of 65 thousand words (65 K) is used in LVCSR. Large corpora of text data are needed to train language model probabilities for the words in the vocabulary.

Because of the the requirements for training a LVCSR system, setting up a large vocabulary speech recognition system for a certain language in a specific domain is complex and time consuming. It is crucial that sufficient amounts of in-domain training data are available to enable the capturing of the acoustic and linguistic variability in the task domain and to train robust acoustic models and language models. To give an impression of the amounts of data that are used for typical systems in the English broadcast news benchmark tests, the LIMSI/BBN[11] 2004 English Broadcast News speech recognition system uses for acoustic model training some 140 hours of carefully transcribed broadcast news audio data and for language model training the manual transcriptions of the acoustic BN data (1.8 M words), the American English GigaWord News corpus for a total amount of approximately 1 billion words of texts, and a few hundreds of million words of other text data. A large part of this data became available with the broadcast news benchmark evaluations (Hub4). For other languages than English and for other domains than news such amounts of annotated data can often not be laid hands on easily. In such cases, one has to come up with strategies to deal with this lack of training data.

Especially in the context of retrieval, the out-of-vocabulary (OOV) problem in speech recognition deserves special attention. When a word is not in the speech recognition vocabulary, it cannot be recognized and hence, will not turn up in an annotation of a video document. In Section 7.4 strategies

---

[11] The Computer Sciences Laboratory for Mechanics and Engineering Sciences (LIMSI) is a research laboratory associated to Paris-6 and Paris-11 Universities and is one of the major players in large vocabulary speech recognition research (www.limsi.fr). BBN technologies is a US company that has been performing pioneering research in automatic speech recognition since the early 1970s (www.bbn.com).

that try to deal with this OOV problem are described in detail. One of these strategies is making use of keyword spotting that is addressed next.

## Keyword Spotting

Because of its relative simplicity, earliest attempts to deploy speech recognition technology in SDR made use of word spotting techniques to search for relevant documents in audio material. A keyword spotter searches the audio material for single keywords or multiword expressions (such as "New York" or "football game"). An acoustic model is used to recognize phones and a small vocabulary of keywords with phonetic transcriptions provide the link to the keywords. Keyword searches are often weighted using a simple grammar (such as a Finite State Grammar). Weighting can be uniform for all keywords or be based on the probability distribution of the keywords in the database. Normally the spotter has a facility to reduce incorrect keyword hypotheses (false alarms). This may be one single "garbage" model matching all non-keywords or even a vocabulary of non-keywords.

A speech recognizer in keyword-spotter mode has the advantage of being relatively light-weight as it does not use a computationally costly language model. Therefore, keyword spotting was a feasible approach at times when computer power was still limited. In early systems, keywords were usually carefully fixed in advance. After the keyword spotting process was performed, the spoken documents in the collection could be represented in terms of the keywords found in the documents. Although, this method worked well within a very restricted domain (such as the detection of weather reports) or topic identification in speech messages, the fixed set of keywords often appeared to be too limited for realistic tasks.

As computer power increased, keyword spotting could also be deployed at retrieval time, enabling the search for any keyword given by the user. However, keyword spotting at retrieval time may result in unacceptable delays in response time, especially when the document collection is large. To avoid this, an alternative word spotting technique called phone lattice scanning (PLS) can be deployed. In PLS word spotting, phone lattices are created and searched for the sequence of phones corresponding to a particular search term. In this way keywords do not need to be chosen a priori so that any set of words can be searched, and as the phone lattices are created before retrieval time, delays in response time can be minimized.

But using keyword spotting for retrieval purposes has disadvantages. Retrieval will suffer from false alarms and missed keywords and especially short words are hard to spot as keyword spotting relies solely on acoustic information. This attracted SDR researchers to use large vocabulary speech recognition systems (LVCSR, discussed below) that can benefit from the restrictive power of language models or to combine other speech recognition techniques with word spotting. Especially when the mismatch between speech recognition vocabulary and domain vocabulary is hard to model and tends to produce many out-of-vocabulary words, having word spotting functionality available as an *ad hoc* tool for searching either the audio directly or a phone or phone lattice representation of the document be profitable. A typical example of a deploying word spotting approach in combination with a full text transcription approach would be the following strategy to recover names that were misrecognized: (i) the initial speech recognition transcript is used to find related collateral text data; (ii) named entity detection in the collateral data source provides relevant named entities given the document topic; (iii) the occurrence (and timings) of these named entities in the source data are recovered using a word spotting approach.

In spite of its disadvantages, keyword spotting can be regarded as a useful technique for the retrieval of spoken documents. The focus of the SDR community however shifted toward large vocabulary speech recognition in the late nineties due to massive research efforts resulting in substantial improvements in speech recognition performance in SDR. But utilizing word spotting techniques, either alone or in combination with other speech recognition techniques, remains a good choice for a variety of applications, especially when heavy-weight speech recognition is not feasible or useful.

## SDR using Subword Unit Representations

While keyword spotting and LVCSR approaches largely focus on words as representation units of the decoded speech in the document, an alternative category of SDR approaches use subword unit representations such as phones, phone *n*-grams, syllables or broad phonetic classes to deal with the retrieval of spoken documents. Subwords are generated by either taking the output of a phone recognizer directly (phones) or by post-processing this output to acquire phone *n*-grams or other representations. A significant characteristic of subword based approaches is that the document is represented in terms of these subword units. At retrieval time, query words are translated into a sequence of subword units which are matched with subword document representations.

Note that keyword spotting using a phone lattice as described earlier, resembles this type of approaches in the way that the query is translated into a sequence of subword units, namely phones, that are matched with the phone representation of the documents. However, keyword spotting aims at matching particular sequences of phones in the document representations themselves in order to map them to words, whereas in subword based approaches, the matching is done using subword indexing terms.

As a phone recognizer requires only an acoustic model and a small phone grammar to generate sequences of phones, the recognition process can do with a relatively simple decoding algorithm. Compared to computationally expensive large vocabulary speech recognition approach, the decoding step of a subword based approach is much faster. Also, by deploying a phone recognizer, collecting large amounts of domain specific text data (that may be unavailable) for language model training can be circumvented, which reduces training requirements to the acoustic model training. Finally, as the phone recognizer does not need a vocabulary of words, a subword based approach is less sensitive to out-of-vocabulary words, provided that the query words can be converted to the subword representations using grapheme-to-phoneme conversion tools.

However, depending solely on acoustic information, phone recognition systems tend to produce higher error rates, resulting in less accurate document representations. To compensate for the decrease in precision, hybrid approaches have been proposed where for example the subword unit approach is used as a pre-selection step for a word spotting approach.

## 7.4 Robust Speech Recognition and Retrieval

If speech recognition technology is deployed to support retrieval tasks, the recognition accuracy must be analyses in this context. Whereas in dictation systems for example, it is of utmost importance to have a high speech recognition accuracy level for all words, for retrieval purposes it is important to have at least the *content words* right, e.g., nouns, proper names, adjectives and verbs. During the indexing process, function words (articles, auxiliary verbs, etc.) are filtered out anyway. The usually smaller function words bear less acoustic information and therefore have a high change to be misrecognized by speech recognition systems. Therefore, analyzing the global word error rate of an ASR system for evaluating its feasibility for retrieval may not always be adequate. The word error rate is based upon a comparison of a *reference* transcription of the test material with the output of the recognizer referred to as the *hypothesis* transcription. The scoring algorithm searches for the *minimum edit distance* in words between the hypothesis and reference and produces the number of substitutions, insertions and deletions that are needed to align the reference with the hypothesis. The word error rate $WER$ is then defined as:

$$WER = \frac{\text{Insertions} + \text{Deletions} + \text{Substitutions}}{\text{Total words in reference}}. \tag{7.8}$$

Disregarding words that are in a list of stop-words during evaluation is one of the strategies that can be used for scaling the word error rate. Another strategy is to compute the *term error rate $TER$*, that is defined as:

$$TER = \frac{\sum_{t \in T} |R(t) - H(t)|}{|T|}, \tag{7.9}$$

where $R(t)$ and $H(t)$ represent the number of occurrences of query term $t$ in the reference and the hypothesis respectively, and $|T| = \sum_{t \in T} R(t)$. The $TER$ gives a more accurate measure of speech recognition performance conditioned on a retrieval system as it takes only the misrecognized query terms into account.

In practice, the word error rate is nevertheless frequently used as an indication of quality. In general, a word error rate of 50% is regarded as an adequate baseline for retrieval. However, for certain collections, it can be hard enough to achieve this goal of having at least half of the words right. In the following section, we describe a strategy that aims at improving retrieval based on noisy speech recognition transcripts itself by making use of parallel text corpora (Section 7.4.1). Next, three strategies to reach optimal speech recognition are described: optimization of the speech recognition vocabulary in Section 7.4.2, generation of topic specific language models in Section 7.4.3, and acoustic model adaptation in Section 7.4.4.

### 7.4.1 Query and Document Expansion

A technique applied in information retrieval that is specifically worth mentioning in the context of spoken document retrieval, is *query expansion*. As the term already suggests, this technique simply adds words to the query in order to improve retrieval performance. In query expansion the document search is basically performed twice. After an initial run, a selection of the top $N$ most relevant documents generates a list of terms ranked by their weight (e.g., a tf.idf weight). The top $T$ terms of this list are then added to the query and the search is repeated using the enriched query. Query expansion can be performed using retrieved documents from the same collection, or using retrieved documents from another (parallel) corpus. In the former case, query expansion is referred to as *blind relevance feedback*, in the latter it is called *parallel blind relevance feedback*. As the speech recognition system in a spoken document retrieval task may have produced errors or may have missed important words, it can be useful to apply parallel blind relevance feedback using a corpus without errors, such as a manually transcribed corpus, in order to reduce retrieval misses due to speech recognition errors. In other approaches to query expansion, compound words are split, geographic names are expanded (e.g., "The Netherlands" to "Amsterdam, ..., Zaandam") and hyponyms of unambiguous nouns are added (e.g., "flu, malaria, etc." are added given "disease") using thesauri and dictionaries. Also the opposite approach, *document expansion* is applied to alleviate the effect of speech recognition errors on retrieval performance. However, this approach does not work that well when story segmentation is unknown.

### 7.4.2 Vocabulary Optimization

For successful retrieval, the minimization of out-of-vocabulary (OOV) words in the speech-to-text conversion step is important. OOV words may result in OOV query words (QOV): words that appear in a user's query and also occurred in the audio document but – as they were OOV – could not be recognized correctly. OOV's damage retrieval performance in two ways: firstly, given a query with a QOV word, the QOV word leads to a word *miss* in searching. Secondly, its replacement potentially induces a *false alarm* for other queries. Document expansion and query expansion techniques are often deployed to compensate for QOV's in information retrieval. However, especially when OOV words are named entities, attempts to minimize the number of OOV words beforehand is beneficial. To enable the selection of an appropriate set of vocabulary words, typically text data that closely resemble the task domain are deployed to obtain an indication of the word usage in the task domain. The broadcast news (BN) domain is a relatively "open" with respect to word usage. Predicting exactly which words are to be used in news items is virtually impossible and as a result of this, the usual approach is to include as many words as possible in the vocabularies so that at least the majority of the words occurring are covered. The maximum number of words that can be included in the vocabulary is restricted by the number of words a speech recognition system can deal with, typically 65 K words[12] But as news topics are constantly changing, it is necessary to revise the selection of vocabulary words with regular intervals. By doing so, words that have shown an increased news value due to recent events, but were not in a vocabulary created earlier, can be recognized as well. On the other hand, words that become outdated, such as for example the name of a former minister that has a very low chance to appear in the news again, should be removed in order to avoid that these obsolete words are confused acoustically with other words in the vocabulary.

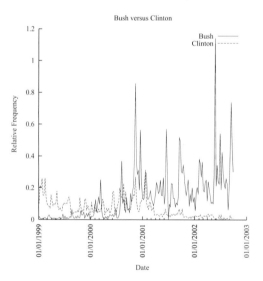

**Fig. 7.4.** Relative frequency statistics plotted in time of the words "Clinton" and "Bush". "Clinton" is showing a decreasing news value, whereas "Bush" is increasing.

---

[12] The reason for limiting the vocabulary to 65 K words in large vocabulary speech recognition is often for efficiency reasons. Words in the language model are represented by an integer index, which fit in 16-bit integers when the vocabulary size is limited to $2^{16} = 65536$.

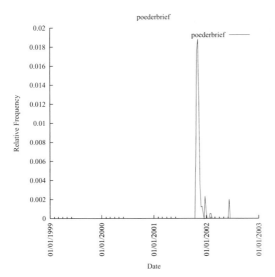

**Fig. 7.5.** Relative frequency statistics plotted in time of "Poederbrief" showing that word suddenly appears in the news.

In Figures 7.4–7.6 the changing news value of words are visualized. Relative frequency statistics of word occurrences in a newspaper database are plotted in time (1999–2003). Figure 7.4 shows the decrease in news value of the word "Clinton" in favor of "Bush", whereas Figure 7.5 shows the word "poeder-brief" (letter containing possibly poisonous powder) that suddenly appears after the 9/11 terrorist attacks. In the first example, one could think of removing "Clinton" from the vocabulary after a certain period of time. The appearance of word in the second example however cannot be "foreseen" (it suddenly appears) and can only be incorporated in the speech recognition vocabulary after it is first seen. Another category of words appear only (or mostly) in certain times of the year such as "Santa-Claus", "Christmas" and "Prinsjesdag"(see Figure 7.6). One could decide to include such words in the vocabulary only during the relevant periods with a certain overlap.

In order to use a dynamic vocabulary that is updated on the basis of the news value of words, a parallel text corpus is needed for generating word occurrence statistics. An obvious approach is to extract text data from Internet news sites on a daily basis. Having such a corpus available a vocabulary selection strategy has to be chosen. Typically new words that exceed a certain frequency threshold are added to the vocabulary but other, more fine-grained strategies are conceivable, depending on available parallel text corpora. Note however that for commercial applications, intellectual property rights (IPR) can make the exploitation of text corpora difficult.

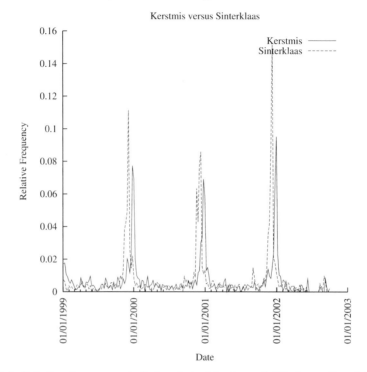

**Fig. 7.6.** Relative frequency statistics plotted in time of "Christmas" and "Santa-Claus".

### 7.4.3 Topic-based Language Models

The use of topic-based language models is a somewhat different approach towards domain adaptation on the word level then the vocabulary selection approach discussed in the previous section. Here, instead of selecting words that are expected to appear in a task domain globally, words are selected with a focus on a specific segment of an audio document. Moreover, topic-based language model also try to incorporate those $n$-gram that are specific for a certain topic. A very simple example would be $n$-grams concerning the word 'bank': in a financial topic the four-gram "go to the bank" is more likely then "sit on the bank". A financial-specific language model should reflect these topic specific statistics. More generally, one could interpret topic-specific language models as attempts to model topic-specific "matters of speaking", more accurately.

Building topic-based language models in principle requires five steps:

- segmentation of the audio file;
- initial speech recognition on the audio segments;
- defining the "topic" on the basis of the speech transcripts;
- creating a topic specific language model;
- final speech recognition run using topic-based language model.

Ideally a *segmentation* of the audio file in order to apply topic-based language models results in a number of subsequent segments that can be interpreted to be on one single topic. In practice, real topic segmentations are usually not known a priori so that often readily available segmentations, such as on the change of speaker, on longer silence intervals or even fixed time windows (see also Section 7.5 below), are chosen to divide the audio document in smaller parts. These parts are then further regarded as representing single topics. For each segment, a baseline speech recognition system provides an initial textual transcription.

On the basis of the speech transcript a topic must be assigned to the segment, either implicitly or explicitly. An explicit topic assignment refers to using specific topic labels, for example generated on the basis of a topic-classification system that assigns thesaurus terms. From a collateral text corpus (e.g., a newspaper corpus) that is labeled with the same thesaurus terms documents that are similar to the topic in the segment can be harvested for creating a topic-specific language model. For implicit topic assignment, an information retrieval system is used for the selection of documents from an unstructured collateral text source that have a similar topic: on the basis of the speech transcript (stop-words removed) that serves as a query, a ranked list of similar documents is generated; the top $N$ documents of the list in turn serve as input for language modeling. Having created a topic specific language model a second speech recognition run is performed on the same segment with the new language model to generate the final transcript. The procedure is visually depicted in Figure 7.7.

A drawback of the procedure is that the two recognition runs, the search for related text documents and building the language models takes quite some time. When the topics are broadly defined (e.g., economics, sports, etc.) the language models could best be created a priori therefore. Note also that in an alternative set-up, the segmentation can in theory be done on the basis of topic segmentation on the speech transcript of the complete audio document. However, as the initial speech transcripts has errors, the accuracy of the text-based topic segmentation may be low.

### 7.4.4 Acoustic Adaptation

A robust speech recognition system can be defined as a system that is capable of maintaining good recognition performance even when the quality of the speech input is low (environment, background noises, cross-talk, low audio quality) or when the acoustical, articulatory, or phonetic characteristics of the speech encountered in the training data differ from the speech in the task data. Speaker-to-speaker characteristics may vary enormously due to a number of factors, including:

- vocal tract length difference (gender);
- age;
- speaking style (pronunciation, speed);

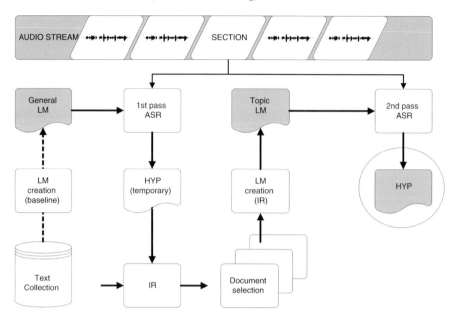

**Fig. 7.7.** Creation of topic based LM.

- regional accents;
- emotion;
- non-nativeness.

Even systems that are designed to be speaker independent cannot cover all the speaker variations that may occur in the task domain. A possible strategy to deal with the variation encountered in the task domain would be to collect domain specific data for additional training in order to capture the environment characteristics or, when there are only a few speakers, train speaker dependent models. This strategy however has some drawbacks. Firstly, setting up a domain specific training collection is costly. For acoustic training purposes the speech data needs to be annotated on the word level, which takes an experienced annotator approximately 10 hours for every hour. Secondly, the variability in the task domain can simply be too large for additional training to be successful (multiple acoustic conditions, large number of speakers of varying signature, etc.).

The alternative of doing additional training is to apply *normalization* procedures (speaker normalization, noise suppression) and *dynamic adaptation* procedures. The idea is to start with a general, relatively stable baseline system and tune this system to the specific conditions in the task domain automatically. Below, three frequently used techniques are discussed in brief.

## Vocal Tract Length Normalization

The vocal tract is the area in between the lips and the glottis. It is often imagined as a tube which length and shape have a determining effect on the resonance characteristics and hence the characteristics of the speech. The length of the vocal tract of speakers differs. The average length for white American adult males is said to be 17 cm, but this varies strongly with the physical dimension of the person. A short vocal tract tends to result in formants at a higher frequency and long vocal track lengths with lower formant frequencies.

Over the past 10 years VTLN has become a standard normalization technique in speaker-independent speech recognition. With vocal tract length normalization (VTLN) the aim is to compensate for the acoustic difference due to vocal tract length by normalizing the spectra of speakers or clusters of speakers to that of a "generic" speaker during training and testing. The normalization is done by *warping* the frequency axis of the spectra by an appropriate *warp factor* prior to the feature extraction procedure. Different warping techniques have been reported: frequency warping both linear and exponential nonlinear and Bark/Mel scale warping.

## MAP and MLLR Adaptation

Whereas with VTLN the adaptation is done by normalizing *spectral information* (feature space normalization), other adaptation methods aim at adjusting the *model parameters* (model-space transformation). The advantage of the model-space transformation is that the normalization has to be performed only once instead of every time new speech input has to be decoded. A disadvantage however is that one may end up with a variety of adapted models.

Model adaptation can be done *off-line* or at preparation time and *online*, at runtime. Off-line (or batch) adaptation refers to situations in which is known that the acoustic model has to be adapted for one single speaker or acoustic condition (typically in dictation tasks). The approach here is to collect as little adaptation data as possible to achieve an acceptable performance as collecting the adaptation data can be expensive (as discussed above). In on-line adaptation, the adaptation is during at recognition time. As a consequence only very little data is available and the adaptation algorithms should not be too complex in order to avoid huge delays. Often, online-adaptation requires multiple decoding passes.

As in the context of spoken document retrieval on-line adaptation is most needed, we restrict ourselves to this adaptation mode. A very effective and popular model adaptation technique is *Maximum Likelihood Linear Regression* (MLLR). With MLLR estimation the aim is to capture the general relationship between the speaker independent modal set and the current speaker by transforming the model means to fit the adaptation data. This is done by estimating a global linear model transformation matrix in order to maximize the likelihood of generating the adaptation data.

In MLLR adaptation clusters of model parameters are transformed simultaneously using a shared function that is estimated from available adaptation data. Because of this sharing, transformation-based adaptation techniques are especially attractive in situations where the amount of adaptation data is limited. MLLR adaptation is an indirect model adaptation approach. Direct model adaptation techniques do not assume any underlying functional transformation. Here, acoustic units are re-estimated for which adaptation data is available. As acoustic units that are not observed in the adaptation are not modified, this type of adaptation leads to local adaptation. In direct adaptation *Bayesian learning*, often implemented via *maximum a posteriori* (MAP) estimation, is a commonly used approach. MAP adaptation combines the information provided by the adaptation data with some prior knowledge about the model parameters described by a prior distribution. When the amount of adaptation data increases, MAP converges slowly to maximum likelihood estimation. A large amount of adaptation data is needed however to observe a significant performance improvement.

## 7.5 Audio Segmentation

Although timelabeled speech transcripts can directly be used to identify relevant items in within an audio collection, segmenting of longer audio documents is a helpful intermediate step. Segmentation can be done according to a particular condition such as speaker, speech/non-speech, silence, or even topic, into homogeneous subdocuments that can be accessed individually. This is convenient, as scrolling through a large unstructured audio or video fragment to identify interesting parts can be cumbersome. Audio segmentation can be advantageous from a speech recognition point of view as well, as it allows for segment based adaptation of the recognition models as will be discussed below. A frequently applied adaptation scheme is based on speaker identity.

Using a fixed overlapping time window, or fixed number of words to segment an audio stream is a simple but in cases very effective segmentation approach that does not rely on special segmentation tools. When the window and overlap ranges are chosen well, it can provide a document structure that can already usefully be deployed for certain retrieval tasks, such as word-spotting. But a segmentation based on audio features is much more informative and helpful both from a retrieval and speech recognition point of view. With a segmentation according to speaker for example, a retrieval results can be structured and presented according to speaker identity (using an ID or even a name when combined with speaker identification). In addition speaker dependent modeling schemes can be applied in order to improve speech recognition performance. Useful segmentation cues are in general provided by techniques that aim at the labeling of the source of audio data (e.g., acoustic environment, bandwidth, speaker, gender), often referred to as "diarization" or "non-lexical information generation".

## 7.6 Cross-media Mining

In Section 7.3.3 the alignment of collateral data such as subtitling information to the audiovisual source was discussed as a convenient metadata generation approach. Ideally one would not only synchronize audiovisual material with content that approximates the speech in the data such as with subtitles or minutes, but take even one step further and exploit *any* collateral textual resource, or even better: any kind of textual resource that is accessible, including open source titles and proprietary data (e.g., trusted Web pages and newspaper articles). Another way of putting it is to shift the focus from indexing individual multimedia documents to video-mining in truly multimedia distributed databases. In the context of meetings for example, usually an agenda, documents on agenda topics and CVs of meeting participants can be obtained and added to the repository. Mining these resources can support information search because it yields annotations that offers the user not just access to a specific media type, but also different perspectives on the available data. An agenda could help to add structure that can for example be presented in a network representation, whereas CVs can be linked to annotations resulting from automatic speaker segmentation. In addition, both documents and CVs would allow for multisource information extraction.

A typical example of what the cross-media perspective can yield in the broadcast news domain is the linking of newspaper articles with broadcast items and *vice versa*. Links can be established between two news objects which count is similar on the basis of the language models assigned to them via statistical analysis. Typically such language models are determined by the frequency of the linguistic units such as written or spoken words and their co-occurrences. The similarity between two documents can be decided for each pair of documents, but a more common approach is to pre-structure a document collection into clusters of documents with similar language models. Similarity of language models predicts similarity of topic, and therefore this technique is known as topic clustering.[13]

In addition to linking documents with a similar topic profile, which can be supportive in a browser environment, also the available semantic annotation for documents with similar profiles can be exchanged and exploited for conceptual search. If a newspaper article has been manually classified as belonging to, e.g., economy or foreign politics, a broadcast item with a similar language model can be classified with these conceptual labels as well.

## 7.7 Summary

In this chapter the focus was on the automatic extraction of information from the speech in multimedia documents. The larger part of this chapter was concerned with the use of speech recognition technology for automatic metadata

---

[13] The functionality commonly known as *topic detection and tracking* (TDT) for dynamic news streams has been built upon it and plays a central role in the evaluation series for TDT organized by DARPA.

extraction. After a brief introduction to speech recognition a number of spoken document retrieval techniques have been discussed: alignment of available textual data sources, keyword spotting, subword unit based approach, and finally large vocabulary speech recognition. It was shown that for certain domains acquiring a speech recognition performance that is suitable for retrieval purposes can be hard and that approaches aiming at robust speech recognition on the one hand, and search error minimization on the other hand can be deployed in such difficult domains. The chapter was finalized by discussing some properties of segmentation, an important topic from both a information retrieval and speech recognition development point of view, and by introducing the concept of cross-media mining where the focus is less on searching (an index of) a multimedia database, but on enabling new views on the data by cross-linking all the available multifaceted information sources in a multimedia database.

## 7.8 Further Reading

Given the large amount of topics that are relevant in the context of information extraction from speech, it is hardly feasible to provide a list of interesting (key) publications for further reading. A lot of information on large vocabulary speech recognition and spoken document retrieval can be obtained via the Internet, for example via NIST (`http://www.nist.gov/speech/tests/rt/` or `http://www.nist.gov/speech/publications/index.htm`) and via the publication lists of important players in the field such as the LIMSI Spoken Language Processing Group (`http://www.limsi.fr/tlp/`), BBN technologies (`http://www.bbn.com/`), the SRI Speech Technology and Research Laboratory (`http://www.speech.sri.com/`) or the Speech Research Group at Cambridge (`http://mi.eng.cam.ac.uk/research/speech/`), to name only a few.

A selection of journals in the area of speech recognition and spoken document retrieval are:

- *Speech Communication*;
- *Computer, Speech and Language*;
- *Journal of the Acoustical Society of America*;
- *IEEE Transactions on Speech and Audio Processing*.

A large number of text books are available on topics such as speech processing, signal analysis, and speech recognition. Two examples are:

- *Speech and Language Processing, An Introduction to Natural Language Processing, Computational Linguistics, and Speech Recognition*, Daniel Jurafsky and James H. Martin, Prentice Hall, 2000.
- *Statistical Methods for Speech Recognition*, Frederick Jelinek, The MIT Press, January 1998.

# 8

# Semantic Video Indexing*

Cees G.M. Snoek, Marcel Worring, Jan-Mark Geusebroek, Dennis C. Koelma, Frank J. Seinstra, and Arnold W.M. Smeulders

University of Amsterdam

## 8.1 Introduction

Query-by-keyword is the paradigm on which machine-based text search is still based. Elaborating on the success of text-based search engines, query-by-keyword also gains momentum in multimedia retrieval. For multimedia archives it is hard to achieve access, however, when based on text alone. Multimodal indexing is essential for effective access to video archives. For the automatic detection of specific concepts, the state-of-the-art has produced sophisticated and specialized indexing methods. Other than their textual counterparts, generic methods for semantic indexing in multimedia are neither generally available, nor scalable in their computational needs, nor robust in their performance. As a consequence, semantic access to multimedia archives is still limited. Therefore, there is a case to be made for a new approach to semantic video indexing.

The main problem for any semantic video indexing approach is the semantic gap between data representation and their interpretation by humans, as identified by Smeulders et al. [32]. In efforts to reduce the semantic gap, many video indexing approaches focus on specific semantic concepts with a small intra-class and large inter-class variability of content. Typical concepts and their detectors are *sunsets* by Smith and Chang [33] and the work by Zhang et al. on *news anchors* [43]. These concepts have become icons for video indexing. Although they have aided in achieving progress, this approach is limited when considering the plethora of concepts waiting to be detected. It is simply impossible to bridge the semantic gap by designing a tailor-made solution for each concept.

In this chapter we present a generic semantic video indexing method, which builds on the observation that produced video is the result of an authoring process. When producing a video, an author departs from a conceptual idea.

* © 2006 IEEE. Reprinted, with permission, from *IEEE Transactions on Pattern Analysis and Machine Intelligence*, 28(10):1678–1689, October 2006 [38].

The semantic intention is then articulated in (sub) consciously selected conventions and techniques for the purpose of emphasizing aspects of the content. The intention is communicated in context to the audience by a set of commonly shared notions. We aim to link the knowledge of years of media science research to semantic video analysis, see for example Boggs and Petrie [7] and Bordwell and Thompson [9]. We use the authoring-driven process of video production as the leading principle for generic video indexing.

Viewing semantic video indexing from an authoring perspective has the advantage that the most successful existing video indexing methods may be combined in one architecture. We first consider the vast amount of work performed in developing detection methods for specialized concepts [2, 5, 16, 18, 33, 43, 41]. If we measure the success of these methods in terms of benchmark detection performance, Informedia [18, 41] stands out. They focus on combining techniques from computer vision, speech recognition, natural language understanding, and artificial intelligence into a video indexing and retrieval environment. This has resulted in a large set of isolated and specialized concept detectors [18]. We build our generic indexing approach in part on the outputs of their detectors, but we do not use them in isolation.

In comparison to specialized detection methods, generic semantic indexing is rare. We discuss three successful examples of generic semantic indexing approaches [3, 13, 39]. Firstly, Fan et al. [13] propose the *ClassView* framework. The framework combines hierarchical semantic indexing with hierarchical retrieval. At the lowest level, the framework supports indexing of shots into concepts based on a large set of low-level visual features. At the second level a Bayes classifier maps concepts to semantic clusters. By assigning shots to a hierarchy of concepts, the framework supports queries based on semantic and visual similarity. As the authors indicate, the framework will provide more meaningful results if it would support multimodal content analysis. We aim for generic semantic indexing also, but we include multimodal analysis from the beginning. Secondly, Amir et al. [3] propose a system for semantic indexing using a detection pipeline. The pipeline starts with feature extraction, followed by consecutive aggregations on features, multiple modalities, and concepts. The pipeline optimizes the result by rule-based post filtering. We interpret the success of the system by the fact that all modules in the pipeline select the best of multiple hypotheses, and the exhaustive use of machine learning. Moreover, the authors were among the first to recognize that semantic indexing profits substantially from context. We adopt and extend their ideas related to hypothesis selection, machine learning, and the use of context for semantic indexing. All of the above generic methods ignore the important influence of the video production style in the analysis process. In addition to content and context, we identify layout and capture in [39] as important factors for semantic indexing of produced video. We propose in [39] a generic framework for produced video indexing combining four sets of style detectors in an iterative semantic classifier. Results indicate that the method obtains high accuracy for rich semantic concepts, rich meaning that concepts share many similarities in their video production process. The framework is less suited for concepts that are not stylized. In the current paper, we generalize the idea of using style for semantic indexing.

We propose a generic approach for semantic indexing, we call the *semantic pathfinder*. It combines the most successful methods for semantic video indexing [3, 18, 39, 41] into an integrated architecture. The design principle is derived from the video production process, covering notions of content, style, and context. The architecture is built on several detectors, multimodal analysis, hypothesis selection, and machine learning. The semantic pathfinder combines analysis steps at increasing levels of abstraction, corresponding to well-known facts from the study of film and television production [7, 9]. Its virtue is its ability to learn the best path, from all explored analysis steps, on a per-concept basis. To demonstrate the effectiveness of the semantic pathfinder, the semantic indexing experiments are evaluated within a case study, using 85 hours of broadcast news video [30, 31].

### 8.1.1 Relation to Other Chapters
Chapter 2 discussed the important issue of multimedia management using metadata standards. An overview of basic machine learning techniques for recognizing patterns in multimedia content was presented in Chapter 3. Chapters 4, 5, and 7 presented an in-depth coverage of unimodal media analysis approaches on text, image, and speech respectively. In this chapter we present a unifying view to automatic extraction of metadata from multimedia sources, specifically focusing on multimodal video analysis in combination with machine learning.

### 8.1.2 Outline
The organization of this chapter is as follows. First, we introduce the broadcast news case study in Section 8.2. We highlight the data set used and elaborate on the lexicon of concepts that we index in a generic fashion. Our system architecture for semantic video indexing is presented in Section 8.3. We discuss its general machine learning architecture and its successive analysis steps. We present results in Section 8.4.

## 8.2 A Case Study on Broadcast News Video
### 8.2.1 Multimedia Archive
We focus on news video as a case study to study the problem of generic semantic indexing. The archive of choice is composed of 184 hours of ABC World News Tonight and CNN Headline News and is recorded in MPEG-1 format. The training data contains approximately 120 hours covering the period of January until June 1998. The 2004 test data contains the remaining 64 hours, covering the period of October until December 1998. Together with this video archive, CLIPS-IMAG [26] provided a camera shot segmentation.

We evaluate our semantic indexing approach on this data set to demonstrate the effectiveness of the semantic pathfinder for semantic access to multimedia archives.

### 8.2.2 Concept Lexicon

Before we elaborate on the video indexing architecture, we first define a lexicon $\Lambda_S$ of 32 semantic concepts. The lexicon is indicative for future efforts to detect as much as 1000 concepts [17]. At present, it serves as a non-trivial illustration of concept possibilities. The semantic concept lexicon consists of the following concepts:

$\Lambda_S = \{$ *airplane take off, American football, animal, baseball, basket scored, beach, bicycle, Bill Clinton, boat, building, car, cartoon, financial news anchor, golf, graphics, ice hockey, Madeleine Albright, news anchor, news subject monologue, outdoor, overlayed text, people, people walking, physical violence, road, soccer, sporting event, stock quotes, studio setting, train, vegetation, weather news* $\}$.

Instantiations of the concepts in the lexicon are portrayed in Figure 8.1. The lexicon contains both general concepts, like *building*, *boat*, and *outdoor*, as well as specific concepts such as *news subject monologue* and *people walking*. We aim to detect all 32 concepts with the proposed system architecture.

## 8.3 Semantic Pathfinder

The semantic pathfinder is composed of three analysis steps. It follows the reverse authoring process. Each analysis step in the path detects semantic concepts. In addition, one can exploit the output of an analysis step in the

**Fig. 8.1.** Instances of the 32 concepts in the lexicon, which we aim to detect with the semantic pathfinder.

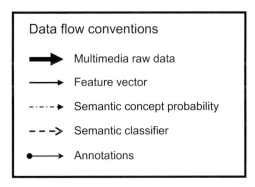

**Fig. 8.2.** Data flow conventions as used in this chapter. Different arrows indicate difference in data flows.

path as the input for the next one. The semantic pathfinder starts in the *content analysis step*. In this analysis step, we follow a data-driven approach of indexing semantics. The *style analysis step* is the second analysis step. Here we tackle the indexing problem by viewing a video from the perspective of production. This analysis step aids especially in indexing of rich semantics. Finally, to enhance the indexes further, in the *context analysis step*, we view semantics in context. One would expect that some concepts, like *vegetation*, have their emphasis on content where the style (of the camera work that is) and context (of concepts like *graphics*) do not add much. In contrast, more complex events, like *people walking*, profit from incremental adaptation of the analysis to the intention of the author. The virtue of the semantic pathfinder is its ability to find the best path of analysis steps on a per-concept basis.

The analysis steps in the semantic pathfinder exploit a common architecture, with a standardized input-output model, to allow for semantic integration. The conventions to describe the system architecture are indicated in Figure 8.2. An overview of the semantic pathfinder is given in Figure 8.3.

### 8.3.1 Analysis Step General Architecture

We perceive semantic indexing in video as a pattern recognition problem. We first need to segment a video. We opt for camera shots, indicated by $i$, following the standard in literature. Given pattern $x$, part of a shot, the aim is to detect a semantic concept $\omega$ from shot $i$ using probability $p(\omega|x_i)$. Each analysis step in the semantic pathfinder extracts $x_i$ from the data, and exploits a learning module to learn $p(\omega|x_i)$ for all $\omega$ in the semantic lexicon $\Lambda_S$. We exploit supervised learning to learn the relation between $\omega$ and $x_i$. The training data of the multimedia archive, together with labeled samples, are for learning classifiers. The other data, the test data, are set aside for testing. This division prevents overtraining of the classifier. The general architecture for supervised learning in each analysis step is illustrated in Figure 8.4.

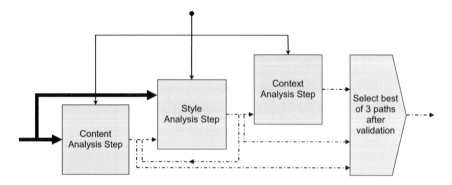

**Fig. 8.3.** The semantic pathfinder for one concept, using the conventions of Figure 8.2.

Supervised learning requires labeled examples. In part, we rely on the ground truth, which accompanies our news video data, provided by [20]. We remove the many errors from this manual annotation effort. It is extended to arrive at an incomplete, but reliable ground truth for all concepts in lexicon $\Lambda_S$. We split the training data a priori into a non-overlapping training set and validation set to prevent overfitting of classifiers in the semantic pathfinder. It should be noted that a reliable validation set would ideally require an as large as possible percentage of positively labeled examples, which is comparable to the training set. In practice this may be hard to achieve, however, as some

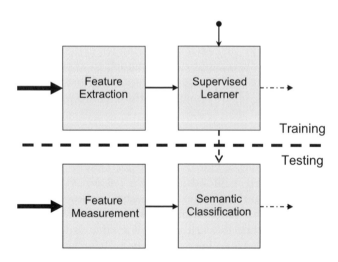

**Fig. 8.4.** General architecture of an analysis step in the semantic pathfinder, using the conventions of Figure 8.2.

concepts are sparse. The training set we use contains 85% of the training data, the validation set contains the remaining 15%. We summarize the percentage of positively annotated examples for each concept in training and validation set in Table 8.1.

We choose from a large variety of supervised machine learning approaches to obtain $p(\omega|x_i)$. For our purpose, the method of choice should be capable of handling video documents. To that end, ideally it must learn from a limited number of examples, it must handle unbalanced data, and it should account for unknown or erroneously detected data. In such heavy demands, the *Support Vector Machine* (SVM) framework [12, 40] has proven to be a solid choice [3, 35]. In this framework each pattern $x$ is represented in an $n$-dimensional space, spanned by extracted features. Within this feature space an optimal hyperplane is searched that separates it into two different categories, where the categories are represented by +1 and −1 respectively. The hyperplane has the following form: $\omega|(\mathbf{w} \cdot x + b)| \geq 1$, where $\mathbf{w}$ is a weight vector, and $b$ is a threshold. A hyperplane is considered optimal when the distance to the closest training examples is maximum for both categories. This distance is called the margin, see the example in Figure 8.5. The problem of finding the optimal hyperplane is a quadratic programming problem of the following form [40]:

$$\min_{\mathbf{w},\xi} \left\{ \frac{1}{2}\mathbf{w} \cdot \mathbf{w} + C\left( \sum_{i=1}^{l} \xi_i \right) \right\}, \tag{8.1}$$

under the following constraints:

$$\omega|(\mathbf{w} \cdot x_i + b)| \geq 1 - \xi_i, \quad \text{for } i = 1, 2, \dots, l , \tag{8.2}$$

where $C$ is a parameter that allows us to balance training error and model complexity, $l$ is the number of shots in the training set, and $\xi_i$ are slack variables that are introduced when the data is not perfectly separable. These slack variables are useful when analyzing multimedia, since results of individual feature detectors typically include a number of false positives and negatives. The usual SVM method provides a margin, $\gamma(x_i)$, in the result. We prefer Platt's conversion method [25] to achieve a posterior probability of the result. It is defined as:

$$p(\omega|x_i) = \frac{1}{1 + \exp(\alpha\gamma(x_i) + \beta)}, \tag{8.3}$$

where the parameters $\alpha$ and $\beta$ are maximum likelihood estimates based on training data. SVM classifiers thus trained for $\omega$, result in an estimate $p(\omega|x_i, \mathbf{q})$, where $\mathbf{q}$ are parameters of the SVM yet to be optimized.

The influence of the SVM parameters on concept detection is significant [22]. We obtain good parameter settings for a classifier, by using an iterative search on a large number of SVM parameter combinations. We measure average precision performance of all parameter combinations and select the combination that yields the best performance, $\mathbf{q}^*$. Here we use a three-fold cross-validation [19] to prevent overfitting of parameters. The result of

**Table 8.1.** Semantic concepts and the percentage of positively labeled examples used for the training set and the validation set.

| Semantic concept | Training (%) | Validation (%) |
|---|---|---|
| Weather news | 0.51 | 0.43 |
| Stock quotes | 0.26 | 0.30 |
| News anchor | 3.91 | 3.99 |
| Overlayed text | 0.26 | 0.17 |
| Basket scored | 1.07 | 0.97 |
| Graphics | 1.06 | 1.05 |
| Baseball | 0.74 | 0.66 |
| Sporting event | 2.27 | 2.44 |
| People walking | 1.92 | 1.97 |
| Financial news anchor | 0.35 | 0.35 |
| Ice hockey | 0.36 | 0.47 |
| Cartoon | 0.60 | 0.73 |
| Studio setting | 4.94 | 4.65 |
| Physical violence | 2.73 | 3.14 |
| Vegetation | 1.60 | 1.59 |
| Boat | 0.55 | 0.45 |
| Golf | 0.14 | 0.25 |
| People | 3.89 | 3.99 |
| American football | 0.05 | 0.10 |
| Outdoor | 7.52 | 8.60 |
| Car | 1.57 | 2.10 |
| Bill Clinton | 0.97 | 1.41 |
| News subject monologue | 3.84 | 3.96 |
| Animal | 1.35 | 1.34 |
| Road | 1.44 | 1.98 |
| Beach | 0.42 | 0.61 |
| Train | 0.21 | 0.36 |
| Madeleine Albright | 0.18 | 0.02 |
| Building | 4.95 | 4.81 |
| Airplane take off | 0.89 | 0.87 |
| Bicycle | 0.28 | 0.27 |
| Soccer | 0.06 | 0.09 |

the parameter search over $\mathbf{q}$ is the improved model $p(\omega|x_i, \mathbf{q}^*)$, contracted to $p^*(\omega|x_i)$.

This concludes the introduction of the general architecture of all analysis steps in the semantic pathfinder.

### 8.3.2 Content Analysis Step

We view video in the content analysis step from the data perspective. In general, three data streams or modalities exist in video, namely the auditory modality, the textual modality, and the visual one. As speech is often the most informative part of the auditory source, we focus on textual features

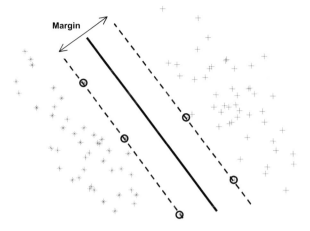

**Fig. 8.5.** Visual representation of the support vector machine framework. Here a two-dimensional feature space consisting of two categories is visualized. The solid bold line is chosen as optimal hyperplane because of the largest possible margin. The circled data points closest to the optimal hyperplane are called the support vectors.

obtained from transcribed speech and visual features. After modality specific data processing, we combine features in a multimodal representation. The data flow in the content analysis step is illustrated in Figure 8.6.

**Visual Analysis**

In the visual modality, we aim for segmentation of an image frame $f$ into regional visual concepts. Ideally, a segmentation method should result in a precise partitioning of $f$ according to the object boundaries, referred to as strong segmentation. However, weak segmentation, where $f$ is partitioned into internally homogenous regions within the boundaries of the object, is often the best one can hope for [32]. We obtain a weak segmentation based on a set of visual feature detectors. Prior to segmentation we remove the border of each frame. The basis of feature extraction in the visual modality is weak segmentation.

Invariance was identified in [32] as a crucial aspect of a visual feature detector, e.g., to design features which limit the influence of accidental recording circumstances. We use color invariant visual features [15] to arrive at weak segmentation. The invariance covers the photometric variation due to shadow and shading, and geometrical variation due to scale and orientation. This invariance is needed as the conditions under which semantic concepts appear in large multimedia archives may vary greatly.

The feature extraction procedure we adhere to, computes per pixel a number of invariant features in vector **u**. This vector then serves as the input for

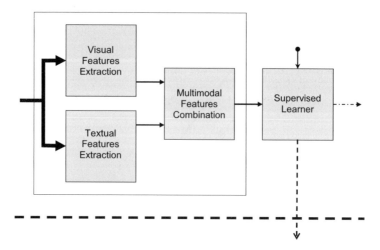

**Fig. 8.6.** Feature extraction and classification in the content analysis step, special case of Figure 8.4.

a multiclass SVM [12] that associates each pixel to one of the regional visual concepts defined in a visual concept lexicon $\Lambda_V$, using a labeled training set. Based on $\Lambda_S$, we define the following set of regional visual concepts:

$\Lambda_V = \{$ *colored clothing, concrete, fire, graphic blue, graphic purple, graphic yellow, grassland, greenery, indoor sport court, red carpet, sand, skin, sky, smoke, snow/ice, tuxedo, water body, wood* $\}$.

As we use invariant features, only a few examples per visual concept class are needed; in practice less than 10 per class. This pixel-wise classification results in the image vector $\mathbf{w}_f$, where $\mathbf{w}_f$ contains one component per regional visual concept, indicating the percentage of pixels found for this class. Thus, $\mathbf{w}_f$ is a weak segmentation of frame $f$ in terms of regional visual concepts from $\Lambda_V$, see Figure 8.7 for an example segmentation.

We use Gaussian color measurements to obtain $\mathbf{u}$ for weak segmentation [15]. We decorrelate $RGB$ color values by linear transformation to the opponent color system [15]:

$$\begin{bmatrix} E \\ E_\lambda \\ E_{\lambda\lambda} \end{bmatrix} = \begin{pmatrix} 0.06 & 0.63 & 0.27 \\ 0.3 & 0.04 & -0.35 \\ 0.34 & -0.6 & 0.17 \end{pmatrix} \begin{bmatrix} R \\ G \\ B \end{bmatrix}. \tag{8.4}$$

Smoothing these values with a Gaussian filter, $G(\sigma)$, suppresses acquisition and compression noise. Moreover, we extract texture features by applying Gaussian derivative filters. We vary the size of the Gaussian filters, $\sigma = \{1, 2, 3.5\}$, to obtain a color representation that is compatible with variations in the target object size (leaving out pixel position parameters):

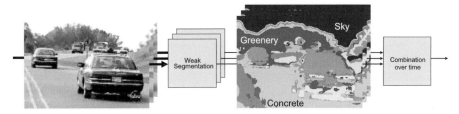

**Fig. 8.7.** Computation of the visual features, see Figure 8.6, is based on weak segmentation of an image frame into regional visual concepts. A combination over time is used to select one frame as representative for the shot.

$$\hat{E}_j(\sigma) = G_j(\sigma) * E, \quad \hat{E}_{\lambda j}(\sigma) = G_j(\sigma) * E_\lambda, \quad \hat{E}_{\lambda\lambda j}(\sigma) = G_j(\sigma) * E_{\lambda\lambda}, \quad (8.5)$$

where $j \in \{\varnothing, x, y\}$ indicates either spatial smoothing or spatial differentiation and that from now on the hat symbol $(\hat{\cdot})$ implies a dependence on $\sigma$. Normalizing each opponent color value by its intensity suppresses global intensity variations. This results in two chromaticity values per color pixel:

$$\hat{C}_\lambda = \frac{\hat{E}_\lambda}{\hat{E}}, \quad \hat{C}_{\lambda\lambda} = \frac{\hat{E}_{\lambda\lambda}}{\hat{E}}. \quad (8.6)$$

Furthermore, we obtain rotationally invariant features by taking Gaussian derivative filters and combining the responses into two chromatic gradients:

$$\hat{C}_{\lambda w} = \sqrt{\hat{C}_{\lambda x}^2 + \hat{C}_{\lambda y}^2}, \quad \hat{C}_{\lambda\lambda w} = \sqrt{\hat{C}_{\lambda\lambda x}^2 + \hat{C}_{\lambda\lambda y}^2}, \quad (8.7)$$

where $\hat{C}_{\lambda x}$, $\hat{C}_{\lambda y}$, $\hat{C}_{\lambda\lambda x}$, and $\hat{C}_{\lambda\lambda y}$ are defined as:

$$\hat{C}_{\lambda x} = \frac{\hat{E}_{\lambda x}\hat{E} - \hat{E}_\lambda \hat{E}_x}{\hat{E}^2}, \quad \hat{C}_{\lambda\lambda x} = \frac{\hat{E}_{\lambda\lambda x}\hat{E} - \hat{E}_{\lambda\lambda}\hat{E}_x}{\hat{E}^2},$$

$$\hat{C}_{\lambda y} = \frac{\hat{E}_{\lambda y}\hat{E} - \hat{E}_\lambda \hat{E}_y}{\hat{E}^2}, \quad \hat{C}_{\lambda\lambda y} = \frac{\hat{E}_{\lambda\lambda y}\hat{E} - \hat{E}_{\lambda\lambda}\hat{E}_y}{\hat{E}^2}. \quad (8.8)$$

The seven measurements computed in (8.5)–(8.7), and each calculated over three scales, yield a 21-dimensional invariant feature vector **u** per pixel.

Segmenting image frames into regional visual concepts at the granularity of a pixel is computationally intensive. We estimate that the processing of the entire case study data set would have taken around 250 days on the fastest sequential machine available to us. As a first reduction of the analysis load, we analyze 1 out of 15 frames only. For the remaining image processing effort we apply the Parallel-Horus software architecture [29]. This architecture, consisting of a large collection of low-level image processing primitives, allows the programmer to write sequential applications with efficient parallel execution on commonly available commodity clusters. Application of Parallel-Horus, in combination with a distributed cluster consisting of 200 dual 1-GHz Pentium-III CPUs [6], reduced the processing time to less than 60 hours [29].

The features over time are combined into one vector for the shot $i$. Averaging over individual frames is not a good choice, as the visual representation should remain intact. Instead, we opt for a selection of the most representative frame or visual vector. To decide which $f$ is the most representative for $i$, weak segmented image $\mathbf{w}_f$ is the input for an SVM that computes a probability $p^*(\omega|\mathbf{w}_f)$. We select $\mathbf{w}_f$ that maximizes the probability for a concept from $\Lambda_S$ within $i$, given as:

$$\mathbf{v}_i = \arg \max_{f \in f_i} p^*(\omega|\mathbf{w}_f). \qquad (8.9)$$

The visual vector $\mathbf{v}_i$, containing the best weak segmentation, is the final result of the visual analysis.

**Textual Analysis**

In the textual modality, we aim to learn the association between uttered speech and semantic concepts. A detection system transcribes the speech into text. From the text we remove the frequently occurring stopwords. After stopword removal, we are ready to learn semantics.

To learn the relation between uttered speech and concepts, we connect words to shots. We make this connection within the temporal boundaries of a shot. We derive a lexicon of uttered words that co-occur with $\omega$ using the shot-based annotations of the training data. For each concept $\omega$, we learn a separate lexicon, $\Lambda_T^\omega$, as this uttered word lexicon is specific for that concept. We modify the procedure for Person $X$ concepts, i.e., *Madeleine Albright* and *Bill Clinton*, to optimize results. In broadcast news, a news anchor or reporter mentions names or other indicative words just before or after a person is visible. To account for this observation, we stretch the shot boundaries with five seconds on each side for Person $X$ concepts. For these concepts, this procedure assures that the textual feature analysis considers even more textual content. For feature extraction we compare the text associated with each shot with $\Lambda_T^\omega$. This comparison yields a text vector $\mathbf{t}_i$ for shot $i$, which contains the histogram of the words in association with $\omega$.

**Multimodal Analysis and Classification**

The result of the content analysis step is a multimodal vector $\mathbf{m}_i$ that integrates all unimodal results. We concatenate the visual vector $\mathbf{v}_i$ with the text vector $\mathbf{t}_i$, to obtain $\mathbf{m}_i$. After this modality fusion, $\mathbf{m}_i$ serves as the input for the supervised learning module. To optimize parameter settings, we use three-fold cross-validation on the training set. The content analysis step associates probability $p^*(\omega|\mathbf{m}_i)$ with a shot $i$, for all $\omega$ in $\Lambda_S$.

**8.3.3 Style Analysis Step**

In the style analysis step we conceive of a video from the production perspective. Based on the four roles involved in the video production process [39, 34], this step analyzes a video by four related style detectors. Layout detectors analyze the role of the editor. Content detectors analyze the role of production design. Capture detectors analyze the role of the production recording unit. Finally, context detectors analyze the role of the preproduction team, see Figure 8.8. Note that in contrast to the content analysis step, where we learn specific content features from a data set, content features in the style analysis step are generic and independent of the data set.

**Style Analysis**
We develop detectors for all four production roles as feature extraction in the style analysis step. Each style detector uses an existing software implementation as a basis. The output of such a base detector is then aggregated and synchronized to a camera shot. We categorize the resulting production-derived features based on experimentally obtained thresholds. Together, these three components define a style detector. We refer to our previous work for specific implementation details of the detectors [34, Appendix A],[39]. We have chosen to convert the output of all style detectors to an ordinal scale, as this allows for easy fusion.

For the layout $\mathcal{L}$ the length of a camera shot is used as a feature, as this is known to be an informative descriptor for genre [36]. Overlayed text is another informative descriptor. Its presence is detected by a text localization algorithm [27]. To segment the auditory layout, periods of speech and silence are detected based on an automatic speech recognition system [14]. We obtain a voice-over detector by combining the speech segmentation with the camera shot segmentation [39]. The set of layout features is thus given by: $\mathcal{L} = \{$ *shot length, overlayed text, silence, voice-over* $\}$.

As concerns the content $\mathcal{C}$, a frontal face detector [28] is applied to detect people. We count the number of faces, and for each face its location is derived [39]. Apart from faces, we also detect the presence of cars [28]. In addition, we measure the average amount of object motion in a camera shot [35]. Based on speaker identification [14] we identify each of the three most frequent speakers. The camera shot is checked for the presence on the basis of speech from one of the three [39]. The length of text strings recognized by Video Optical Character Recognition [27] is used as a feature [39]. In addition, the strings are used as input for a named entity recognizer [41]. On the transcribed text obtained by the LIMSI automatic speech recognition system [14], we also apply named entity recognition. The set of content features is thus given by: $\mathcal{C} =\{$ *faces, face location, cars, object motion, frequent speaker, overlayed text length, video text named entity, voice named entity* $\}$.

For capture $\mathcal{T}$, we compute the camera distance from the size of detected faces [28, 39]. It is undefined when no face is detected. In addition to camera distance, several types of camera work are detected [4], e.g., pan, tilt, zoom, and so on. Finally, for capture we also estimate the amount of camera motion [4]. The set of capture features is thus given by: $\mathcal{T} = \{$ *camera distance, camera work, camera motion* $\}$.

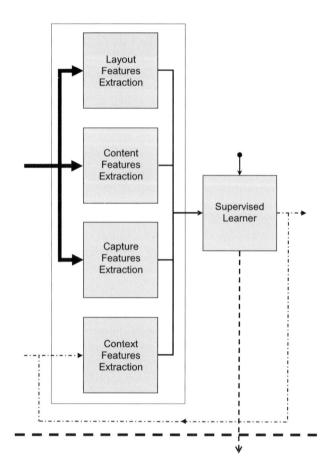

**Fig. 8.8.** Feature extraction and classification in the style analysis step, special case of Figure 8.4.

The context $\mathcal{S}$ serves to enhance or reduce the correlation between semantic concepts. Detection of *vegetation* can aid in the detection of a *forest* for example. Likewise, the co-occurrence of a *space shuttle* and a *bicycle* in one shot is improbable. As the performance of semantic concept detectors is unknown and likely to vary between concepts, we exploit iteration to add them to the context. The rationale here is to add concepts that are relatively easy to detect first. They aid in detection performance by increasing the number of true positives or reducing the number of false positives. As initial concept we detect news reporters. We recognize news reporters by edit distance matching of strings, obtained from the transcript and video text, with a database of names of CNN and ABC affiliates [39]. The other concepts that are added to the context stem from $\Lambda_S$. To prevent bias from domain knowledge, we use the performance on the validation set of all concepts from $\Lambda_S$ in the content analysis step as the ordering for the context. For this ordering we again refer to Table 8.1. To assign detection results for the first and least difficult concept, $\omega_1 = weather\ news$, we rank all shot results on $p_i^*(\omega_1|\mathbf{m}_i)$. This ranking is then exploited to categorize results for $\omega_1$ into one of five levels. The basic set of context features is thus given by: $\mathcal{S} = \{news\ reporter,\ content\ analysis\ step\ \omega_1\}$.

The concatenation of $\{\mathcal{L}, \mathcal{C}, \mathcal{T}, \mathcal{S}\}$ for shot $i$ yields the style vector $\mathbf{s}_i$. This vector forms the input for an iterative classifier that trains a style model for each concept in lexicon $\Lambda_S$.

**Iterative Style Classification**

We start from an ordering of concepts in the context, as defined above. The iteration of the classifier begins with concept $\omega_1$. After concatenation with the other style features this yields $\mathbf{s}_{i,1}$ the first style vector of the first iteration. $\mathbf{s}_{i,1}$ contains the combined results of the content analysis step and the style analysis step. We classify $\omega_1$ again based on $\mathbf{s}_{i,1}$. This yields the a posterior probability $p^*(\omega_1|\mathbf{s}_{i,1})$. When $p^*(\omega|\mathbf{s}_i) \geq \delta$ the concept $\omega_1$ is considered present in the style representation, else it is considered absent. The threshold $\delta$ is set a priori at a fixed value of 0.5. In this process the classifier replaces the feature for concept $\omega_1$, from the content analysis step, by the new feature $\omega_1^+$. The style analysis step adds more aspects of the author influence to the results obtained with the content analysis step. In the next iteration of the classification procedure, the classifier adds $\omega_2 = stock\ quotes$ from the content analysis step to the context. This yields $\mathbf{s}_{i,2}$. As explained above, the classifier replaces the $\omega_2$ feature from the content analysis step by the styled version $\omega_2^+$ based on $p^*(\omega_2|\mathbf{s}_{i,2})$. This iterative process is repeated for all $\omega$ in lexicon $\Lambda_S$.

We classify all $\omega$ in $\Lambda_S$ again in the style analysis step. As the result of the content analysis step is only one of the many features in our style vector representation in the style analysis step, we also use three-fold cross-validation on the training set to optimize parameter settings in this analysis step. We use the resulting probability as output for concept detection in the style analysis step. In addition, it forms the input for the next analysis step in our semantic pathfinder.

### 8.3.4 Context Analysis Step

The context analysis step adds context to our interpretation of the video. Our ultimate aim is the reconstruction of the author's intent by considering detected concepts in context.

**Semantic Analysis**

The style analysis step yields a probability for each shot $i$ and all concepts $\omega$ in $\Lambda_S$. The probability indicates whether a concept is present. We use the 32 concept scores as semantic features. We fuse them into context vector $c_i$, see Figure 8.9.

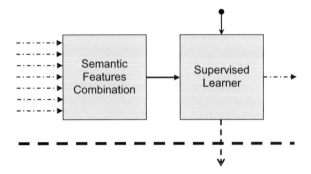

**Fig. 8.9.** Feature extraction and classification in the context analysis step, special case of Figure 8.4.

From $c_i$ we learn relations between concepts automatically. To that end, $c_i$ serves as the input for a supervised learning module, which associates a contextual probability $p^*(\omega|c_i)$ to a shot $i$ for all $\omega$ in $\Lambda_S$. To optimize parameter settings, we use three-fold cross-validation on the previously unused data from the validation set.

The output of the context analysis step is also the output of the entire semantic pathfinder on video documents. On the way we have included in the semantic pathfinder, the results of the analysis on raw data, facts derived from production by the use of style features, and a context perspective of the author's intent by using semantic features. For each concept we obtain a probability based on content, style, and context. We select from the three possibilities the one that maximizes average precision based on validation set performance. The semantic pathfinder provides us with the opportunity to decide whether a one-shot analysis step is best for the concept only concentrating on content, or a two-analysis step classifier increasing discriminatory power by adding production style to content, or that a concept profits most from a consecutive analysis path using content, style, and context.

## 8.4 Indexing Results on 32 Semantic Concepts

We evaluated detection results for all 32 concepts in each analysis step. Given the already enormous size of the data sets and the large amounts of annotation – yet limited in terms of completeness – we have performed one pass for 32 concepts through the entire semantic pathfinder. We report the *precision at 100*, which indicates the number of correct shots within the first 100 results in Table 8.2.

**Table 8.2.** Test set precision at 100 after the three steps, for a lexicon of 32 concepts. The best result is given in bold. The corresponding path is selected in the semantic pathfinder.

| Semantic concept | Content analysis step | Style analysis step | Context analysis step | Semantic pathfinder |
|---|---|---|---|---|
| News subject monologue | 0.55 | **1.00** | 1.00 | 1.00 |
| Weather news | **1.00** | 1.00 | 1.00 | 1.00 |
| News anchor | 0.98 | 0.98 | **0.99** | 0.99 |
| Overlayed text | 0.84 | **0.99** | 0.93 | 0.99 |
| Sporting event | 0.77 | **0.98** | 0.93 | 0.98 |
| Studio setting | 0.95 | 0.96 | **0.98** | 0.98 |
| Graphics | 0.92 | 0.90 | **0.91** | 0.91 |
| People | 0.73 | 0.78 | **0.91** | 0.91 |
| Outdoor | 0.62 | 0.83 | **0.90** | 0.90 |
| Stock quotes | **0.89** | 0.77 | 0.77 | 0.89 |
| People walking | 0.65 | 0.72 | **0.83** | 0.83 |
| Car | 0.63 | 0.81 | **0.75** | 0.75 |
| Cartoon | 0.71 | 0.69 | **0.75** | 0.75 |
| Vegetation | **0.72** | 0.64 | 0.70 | 0.72 |
| Ice hockey | **0.71** | 0.68 | 0.60 | 0.71 |
| Financial news anchor | 0.40 | **0.70** | 0.71 | 0.70 |
| Baseball | **0.54** | 0.43 | 0.47 | 0.54 |
| Building | **0.53** | 0.46 | 0.43 | 0.53 |
| Road | 0.43 | 0.53 | **0.51** | 0.51 |
| American football | **0.46** | 0.18 | 0.17 | 0.46 |
| Boat | 0.42 | 0.38 | **0.37** | 0.37 |
| Physical violence | 0.17 | 0.25 | **0.31** | 0.31 |
| Basket scored | 0.24 | 0.21 | **0.30** | 0.30 |
| Animal | 0.37 | 0.26 | **0.26** | 0.26 |
| Bill Clinton | **0.26** | 0.35 | 0.37 | 0.26 |
| Golf | **0.24** | 0.19 | 0.06 | 0.24 |
| Beach | 0.13 | 0.12 | **0.12** | 0.12 |
| Madeleine Albright | **0.12** | 0.05 | 0.04 | 0.12 |
| Airplane take off | 0.10 | 0.08 | **0.08** | 0.08 |
| Bicycle | 0.09 | **0.08** | 0.07 | 0.08 |
| Train | **0.07** | 0.07 | 0.03 | 0.07 |
| Soccer | **0.01** | 0.01 | 0.00 | 0.01 |
| Mean | 0.51 | 0.53 | 0.54 | 0.57 |

We observe from the results that the learned best path (printed in bold) indeed varies over the concepts. The virtue of the semantic pathfinder is demonstrated by the fact that for 12 concepts, the learning phase indicates it is best to concentrate on content only. For five concepts, the semantic pathfinder demonstrates that a two-step path is best (where in 15 cases addition of style features has a marginal positive or negative effect). For 15 concepts, the context analysis step obtains a better result. Context aids substantially in the

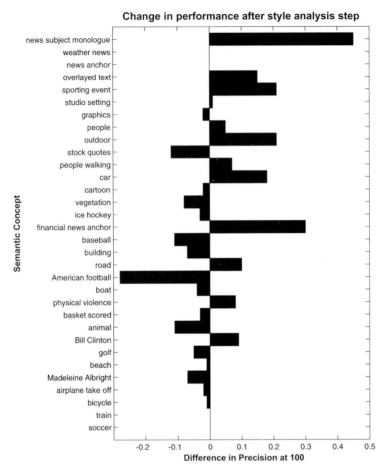

**Fig. 8.10.** Influence of the style analysis step on precision at 100 performance for a lexicon of 32 semantic concepts. Note a considerable decrease (American football) or increase (news subject monologue) in performance when adding production style information.

performance for five concepts. As an aside we note that the precision at 100, when averaged over all concepts, steadily increases from 0.51 to 0.57 while traversing the different semantic analysis paths.

The results demonstrate the virtue of the semantic pathfinder. Concepts are divided by the analysis step after which they achieve best performance. Some concepts are just content, style does not affect them. In such cases as *American football* there is style-wise too much confusion with other sports to add new value in the path. Shots containing *stock quotes* suffer from a similar problem. Here false positives contain many stylistically similar results like graphical representations of survey and election results. For complex con-

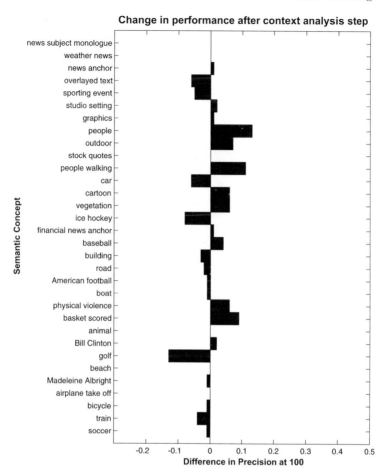

**Fig. 8.11.** Influence of the context analysis step on precision at 100 performance for a lexicon of 32 semantic concepts. Note a considerable decrease (golf) or increase (people) in performance when adding context information.

cepts, analysis based on content and style is not enough. They require the use of context. The context analysis step is especially good in detecting named events, like *people walking, physical violence,* and *basket scored.* The results offer us the possibility to categorize concepts according to the analysis step of the semantic pathfinder that yields the best performance.

The content analysis step seems to work particularly well for semantic concepts that have a small intra-class variability of content: *weather news* and *news anchor* for example. In addition, this analysis step aids in detection of accidental content like *building, vegetation, bicycle,* and *train.* However, for some of those concepts, e.g., *bicycle* and *train,* the performance is still disappointing. Another observation is that when one aims to distinguish subgenres, e.g., *ice hockey, baseball,* and *American football,* the content analysis step is the best choice.

After the style analysis step, we obtain an increase in performance for 12 concepts, see Figure 8.10. Especially when the concepts are semantically rich: e.g., *news subject monologue, financial news anchor,* and *sporting event,* the style helps. As expected, index results in the style analysis step improve on the content analysis step when style is a distinguishing property of the concept and degrade the result when similarity in style exists between different concepts.

Results after the context analysis step in Figure 8.11 show that performance increases for 13 concepts. The largest positive performance difference between the context analysis step and the style analysis step occurs for concept *people.* Concept *people* profits from sport-related concepts like *baseball, basket scored, American football, ice hockey,* and *sporting event.* In contrast, *golf* suffers from detection of *outdoor* and *vegetation.* When we detect *golf,* these concepts are also present frequently. The inverse, however, is not necessarily the case, i.e., when we detect *outdoor* it is not necessarily on a golf course. Based on these observations we conclude that, apart from named events, detection results of the context analysis step are similar to those of the style analysis step. Index results improve based on presence of semantically related concepts, but the context analysis step is unable to capture the semantic structure between concepts and for some concepts, this is leading to a drop in performance.

The above results show that the semantic pathfinder facilitates generic video indexing. In addition, the semantic pathfinder provides the foundation of a technique taxonomy for solving semantic concept detection tasks. The fact that subgenres like *ice hockey, golf,* and *American football* behave similarly indicate the predictive value of the pathfinder for other subgenres. The same holds for semantically rich concepts like *news subject monologue, financial news anchor,* and *sporting event.* We showed that for named events, such as *basket scored, physical violence,* and *people walking,* one should apply a detector that is based on the entire semantic pathfinder. The significance of the semantic pathfinder is its generalizing power combined with the fact that addition of new information in the analysis can be considered by concept type.

### 8.4.1 Usage Scenarios

The results from the semantic pathfinder facilitate the development of various applications. The lexicon of 32 semantic concepts allows for querying a video archive by concept. Elswhere [37] we combined into the *MediaMill* semantic video search engine query-by-concept, query-by-keyword, query-by-example, and interactive filtering, see Figure 8.12. In addition to interactive search, the set of indexes is also applicable in a personalized retrieval setting. A feasible scenario is that users with a specific interest in sports are provided with personalized summaries when and where they need it. The sketched applications provide a semantic access to multimedia archives.

**Fig. 8.12.** Interface of the MediaMill semantic video search engine. The system allows for interactive query-by-concept using 32 concepts. In addition, it facilitates query-by-similarity in the form of query-by-keyword, and query-by-example. Results are presented in a storyboard.

## 8.5 Summary

In this chapter, we present the semantic pathfinder for semantic access to multimedia archives. The semantic pathfinder is a generic approach for video indexing. It is based on the observation that produced video is the result of an authoring process. The semantic pathfinder exploits the authoring metaphor in an effort to bridge the semantic gap. The architecture is built on a variety of detector types, multimodal analysis, hypothesis selection, and machine learning. The semantic pathfinder selects the best path through content analysis, style analysis, and context analysis. After machine learning it appears that the analysis is completed after content analysis only when concepts share many similarities in their multimodal content. It appears also that the semantic path runs up to style analysis when the professional habits of television are evident to the concept. Finally, it exploits a path based on content, style, and context for concepts that are primarily intentional, see Table 8.2 and Figures 8.10 and 8.11.

Experiments with a lexicon of 32 semantic concepts demonstrate that the semantic pathfinder allows for generic video indexing, while confirming the value of the authoring metaphor in indexing. In addition, the results over the various analysis steps indicate that a technique taxonomy exists for solving semantic concept detection tasks; depending on whether content, style, or context is most suited for indexing. For some concepts the precision at 100 performance is still quite low. For selecting illustrative footage, this may already be sufficient. This is not yet so for tasks that require accurate retrieval.

However, the trend in results over the past years indicates that automated search in video archives lures at the horizon.

## 8.6 Further Reading

Basic techniques for video indexing are discussed in the review papers by Bolle et al. [8] and Brunelli et al. [10]. Smeulders et al. [32] present an in depth overview of content-based image retrieval. Where these papers emphasize the visual analysis in video indexing, the review paper of Wang et al. [42] stresses audio analysis. For an overview of text analysis methods we refer to the book by Manning and Schütze [21]. A broad introduction to multimodal semantic video indexing literature can be found in our previous work [36] and the work of Naphade and Huang [23].

Statistical pattern recognition is an indispensable tool for anyone working in semantic video indexing. An excellent introduction and overview is in the paper by Jain et al. [19]. At present, the support vector machine framework is the classifier of choice in the most successful semantic video indexing systems [1, 3, 38] An in depth theoretical discussion on the support vector machine is in the book by its inventor Vapnik [40]. A more accessible tutorial is the paper by Burges [11].

For recent updates on the state-of-the-art in the field we refer to the proceedings of the yearly *ACM Multimedia Conference*, the *International Conference on Image and Video Retrieval*, and the *IEEE International Conference on Multimedia & Expo*. The most important journals in the field are *IEEE Transactions on Pattern Analysis and Machine Intelligence*, *IEEE Transactions on Multimedia*, *IEEE Multimedia*, and *ACM Transactions on Multimedia Computing, Communications and Applications*.

We have deliberately left out the NIST TRECVID video retrieval benchmark in our discussion on semantic video indexing, as this benchmark is the topic of Chapter 13. The benchmark aims to promote progress in video retrieval via open, metrics-based evaluation [30, 31]. Tasks include camera shot segmentation, story segmentation, semantic concept detection, and several search tasks. Because of its widespread acceptance in the field, resulting in large participation of teams from both academic and corporate research labs worldwide, the benchmark can be regarded as the *de facto* standard to evaluate performance of semantic video indexing and retrieval research. The most recent developments in semantic video indexing are accessible via the electronic proceedings of the TREC workshop on Video Retrieval Evaluation [24].

## References

1. W. H. Adams, G. Iyengar, C.-Y. Lin, M.R. Naphade, C. Neti, H.J. Nock, and J.R. Smith. Semantic indexing of multimedia content using visual, audio, and text cues. *EURASIP Journal on Applied Signal Processing*, (2):170–185, 2003.

2. A.A. Alatan, A.N. Akansu, and W. Wolf. Multimodal dialogue scene detection using hidden Markov models for content-based multimedia indexing. *Multimedia Tools Applicat.*, 14(2):137–151, 2001.
3. A. Amir, M. Berg, S.-F. Chang, W. Hsu, G. Iyengar, C.-Y. Lin, M.R. Naphade, A.P. Natsev, C. Neti, H.J. Nock, J.R. Smith, B.L. Tseng, Y. Wu, and D. Zhang. IBM research TRECVID-2003 video retrieval system. In *Proc. TRECVID Workshop*, NIST Special Publication, Gaithersburg, USA, 2003.
4. J. Baan, A. van Ballegooij, J.-M. Geusebroek, D. Hiemstra, J. den Hartog, J. List, C. Snoek, I. Patras, S. Raaijmakers, L. Todoran, J. Vendrig, A. de Vries, T. Westerveld, and M. Worring. Lazy users and automatic video retrieval tools in (the) lowlands. In E.M. Voorhees and D.K. Harman, editors, *Proc. 10th Text REtrieval Conference*, volume 500-250 of *NIST Special Publication*, Gaithersburg, USA, 2001.
5. N. Babaguchi, Y. Kawai, and T. Kitahashi. Event based indexing of broadcasted sports video by intermodal collaboration. *IEEE Trans. Multimedia*, 4(1):68–75, 2002.
6. H.E. Bal et al. The distributed ASCI supercomputer project. *Operating Syst. Review*, 34(4):76–96, 2000.
7. J.M. Boggs and D.W. Petrie. *The Art of Watching Films*. Mayfield Publishing Company, Mountain View, USA, 5th edition, 2000.
8. R.M. Bolle, B.-L. Yeo, and M.M. Yeung. Video query: Research directions. *IBM Journal of Research and Development*, 42(2):233–252, 1998.
9. D. Bordwell and K. Thompson. *Film Art: An Introduction*. McGraw-Hill, New York, USA, 5th edition, 1997.
10. R. Brunelli, O. Mich, and C.M. Modena. A survey on the automatic indexing of video data. *J. Visual Commun. Image Representation*, 10(2):78–112, 1999.
11. C.J.C. Burges. A tutorial on support vector machines for pattern recognition. *Data Mining and Knowledge Discovery*, 2(2):121–167, 1998.
12. C.-C. Chang and C.-J. Lin. *LIBSVM: a library for Support Vector Machines*, 2001. http://www.csie.ntu.edu.tw/~cjlin/libsvm/.
13. J. Fan, A.K. Elmagarmid, X. Zhu, W.G. Aref, and L. Wu. *ClassView*: hierarchical video shot classification, indexing, and accessing. *IEEE Trans. Multimedia*, 6(1):70–86, 2004.
14. J.L. Gauvain, L. Lamel, and G. Adda. The LIMSI broadcast news transcription system. *Speech Commun.*, 37(1–2):89–108, 2002.
15. J.M. Geusebroek, R. van den Boomgaard, A.W.M. Smeulders, and H. Geerts. Color invariance. *IEEE Trans. Pattern Anal. Machine Intell.*, 23(12):1338–1350, 2001.
16. N. Haering, R. Qian, and I. Sezan. A semantic event-detection approach and its application to detecting hunts in wildlife video. *IEEE Trans. Circuits Syst. Video Technol.*, 10(6):857–868, 2000.
17. A.G. Hauptmann. Towards a large scale concept ontology for broadcast video. In *CIVR*, volume 3115 of *LNCS*, pages 674–675. Springer-Verlag, 2004.
18. A.G. Hauptmann, R.V. Baron, M.-Y. Chen, M. Christel, P. Duygulu, C. Huang, R. Jin, W.-H.Lin, T. Ng, N. Moraveji, N. Papernick, C.G.M. Snoek, G. Tzanetakis, J. Yang, R. Yang, and H.D. Wactlar. Informedia at TRECVID 2003: Analyzing and searching broadcast news video. In *Proc. TRECVID Workshop*, NIST Special Publication, Gaithersburg, USA, 2003.
19. A.K. Jain, R.P.W. Duin, and J. Mao. Statistical pattern recognition: A review. *IEEE Trans. Pattern Anal. Machine Intell.*, 22(1):4–37, 2000.

20. C.-Y. Lin, B.L. Tseng, and J.R. Smith. Video collaborative annotation forum: Establishing ground-truth labels on large multimedia datasets. In *Proc. TRECVID Workshop*, NIST Special Publication, Gaithersburg, USA, 2003.

21. C.D. Manning and H. Schütze. *Foundations of Statistical Natural Language Processing*. The MIT Press, Cambridge, USA, 1999.

22. M.R. Naphade. On supervision and statistical learning for semantic multimedia analysis. *J. Visual Commun. Image Representation*, 15(3):348–369, 2004.

23. M.R. Naphade and T.S. Huang. Extracting semantics from audiovisual content: The final frontier in multimedia retrieval. *IEEE Trans. Neural Networks*, 13(4):793–810, 2002.

24. NIST. TREC Video Retrieval Evaluation. `http://www-nlpir.nist.gov/projects/trecvid/`.

25. J.C. Platt. Probabilities for SV machines. In A.J. Smola, P.L. Bartlett, B. Schölkopf, and D. Schuurmans, editors, *Advances in Large Margin Classifiers*, pages 61–74. MIT Press, 2000.

26. G.M. Quénot, D. Moraru, L. Besacier, and P. Mulhem. CLIPS at TREC-11: Experiments in video retrieval. In E.M. Voorhees and L.P. Buckland, editors, *Proc. 11th Text REtrieval Conference*, volume 500-251 of *NIST Special Publication*, Gaithersburg, USA, 2002.

27. T. Sato, T. Kanade, E.K. Hughes, M.A. Smith, and S. Satoh. Video OCR: Indexing digital news libraries by recognition of superimposed caption. *Multimedia Syst.*, 7(5):385–395, 1999.

28. H. Schneiderman and T. Kanade. Object detection using the statistics of parts. *Int'l J. Comput. Vision*, 56(3):151–177, 2004.

29. F.J. Seinstra, C.G.M. Snoek, D. Koelma, J.M. Geusebroek, and M. Worring. User transparent parallel processing of the 2004 NIST TRECVID data set. In Proceedings of the 19th IEEE International Parallel and Distributed Processing Symposium (IPDPS'05), pages 90–98, Denver, USA, 2005.

30. A.F. Smeaton, W. Kraaij, and P. Over. The TREC VIDeo retrieval evaluation (TRECVID): A case study and status report. In *Proc. RIAO 2004*, Avignon, France, 2004.

31. A.F. Smeaton, P. Over, and W. Kraaij. TRECVID: Evaluating the effectiveness of information retrieval tasks on digital video. In *Proceedings of the ACM MM'04 (Multimedia)*, pages 652–655, New York, USA, 2004.

32. A.W.M. Smeulders, M. Worring, S. Santini, A. Gupta, and R. Jain. Content based image retrieval at the end of the early years. *IEEE Trans. Pattern Anal. Machine Intell.*, 22(12):1349–1380, 2000.

33. J.R. Smith and S.-F. Chang. Visually searching the Web for content. *IEEE Multimedia*, 4(3):12–20, 1997.

34. C.G.M. Snoek. *The Authoring Metaphor to Machine Understanding of Multimedia*. PhD thesis, University of Amsterdam, 2005.

35. C.G.M. Snoek and M. Worring. Multimedia event-based video indexing using time intervals. *IEEE Trans. Multimedia*, 7(4):638–647, 2005.

36. C.G.M. Snoek and M. Worring. Multimodal video indexing: A review of the state-of-the-art. *Multimedia Tools Applicat.*, 25(1):5–35, 2005.

37. C.G.M. Snoek, M. Worring, J. van Gemert, J.M. Geusebroek, D. Koelma, G.P. Nguyen, O. de Rooij, and F. Seinstra. MediaMill: Exploring news video archives based on learned semantics. In *Proceedings of the ACM International Conference on Multimedia*, pages 225–226, Singapore, November 2005.

38. C.G.M. Snoek, M. Worring, J.M. Geusebroek, D.C. Koelma, F.J. Seinstra, and A.W.M. Smeulders. The semantic pathfinder: Using an authoring metaphor for generic multimedia indexing. *IEEE Trans. Pattern Anal. Machine Intell.*, 28(10):1678–1689, 2006.

39. C.G.M. Snoek, M. Worring, and A.G. Hauptmann. Learning rich semantics from news video archives by style analysis. *ACM Trans. Multimedia Computing, Comm. Applications*, 2(2):91–108, 2006.

40. V.N. Vapnik. *The Nature of Statistical Learning Theory.* Springer-Verlag, New York, USA, 2nd edition, 2000.

41. H.D. Wactlar, M.G. Christel, Y. Gong, and A.G. Hauptmann. Lessons learned from building a terabyte digital video library. *IEEE Computer*, 32(2):66–73, 1999.

42. Y. Wang, Z. Liu, and J. Huang. Multimedia content analysis using both audio and visual clues. *IEEE Signal Processing Magazine*, 17(6):12–36, 2000.

43. H.-J. Zhang, S.Y. Tan, S.W. Smoliar, and Y. Gong. Automatic parsing and indexing of news video. *Multimedia Syst.*, 2(6):256–266, 1995.

# A Spatio-Temporal and a Probabilistic Approach for Video Retrieval

Milan Petković[1], Willem Jonker[1,2], and Henk Blanken[2]

[1] Philips Research
[2] University of Twente

## 9.1 Introduction

In this chapter we address two approaches to extract high-level concepts from video footage and show the integrated use of both. We also describe an experiment used for validation.

The spatio-temporal approach deals with space and time. Reasoning about space and time is a major field of interest in many areas, for instance in navigation of autonomous mobile robots. Its overall goal is to increase the understanding of reasoning processes that apply to moving objects in space. Spatio-temporal formalization is also used to infer semantics from low-level video features. The formalization presented in this chapter has been validated in at least three case studies. A medical case deals with modeling of walking persons defining events like "walking on toes", "wide walking", etc. In the sports domain there are two case studies dealing with soccer and tennis respectively. The soccer case describes formalizations for events such as "player has the ball", "pass", "scoring a goal", etc. Elsewhere we have described the soccer and the medical case [11].

Here we concentrate on the tennis case. We encounter high-level objects ("player", "ball", "net") together with spatial ("covered by", "east of") and temporal relations ("before", "during"). Using these objects and relations, we formalize and derive events like "net playing" and "rally". We may apply this approach to even more complex events, like strokes ("forehand", "backhand", and so on). Unfortunately, we then run into accuracy problems, as shown by Sudhir et al. [17], for example.

So, how to recognize strokes? Some recent research shows that it is possible to recognize human activities from their binary representations, see for example [14]. Moreover, we notice that probabilistic methods often exploit automatic learning capabilities to derive knowledge. For example, Naphade et al. [9] use hierarchical hidden Markov models to extract events like explosions. This motivates us to train and use hidden Markov models. In order to achieve this goal we start to extract the player from the background and to derive informative features from the player's binary representation. So, in this chapter we explain the use of hidden Markov models to recognize strokes and we describe some experiments to validate the approach.

To experiment with, we have built a prototype system with a general architecture that allows the development of video applications from several areas. Experiments reported in this chapter are based on video footage taken from ordinary TV broadcast tennis videos with different players at different tennis tournaments, like the Australian Open, Swisscom Challenge, Vienna Open, etc. Objects and events are high-level concepts (metadata) that are stored within a database management system. We give an example of a query which requires exploitation of both approaches.

### 9.1.1 Relation to Other Chapters

In this chapter we deal with video. Some of the image processing techniques described in Chapter 5, are used here. To capture high-level concepts we also follow a probabilistic approach. The approach is based on hidden Markov models, which are explained rather extensively in Chapter 3. Text processing is applied to frames to detect names of players. In Chapter 10 text processing is discussed in more detail.

### 9.1.2 Outline

The remainder of this chapter is organized as follows. Next three sections investigate the practical exploitation of spatio-temporal reasoning and hidden Markov models in a real situation using ordinary TV broadcasts of tennis matches. Section 9.2 details some necessary video analysis techniques regarding shot detection, low-level features, and object detection and tracking. Section 9.3 is dedicated to the detection and recognition of video events using spatio-temporal formalizations, while in Section 9.4, we introduce hidden Markov models and demonstrate how they can be used for recognition of tennis strokes. In Section 9.5, we describe a prototype system that implements the approaches. We present an example of integrated querying. The last two sections summarize the chapter and give some hints for further reading.

## 9.2 Tennis Video Analysis

Before we extract high-level concepts we have to do some preprocessing. This includes reconstruction of the video structure, i.e., shot detection and classification, but also object segmentation and tracking, and finally low-level feature extraction. We explain this process with help of Figure 9.1. In this figure the tennis video is pictured by the frames at the top.

### 9.2.1 Shot Detection and Classification

A typical video of a tennis match consists of different video shots (do not confuse a video shot with a tennis shot!). The majority of shots show a tennis court with two players (we only consider single matches). These shots are called playing shots. However, there are also some advertisement and close up shots, as well as shots showing audience, which are usually taken during game breaks. This can be seen in the second row of frames in Figure 9.1. Selection of video shots containing a tennis court from other shots is necessary, since our analysis is limited to playing shots. As video segmentation and shot classification is already described in Chapter 3 we only briefly explain how it is applied here. A tennis video is first segmented into different shots using differences in color histograms of neighboring frames. For each shot, we extract its dominant color. A simplified robust M-estimator is used to estimate the parameters of the Gaussian, discarding other color pixels as outliers. The dominant color that repeats the most number of times is supposed to be the color of the tennis court. By analyzing the dominant color of shots on other surfaces, we generalize our segmentation algorithm to different classes of tennis courts: clay, grass, and so on.

Counting the number of skin-colored pixels and using a certain threshold helps us to define close up shots. Also audience shots have a high number of skin-colored pixels, but now entropy (mean and variance) are used as distinguishing characteristics. Remaining shots are called "other". From now on we concentrate on playing shots.

### 9.2.2 Player Segmentation and Tracking

The first step in the segmentation of players is to filter the dominant color (in a playing shot this is the color of tennis court). Assume the leftmost frame of the second row of Figure 9.1 to be the first frame of a playing shot. We carry out the initial quadratic segmentation of the first two frames of the playing shot using estimated statistics of the dominant color. The obtained black-white frame is shown in the third row. Then, the player is detected as the largest compact region in the lower half of the frame using some morphological operations [10]. The other player and the ball may be detected too.

We fit the 3D tennis court model to the actual lines in the image. The new knowledge about the scene is used to form the start values for robust estimation of the parameters of a number of Gaussian models. Model parameters for the color of the field, the lines and eventually the net are estimated using the data from some neighborhood of the initially detected player. These values are used to refine the player segmentation [19]. (Having the human figure in this particular application, we extract special parameters trying to maximize their informative content.) The center of mass of the region is taken as the player position. The algorithm processes the next frame and searches for a region similar to the region of the detected player using the player's position. Doing this for more frames delivers an estimate for the speed. This segmentation and tracking algorithm is a bit rough, but satisfactory, and is described by Petković et al. [12].

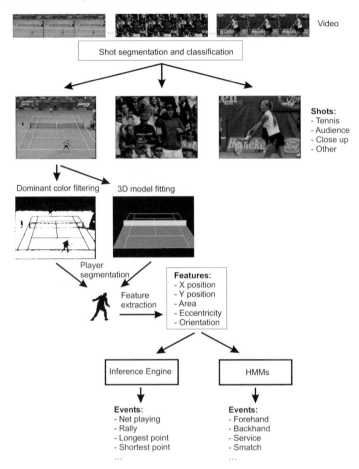

**Fig. 9.1.** Tennis video analysis.

### 9.2.3 Audio and Text

Until now we have focused on images. The audio signal, as one of the essential video components, provides a rich source of information to supplement understanding of a video. Combining audio with other modalities gives more information than any modality alone. The raw audio data can be divided into speech and non-speech parts. Speech recognition results into a time-aligned transcript of spoken words. Non-speech parts can be put into clusters with textual descriptions like cheering and stroke sound. See Chapter 10 for more information.

We observe that at the start of the match the names of the players appear in a frame sequence. Using OCR techniques we detect which players are playing and are able to keep these names during the match using player specific characteristics. The text showing names of players has to be distinguished from text appearing in advertisements, and so on. These and other problems are extensively dealt with in Chapter 10.

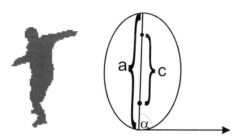

**Fig. 9.2.** Orientation and eccentricity.

### 9.2.4 Low-Level Image Features

In previous sections we already introduced some low-level features. The list of features includes the color histogram ($f_1$), which is in fact a list of 256 values, the dominant color ($f_2$), entropy characteristics mean ($f_3$), and variance ($f_4$), number of skin colored pixels ($f_5$), player position ($f_6$), area ($f_7$), orientation ($f_8$), and eccentricity ($f_9$). Area denotes the actual number of pixels in the region. Orientation is the angle between the X-axis and the major axis of the ellipse that has the same second moment as the region (in Figure 9.2 it is called $\alpha$). Eccentricity is the ratio of the distance between the foci of the ellipse and its major axis length (in Figure 9.2 this is $c/a$). The eccentricity takes a value between zero and one; these values are actually degenerate cases. An ellipse with eccentricity zero is a circle, while an ellipse with eccentricity one is a line segment.

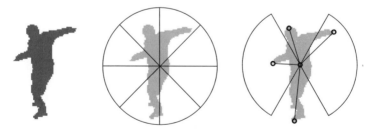

**Fig. 9.3.** Specific features: (a) extracted shape; (b) pie features; (c) skeleton features.

The features defined until now are used by both the spatio-temporal and the hidden Markov model approach. We have, however, also some features which are used by the second approach alone. The latter features are:

- The position of the upper half of the mask with respect to the mass center ($f_{10-11}$), its orientation ($f_{12}$), and the eccentricity ($f_{13}$). Those features describe the upper part of the body that contains most of the information.
- For each circle sector that is centered at the mass center, we count the percentage of pixels in the pie ($f_{14-21}$) as shown in Figure 9.3b.
- The sticking-out parts ($f_{22-23}$) are extracted by filtering and finding local maxima of the distance from a point on the contour to the mass center. Only certain angles are considered, as indicated in Figure 9.3c.

## 9.3 Spatio-temporal Approach

Now we turn our attention to the spatio-temporal approach. First, we define spatial and temporal relations that can hold between spatial objects. Then we give rules to describe object and event types and we conclude with an example query.

### 9.3.1 Spatial Relations

The concept of neighborhood is defined by topological relations which stay invariant under transformations such as translation, rotation, and scaling. Order in space is defined by direction relations. A notion of distance between points is the last element of spatial relations. The most often used distance metric is the well-known Euclidian metric.

### Topological Relations

Each object is represented in two-dimensional space as a point set, which has an interior, a boundary, and an exterior. The nine intersections of the three properties of each of two objects describe the topological relations between any two objects. The following eight relations are meaningful for region objects [3]: "disjoint", "meet", "equal", "overlap", "contains", "inside", "covers", and "covered by".

### Directional Relations

A video object is very often represented by a polygon. However, it is a common strategy when dealing with spatial objects to use the Minimum Bounding Rectangle approximation to increase efficiency. The reason is that we need to store only two points (one corresponding to the lower left and another to the upper right corner of the Minimum Bounding Rectangle). We base directional relations on the cone-shaped concept of directions. They are defined using angular regions between objects, which are abstracted as single points based on the center of mass. Therefore, there are eight directional relations, namely "north", "east", "north-east", and so on.

### 9.3.2 Temporal Relations

Video shots take time and so do actions of tennis players. A time interval has a start time, an end time, and a duration. Tracking spatial objects defines time intervals in which certain conditions like "player near the net" may hold. Allen [1] defines thirteen relations between two time intervals. They can be represented by the following seven: "before", "meets", "overlaps", "during", "starts", "finishes", "equal". The other six are inverse relations. For example, "after" is the inverse relation of "before". Only the equality relation has no inverse. We refer to Allen [1] for a formal definition of the temporal relations.

### 9.3.3 Rules for Object and Event Types

To describe object and event types we use rules expressed in a syntax. These rules form a part of an object and event grammar. Low-level features and spatio-temporal relations form rules. The grammar is described by Petković [10]. Below we will use a *simplified* form of the syntax.

We distinguish between simple and compound objects. In a soccer match we may consider a ball to be a simple object and a goal post a compound one. A goal post is then composed of two vertical bars and one horizontal bar with their well-known spatial relationships. We also distinguish between simple and compound event types. Simple event types are defined with help of features types, object types, and all kinds of relations, but no event types. Compound event types have event types in their defining rule.

The video analysis delivers a set of feature types:

```
{f1, f2, f3, f4, f5, f6, f7, f8, f9}
```

Moreover, we assume that the video analysis also established two sets of basic visual object and audio event types:

```
{SpatialObject, Ball, Net}
{Cheering, StrokeSound, SighSound}
```

In the remainder of this section, we first give some rules to describe simple object and event types. Then we present some rules to define compound types that build on already defined concepts.

### Simple Types

Consider a video frame. A simple object description that defines the player closer to the camera (than the other one) using shape features and the spatial relation `contain` is defined as:

```
PlayerCloserToCamera ::=
    {r1: SpatialObject, r2: rect(0, 144, 384, 288)},
    {700 < f7(r1) < 1200}, {contain(r2, r1)}
```

In fact, in all frames of a playing shot the same player would be the `PlayerCloserToCamera`. There are two regions involved: `r1` corresponds to a spatial object and `r2` to the lower half of the frame. The criterion concerning the area feature `f7` has to be fulfilled. Furthermore, the region `r2` has to contain the region `r1`.

Let us consider a simple event type. The rule defines events in which Venus Williams is playing close to the net for a given period of time:

```
PlayerNearTheNet  ::=
    {o1: PlayerCloserToCamera}, {o1.name = ''V.Williams''},
    {y_distance (o1, Net) < 50}, {duration > 60})
```

Assume that the object types `PlayerCloserToCamera` and `Net` are already defined. The new `PlayerNearTheNet` event type is expressed in terms of spatio-temporal object interactions. Among others the distance to the net along the Y-axis must be smaller than 10. The temporal relation says that this event type should last for a specific period, as well as that the spatial relation should be valid for that period of time. This description also shows how event types can be parameterized (a user might be interested not only in Venus Williams, but in other players playing as well).

**Compound Types**
In the description of the event type `PlayerNearTheNet` audio characteristics do not play a part. The following event type descriptions use an audio event type:

```
ForehandTouch  ::=
    {o1:PlayerCloserToCamera, o2:Ball}, {s:StrokeSound},
    {IsRightHanded(o1)}, {overlap(o1, o2), east(o2, o1)}
BackhandTouch  ::=
    {o1:PlayerCloserToCamera, o2:Ball}, {s:StrokeSound},
    {IsRightHanded(o1)}, {overlap(o1, o2), west(o2, o1)}
```

The rules define event types based on the occurrence of an event of type `StrokeSound`, some conceptual information about the player, the topological operator `overlap`, and the direction operators `east` and `west`. The direction operators ensure that the ball is on the correct side of the player.

A user can also reuse already defined event types in order to define other ones. For example, in our case study the "rally" event is defined as a compound event type. First, we define simple event types `PlayerInRightCorner` and `PlayerInLeftCorner`. An event like `PlayerInRightCorner` lasts as long as the defining conditions remain true:

```
PlayerInRightCorner  ::=
    {o1:PlayerCloserToCamera}, { f6.x(o1)>=190, f6.y(o1)>=170}
PlayerInLeftCorner   ::=
    {o1:PlayerCloserToCamera}, { f6.x(o1)<190, f6.y(o1)>=170}
```

Notice that these rules use feature f6, the position of the player. Having defined these two event types, we create a compound event type that can be used to extract all frame sequences in which a player goes two times from the left part of the court to the right part and back. This event type is called left-to-right rally. The rule includes the temporal relation meet: the relation meet means that the first event has to finish at the moment the second event starts:

```
LtRRally  ::=
    {e1,e2:PlayerInLeftCorner, e3,e4:PlayerInRightCorner},
    {e1.o1 = e2.o1 = e3.o1 = e4.o1},
    {meet(e1,e3), meet(e3,e2), meet(e2,e4)}
```

So, a user can build new event types. The list of described event types grows very quickly. For example, in the following event description, some lobs are retrieved by describing a new event type using the already defined event types PlayerNearTheNet and PlayerNearTheBaseline and some additional criteria:

```
Lob ::=
    {e1: PlayerNearTheNet, e2: PlayerNearTheBaseline},
    {e1.o1 = e2.o1}, {meet (e1, e2)}
```

This rule captures the situations that a player is near the net and has to run back to the baseline to fetch the ball. However, a query with this event type will not retrieve all lobs (for example, the ones where the player stays at the net or smashes the ball at the service line will not be retrieved). To be able to retrieve all lobs, the position of the ball must be taken into account.

### 9.3.4 Discussion

The spatio-temporal approach works for "simple" object and event types and is easy to understand for the end user. In Section 9.1 we already mentioned a major drawback of the spatio-temporal approach: the difficult task of defining object and event types. An expert can help, but even then for some events the approach will not grant the best results. Furthermore, we are able to specify rules for forehand and backhand, but to recognize more different strokes will not result in reasonable accuracy (as shown by Sudhir [17], for example). We can enrich the rules with the concept of "ball position" together with some other features. This might increase the accuracy, but, unfortunately, this will make these descriptions even more complicated. Finally, it is very difficult to find and track the ball because of its high speed (can be more than 200 km/h) and occlusion problems. So, for the recognition of tennis strokes we try the probabilistic approach.

## 9.4 Stroke Recognition Using Hidden Markov Models

In this section we concentrate on hidden Markov models to map strokes into classes such as forehand, smash, and service. To this end we use low-level visual features.

Performing a stroke, the shape of a player is changing over time. So, we have to map time-varying patterns into stroke classes.

### 9.4.1 Feature Extraction

The first step is to extract specific features from the player silhouette to reduce the dimensionality of the problem. For each frame we obtain a vector of feature values as described in Section 9.2.4. In Figure 9.4 each dot or + sign represents a feature value in an $n$-dimensional space.

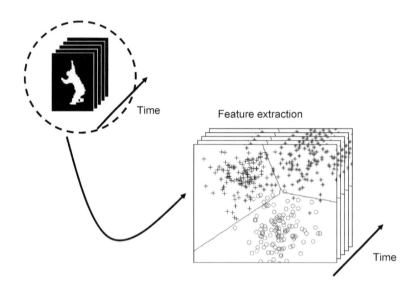

**Fig. 9.4.** Feature values extracted from a stroke.

### Codebook

Having the low-level features extracted as described in Section 9.2.4, we proceed with vector quantization. This means that a vector of feature values that characterizes the shape of the player is represented by only one discrete symbol. The set of possible discrete symbols is called the codebook. This step is required by the used discrete hidden Markov models, see further on.

Vector quantization is the joint quantization of a vector of feature values. This process implies that $n$-dimensional space is partitioned into $M$ clusters, where $n$ is the number of feature types, while $M$ is the codebook size. A simple example of a quantization process, where two feature types are jointly quantized using a codebook size of three symbols (A, B, C), is given in Figure 9.5.

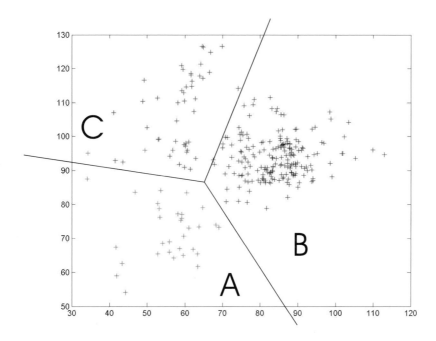

**Fig. 9.5.** Example of vector quantization.

In order to design a codebook we use an iterative clustering algorithm known in the pattern-recognition literature as the $k$-means algorithm. However, the $k$-means algorithm can only converge to a local minimum of the quantization error. Hence, it is wise to repeat it a number of times with different initial values for cluster centers, and then choose the clustering with the minimum overall quantization error. Selection of the codebook size is a trade-off between a smaller quantization error (larger codebook size) and faster operations (smaller codebook size).

### 9.4.2 Hidden Markov Models

Hidden Markov models are very effective tools for modeling time-varying patterns with automatic learning capabilities. They are applied in many fields, such as speech recognition, and more recently in human gesture recognition and handwriting recognition.

262     Milan Petković, Willem Jonker, and Henk Blanken

Hidden Markov models are explained in Chapter 3. Figure 9.6 pictures some parameters of a stroke considered as a hidden Markov model. The number of hidden states $N_S = 3$, the number of observation symbols, i.e., the codebook size, $K = 20$, the sequence of observed symbols is pictured by the line of numbers, and so on.

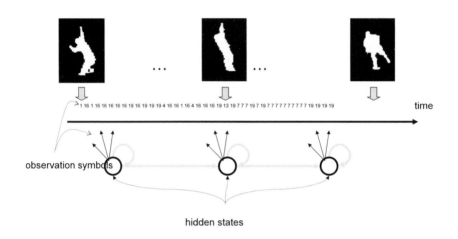

**Fig. 9.6.** A stroke and some related HMM parameters.

We observe that a stroke is a continuous movement of the player. In a stroke it is unlikely that a certain posture recurs. This property leads us to an important class of Hidden Markov models, namely a first order left-to-right hidden Markov model. A left-to-right model always starts from the first state to the left and is allowed to make transitions only toward right states or to the same state, see Figure 9.7.

In Chapter 3 the learning, evaluation, and decoding problems are introduced. In that chapter a general discussion on solutions to these three problems is given. Our aim is to recognize strokes and we do this is two steps. First, we solve the learning problem using training video sequences with strokes. This results in a hidden Markov model for each stroke class. Then we use the obtained models to evaluate strokes in new video sequences.

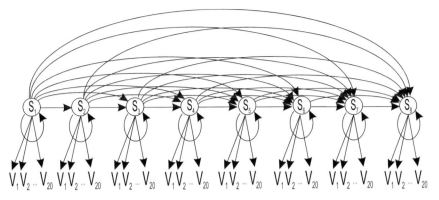

**Fig. 9.7.** A left-to-right model.

### 9.4.3 Learning Process

For each stroke class (forehand, volley, etc.) we have to find the optimal hidden Markov model, meaning that we have to optimally estimate the probabilities of the model by using the observations in the training process.

Training sequences with strokes were manually selected, using a tool that was developed for video annotation and pre-processing. Then we set up the hidden Markov model parameters, which include the number of states and the size of a codebook, based on some heuristics. Subsequently, we trained 50 different models for each stroke class using the Baum–Welch algorithm with the modified re-estimation formula for the training with multiple observation sequences [2]. Finally, after trying different codebook sizes and number of states from 4 to 48, we selected the codebook size of 24 symbols and hidden Markov models with 8 states. This gave the models with the highest probability to represent a class of strokes.

The experiments, we carried out, are divided into two series based on the number of stroke classes used.

### 9.4.4 Recognizing Strokes of Six Classes

Having a model for each class of strokes, we perform stroke recognition using the first order, left-to-right, discrete hidden Markov models.

In the first experiment, we aimed at achieving of two goals: (1) determine the best feature set and (2) investigate person independence of different feature sets. Hence, we have performed a number of experiments with different feature combinations. In order to examine how invariant they are on different male or female players, two series of experiments have been conducted: 1a and 1b. In the series 1a, we used the same player in the training and evaluation sets, while in 1b hidden Markov models were trained with one group of players, but strokes performed by another group were evaluated. In both cases, the training set contained 120 different sequences, while the evaluation set contained 240 sequences.

We selected stroke classes to be recognized: forehand, backhand, service, smash, forehand volley, and backhand volley. In each experiment, six hidden Markov models were constructed – one for each stroke class we would like to recognize. Each stroke sequence was evaluated by all six hidden Markov models. The one with the highest probability was selected as the result. This is called parallel evaluation.

**Table 9.1.** Recognition results (%).

| Feature/Experiment | 1a | 1b | 2 |
|---|---|---|---|
| $f_{8-11}$ | 82 | 79 | 76 |
| $f_{8-13}$ | 85 | 82 | 80 |
| $f_{8-9,12-13}$ | 81 | 78 | 76 |
| $f_{8-9,22-23}$ | 89 | 88 | 87 |
| $f_{8-23}$ | 86 | 82 | 79 |
| $f_{9-11,22-23}$ | 91 | 89 | 88 |
| $f_{14-21}$ | 85 | 78 | 78 |
| $f_{14-23}$ | 93 | 87 | 86 |

The recognition accuracies in Table 9.1 (percentages of rightly classified strokes using parallel evaluation) show that the combination of pie and skeleton features ($f_{14-23}$) achieved the highest accuracy in experiment 1a. The recognition rates dropped in experiment 1b as expected. Two feature combinations showed to be the most person independent, i.e., invariant on different player constitutions. The first is the combination of eccentricity, the mass center of the upper part, and skeleton features, while another is the combination of orientation, eccentricity, and skeleton features.

### 9.4.5 Recognizing Strokes of Eleven Classes

In the second experiment, we investigated recognition rates of different feature combinations using an extensive classification of strokes from tennis literature [20]. There are 11 different stroke classes: service, backhand slice, backhand spin, backhand spin two-handed, forehand slice, forehand spin, smash, forehand volley, forehand half-volley, backhand volley, and backhand half-volley. The training and the evaluation set remained the same as in experiment 1b, only the new classification was applied. Although at first glance some strokes in this new classification are very similar to each other (for example volley and half-volley or backhand slice and spin), the performance (Table 9.1, last column) dropped only slightly. The results have proved that there is an evident difference between, for example, backhand slice and spin stroke. The arm position and the swing are different. In this experiment, the majority of false recognitions remained the same as in experiment 1. Nearly 65% comes from forehands recognized as backhands and vice versa, as well as from forehand-volleys recognized as forehands and vice versa. A reason for that can also be an unbalanced number of strokes in different stroke classes in our test set. A bigger test collection with the exactly same number of strokes in each stroke groups would lead to a more comprehensive analysis of mis-recognition in this experiment with expanded classification of tennis strokes.

### 9.4.6 Discussion

The recognition rate did not drop much from experiment 1a to experiment 1b. We believe that this is due to the advanced, very informative, invariant features (in the first place novel skeleton features). The high recognition rate we achieved is certainly more significant taking into account that we used TV video scenes with a very small player's shape. In order to improve the performance of our approach, one could further fine-tune feature extraction taking into consideration human body parts and their kinematics. The use of shape axis model introduced by Liu and Geiger [8] would be interesting in this context. On the other hand, having the ball position known (an attempt is reported by Pingali [13]) would certainly make the distinction between fore-hand and backhands as well as between volleys and half-valleys more robust and significantly increase the recognition rate. The approach presented here has some limitations. The performance of stroke recognition depends on the camera position and the noise strength, as skeleton features are very sensitive on video quality. Some features are also dependent on the resolution of input images. Furthermore, we used only right-handed players in our experiments. Introducing left-handed players would require training of additional hidden Markov models and further experiments to assess the accuracy of stroke recognition of mixed right- and left-handed players. However, an easier way is to use conceptual information from the player profile and then choose the right hidden Markov models for recognition.

## 9.5 Prototype

Based on the architecture shown in Figure 9.8 we implemented a prototype system. In this system raw video data are stored as files. As metadata server we choose the MONET database system, which has been extended with modules to deal with hidden Markov models, (dynamic) Bayesian networks, and rules. We added also an interface to simplify definition of object and event types and the formulation of queries.

Using the interface, a user can easily define a query by selecting particular features and by setting constraints on them. Moreover, the event grammar allows users to define new events types and build the metadata themselves. For example, a user can define a new event called "rallies with net playing" by introducing the "overlap" temporal operation between the "playing on the net' and "rally" event types. After the evaluation of the query, results are added to the metadata. This speeds up further querying of this event, which is resolved directly in the event layer of metadata without performing costly join operation for resolving the temporal relation.

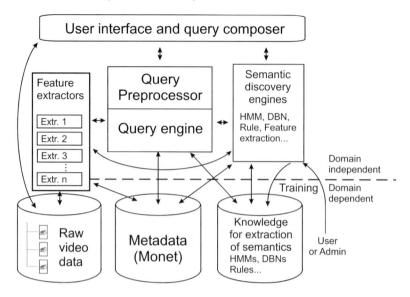

**Fig. 9.8.** Architecture of prototype.

The feature extraction component is used for video segmentation and feature extraction purposes.

The advantage of this framework is that it supports the integrated use of different techniques for semantic extraction (elsewhere we give more details about the integrated use [10, 11]). Therefore, we can benefit from using the spatio-temporal event formalization together with the stochastic formalization. The system can answer very detailed complex queries, such as "Select all video sequences from the game between Kournikova and Kuti Kis where one of the players smashes being near the net". Figure 9.9 shows a graphical user interface that allows to formulate a query like this one:

```
SELECT vi.frame_seq
FROM video vi
WHERE s_contains (vi.frame_seq,
     SmashOnNet = ({e1: PlayerNearTheNet, e2: Smash},
     {overlap (e2, e1)},e1.o1= e2.o1)) = 1 AND
     vi.name = 'KournikovaKutiKis'
```

The query retrieves all video segments from the game between Kournikova and Kis. The name of the video is "KournikovaKutiKis". The query is formulated using an extended OQL, where s_contains is a function that checks whether a frame sequence contains requested objects or events. The query comprises a new event type, namely the SmashOnNet event type that consists of two event types. PlayerNearTheNet is defined using the spatio-temporal approach, while `Smash` has been detected with the hidden Markov model approach.

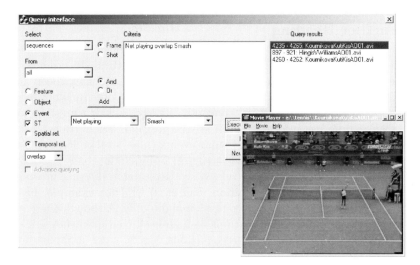

**Fig. 9.9.** Graphical user interface for combined queries.

## 9.6 Summary

We have presented a framework for automatic extraction of high-level concepts (objects and events) from raw video data. The extraction is supported by two components. The rule-based component formalizes descriptions of high-level concepts using spatio-temporal reasoning. The stochastic component exploits the learning capability of hidden Markov models to recognize events in video data automatically. By integrating these techniques within the database management system, the users are provided with ability to define and extract events dynamically. These two approaches have been applied for retrieval in the particular domain of tennis game videos. The spatio-temporal approach is used for retrieval of more "exact" events such as "net-playing" and "rally", while hidden Markov models are used for the retrieval of more "fuzzy" events like "forehand", "service", etc. Consequently, the complete set of video processing tools for the Tennis domain has been introduced, starting from shot segmentation and classification, through player segmentation and tracking, to feature extraction. A number of experiments with hidden Markov models have been carried out in order to find which combination of features, but also which hidden Markov model parameters give the best results. The results have proved that specific features, such as the skeleton and the pie features are of the greatest importance. Furthermore, experimental results with a regular classification of tennis strokes demonstrated that our hidden Markov model approach is promising to realize statistics of tennis games automatically using normal TV broadcast videos.

## 9.7 Further Reading

The problem addressed in this chapter is to automatically derive high-level representation of video content based on low-level features. In order to solve this problem, several domain-dependent research efforts have been undertaken. These approaches take an advantage of using domain knowledge to facilitate extraction of high-level concepts directly from features. In particular, they mainly use information on object positions, their transitions over time, etc., and relate them to particular events (high-level concepts). For example, methods have been proposed to detect events in football [7], soccer [5], and hunting [6], etc. Motion (for review see [16]) and audio are, in isolation, very often used for event recognition. Rui et al. [15] for example, base extracting highlights from baseball games on audio only. Although these efforts resulted in the mapping from features to high-level concepts, they are essentially restricted to the extent of recognizable events, since it might become difficult to formalize complex actions of non-spatial objects using rules. Furthermore, rules require expert knowledge and have problems when dealing with uncertainty.

On the other hand, some other approaches use probabilistic methods that often exploit automatic learning capabilities to derive knowledge. For example, Naphade et al. [9] used hierarchical hidden Markov models to extract events like explosions. Structuring of video using Bayesian networks alone [18] or together with hidden Markov models [4] has been also proposed.

## References

1. J. F. Allen. Maintaining Knowledge about Temporal Intervals. *Communications of ACM*, 26(11):832–843, 1983.
2. L. Baum, T. Petrie, G. Soules, and N. Weiss. A maximization technique occurring in the statistical analysis of probabilistic functions of markov chains. *Annals of Mathematical Statistics*, 41(1):164–171.
3. M. Egenhofer and R. Franzosa. Point-set topological spatial relations. *International Journal of Geographic Information Systems*, 5(2):161–174.
4. A.M. Ferman and A.M. Tekalp. Probabilistic Analysis and Extraction of Video Content. In *Procceeding of IEEE ICIP*, volume 2, pages 536–540, Tokyo, Japan, 1998.
5. Y. Gong, L.T. Sin, C.H. Chuan, H-J. Zhang, and M. Sakauchi. Automatic Parsing of TV Soccer Programs. In *Procceeding of IEEE International Conference on Multimedia Computing and Systems*, pages 167–174, Washington D.C., 1995.
6. N. Haering, R.J. Qian, and M.I. Sezan. A Semantic Event-Detection Approach and its Application to Detecting Hunts in Wildlife Video. *IEEE Transactions on Circuits and Systems for Video Technology*, 10(6):857–868, 2000.

7. S. Intille and A. Bobick. Visual Tracking Using Closed-Worlds. Technical Report 294, MIT Media Laboratory, 1994.
8. T-L. Liu and D. Geiger. Approximate Tree Matching and Shape Similarity. In *Proceedings of the 7th Intl. Conference on Compute Vision*, pages 456–462, Greece, 1999.
9. M. Naphade, T. Kristjansson, B. Frey, and T.S. Huang. Probabilistic Multimedia Objects (Multijects): A Novel Approach to Indexing and Retrieval in Multimedia Systames. In *Procceeding of IEEE ICIP*, volume 3, pages 536–540, Chicago, IL, 1998.
10. M. Petković. *Content-Based Video Retrieval Supported by Database Technology*. PhD thesis, Centre for Telematich and Information Technology, Enschede, The Netherlands, 2003.
11. M. Petković and W. Jonker. Content-Based Video Retrieval by Integrating Spatio Temporal and Stochastic Recognition of Events. In *Procceeding of IEEE Intl. Workshop on Detection and Recognition of Events in Video*, pages 75–82, Vancouver, Canada, 2001.
12. M. Petkovic, M. A. Windhouwer, R. van Zwol, H. E. Blok, P. M. G. Apers, M. L. Kersten, and W. Jonker. Content-based video indexing for the support of digital library search. In *Proceedings of the 18th International Conference on Data Engineering (ICDE 2002), San Jose, CA, USA*, pages 494–495, Washington, DC, USA, 2002. IEEE Computer Society. http://doi.ieeecomputersociety.org/10.1109/ICDE.2002.994766, issn 1063-6382.
13. G. Pingali, Y. Jean, A. Opalach, and I. Carlbom. LucentVision: Converting Real World Events into Multimedia Expiriences. In *Procceeding of IEEE Intl. Conference on Multimedia and Expo (ICME)*, volume 3, pages 1433–1436, New York, 2000.
14. R. Rosales and A. Sclaroff. Specialized Mappings and the Estimation of Human Body Pose from a Single Image. In *Workshop on Human Motion (HUMO)*. IEEE.
15. Y. Rui, A. Gupta, and A. Acero. Automatically Extracting Highlights for TV Baseball Programs. In *Procceeding of ACM Multimedia*, pages 105–115, Los Angeles, CA, 2000.
16. M. Shah and R. Jain. *Motion-Based Recognition*. Kluwer Academic Publisher, 1997.
17. G. Sudhir, J. Lee, and A. Jain. Automatic Classification of Tennis Video for High-level Content-based Retrieval. In *Proceedings of IEEE Intl. Workshop on Content-based Access and Image and Video Databases*, pages 81–90, Bombay, India, 1998.
18. N. Vasconcelos and A. Lippman. Bayesian Modeling of Video Editing and Structure: Semantic Features for Video Sumarization and Browsing. In *Procceeding of IEEE ICIP*, volume 2, pages 550–555, Chicago, IL, 1998.
19. Z. Živković, F. van der Heijden, M. Petković, and W. Jonker. Image Processing and Feature Extraction for Recognizing Strokes in Tennis Game Videos. In *Proceedings of 7th Annual Conference of the Advances School for Computing and Imaging*, pages 262–266, The Netherlands, 2001.
20. J. Yandell. *Visual Tennis*. Human Kinetics, 1999.

# Multimodal Content-based Video Retrieval

Vojkan Mihajlović[1], Milan Petković[1], Willem Jonker[1,2], and Henk Blanken[2]

[1] Philips Research
[2] University of Twente

## 10.1 Introduction

This chapter is a case study showing how important events (highlights) can be automatically detected in video recordings of Formula 1 car racing. Numerous approaches presented in literature have shown that it is becoming possible to extract interesting events from video. However, the majority of the approaches uses individual visual or audio cues. According to the current understanding of human perception it is expected that using evidence obtained from different modalities should result in a more robust and accurate perception of video. On the other hand, fusion of multimodal evidence is quite challenging, since it has to deal with indications which may contradict each other. In this chapter we deal with three topics, one being fusion of evidence from different modalities.

Firstly, we explain how Bayesian and dynamic Bayesian networks (DBNs) can use the evidence obtained from audio signal analysis in detecting interesting events in the race. We observe that as soon as the voice of the commentator of the race becomes excited, probably a highlight has occurred. We use low-level features first to localize speech in the audio signal and then to detect excited speech. Furthermore, certain words uttered by the commentator may also indicate excitement. To recognize words, we do not use, however, a full-blown speech recognizer. Instead we use a simple recognizer that is able capture only a very limited set of words frequently used to describe highlights in car racing. To process recognized words and detected low-level features, we design BNs and DBNs. By experimentation, we try to get an idea of the influence of the structure of a (D)BN on detection of excited speech.

Secondly, we focus on the problem of fusion of information coming from different modalities. By exploiting audio only, some highlights may have been unnoticed. So, we also analyze the image stream of the video to obtain cues for highlights like the start of the race. DBNs may also fuse evidence obtained from audio and video cues in order to detect time-boundaries of highlights automatically.

Thirdly, we also deal with superimposed text. In order to improve user understanding, text is projected on the TV screen. This text contains information about the name of a driver (e.g., Schumacher), the position of a driver in the race, and so on. Of course this information is related to the highlights obtained from audio/video analysis. Combining all information obtained so far we are able to answer queries like: "Give video sequences showing Michael Schumacher passing another car".

A more elaborate version of this chapter can be found in a technical report belonging to this project [10].

### 10.1.1 Information Sources

The approach described in this chapter is validated in the domain of Formula 1 races. For that domain, we introduce a robust audio-visual feature extraction scheme, as well as a text recognition and detection method.

We digitized three Formula 1 races of the 2001 season, namely the German, Belgian, and USA Grand Prix (GP). The average duration of these Formula 1 races was about 90 minutes or 135,000 frames for a PAL video. Videos were digitized as a quarter of the PAL standard resolution (384×288). Audio was sampled at 22 kHz with 16 bits per audio sample.

Several low-level features are extracted from both the audio and video signals. Together with domain knowledge these features form the basis for the derivation of highlights such as start of the race, and passing and fly-out of cars.

### 10.1.2 Relation to Other Chapters

This chapter deals among others with speech, so there is a relationship with Chapter 7. Chapter 4 introduces Bayesian networks, and among others it is shown how the probability is computed that a query is answered by a document. To this end many conditional probabilities have to be given. Recall how Chapter 3 and 6 give algorithms that compute the conditional probabilities in hidden Markov models from observed low-level features in a training set of video data. In the current chapter we use a similar approach and compute probabilities for (D)BNs given features from training data.

### 10.1.3 Outline

Sections 10.2 and 10.3 aim to detect moments of excited speech occurring in the voice of the commentator. The assumption is that excited speech indicates a highlight. We use (dynamic) Bayesian networks to capture moments of excitement and try to detect the influence of network structure on retrieval results.

Exploiting only audio may leave some highlights undetected. So, in Section 10.4 we also take images into account and in Section 10.5 we fuse image and audio cues. As *dynamic* Bayesian networks are shown to be more robust and more effective for detecting excited speech we use them for highlights detection.

The third modality is superimposed text. Detection and usage of this text is the topic of Section 10.6.

Combining the results derived from audio and images together with the knowledge obtained from superimposed text allows answering complex queries. We give some examples in Section 10.7. The chapter ends with a summary section and a section that gives some hints for further reading.

## 10.2 Processing the Audio Signal

The Formula 1 audio signal is complex and ambiguous. It consists of human speech, car noise, and various background noises, such as crowd cheering, horns, etc. To deal with this complexity, we focus on low-level features that allow to filter speech from other sounds. Moreover, dependent on the sport, keywords derived from speech may suggest highlights. For instance, in Formula 1 racing a keyword like `start` or `accident` may suggest an interesting event. So, keyword spotting techniques get attention in this section. Finally, we give a brief overview of other relevant low-level features and integrate them into (dynamic) Bayesian networks. We describe experiments in which the quality of search results of several networks is compared and evaluated.

### 10.2.1 Low-Level Audio Features

We use low-level features to try to locate speech segments in the audio signal. A great number of features can be extracted from audio signals. We select four of them, namely Short Time Energy (STE), pitch, Mel-Frequency Cepstral Coefficients (MFCCs), and pause rate. For the recognition of specific keywords in commentator's speech, we use a keyword-spotting tool based on a finite state grammar. Below we give a brief summary.

### Short Time Energy (STE)

The main usage of this feature is to separate speech from non-speech segments. It is useful in noisy environments, because noise signals have lower average short time energy than regular speech. Short time energy represents average waveform amplitude, defined over a specific time interval. Usually it is computed after performing sub-band division of the audio signal. Indicative bands for audio characterization are lower sub-bands that is with a frequency of less than 4400 Hz. The average short time energy of the interval with $N$ samples preceding sample $m$ can be mathematically expressed as follows:

$$E_m \; = \; \frac{1}{N} \sum_{n=m-N+1}^{m} (x(n)^2 \cdot w(m-n)), \qquad (10.1)$$

where $x(n)$ is the input audio sample, and $w(m-n)$ is a window function. The sample values may vary a lot. Window functions allow to manipulate the sample values. There are many of those functions and in Figure 10.1 we picture two of them, namely the rectangular and the Hamming window (notice that the considered interval is pictured here as $[-1, 1]$). A rectangular window simply weights all values in the interval the same. A Hamming window uses the function $0.54 + 0.46 \cos(\pi t)$ resulting in less weight for values at the borders of the interval. In other words, it avoids the sharp discontinuity at the end of the segments, resulting in better description of a harmonic structure of the speech signal when applying fast Fourier transform (FFT). Therefore, we employed Hamming window in our approach.

**Fig. 10.1.** A rectangular window and a Hamming window.

**Pitch**

Pitch (fundamental frequency, F0) is an important feature for audio analysis, especially for detection of emphasized human speech. It represents the leading frequency of a complex audio signal. In speech, the pitch often gets higher values when the speaker is excited. Many techniques have been proposed for pitch estimation and tracking, such as cepstrum analysis, harmonic product analysis, autocorrelation analysis, maximum a posterior (MAP) pitch estimation, difference analysis, etc.

All these techniques for pitch estimation demand appropriate bandwidth of audio signal for accurate estimation of the pitch. Since human speech is usually under 1000 Hz, we are particularly interested in determining pitch that is under this frequency range. We decided to use the autocorrelation function in our approach of pitch estimation. The autocorrelation function for a random signal is defined as:

$$A(k) \;=\; \frac{1}{2N+1} \sum_{n=-N}^{N} x(n) \cdot x(n+k), \qquad (10.2)$$

where $k$ is the number of overlapping samples. The autocorrelation function of a periodic signal (like, e.g., the speech signal) is also periodic. The first value $A(0)$ is the average energy of the signal. From (10.2) we can compute peak values for different values of $k$. Pitch for a particular window is defined as the largest peak value $max(A(k))$, only if the autocorrelation function is above a certain threshold (0.3 in our case). Otherwise the pitch is unknown.

It is shown that detection of emphasized human speech for complex sounds can be achieved by pitch tracking. We can even learn these pitch characteristics for a particular talker (see for an example [1]). The only thing we have to do is to carefully determine the pitch threshold for every talker. In our approach we use the pitch as evidence in a DBN for finding the segments of excited speech.

**Mel-frequency Cepstral Coefficients**

Mel-frequency cepstral coefficients (MFCCs) is a type of phoneme-level feature for characterizing audio signals. It is based on a sub-band division of entire frequency spectrum, and uses Mel-scale. Mel-scale is a gradually warped linear spectrum, with coarser resolution on higher, and finer resolution on lower frequencies. It is metrically adapted to the human perception system.

MFCCs are a simple cosine transform of the Mel-scale energy for different filtered sub-bands. For audio characterization, MFCCs (especially their first derivatives) bring good results for determining speech phonemes, and are very useful for speech recognition and speaker detection. More details on usage of MFCC and their first derivatives can be found in the book by Rabiner and Juang [12].

**Pause Rate**

The feature pause rate intends to determine the quantity of speech in an audio clip. The pause rate can be used as an indication of emphasized human speech. The higher the pause rate, the lower the indication for excitement. Pause rate can easily calculated by counting the number of silent audio frames in an audio clip and dividing this number by the total number of frames. Silent audio frames can be detected based on low short-term energy values and low values of first derivatives of MFCCs (see below).

**10.2.2 Speech Sequence Detection**

We use short time energy (STE) and Mel-frequency cepstral coefficients (MFCC) to detect speech sequences. These low-level features are also used by Rui et al. [13], where the audio signal was extracted from a baseball game. The Formula 1 signal seems to be similar to that of a baseball game. We divide the audio signal into audio frames of 10 ms. Ten frames add up to an audio segment of 100 ms.

First, we have to filter background noises: sounds made by engines, and so on. To this end we process the audio signal so that only a signal of 0–882 Hz remains. This elimination is important, especially when we have to determine silent segments. We decide to employ the Hamming window for processing STE because it showed higher accuracy in speech sequence detection than the rectangular one.

For MFCC calculations we use only first three coefficients, because experiments show that they are the most indicative for speech detection.

We calculate STE and MFCC values for audio frames. Moreover, for a segment we compute the average and maximum value as well as dynamic range of STE. For MFCC only the average and maximum value are interesting.

Figure 10.2 shows STE values for an audio signal of 1000 audio frames (in total 10 s). Appropriate thresholds for audio features are based on experiments. As a result we receive an indication for each 100 ms segment whether it is a non-speech segment or not.

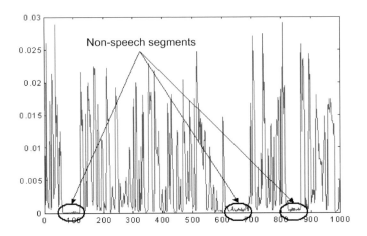

**Fig. 10.2.** Short-term energy calculations for 1000 audio frames with indications for non-speech segments.

### 10.2.3 Keyword Spotting
The commentator reports on the events of the race. In the previous section we demonstrated how we can detect speech in the audio signal.

Chapter 7 addresses speech recognition techniques. It appeared that these techniques are still not perfect today. We now have two options: either we go for a general speech recognizer or for one that focuses on the recognition of a limited number of words. The first approach recognizes in principle every word at the cost of generating false alarms. The second approach is more limited, but has less false alarms assuming sufficient training data. We decided for the second approach and selected about 30 words that may be used when a commentator of a Formula 1 race gets excited. We tried two different acoustic models, see Chapter 7, for this purpose. One was trained for the clean speech, and the other was aimed for word recognition in TV news. The latter showed better results, so it has been chosen.

## 10.3 Detection of Excited Speech using (D)BNs
We now face the task to detect those parts of the audio signal in which the commentator is excited. We hope that this is an indication for an interesting

event, a highlight. In previous subsections we have already gathered indications for excited speech. For instance, in Figure 10.3 we see pitch values for 1000 audio frames of 10 ms; as known, high values suggest excited speech.

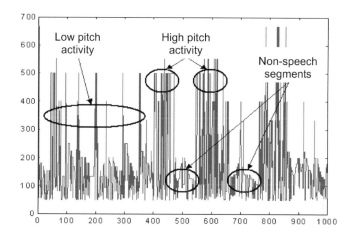

**Fig. 10.3.** High pitch values indicating excited speech.

We split the audio signal into segments, also called time slices. For each segment we derive many features: keywords ($f_1$), pause rate ($f_2$), average values of STE ($f_3$), dynamic range of STE ($f_4$), maximum values of STE ($f_5$), average values of pitch ($f_6$), dynamic range of pitch ($f_7$), maximum values of pitch ($f_8$), average values of MFCCs ($f_9$), and the maximum values of MFCCs ($f_{10}$).

This information forms an input to a probabilistic framework, namely a (dynamic) Bayesian network (see also Section 4.3.4). Therefore, these features are considered as evidence nodes for a BN or a DBN. The features within a segment (i.e., time instance) have certain dependencies which are captured in the (dynamic) Bayesian network through the hidden nodes that are stochastic variables.

A dynamic BN (DBN) is a Bayesian network that deals with the time aspect. This implies that features and stochastic variables from one segment (time instance) may depend on features and stochastic variables in other segments. A DBN satisfies the first order Markov property. So, a stochastic variable at time $t$ may depend on one or more stochastic variables (or features) at time $t-1$ and/or some at time $t$. The conditional probabilities between hidden and evidence nodes (stochastic variables and features) define the evaluation model.

A Bayesian network (BN) is a network where dependencies between variables from one segment and from the segment before it are not allowed. Therefore, only conditional probabilities between hidden and evidence nodes exist.

The probabilities in a (D)BN can be learned from a training data set. We follow an approach that has some similarities with the one described in Chapter 9, where hidden Markov models were trained. Note that an HMM is a special case of a DBN.

As we work with DBNs that have hidden states we employ the Expectation Maximization learning algorithm. In the inferencing process, we use the modified Boyen–Koller algorithm for approximate inference [3].

### 10.3.1 Influence of Network Structure

Many different networks can be used to describe the problem of the case study. Figure 10.4 proposes three possible network structures, and we investigate how these perform the task of detecting excited speech. We use either "simple" BNs (Figure 10.4) or DBNs where temporal dependencies between nodes from two consecutive time slices of DBNs are defined as in Figure 10.5, resulting in six candidate networks.

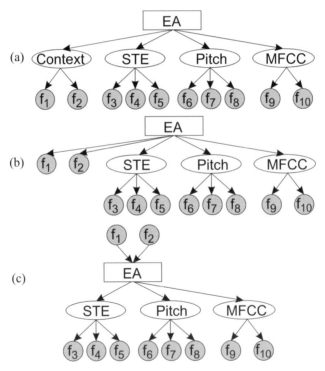

**Fig. 10.4.** Different structures for processing of audio features: (*a*) fully parameterized structure; (*b*) structure with direct influence from evidence to query node; (*c*) input/output BN structure.

The query node is Excited Announcement (EA), since we want to determine whether the commentator raises his voice which may be caused by an interesting event that is taking place. The shaded nodes represent evidence nodes, which receive their values based on features extracted from the audio signal of the Formula 1 video. Other nodes represent hidden nodes.

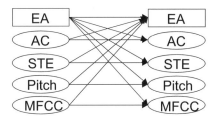

**Fig. 10.5.** Temporal dependencies for the DBNs.

We learned the BN conditional probabilities on a video segment, consisting of 3000 evidence values, 100 ms each (300 s in total) extracted from the audio signal. For the DBNs, we used the same video segment of 300 s, which was divided into 12 subsegments with 25 s duration each. The inference was performed on audio evidence extracted from the digitized German Grand Prix (GP). The evaluation is then performed on the same Grand Prix as well as the two others: Belgian Grand Prix and USA Grand Prix. For each network structure we computed precision and recall.

Note that we had to process the results obtained from BNs since the output values cannot be directly employed to distinguish the presence and time boundaries of the excited speech. This is shown in Figure 10.6a. Therefore, we accumulated values of a query node over time to make a conclusion whether the commentator is excited.

The results obtained from a DBN were much smoother (see Figure 10.6), as DBNs perform a kind of smoothing when propagating probabilities from the previous to the current time slice. Therefore, we did not have to process the output. The results from conducted experiments with previously described networks are shown in Table 10.1. As the effectiveness of DBNs corresponding to BNs given in Figures 10.4b and 10.4c were poor (less than 50% for both precision and recall) we do not report them.

**Table 10.1.** BNs and a DBN for detection of excited speech.

| Network structure | BN (Fig. 10.4a) | BN (Fig. 10.4b) | BN (Fig. 10.4c) | DBN (Fig. 10.4a, Fig. 10.5) |
|---|---|---|---|---|
| Precision | 60% | 54% | 50% | 85% |
| Recall | 66% | 61% | 76% | 81% |

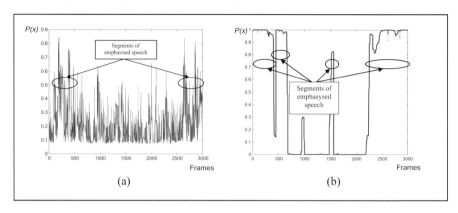

**Fig. 10.6.** Results of audio BN (*a*) and DBN (*b*) inference for 300 s of audio.

By comparing different BN structures we can see that there is no significant difference in precision and recall obtained from them (Table 10.1). The corresponding DBNs perform worse than BNs, except for the DBN that corresponds to the BN with fully parameterized structure (Figure 10.4a). It gives much better results than the other BN/DBN networks (last column in Table 10.1).

### 10.3.2 Influence of Temporal Dependencies

Next, we explored the influence that different temporal dependencies have on learning and inference procedures in DBNs. We developed three DBNs with the same structure of one time slice (Figure 10.4a), but different temporal dependencies between two consecutive time slices: (1) the structure with emission query node (Figure 10.7a), (2) one with collecting query node (Figure 10.7b), and (3) one with dependencies as in Figure 10.5.

The first introduces conditional dependencies only between hidden nodes from the previous time slice and EA node in the current time slice, as well as the EA node from the previous time slice to all hidden nodes in the current time slice. The second one assumes that each hidden node from the previous time slice has influence on corresponding node from the current time slice and on EA node. Finally, the third one is the same as the second except that EA node has influence to all nodes in the current time slice. Therefore, the first two DBNs are a less connected versions of the third DBN.

The evaluation showed that the third DBN (Figure 10.5) significantly outperforms the first and slightly the second DBN.

Finally, we selected the fully parameterized DBN structure (Figure 10.5) as the most powerful DBN structure for detection of the emphasized announcements. To evaluate the chosen network structure we employed it for detecting the emphasized speech in the audio signal of all three races (Table 10.2).

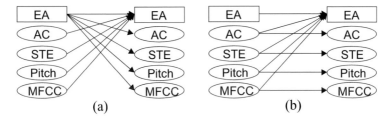

**Fig. 10.7.** Temporal dependencies: emission (a), collecting (b).

**Table 10.2.** Evaluation results for the audio DBN.

| Race | German GP | Belgian GP | USA GP |
|---|---|---|---|
| Precision | 85% | 77% | 76% |
| Recall | 81% | 79% | 81% |

### 10.3.3 Discussion

Conclusions from experiments performed are twofold. From the first group of experiments we conclude that the DBN learning and inference procedures depend a lot on the selected DBN structure for one time slice. We observe that this is not the case when inference and learning are performed with BNs. These experiments also showed the advantages of the fully parameterized DBN structure over the other BN/DBN networks. Secondly, we conclude that chosen temporal dependencies between nodes of two consecutive time slices have strong influence on the results of DBN inference. The best result was obtained with temporal dependencies depicted in Figure 10.5.

## 10.4 Analyzing the Image Stream

In the previous section we focused on audio only. We extracted segments of the Formula 1 race where the commentator raises his voice. However, interesting events missed by the commentator could not be detected. This leads to high precision and low recall. The aim of this section is to improve recall by taking into account the images of a video as well.

Visual features such as color histogram, dominant color, shape moments, etc., characterize low-level visual content. In Chapter 5 low-level features are extensively described. One feature not covered is the motion feature, which is related to video. In this section we briefly introduce the techniques used for the extraction of motion feature.

Subsequently we describe the segmentation of a video into shots, which is a familiar technique and is based on the differences of color histograms among several consecutive frames.

Afterwards we present replay detection approaches, and the simple approach that we use. Finally, we pay attention to the semantic content of a video. Detection of the content is based on low-level features and domain dependent characteristics of the video. Our domain is car racing, so we apply detectors related to car racing to characterize events like passing, start, fly-out, and replay.

The features extracted from video frames and used as input to a (D)BN are simple low-level features that do not require much computational power. We emphasize that the usage of more advanced image feature would lead to higher effectiveness.

### 10.4.1 Motion

Motion information is based on block-matching or optical flow techniques. Motion features can be seen as low- or high-level features. Low-level features are moments of the motion field, motion histogram, and global motion parameters. They can be extracted from the motion vectors. High-level features reflect the camera motion such as panning, tilting, and zooming. For our purpose, we used optical flow techniques based on motion vectors formed from pixel colors.

### 10.4.2 Shot Segmentation

For shot segmentation we employed a simple histogram based algorithm. According to Chang et al. [4], shot cuts can be detected by comparing histograms from two consecutive frames. If these two frames are substantially different we could separate them as belonging to different shots. This histogram difference $HD$ is defined as:

$$HD(H_i, H_{i-1}) = \sum_{i=1}^{N} \frac{(H_t(i) - H_{t-1}(i))^2}{H_t(i)}, \tag{10.3}$$

where $H_t$ is the histogram for the time $t$, and $N$ is the total number of colors in an image. If we put an appropriate threshold for this histogram difference, based on experiments in the specified domain, we will be able to separate shots with the high accuracy. Unfortunately, if we have the digital shot change effects (such as fade, morphing, etc.) this technique will yield poor results. Therefore, we modified it in sense that we calculate histogram difference among several consecutive frames in the multimedia document. This algorithm resulted in over 90% of accuracy, which we considered satisfactory.

### 10.4.3 Replay Detection

Broadcast sport videos usually contain a large amount of replay scenes. Extraction of these scenes is not an easy task. Domain knowledge about the production of TV sport programmes plays a significant role in replay detection. The simplest way to detect replays is to detect when the superimposed text Replay is put on the screen. However, this will not always happen. Sometimes replays are a slowed down representation of live scenes. Replays may also be characterized by special shot change operations. They are termed Digital Video Effects (DVEs) and are present in the beginning and at the end of a replay scene. A technique for replay detection based on DVEs is described by Babaguchi et al. [2].

We could employ the DVE-based detection, but the problem is that these DVEs must be learned for every race. Even then, since they may vary, and even be omitted for some replays, this would lead to small replay recognition accuracy. Moreover, these algorithms are time consuming and computationally expensive. Therefore, we decided to employ a simpler algorithm based on color difference between two consecutive frames. We computed the differences of RGB color components for each pixel in the central area (usually depicting Formula 1 cars) for two consecutive frames. As our algorithm was not perfect, we manually improved the results if necessary. We call this feature $f_{12}$.

### 10.4.4 Start of Race

We consider the start of a race to be defined by two parameters, namely the amount of motion in the scene, and the semaphore presence in the image. To detect the amount of motion we used pixel color difference between two consecutive frames. By experimentation we observed that red, green, and blue pixel color difference brings good results. We called the feature $f_{13}$.

In car racing a semaphore is used to indicate the start of the race. It is a red colored rectangular shape that increases and decreases along the vertical dimension. As soon as the red color disappears cars may start. We try to filter the red component of RGB pixel color representation of a still image which results in feature $f_{14}$.

### 10.4.5 Passing

We did not try to use powerful motion analysis, instead we used some less computationally demanding features. We calculate the movement properties on several consecutive pictures, based on motion histogram obtained from them. Such obtained outputs enable us to derive an indication that one car passes another one. Note, that we employed a very simple and naïve approach for passing detection. By applying more powerful techniques for object tracing we could obtain much better results. As evidence we exploit the features color difference $f_{13}$, like for the start highlight, and amount of motion $f_{17}$.

### 10.4.6 Fly-outs

Fly-outs usually come with a lot of sand and dust. Therefore, we had to recognize presence of these two characteristics in the picture. We resolve this problem using the filtered RGB image for dominant colors. First we determined a dominant color in several still images of fly-outs. Then, we employ color filtering to extract the amount of presence of these dominant colors in the still image of Formula 1 video. An example of a color histogram of such an image is given in Figure 10.8. The evidence comes from two features, dust $f_{15}$ and sand $f_{16}$.

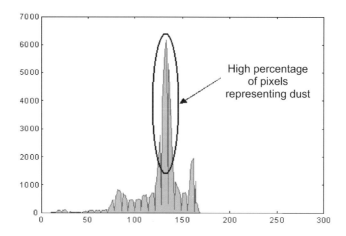

**Fig. 10.8.** Fly-out suggested by dust colors.

## 10.5 Highlight Detection using DBNs

To improve the results obtained solely from audio cues we developed an audio-visual DBN for highlight detection. The structure that represents one time slice of this network is depicted in Figure 10.9. The Highlight node was chosen to be the main query node; other nodes are Start, Fly-out, and Passing. We used the same kind of temporal dependencies as for the audio network. Evidence nodes in audio-visual DBN obtain the values from the various audio and video features mentioned before.

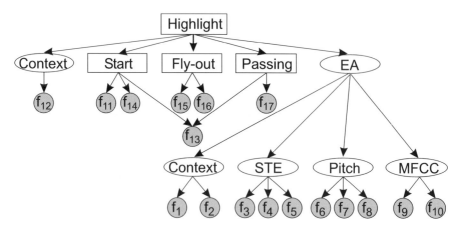

**Fig. 10.9.** Audio-visual DBN for one time slice.

We employed the learning algorithm on 6 sequences with 50 s duration each using the German Grand Prix (similar to audio DBN). The evaluation is done again on the three races: German Grand Prix, Belgian Grand Prix, and USA Grand Prix. The results are shown in Table 10.3. Based on the value of the main query node depicting the highlight in the race, the values of the other query nodes are calculated. We calculated the most probable candidates during each "highlight" segment, and pronounce it as a start, fly-out, or passing based on values of corresponding nodes. For segments longer than 15 s we performed this operation for each 5 s segment to enable multiple selections.

The supplemental query nodes are incorporated in the scheme in order to classify different interesting events that take place in the Formula 1 race. We can see from Table 10.3 that for the German GP we gained high accuracy for highlights and start, while the most misclassifications were for fly-out and passing events. Main reason for this is that we used very general and less powerful video cues for fly-out, and especially passing.

**Table 10.3.** Evaluation results for audio-visual DBN.

| Audio/video DBN | | German GP | Belgian GP | USA GP |
|---|---|---|---|---|
| Highlights | Precision | 84% | 43% | 73% |
| | Recall | 86% | 53% | 76% |
| Start | Precision | 83% | 100% | 100% |
| | Recall | 100% | 67% | 50% |
| Fly-out | Precision | 64% | 100% | – |
| | Recall | 78% | 36% | – |
| Passing | Precision | 79% | 28% | |
| | Recall | 50% | 31% | |

(Note: There were no fly-outs in the USA GP, denoted with "–". Moreover, the results in that column are obtained by the audio-visual DBN that excludes the passing subnetwork.)

For the Belgium and the USA GP we had a big decrease in effectiveness for highlights detection. This is mostly because of the "passing" part of the network, as depicted in the second column of Table 10.3 where precision and recall values for passing are around 30%. Therefore, we simplified the overall audio-visual network, and excluded the "passing" subnetwork for the USA Grand Prix. A significant difference in results obtained *with* (Belgian) and *without* the passing subnetwork (USA) can be seen in Table 10.3.

The network with the passing subnetwork worked fine in the case of the German GP, but failed with the other two races. The explanation for this might be different camera work in the German GP than in other two races, as well as the usage of basic image features. This just confirms the fact that general low-level visual features might yield very poor results in the context of high-level concepts (to characterize passing we used pixel color difference). Obviously, more domain dependent features, which characterize the trajectories of Formula 1 cars, would be more robust and give better results for the passing event.

## 10.6 Superimposed Text

The third modality we used is the text that is superimposed on the screen. This is another type of on-line annotation offered by the TV programme producer. The text is intended to help viewers to better understand the video content. The superimposed text often brings some additional information that is difficult or even impossible to deduce otherwise.

Text appearing in digital videos can be broadly divided into two classes, namely scene text and superimposed (overlay) text [9]. Scene text occurs as a natural part of the actual scene captured by the camera. Examples of scene text include billboards, text on vehicles, writings on human clothes, etc. Superimposed text on the other hand is text manually added to video frames in order to supplement the visual and audio content.

Before superimposed text can be recognized, it has to be detected and that is a major problem. One characteristic of superimposed text is that it has certain spatial properties (see Lienhart's survey for a number of properties [9]). For instance, regions with superimposed text satisfy certain constraints with respect to the minimum and maximum bounds. Detected text regions which do not satisfy these constraints can be eliminated.

Since the process of text detection and recognition is complex, we will divide it into three steps, namely detection of text region, refinement of the detected regions, and recognition of the text itself.

In Figure 10.10 a summary of the process is given. In the lower part of the scene we detect the region where text is projected. First, the region is magnified by means of interpolation. Then the colors are mapped to black and white in a process that is called *binarization*. Subsequently, we extract words from the text region. Finally, we perform text recognition. A limited number of words characteristic for the race is determined. By pattern matching the projected word on the screen is recognized (see lower part of the figure).

### 10.6.1 Detection of Text Region

A useful characteristic of superimposed text is that it usually spans quite some time. So, many frames have the same superimposed text, which is important as text detection on every frame would be computationally too expensive.

A text region can be defined as a horizontal rectangular structure of clustered sharp edges. To detect regions we use a horizontal differential filtering. This filtering searches for horizontal rectangular structures of clustered sharp edges, which in most cases represents text regions. Usually filter magnitude is

**Fig. 10.10.** Text recognition.

$3 \times 3$ pixels. By applying appropriate binary thresholds we are able to extract vertical edge features and based on them we can define text regions.

In our case superimposed text is placed in the bottom of the picture. To ease reading, the background is shaded and the characters are bright (light blue, yellow, or white) for contrast.

Our algorithm is a two-pass text detection algorithm. In the first part we determine whether a shaded region is present in the bottom part of every frame in a video sequence. We conclude that a frame is shaded based on the color feature for every pixel in the bottom part of the frame. Since shaded regions in Formula 1 video can have two different sizes we employ synthesized

288 Vojkan Mihajlović, Milan Petković, Willem Jonker, and Henk Blanken

detection for both of them. Computing the number of these shaded regions in consecutive frames, we skip all the short segments that do not satisfy the duration criteria.

The second part analyzes the same time-dependent properties of shaded regions. We calculate the duration, number, and variance of bright pixels present in these shaded regions. If computed values for the video sequence satisfy constraints defined for the text detection algorithm then this video sequence is marked as a sequence with superimposed text.

### 10.6.2 Refinement of Text Regions

A text region that we receive as a result of region detection usually contains the text of similar intensities and same background. Therefore, we can put a simple threshold to distinguish characters from the background. Then we could binarize the text region, to make characters stand out. The binarization threshold is based on histogram values obtained from the text region. This is one way of cleaning up the text. However, it does not always supply us with clean and regular character forms, especially if the size of characters in the text is small. To overcome this problem, we employed some algorithms. The refinement process consists of two steps, namely filtering of text regions, and interpolation of text regions.

We need to filter the text regions in order to enable better separation from the background, as well as for sharpening the edges of characters. Filtering was executed through minimizing or maximizing pixel intensities over several consecutive frames. However, this filtering is not sufficient for text recognition. Therefore, we had to employ an interpolation algorithm to enlarge characters and make them clearer and cleaner. In this interpolation algorithm the text area is magnified four times in both directions.

After this refinement, we have magnified text regions with much better character representations. After these actions, the text is ready for the text recognition step. Elsewhere we have described the filtering and interpolation algorithms [10].

### 10.6.3 Text Recognition

Given a text printed against a clean background, current optical character recognition (OCR) techniques perform rather well and give good recognition accuracy. However, since we are interested in recognition of the text printed against shaded and textured backgrounds, OCR technology cannot handle such texts. Hence, we developed a specific algorithm.

The text recognition task should enable extracting words and sentences from purposely-added superimposed text. This procedure should supply us with additional information about a video scene that can be used for conclusions about the content of a video sequence (in our case also as an input for probabilistic framework). In the Formula 1 domain, two important properties can be exerted about the superimposed text:

- there are not many different words superimposed on the screen, and
- the font used for superimposed text is the same.

Based on these properties we developed our text recognition algorithm. Assuming that we received a clean and sharpened text from the previous step, we can now begin character/word recognition process.

The character recognition process is somewhat more complex and time consuming, but it is more robust and more general, because we can employ it on any font size. On the other hand, word recognition is limited on a specified number of defined words (extracted reference patterns), but it is less computationally demanding. We decided to recognize words based on extracted text regions with one or several successive characters.

Our algorithm is based on pattern matching techniques, mainly because of a small number of different words superimposed on the screen. These words are names of the Formula 1 drivers, and some informative words, such as pit stop, final lap, classification, winner, etc. Therefore, the first task was to extract patterns for these words. Since the processing of a color image is computationally expensive and slow, we decided to extract reference patterns, and to perform matching with black–white pictures. Black–white text regions are obtained from the color text regions by filtering RGB components on a text region. After applying thresholds on the text region, we marked characters as white space on the black background. For character extraction we used the horizontal and vertical projection of white pixels. Since characters can have different heights we used double vertical projection in order to refine the characters better. However, we did not match characters to reference patterns because they are usually irregular and can be occluded or deformed. Thus, we connect characters that belong to one word into a region. This was done based on the pixel distance between characters. Regions that are close to each other are considered as characters that belong to the same word. Having the regions containing one word, we perform pattern matching. To make this matching algorithm faster and more powerful, we separate words into several categories based on their length, and perform matching procedures only for reference patterns with similar length. Simple metric of pixel difference $PD$ that is used for pattern matching is described by the following equation:

$$PD = \sum_{(x,y)} I_{ref}(x,y)(n) \cdot I_{extr}(x,y), \tag{10.4}$$

where the black and white images of the referenced and extracted regions are compared. By specifying an appropriate threshold for similarity matching (0.225 in our case), we were able to recognize the superimposed word. Thus, a reference pattern with largest metric above this threshold is selected as the matched word or character.

## 10.7 Integrated Querying

In this section we give some examples that show integrated use of different semantic extraction techniques. We modeled by DBNs the following concepts: highlights, excited speech, start, passing, and fly-out.

Except for those concepts, the videos can be queried based on recognized superimposed text. For example, a user can ask for the race winner, the classification in the $i$th lap, the position of a driver in the $i$th lap, relative positions of two drivers in the $i$th lap, pit stop of a specific driver, the final lap, etc. All this information is extracted from the superimposed text. To give the reader an impression, some query examples follow:

> "Retrieve the video sequences showing the car of Michael Schumacher"
> "Retrieve the video sequences with Michael Schumacher leading the race"
> "Retrieve the video sequences showing Barrichello in the pit stop"
> "Retrieve all fly-outs".

For querying the superimposed text, we can imagine a suitable user interface (see Figure 10.11). In this way, the user benefits of combining the results obtained from different techniques for semantic extraction. In the following examples, the user sees results acquired from dynamic Bayesian networks and text recognition, and gets an answer to very detailed complex queries, such as:

> "Retrieve all highlights showing the car of Barrichello" (see Figure 10.11)
> "Retrieve all fly-outs of Mika Hakkinen in this season"
> "Retrieve all highlights at the pit line involving Juan Pablo Montoya".

The answer to the query defined in Figure 10.11 is composed by intersecting all video sequences annotated as highlights with the segments in which the text "Barrichello" is superimposed in the screen as a driver signature.

## 10.8 Summary

This chapter addresses the problem of automatic derivation of high-level video content representations from raw video data.

Videos from Formula 1 car racing provide experimental data. We consider these videos to contain three modalities, namely audio, the stream of video frames, and superimposed text projected by the producer on the frames. From these modalities we can derive low-level features that may contain cues for certain events, for instance the start of a race or a fly-out of a car. It is important to find techniques that can be effectively used to fuse evidence obtained from the modalities present in video.

In this chapter, we focused on (dynamic) Bayesian networks. Bayesian networks model excited speech based on cues (low-level features) derived from videos. Moreover, dynamic Bayesian networks take the time aspect into account by splitting the video into a number of segments or time slices.

**Fig. 10.11.** Pit stop with Barrichello.

First, we focused on the audio signal and detected the parts with speech. Interesting events may occur when the commentator becomes excited. Modeling the cues that may indicate excited announcements, we evaluated the influence of the network structure and temporal dependencies. We carried out numerous experiments with different atemporal and temporal connections within BNs/DBNs. They have shown that the inference in BNs does not vary much with the change of atemporal connections. However, the chosen atemporal, but also temporal dependencies between the nodes of two consecutive time slices, have strong influence on the results of *dynamic* BN inference. This demonstrates the importance of taking time into account meaning that a video should not be considered as a set of independent frames.

With BNs we obtained results for precision and recall in the range from 50% to 75%, while the best DBN reached around 80% for both precision and recall, in detecting excited announcer speech.

Next, we analyzed video frames, the second modality. Again, low-level features may contain cues for interesting high-level concepts. We integrated these cues into an audio-visual DBN. The aim was to detect all highlights (and not only the ones where announcer is excited) as well as which highlight can be considered as a start, fly-out or passing.

Results varied a lot depending on the event and on the race. On German Grand Prix precision and recall were above 50% for all events, and more than 80% for highlights detection. Due to the usage of basic low-level features precision and recall on Belgian and USA Grand Prix were lower than 50% for passing. Eliminating the passing subnetwork resulted in the increase of precision and recall (more than 70% on USA Grand Prix).

Finally, we introduced text extraction schemes, which are applied to superimposed text. Names of drivers, position in the race, lap information, and so on are projected on the screen with a strong varying background. The used optical character recognition techniques make this valuable and otherwise difficult to grasp information available. The effectiveness of text recognition algorithm was almost perfect.

Together, the techniques described in this chapter automatically derive interesting events in Formula 1 racing. This allows us to answer queries like: "In which lap did Schumacher make a fly-out?".

## 10.9 Further Reading

To solve the gap between low-level features and high-level concepts, several domain-dependent research efforts have been undertaken. They mainly use information on object positions, their transitions over time, etc., and relate them to particular events (high-level concepts). Methods have been proposed to detect events in football [7], soccer [5], and hunting [6], etc. For example, Chang et al. [4] presented an integrated audio and video analysis for content-based video indexing. The goal was to develop a system for automatic indexing of sports videos based on speech understanding and video analysis. Authors choose to apply their algorithms for extracting touchdowns in a football game. For audio signal analysis authors used word spotting to recognize when the commentator pronounces the word touchdown, and cheering detection. They fused these two features by using a simple logic. They also used video features to detect shot changes. Based on the audio cues they were able to detect touchdown shots. These approaches have a problem of creating the mapping for each domain manually. In addition, many of these methods are not extensible for detecting new events because they are very dependent on specific artifacts used in the broadcasts of domain programmes.

Other approaches use stochastic methods that often exploit automatic learning capabilities to derive knowledge. Structuring of video using Bayesian Networks alone or together with HMMs has been proposed. Syeda-Mahmood and Srinivasan [14] use a probabilistic model to combine results of visual and audio event detection in order to identify topics of discussion in a classroom lecture environment. Another probabilistic framework that comprises multimedia objects within a Bayesian multinet has been proposed by Naphade and Huang [11]. The closest to work described in this chapter is the one presented by Rui et al. [13]. It concentrates solely on the audio analysis for video characterization. The paper describes how audio features can be used to extract highlights for TV baseball programmes. The authors rely only on audio features, but they used a combination of generic audio features, and baseball-specific features as well. Based on these features they developed subsystems for noisy environment, speech endpoint detection, excited speech classification, and baseball hits detection. Some of the algorithms for calculation of these features are used in this chapter, and they yield good results. It is important to state that they did not cut these values by threshold. On the contrary, they employed probabilistic framework and support vector machines to obtain the best results. However, only few of the mentioned approaches use fusion of audio and video cues using a probabilistic framework for such purpose.

Another related problem is the video classification problem. Kobla et al. [8] tackled this problem and presented various techniques for extraction of video features that will enable identification of sports videos. They used the presence of action replays, amount of scene text in video, and computations of various statistics on camera and/or object motion. The authors also presented novel technique for the automatic detection of slow motion action replays. They focused on development of a system that will be able to automatically distinguish sports scenes from other scenes.

# References

1. B. Arons. Pitch-Based Emphasis Detection for Segment Speech Recordings. In *Proceeding of the International Conference on Spoken Language Processing*, pages 1931–1934, Yokohama, Japan, 1994.
2. N. Babaguchi, Y. Kawai, Y. Yasugi, and T. Kitahashi. Linking Live and Replay Scenes in Broadcast Sport Video. In *Proceeding of ACM Multimedia 2000 Workshops*, pages 205–208, Marina del Rey, CA, 2000.
3. X. Boyen, N. Fiderman, and D. Koller. Discovering the Hidden Structure of Complex Dynamic Systems. In *Proceeding of IEEE Intl. Conference on Uncertainty in Artificial Intelligence*, pages 91–100, 1999.
4. Y.L. Chang, W. Zeng, I. Kamel, and R. Alonso. Integrated Image and Speech Analysis for Content-Based Video Indexing. In *Proceeding of third IEEE Conference on Multimedia Computing and Systems*, pages 306–313, Hiroshima, Japan, 1996.
5. Y. Gong, L.T. Sin, C.H. Chuan, H-J. Zhang, and M. Sakauchi. Automatic Parsing of TV Soccer Programs. In *Procceeding of IEEE International Conference on Multimedia Computing and Systems*, pages 167–174, Washington D.C., 1995.
6. N. Haering, R.J. Qian, and M.I. Sezan. A Semantic Event-Detection Approach and its Application to Detecting Hunts in Wildlife Video. *IEEE Transactions on Circuits and Systems for Video Technology*, 10(6):857–868, 2000.
7. S. Intille and A. Bobick. Visual Tracking Using Closed-Worlds. Technical Report 294, MIT Media Laboratory, 1994.
8. V. Kobla, D. De Menthon, and D. Doermann. Identifying Sports Video using Replay, Text, and Camera Motion Features. In *Proceeding of SPIE Conference on Storage and Retrieval for Media Datbases*, pages 332–343, Hiroshima, Japan, 2000.
9. R. Lienhart. *Video Mining*, pages 155–184. Kluwer Academic Publisher, 2003.
10. V. Mihajlović and M. Petković. Automatic Annotation of Formula 1 Races for Content Based Video Retrieval. Technical Report TR-CTIT-01-41, Centre for Telematics and Information Technology, 2001.

11. M. Naphade and T.S. Huang. A Probabilistic Framework for Semantic Indexing and Retrieval in Video. In *Proceeding of IEEE Intl. Conference on Multimedia and Expo (ICME)*, volume 1, pages 475–478, New York, 2000.
12. L. Rabiner and B.H. Juang. *Fundamentals of Speech Recognition*. Prentice Hall, Englewood Cliffs, New Yersey, 1993.
13. Y. Rui, A. Gupta, and A. Acero. Automatically Extracting Highlights for TV Baseball Programs. In *Proceeding of ACM Multimedia*, pages 105–115, Los Angeles, CA, 2000.
14. T. Syeda-Mahmood and S. Srinivasan. Detecting Topical Events in Digital Video. In *Procceeding of ACM Multimedia*, pages 85–94, Los Angeles, CA, 2000.

# 11

# Interaction

Erik Boertjes[1] and Anton Nijholt[2]

[1] TNO Information and Communication Technology
[2] University of Twente

## 11.1 Introduction

The challenge of coping with the overload of multimedia data has been growing since the advent of digital cameras and broadband connections to the home. Not only the techniques for storing, annotating and search are essential for helping the user to face this challenge, a well-considered user interaction design and an intuitive user interface are equally important in helping the user to find interesting content.

Some challenges in the domain of user interaction with multimedia systems are:

- Taking into account the mismatch between a user's mental model of a multimedia system and the technical structure of a multimedia system.
- Handling video, which is, because of its linearity and length, a tough medium.
- Coping with bad, incomplete, and inconsistent metadata.
- Helping users express what they need. Users often have a fuzzy understanding of what they are looking. Generally, it is hard for a user to express their information needs in a clear and precise way in a language required by the application.

Following up on the last point, many researchers support the idea that users learn during the search process about their information needs, as opposed to the idea that they are able to precisely express their information need at the start of the search process.

Bates [5] introduces the "berry-picking" model of information seeking, taking picking berries as a metaphor for searching. New information may yield new ideas and new directions. And according to this model, interesting information is scattered like berries among bushes. The information need is therefore not satisfied by a single, final retrieved set; it is satisfied by a series of selections and bits of information found along the way.

Similar to the berry picking model, Pirolli and Stuart [13] propose a theory of "information foraging" as an approach to analyzing human behavior in information retrieval. Information foraging uses the analogy of wild animals gathering food to analyze how humans collect information. The theory links the way in which predators decide which prey to hunt to the way in which humans choose which information resources to pursue. In the real world, strong scents lead animals to food; in information retrieval, "information scents" lead humans to the information they need. Humans are always judging the cues in their environment with respect to their experience, saying what information is relevant to what. Like animals adapting their search strategies, humans adapt their search tactics, and modify their own information environments and information organization to make their searches more productive.

### 11.1.1 Relation to Other Chapters

Many chapters in this book focus on algorithms and techniques that are aimed at efficient and effective metadata generation and query solving. Examples are Chapters 2, 4 and 5. Those issues are not directly visible to the user; they are the "nuts and bolts" of a Multimedia Information Retrieval System (MIRS) and remain hidden to the user. This chapter looks at the part of the system that is visible to the user. It discusses ways of interaction between user and system, the problems that may arise and the algorithms and techniques that take care of efficient and effective communication between user and system. Chapter 1 showed how the components that realize this user interaction relate with the other components of a MIRS. One way of user interaction is by natural speech. While this technique is only briefly discussed in this chapter, the details are discussed in Chapter 7. Content-based queries ("queries by example") are described briefly in this chapter while the principles behind them are discussed extensively in Chapter 9.

### 11.1.2 Outline

This chapter starts with discussing four typical ways of user-system interaction in Section 11.2. Each type of user interaction has its own division of tasks between user and system. The next sections each discuss aspects of user interaction that play an important role in one or more of these interaction types. Section 11.3 shows the different ways in which users can express their information needs. Once the results are presented to the user, the system may ask the user how relevant they find the results so that the system can present even better results in the next iteration. This technique is called Relevance Feedback and is explained in Section 11.4. Section 11.5 discusses a technique called "personalization" that is used to learn the user's taste and needs and tailor the results from a query accordingly. Section 11.6 shows techniques of presenting query results to the user. The same section explains how visualization may help the user with the interpretation of the results in case the result set is large or complex. The last step in multimedia information retrieval is to actually show or play the movie, image or soundtrack. The multimedia item may have to be adapted according to the device it is to be shown on, or according to the situation the user is in. This process is called "content adaptation" and is discussed in Section 11.7.

## 11.2 Interaction Types

This section discusses four ways of user interaction with multimedia systems, varying from one in which the user can ask complex questions, to one in which the user does not have to ask anything but where the system pushes interesting content to the user; see also Van Setten's PhD Thesis [19].

### 11.2.1 Retrieval

The first type of user interaction is simply called "retrieval". It is the most common way of interaction found in applications today. Retrieval starts with a person having an information need. The first task that retrieval systems expect a user to do is to specify that need in a way such that the system understands what the user is looking for. The specification of that information need is called "query". The system then matches the query with the data collection and returns those items that match the query. Two aspects from the user interaction point of view are important here:

- the user should formulate the query in the syntax that the system requires;
- the user should formulate the query such that it correctly represents the information need (semantics).

Since inability of the user or the limitations of the system may cause one or both requirements not to be met in practice, information retrieval is often an iterative process of query specification, examining the results, reformulating the query, etc. until the user is satisfied with the results (or is convinced that the information required is simply not available in the information retrieval system at hand). Some systems allow the user, as part of this iteration, to explicitly express how relevant they find the results found by the system (see Section 11.4). The remainder of this section explains the two types of queries commonly found in retrieval:

- Concept-based queries, e.g., "Find images showing a police car";
- Content-based queries, e.g., "Find images with mainly red colors".

**Concept-based Queries**

Concept-based queries consist of keywords, natural language, or other semantically rich descriptions of what the user is looking for. This type of query is typically solved by matching it with the high-level features of the multimedia content while content-based queries (discussed below) are matched with low-level features (see also Chapter 1). The concept-based query is widely used in both non-multimedia systems as well as multimedia systems like GoogleImages: the user types in one or more keywords, and the system returns objects whose descriptions satisfy the keywords.

The big advantage of these queries is that they are very easy for the user: they are close to the natural language in which the user would express their information need. That makes these types of queries highly expressive and easy to use.

The disadvantage is the possible mismatch between the metadata used to describe the multimedia objects and the keywords in the query. There are two reasons for this mismatch:

- Different people use different words to annotate the same object. For example, an image of a collection of trees may be annotated by different persons as "wood", "forest", or "lots of trees". A solution might be to force the user to use only predefined keywords in their queries ("forced vocabulary"). Another solution is to have the system take care of the mapping between different terms for the same concept (ontologies).
- The metadata might be incomplete; it might not describe the specific property the user is interested in. For example, images of Monica and Bill shot before the hussle about the two are not likely to be annoted as showing "Monica Lewinsky and Bill Clinton", since at the time the image was annotated and stored, Monica was someone unknown.

Another drawback is that these type of queries are less suitable for highly visual information needs that are difficult to describe in text. For instance, a Web designer may be looking for images that fit the style of his Web site in terms of color distribution, and atmosphere. Those search criteria are hard to describe in concepts.

## Content-based Queries

Content-based queries are solved on the level of features. Features are automatically deductible characteristics of a multimedia object, like color histogram, shape, brightness, etc. Features are at a lower semantic level than concept-level queries. Content-based queries are often specified by using the "Query by Example" paradigm, which is a rather intuitive way of constructing content-based queries. The user simply gives one or more examples of what they are looking for and specifies what aspect of the example(s) is important to them. For example: "here is a set of images, find images that have similar colors and preferably similar shapes". Advanced query languages for constructing queries-by-example exist, allowing to give weights to the different aspects (expressing that color is more important than shape) and weights to the different examples (expressing that one image is more representative for what the user is looking for, than another).

Content-based queries are often fuzzy queries, i.e., queries that are not unambiguous. Queries like "Find images with lots of red" are fuzzy because "lots of red" is not a very precise way of expression. Queries by example are in itself fuzzy: the word "similar to" in the query "Find images similar to this example image" is a fuzzy term. Fuzzy querying often needs a few iterations before users find what they need.

## 11.2.2 Dynamic Query Interaction

The characteristic for this type of user interaction is the very visual way of how users specify their information need. Sliders, buttons and other visual user interface components allow the user to compose queries in a very fast way. In dynamic query interaction, results are updated very fast by the system and immediate reflect the changes in user input. Figure 11.1 shows the user interface of the FilmFinder application from Ahlberg [2], an example of a system that uses dynamic query interaction. When the user drags the sliders on the right-hand side, the left-hand side quickly adapts to the new slider settings, showing the movies that comply with the slider settings.

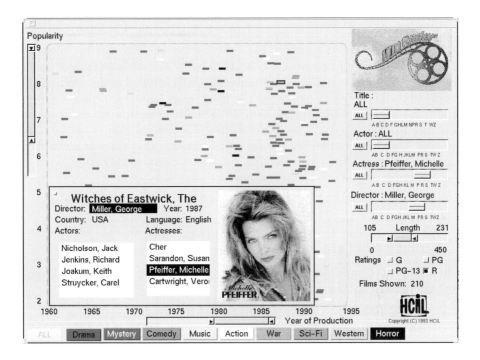

**Fig. 11.1.** The FilmFinder interface (© University of Maryland HCI Lab).

Although the user still poses queries and the system still presents the results, like in the previous section, the iteration cycles in dynamic querying are so short that the user is almost flying through the information space, steering with sliders, buttons and other simple and visual means of input. The separation of action (posting query) and reaction (presenting results) is completely gone. Schneidermann [15] gives these characteristics for dynamic query user interaction:

- visual presentation of the query's components;
- visual presentation of the results;

- rapid, incremental, and reversible control of the query;
- selection by pointing, not typing;
- immediate and continuous feedback.

Queries in this type of interaction are less expressive than those in retrieval where natural language concepts can be used to express rich and precise queries, but more expressive than browsing where the query concept is completely gone.

### 11.2.3 Browsing

The previous section explained how the user can specify their information needs by composing a query. But rather than having a system solve a query and present (hopefully) the items a user is looking for, users may investigate the search space by themselves. Like you browse the Internet by following hyperlinks jumping from Web page to Web page, you can also browse multimedia data. It's like looking for a movie in a video rental store: reading the backs of the DVD boxes, looking at the front image, putting it back, going to the next box, going to another section, etc. Even flipping through TV channels fits into this model: you browse the multimedia content that is broadcasted to you. The characteristic for the browsing model is that there is no explicit specification of information need, like there is in query specification.

Browsing is a useful interaction model:

- to get an impression of the search space;
- to find something without having a clear notion of its characteristics. For example, looking for a "nice" movie, without being able to specify values for title, actors, genre, etc.

Because of the complexity of multimedia objects, there are two levels of browsing multimedia databases:

- browsing through a collection of multimedia objects (e.g., when looking for a movie);
- browsing within a multimedia object (e.g., when looking for a frame within a movie).

A clear visualization of the search space (i.e., the way the multimedia items are presented) is very important, since users have to find their own way in the sometimes large and unstructured search space (see Section 11.6.2).

Browsing can be done on the original search space, but is not limited to that. Browsing the results from a query (so a portion of the search space) is very common: alternating querying and browsing is a powerful interaction model. Browsing can be done on various levels: a user may browse through the metadata of a collection of videos, but may also browse within a video, searching for a certain shot, scene or still image.

Browsing can even be done in a collection of keywords or concepts. Figure 11.2 shows the Aquabrowser; a tool that allows for browsing in predefined

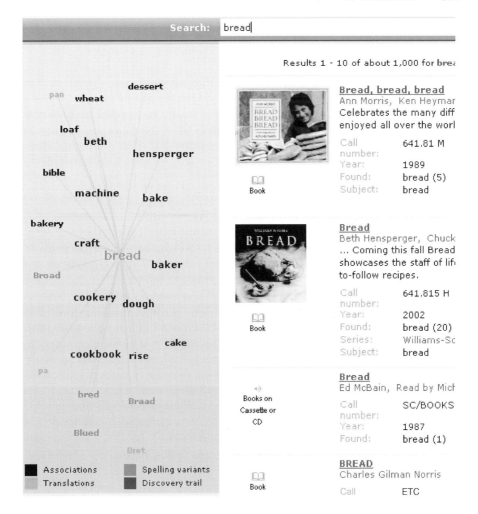

**Fig. 11.2.** A World Cloud in the AquaBrowser (© Medialab Solutions B.V.).

concepts with which the content is annotated. The concepts are represented as nodes in a graph. Two concepts in the graph are connected by a vertex if:

- One concept is the translation of another ("bread" and the French translation "pain" are connected). This allows for quickly browsing from one language to another.
- One concept is a spelling variation of another ("bread" and the German translation "brot" are connected). This allows for quickly correcting mistakes the user may have made in the initial query.

- One concept is semantically related to another ("bread" and "grain" are connected, so are "bread" and "baker"). This allows for quickly browsing the domain the concept is part of.

This visualization gives the user a way to quickly adapt the query while browsing through concepts, their spelling variations, their translations and semantically related concepts. The same principle could be applied to browsing through a collection of multimedia items. Instead of the concepts, you would find movie titles that are connected to each other based on a semantical relation (e.g., having the same genre, actors or subject), spelling variation or translation.

### 11.2.4 Recommendation

The interaction types discussed so far all required initiative from the user: either a query or other input, in response to which the system provides or adapts the results. All these fall in the pull category: the user pulls results from the system. The recommendation interaction model differs from these in that the system itself takes the initiative. As soon as interesting content is available, the system sends them to the user, without the user having to specifically ask for them or having to specify a query. This is called the push scenario. Examples are personal mail advertisements and movie recommendations. The source is often dynamic: new items are added or updated regularly and users are informed when new items appear that are of their interest. This interaction type typically addresses the user's long term interests and taste, and not, like in the previous interaction models their instant and time-specific information need (to be expressed in a query). Personalization is an important technique in systems based on this interaction model. Section 11.5 explains how personalization can be used to select items that match a user's taste and interest.

## 11.3 Modalities for User Input

Modalities refer to the human channels of perception: for example, visual, auditory or tactile modalities. In human–computer interaction the term "modality" is also used to refer to the channels of perception an interface has through the available input devices. For example, a touch screen, an electronic pen, a camera, a microphone, an eyetracker, a locality sensor, a mouse, or a keyboard.

Natural interaction between humans is multimodal and does not require a manual. For the same reason we can aim at multimodal interaction with a computer: use speech to retrieve a speech fragment, point to a preferred item among a list of items, show a picture to retrieve a similar one, hum to retrieve a song and nod to confirm a choice. In these examples there is an almost one-to-one mapping between the input modality and the media type of the item that has to be retrieved. Obviously, there is no need for that. A textual query can retrieve a speech or video fragment and a query that is formulated by drawing a picture can retrieve a text related to that picture. As well, a query for a single-media item can be composed using several modalities and, on the other hand, a single-modality query can retrieve a multimedia item. In current multimedia systems querying is often done using one input modality only. Examples are the traditional textual queries (keywords, a phrase, a sentence or a piece of text), music retrieval by playing or humming a song, picture retrieval by drawing a picture, etc.

Users have to express their information needs and some ways to express these needs are more natural than others. For example, describing spatial relations using speech only is far from easy. If the information is related to a map, displayed on a wall or on a table, speech and pointing are natural ways to formulate queries. If a 3D object has to be retrieved, gestures can be used to describe the object. If we want to retrieve information about a certain person, we can try to describe that person, but we can also try to imitate that person (voice, characteristic postures, and movements) or have a combination of imitation and description.

In particular, in ambient intelligent environments, that is, sensor-equipped environments with embedded intelligence and intelligent and social interfaces a user's actions and behavior can be captured. Being able to perceive the user also allows the computer to better interpret and handle the input the user provides. Queries are often ambiguous. Context to disambiguate and refine the query can be provided by information obtained from the various input modalities the interface distinguishes. Gestures can disambiguate speech and vice versa. Pen input can compensate for errors in speech recognition. From the facial expression of the user the urgency of a request can be determined.

The main problems in modeling multimodal interaction deal with the synchronization and the fusion of the input coming from different channels required to interpret a multimodal request or the feedback by the user. From experiments [8, 10] it has been observed that users not necessarily use all available modalities simultaneously. Rather they switch between modalities. Other problems that are tackled in multimodal interaction research are related to the patterns of multimodality choices. Individual users may have preferences for certain modalities or for sequences and combinations of modalities. These preferences also depend on their management of their cognitive load while interacting [11, 12]. Dynamically adapting the interface to such preferences is an important issue of research.

## 11.4 Relevance Feedback

Some multimedia systems allow the user to give feedback on the results presented by the system. This is called relevance feedback. After the user poses a query, the system solves the query and presents the results. Some systems then allow users to give their opinion on how relevant they find each of the results, or how satisfied they are with the results. Using this feedback, the system can refine the original query and present even better results. This is a form of query expansion, as explained in Chapter 4. Of course, clicking a result from the result list to get more information, or to get directed to the actual content, is an indication of whether the user finds the result promising. When being presented with the result list from Google, for instance, a user probably will click on the results that they think are best. Some systems allow for more precise ways of expressing relevance of results.

### 11.4.1 Binary Relevance Feedback

In the binary relevance feedback scheme, a user can indicate for each of the results whether or not the result is relevant. An example is given in Figure 11.3 showing the user interface of the MetaSeek tool [6]. It shows images that are retrieved in reponse to a query. The user can indicate for each of the images whether they are (more or less) corresponding to what the user is looking for. The positivily rated images serve as a new example set with which the query is expanded. The negatively rated images can serve as a contra-example set. Relevance feedback is especially usefull in fuzzy queries, in which users cannot express precisely what they are looking for. After a few iterations with relevance feedback the results will get better and better.

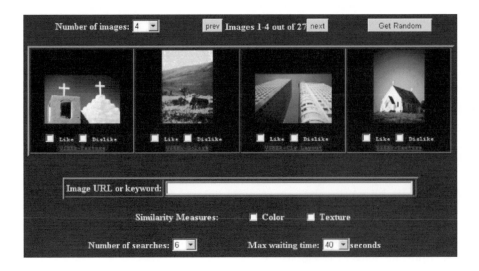

**Fig. 11.3.** User interface of the MetaSEEK system.

### 11.4.2 Weighed Relevance Feedback

In weighed relevance feedback the user can specify the amount of relevance of the results, i.e., a gliding scale from being completely irrelevant, to completely relevant. Figure 11.4 shows a sketch of a corresponding user interface in a query by example system. The distance from the image to the center indicates the amount of relevance of that image. By dragging the images to the middle of the target circle the user indicates that those images are relevant. Dragging them to the outside means that the images are less relevant.

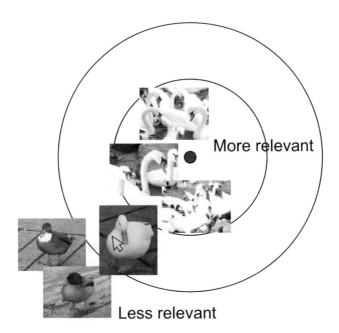

**Fig. 11.4.** Sketch of user interface for weighed relevance feedback.

## 11.5 Personalization

### 11.5.1 Definition

Personalization permits users to adapt a service in a specific context and to individual goals, by providing the users with a high quality product or service they really need and can use at best [14]. This definition is one of many that can be found in literature.

Originally, the term comes from one-to-one marketing, and is used there to indicate the process of trying to pin-point possibly interested users for a new product or service. Closer to the subject of this book, personalization is an important concept in the domain of information delivery. There, personalization means filtering information in such a way that a person only receives relevant information, targeted at the person's unique and individual needs. It is a means of coping with today's information overload, helping finding people what they need and/or like.

## 11.5.2 Examples

Practical use of personalization already can be found on the Web. When entering Amazon's Website for instance, a message like "Hello John, we have new recommendations for you" appears. A list of books and other items is provided that Amazon thinks you will like, based on previous purchases and click-through behavior. This is a so called recommendation system, it recommends possibly interesting items to the user.

Another example of a personalized service is LaunchCast, an Internet radio station that claims to learn the user's taste and only plays music that the user likes. Users can skip a song when they don't like it, or give an explicit rating (good, mediocre, bad). After a while, the system learns from this feedback, playing songs that the user likes more and more.

The previous two examples show how personalization can be used to push interesting content to the user: the initiative is taken by the application. An example in which the user takes the initiative (and not the application) is Google's personalized search. This application orders search results based on what the user has searched for in the past. That way, it tries to learn the domains of interest to the user, so that when a user searches for "java", it shows references to the Indonesian Island instead of the programming language, because it might have learned from previous queries that the user is a-technical and fond of travelling.

## 11.5.3 The personalization process

Figure 11.5 gives the basic steps in the personalization process. Personalization starts with building a user profile (left-hand side of the figure). This user profile is a description of the user and is used to filter metadata and retrieve results that believed to be relevant to that specific user. The right-hand side of the figure shows the two common ways of filtering, which will be explained in more detail below.

### User Profile Building

In order to be able to find information for an individual person, you have to know the user's information needs and store that information as the representation of that user. That representation is called the "user profile", it is the description of the user's taste and needs in a certain domain (e.g., books, movies, etc.)

Building a user profile is a complex task. An application could simply ask users about their information needs. A movie recommender system, for instance, could explicitly ask users about the type of movies they like. There are two problems with this approach:

- Even users themselves might not be able to express their taste in a clear and uniform way in natural language, let alone in a language that the system understands.

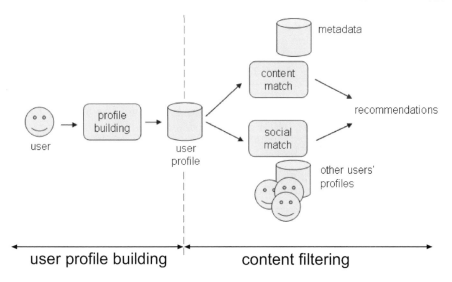

**Fig. 11.5.** The Personalization Process.

- Users tend to be passive and are often not enthusiastic about filling in endless questionnaires before they get to use a recommendation system.

Another approach is to build a user profile by looking at the way users use the application. In an online shop, for instance, a profile can be built based on the items that a user buys or the items that a user clicks on to get more information (click-through behavior). In an intelligent VCR a user profile can be built based on the programmes the user watches, records, replays, etc. This approach is not very reliable either. Most online shops do not make a distinction between users buying things for themselves and users buying gifts for someone else. If someone buys a present for someone else, this purchase information should not be used for adapting the profile of the bying user.

In practice, the two approaches often are combined. Amazon.com for instance, explicitly asks users to rate books (with 1 to 5 stars) and uses in addition implicit information based on user's purchases and click-through behavior.

**Content Filtering**

Once the taste of a user is represented in a user profile, the recommendation system can use it to find interesting content.

There are two well known methods for selecting content, given a user profile. A hybrid version, combining the two, is sometimes also used. We'll explain the two methods by taking an intelligent VCR as a simplified example. This VCR (like TiVo) can record television programmes digitally on a hard disk. It builds user profiles by keeping track of the programmes that its user (John) records and plays back. When John comes home from a long tiring work day and wants to see something interesting on television, it can recommend interesting programmes that will be broadcasted that night and might have recorded some interesting shows. From previous behavior, the VCR stored the following information about John's behavior:

- John recorded *Friends* three times during the past month.
- John recorded the movies *Die Hard*, *The Jackal* and *The Story of Us*.
- John recorded *Soccer: UEFA championship 2005*.
- John watched all three recorded episodes of *Friends*, some of them twice.
- John watched *Die Hard* and *Seven* completely and he watched only two minutes of *The Story of Us*.
- John did not (yet) watch *Soccer: UEFA championship 2005*.

### 11.5.4 Content-based Filtering

Content-based filtering methods select content items that have a high degree of similarity to the user's profile and recommends those items to the user. A user profile in content based filtering consists of attribute-value pairs, together with an indication of how much each attribute-value pair is fitting the user's taste.

Let us take John's behavior profile from above as an example. When using content-based filtering, the information about John's behavior is stored in the following profile:

| Attribute | Value | Fit |
|---|---|---|
| title | *Friends* | 0.9 |
| genre | comedy | 0.9 |
| genre | action | 0.7 |
| actor | Bruce Willis | 0.7 |
| genre | romance | 0.1 |

The first line in this profile means that John likes very much programmes which title equal *Friends*. The last line specifies that he dislikes programmes of the romantic genre.

This is a rather simplified one-dimensional profile. A more accurate representation of the user's taste would store the fact the the user does like Bruce Willis but only in action movies, and not in romantic comedies. Besides, in real life, it takes much more information about user behavior before a profile like this can be derived: to base the assumption that John dislikes romance on just one indication is statistically not plausible. But for the sake of clarity, we will stick with this simple example profile here. Note that the profile is not on the level of multimedia items (televisions programmes), but on the level of their properties (genre, title, etc.). In content-based filtering the attributes are the things that the content is matched with, while in social-based filtering (see below) it is the multimedia items.

Matching of the user profile with multimedia items takes place in vector space. This means that the user profile is an $n$-dimensional vector and so is each individual multimedia item. Each [attribute name, attribute value] pair forms a dimension in this vector space. The dimension [genre, "action"] indicates how well the programme fits the "action" genre, i.e., it indicates how much action there is in the programme. The dimension [actor, Bruce Willis] indicates whether or not Bruce Willis plays a role in the programme. And since vector space is non-binary, this dimension can indicate if Bruce Willis plays a main role (value close to 1), a smaller part (value closer to 0) or does not play at all (value equal to zero).

Figure 11.6 shows how the user profile and a few TV programmes are represented in a simplified vector space with only these two dimensions. For simplicity reasons we only consider two dimensions: in reality there are thousands of dimensions; one for each possible [attribute name, attribute value] pair.

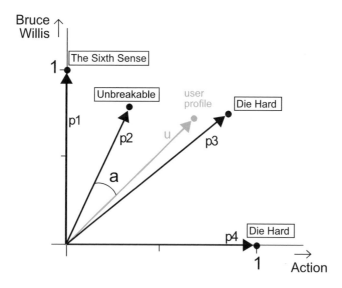

**Fig. 11.6.** User profile and TV programmes in vector space.

The closer a multimedia item is to the user profile, the more likely it is that the item is interesting for the user. This closeness, or similarity, is based on the angle $\alpha$ between the user profile vector $u$ and the item vector $p_i$. The smaller the angle, the more similar the item is to the user profile, and the more likely the user will find the item interesting. This similarity can be calculated as follows:

$$sim(p_i, u) = cos\alpha = \frac{\mathbf{p_i} \bullet \mathbf{u}}{|\mathbf{p_i}| \times |\mathbf{u}|}. \tag{11.1}$$

Disadvantages of content-based filtering are the following:

- Quality of recommendations is dependent on quality and availability of metadata.
- Expressing similarity in terms of properties is tough. One comedy starring Bruce Willis may be very different from another comedy starring Bruce Willis, yet in metadata terms, they may be quite similar.
- New user problem. A new user does not have a profile yet; it takes some time to collect enough information about the user to build a reliable profile. Until then, no reliable recommendations can be provided using this approach.

### 11.5.5 Social-based Filtering: Collaborative Filtering

Collaborative Filtering (CF) techniques draw on the experiences of a group of users rather than on the experience of an individual user. Imagine your friends telling you that they saw this great movie (that you didn't see yet). You might be tempted to go and see that movie as well, since you trust their advice. CF can be seen as the automated version of this "Word of Mouth" principle. In short, this method tries to find people that have similar taste to the user at hand. If those people gave a high rating to a movie that the user at hand did not see, that movie is recommended to that user. In this way, items are recommended on the basis of user similarity rather than item similarity.

Let's go back to John. In CF John's profile would look like:

| Programme | Fit |
|---|---|
| *Friends* | 0.9 |
| *Die Hard* | 0.7 |
| Seven | 0.7 |
| *The Story of Us* | −0.2 |

The first line means that John likes the programme *Friends* very much. The last line means that John dislikes the programme *The Story of Us*. The values in the profile can be seen as ratings. CF now tries to find people with similar profiles as John.

One common way of calculating the similarity $sim_{i,j}$ between two people $i$ and $j$ is by using the Pearson correlation formula (11.2). This formula finds out whether there is a correlation between the ratings $v_{i,p}$ of one person $i$ and those $v_{j,p}$ of another person $j$ on programmes $p$. If two people rate programmes the same way, the value is close to 1. If two people constantly disagree about programmes, their ratings being the opposite of each other, the value is close to −1. When no correlation can be found, the value is zero:

$$sim_{i,j} = \frac{\sum_p (v_{i,p} - \mathbf{v_i})(v_{j,p} - \mathbf{v_j})}{\sqrt{\sum_p (v_{i,p} - \mathbf{v_i})^2 \sum_p (v_{j,p} - \mathbf{v_j})^2}}. \tag{11.2}$$

In this equation $\mathbf{v_i}$ denotes the average of all ratings of person $i$. By using the difference between the actual rating and the average rating, the equation accounts for the effect that some people tend to rate significantly higher than others.

Now the ratings of other users can be used to predict a rating for a programme that the target user did not yet see. If this prediction is high, the programme is probably a good recommendation for the user. If the prediction is low, the programme should not be recommended to the user. A predicted rating $r_{i,p}$ of programme $p$ for user $i$ could be calculated as follows:

$$r_{i,p} = \mathbf{v_i} + \frac{\sum_j (v_{j,p} - \mathbf{v_j}) sim_{i,j}}{\sum_j |sim_{i,j}|}. \tag{11.3}$$

In this equation, the similarity $sim_{i,j}$ between two persons $i$ and $j$ is used as a weight factor: the more two persons $i$ and $j$ are alike, the larger the share of the rating of $j$ will be in the predicted rating for person $i$. Again, $vecv_i$ and $vecv_j$ denote the average ratings of persons $i$ and $j$ respectively.

Advantages of CF are:

- Explicit content representations are not needed. As seen above, in CF the system does not have to store any information about the movie, except for a way to uniquely identify it (title or ID). The knowledge-engineering problem of finding proper characteristics of movies and how to represent and store those is non-existent.
- CF is domain independent: it is equally suitable for recommending movies, as it is for recommending books, holiday destinations or French Cheese.

Disadvantages of CF are:

- Thousands of users are needed, each having rated dozens of items, before enough information is available for generating reliable recommendations.
- Cold start problem: New users have only a small number of ratings in their profile which makes it hard to similar people to base prediction on.
- Unusual user problem: for users that have unusual taste, it is hard to find similar people to base predictions on.
- New item problem: when a new movie is released, no or not many people have rated that movie. This makes it unlikely that that movie will be recommended to anyone.

## 11.6 Presentation

In the context of multimedia information retrieval systems, presentation plays a role on two different levels. First, the results of a query need to be presented to the user. Since multimedia objects are large in general , these results are not presented by the multimedia objects themselves, but by metadata describing those objects (e.g., a list of movie titles). The actual multimedia object (e.g., the movie), is presented after the user selected it from the list of results. So presentation deals with both the description of the multimedia objects found, as well as the multimedia objects themselves.

## 11.6.1 Presentation Modalities

Since an MIRS contains content in various modalities (text, speech, music, images, video, etc.), the results of a query typically consist of various modalities as well. When presenting the items found, the most appropriate modality for each item needs to be selected. This selection is a complex and knowledge intensive process that needs to take into account the type of information that needs to be conveyed, the specific (dis)advantages of each modality, and the preferences and abilities of the user. Further complexity is added because the combination of modalities also needs to be effective.

Given the complexities involved, it is not surprising that human designers need to be involved to balance the different trade-offs. In an MIRS however, this selection has to be done automatically, on-the-fly. Bachvarova et al. [3] discuss an automated system for presentation modality selection. It uses the following rule: Modality combinations that employ different perception channels (visual and auditory) and encode information both verbally and non-verbally are optimal from an information processing perspective.

|  | visual verbal | visual nonverbal | auditory verbal | auditory non-verbal |
|---|---|---|---|---|
| visual verbal (text) | − − two pieces of text | + text and image | − text and speech | + text and music |
| visual non-verbal (image, animation) |  | − two images | ++ image and speech | + image and music |
| (auditory, verbal) speech, songs |  |  | − − two pieces of speech | + speech and music |
| auditory non-verbal (music, environmental sound) |  |  |  | − two pieces of music |

**Fig. 11.7.** Possible binary combinations of modalities in terms of their property values.

Figure 11.7 shows all possible combinations of two modalities as well as how they rank with respect to effective cognitive processing effectiveness. The ranking results from applying the optimal combination rule derived earlier in this section. With ++ we denote the highest ranking position, that is the most preferable combination; − − denotes the most unfavorable ranking position, that is a combination which is almost impossible or impossible to process. A very important assumption we make when analyzing and modeling modality combination process is that we consider the cognitive effect of the simultaneous presentation of different modalities. Thus the combination of two pieces of text is impossible to process simultaneously (in the table this combination is marked with −−) but if the user addresses the two texts one at a time then this turns into an entirely acceptable combination. The described distinction raises questions about the relation between modality combination and temporality which is a further issue we plan to investigate.

### 11.6.2 Visualization

Although the term visualization is close to presentation, there is a slight difference. Visualization is more than presenting results; in visualization, techniques are used to interpret the data and help presenting the data in a more understandable form. Instead of wading through a long list of results, visualization can serve to cluster similar items and identify regions of potential interest. Visualization can also be used for iterating the search process, narrowing in on areas of potential value. Since humans have a highly developed visual ability, visualized data is much faster to understand than text. It helps people gain more insight in a huge collection of data. Sometimes it even reveals information that is hidden in the data.

Goals of visualization:

- enhancing understanding of concepts and processes;
- gaining new (unexpected, profound) insights;
- making invisible visible;
- effective presentation of significant features;
- quality control of simulations, measurements;
- increasing scientific productivity;
- medium of communication/collaboration.

Below we discuss two example visualizations that are suitable for visualizing multimedia collections: treemaps and graphs. Then we discuss 2D and 3D graphics. The last section discusses visualization of video material, which is a complex, linear and long data type.

### Treemaps

Treemaps visualize a hierarchy of data as nested squares. The location and nesting of the squares indicate the position of a data item in the hierarchy. The size of the square can be used to reflect some property of the data item. In addition, color, texture, and even motion can be used to express other properties of the data items.

An example of multimedia data set represented in a treemap can be taken from the TV domain. The classical representation of TV programmes is to list their metadata (title, start-time, genre, description) in an ordered list, one list per channel per day. Browsing such a TV guide would become infeasable when the number of available channels grow to a couple of hundreds or even thousands in the next decade. Using the hierarchy of genres of TV programmes, a treemap can be used to visualize many programmes in one view. This gives the user a better overview of the available programmes in one glance. Figure 11.8 shows an example. The left-hand side of the picture shows the tree of a TV-programme guide. Each node represents a genre, except for the leaves, which are the actual TV programmes. A treemap visualization of this tree is given at the right-hand side.

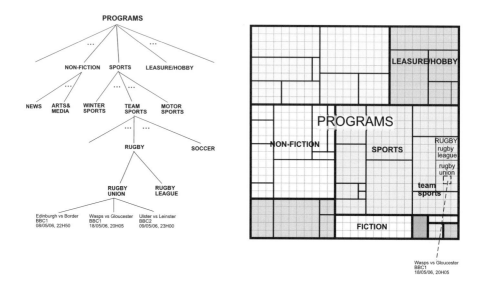

**Fig. 11.8.** A tree representing a collection of TV-programmes (left) and the corresponding treemap (right).

The challenge in using treemaps is how to map $k$-dimensional properties of multimedia items to an $n$-dimensional visualization, where $n$ is the number of visual characteristics of the visualization. Examples of these characteristics are position of the rectangle, its size, its length/width, its color, etc.

A 3D version of Treemaps, called Treecubes, was introduced by Tanaka et al. [17] where instead of rectangular boxes, cubes are used. This gives one extra visual dimension that can be used to visualize an item's property.

**Graphs**

Another popular way of visualizing the search space are 2D or 3D graphs. Each node represents a multimedia item, each vertex represents some relation between the items. The kind of relation chosen is application specific. Figure 11.9 gives an example of a visualization of part of a multimedia database containting audio clips [1]. Each node represents a song or an artist, each songs node is connected to one artist node, and artist nodes are connected to each other according to similarity between artists.

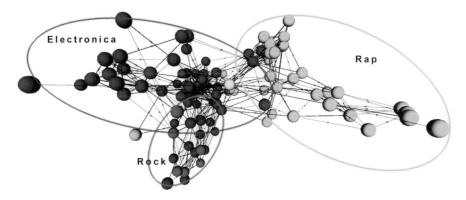

**Fig. 11.9.** Music items represented in a 3D graph.

**Starfield Display**

In the Starfield Display each multimedia item is a dot on a 2D plane, or in a 3D space with the axes representing some attribute of the item. Contrary to the graphs discussed in the previous section, relationship between the items are not explicitly visualized. The FilmFinder (Figure 11.1) shows an example of movies plotted in 2D space. The horizontal axe indicates the year in which the movie is released, the vertical axe gives the average rating on a scale from 0 to 10. Colors of the dots indicate the genre of the movie.

In fact, this visualization plots the items in 2D or 3D vector space. In Section 11.5.4 vector space was mentioned as a way to represent multimedia items. The difference is that here we are stuck to two or three dimensions because in visualization that is the maximum; in storing items, vector space dimensionality can be much larger.

**Visualization for Video Browsing**

Browsing a video in order to get an impression of the visual contents of a video or in order to look for a specific frame in the video is very hard because of the length of the video material and its linear nature. When using a player, one could use the fastforward function to speed up the process, but it would still take an hour to browse through a feature movie.

One way of visualizing video is to break it into segments, and show from each segment one frame. This gives a summarized version of the video, much shorter than the original video. First, a process called shot detection is performed on the video. This breaks the video down into individual shots. Then, for each shot, a representative frame is selected. This frame is called the keyframe of the shot. The video is then presented by displaying all keyframes, similar to a storyboard often used in the production process of a movie.

Some systems group shots into scenes, which are shots that semantically belong together. Like the shots, each scene is represented by a keyframe, chosen from the keyframes that represent each shot within the scene. This allows for a hierarchical visualization of the video, where on the top level the video is represented as a series of scenes. Each scene is represented by the keyframes of its shots. Browsing a video comes down to browsing through the scenes, and once an interesting scene is found, browsing through its shots. Figure 11.10 gives an example of a video browser by Guillemot et al. [9] based on this concept.

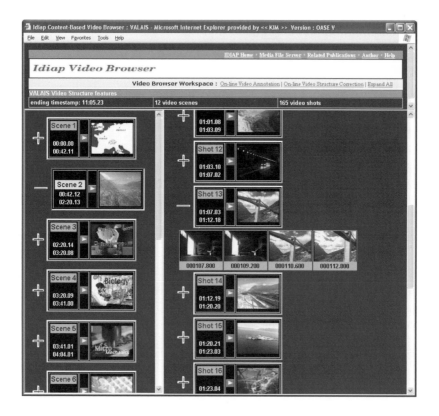

**Fig. 11.10.** User interface of a video browser.

### 11.6.3 Embodied Conversational Agents

Multimedia systems are used more and more by non-professional people. On-line photo-archives, Electronic TV programme guides, have become common tools nowadays. Many people are still reluctant to use these systems since they are "scared" by the apparent complexity of the user interface. Embodied Conversational Agents (ECAs) are one way to solve this problem. An ECA is a computer-generated cartoon-like character that can be used as a guide in helping the user use a system, or as a very easy-to-use interface as an alternative for the existing interface discussed in the book *Embodied Conversational Agents* [7]. ECA demonstrates many of the same properties as humans in face-to-face conversation, which makes them, for some people, more comfortable to interact with than existing interfaces. Experienced users may prefer the more complicated, possibly more efficient, interface without an ECA.

## 11.7 Content Adaptation

Content adaptation plays a role when presenting multimedia content to the user. Whereas Section 11.6 discussed ways to present multimedia query results, often in the form of metadata, this section is about presenting the actual multimedia content itself. The way in which the multimedia content is presented, depends on:

- the capabilities of the device on which the content is played;
- the context the user is in;
- the capabilities of the user.

When the form in which the content is stored does not comply with either of these three factors, the content needs to be adapted to overcome any device/user disabilities. A video for instance may have to be reduced in size or colors, or it may have to be subtitled if the user in question is not able to understand or hear the language spoken in the video. This content adaptation can be seen as the final phase of the content delivery process.

Device capabilities typically refer to properties like

- screen size
- screen resolution
- color depth
- refresh rate
- format support (jpg, mpg, mp3)
- audio quality
- 3D capabilities
- etc.

An example of a user context in which content adaption is needed, is one where the user is driving a car. The user cannot watch video for more than a few seconds nor can read long texts. Audio however, is a much more suitable modality in that context.

Content adaptation is also needed in case of limited user capabilities, e.g., when the user suffers from color vision deficiency or low-vision capabilities. Note that these capabilities are context-independent and user specific.

Some types of content adaptation are:

- Transcoding: bringing content from one storage format to another, e.g., from video in MPEG7 to video in MPEG4. Note that the modality stays the same.

- Transmoding: changing the modality of the content, e.g., from audio to text, from video to still images.
- Content summarization: e.g., from text to textual summarization or from video to a collection of keyframes. In this type of content adaptation information is lost. Both modality and storage format might change.

## 11.8 Summary

Well-considered user interaction design is equally important as the techniques for storing, annotating and search. An MIRS should allow users to express their information needs, formulate their queries, and understand search results. We distinguish four interaction types:

- Retrieval: users formulate their information needs in a (possibly complex) query, which is solved by the MIRS. The system presents the results to the user.
- Dynamic query interaction: the user formulates simple queries by means of sliders, buttons, and other visual user interface components. The system gives instant feedback by continuously updating the visual presentation of the results.
- Browsing: with only an initial query, or no query at all, the user wanders through the search space, selecting the promising items.
- Recommendation: the system takes the initiative by sending the user interesting items. Personalization techniques are used to find items that match the user's personal taste.

Personalization is a technique used to filter information targeted at a person's unique and individual needs. The personal information needs of a user are stored in a user profile. This profile is either matched with the metadata of a collection of items (Content-based filtering) or with other users' profiles (Collaborative Filtering), resulting in personal recommendations.

Relevance feedback allows a user to give feedback on the results presented by the system. The system uses this feedback to improve the resultset in an iterative way.

Interaction with an MIRS is not limited to using keyboard, mouse and monitor. Multimodal interaction allows for visual, auditory and tactile interaction: use speech to retrieve a speech fragment, show a picture to retrieve a similar one, hum to retrieve a song and nod to confirm a choice. A one-to-one mapping between the input modality and the media type of the item to be retrieved is not needed though. When presenting multimedia items, various output modalities can be used as well. The appropriate output modality depends on the type of information, the specific (dis)advantage of each modality, and the preferences and abilities of the user.

Visualization techniques aim at presenting data in a clear and intuitive way. The user will see areas of interest at a glance and may gain new and unexpected insights in the data presented. Treemaps are a common way to visualize hierarchical data, while graphs are typically suitable to visualize (dis)similarity between data items.

Multimedia items may have to be adapted to the capabilities of the user, and to the capabilities of the device they are presented on. Some types of content adaptation are:

- transcoding: changing the storage format, while keeping the modality unchanged;
- transmoding: changing the modality;
- summarization: creating a shorter version of the data (in time or in space).

## 11.9 Further Reading

Baeza-Yates et al. [4, chapter "User Interfaces and Visualization"] give a clear introduction on the interaction aspects of an MIRS, explaining (graphical) ways of query specification, relevance feedback, and user interface specific issues like window management.

Both Soukup et al. [16] and Tufte [18] give a thorough introduction in the area of visualization. The former focuses on visualization of business data with rather traditional tools like column and bar graphs, trees and maps. It also explains visual data mining: the visualization of data in such a way that patterns can be detected easily. The latter is not focused on one data type, but covers a wide range of data types and corresponding ways of visualization. It covers historical aspects of visualization and is more philosophic than the former.

## References

1. Piotr Adamczyk. Seeing Sounds: Exploring Musical Social Networks. In *Proceedings of the 12th annual ACM international conference on Multimedia*, pages 512–515. ACM, 2004.
2. C. Ahlberg and B. Shneiderman. Visual Information Seeking: Tight Coupling of Dynamic Query Filters with Starfield Displays. In *Proceedings of the Human Factors in Computing Systems*, pages 313–317. Association for Computing Machinery, 1994.
3. Yulia Bachvarova, Lynda Hardman, and Jacco van Ossenbruggen. Modeling the process of selecting modalities in automatic generation of multimedia presentations. Presented at the workshop *Interaction Design for the Semantic Web (IDSW)* at the Thirteenth International World Wide Web Conference (WWW2004), New York, 2004.
4. R. Baeza-Yates and B. Ribeiro-Neto, editors. *Modern Information Retrieval*. ACM Press, New York, 1999.
5. Marcia Bates. The design of browsing and berrypicking techniques for the online search interface. *Online Review*, (13):407–424, 1989.
6. A.B. Benitez, M. Beigi, and Shih-Fu Chang. Using relevance feedback in content-based image metasearch. *IEEE Internet Computing*, 2(4):59–69, 1998.

7. J. Cassell, J. Sullivan, S. Provost, and E. Churchill (Eds.). *Embodied Conversational Agents*. The MIT Press, Cambridge, Mass., 2000.
8. P. Cohen, M. Johnson, D.R. McGee, S. Oviatt, J. Pittman, I. Smith, L. Chen, and J. Clow. QuickSet: Multimodal intraction for distributed applications. In *Proceedings Multimedia*, pages 31–40. Association for Computing Machinery, 1997.
9. M. Guillemot, P. Wellner, D. Gatica-Perez, and J-M.Odobez. A hierarchical keyframe user interface for browsing video over the internet. IDIAP-COM 02, IDIAP, 2003.
10. S.L. Oviatt. Ten myths of multimodal interaction. *Communications of the ACM*, 42(11):74–81, November 1999.
11. S.L. Oviatt, R. Coulston, and R. Lunsford. When Do We Interact Multimodally? Cognitive Load and Multimodal Communication Patterns. In *Proceedings of the Sixth International Conference on Multimodal Interfaces*, pages 14–15. Association for Computing Machinery, 2004.
12. S.L. Oviatt, R. Coulston, S. Tomko, B. Xiao, R. Lunsford, M. Wesson, and L. Carmichael. Toward a Theory of Organized Multimodal Integration Patterns during Human-Computer Interaction. In *Proceedings of the International Conference on Multimodal Interfaces*, pages 44–51. Association for Computing Machinery, 2003.
13. Peter Pirolli and Stuart Card. Information Foraging in Information Access Environments. In *Proceedings of the SIGCHI conference on Human Factors in Computing Systems*, pages 51–58. Association for Computing Machinery, 1995. ISBN 0-201-84705-1, `http://acm.org/sigchi/chi95/proceedings/papers/ppp_bdy.htm`.
14. D. Riecken. Personalized Views of Personalization. *Communications of the ACM*, 43(8):26–28, 2000.
15. B. Schneidermann. Dynamic Queries for Visual Information Seeking. *IEEE Software*, 11(6):70–77, nov 1994.
16. T. Soukup and I. Davidson. *Visual Data Mining*. Wiley Publishing, Inc., 2002.
17. Yoichi Tanaka, Yoshihiro Okada, and Koichi Niijima. Interactive interfaces of Treecube for browsing 3D multimedia data. In *Proceedings of the working conference on Advanced visual interfaces*, pages 298–302. Association for Computing Machinery, 2004.
18. E. Tufte. *The Visual Display of Quantitative Information*. Graphics Press, cheshire, Connecticut, 2001.
19. M. van Setten. *Supporting People In Finding Information: Hybrid Recommender Systems and Goal-Based Structuring*. PhD thesis, Telematics Institute, Enschede, The Netherlands, 2005.

# 12

# Digital Rights Management

Paul Koster[1] and Willem Jonker[1,2]

[1] Philips Research
[2] University of Twente

## 12.1 Introduction

Digital Rights Management, or DRM for short, is a much-discussed topic nowadays. The main reason for this is that DRM technology is often mentioned in the context of protection of digital audio and video content, for example to avoid large scale copying of CDs and DVDs via peer-to-peer networks in the Internet. However, DRM technology is much more than a simple copy protection technology. It is one of the enabling technologies that open the way to secure distribution and exchange of digital content over open digital infrastructures such as the Internet.

In order to show how DRM addresses this challenge, we will discuss what DRM technology actually is. There are two main lines of DRM technology based on two different approaches to the problem. The first approach is preventive, while the second approach is reactive.

### 12.1.1 Preventive DRM Technology

Preventive DRM technology aims at preventing behavior that violates the regulations. The technology is based on encryption of the content. The encrypted content can only be accessed through an encryption key. The use of this key is regulated by so called usage rights. A typical electronic distribution system consists of a client-server system. At the server side the content is encrypted and sent to the client. The client needs to be in possession of both the key and the usage right to access the content. The DRM software that runs on the client checks that this is the case. The key and usage right together are typically contained in a data object that we call license. More details and examples can be found in the section on DRM architecture and the case.

### 12.1.2 Reactive DRM Technology

Reactive DRM technology aims at tracing of behavior that violates the regulations. The approach is also called forensic tracking. The technique that is commonly used is that of embedding information in the content itself that allows tracing the origin of the content. The main technology that is exploited in this context is that of watermarking. Watermarking allows inserting information in music or movies in such a way that consumers do not perceive any difference from the original. It is very difficult to remove or detect a watermark when the characteristics of the watermark are not known. A typical reactive DRM system consists of a server that inserts the watermark containing information on the client at the moment a client downloads content. Violations can be detected by using a watermark detector. Such a detector may, for example, be used to monitor content distribution in the network. If, for example, a usage rule does not allow a client to redistribute the content and the content is nevertheless spotted in the distribution network, the watermark can be used to trace the client that originally downloaded the content.

### 12.1.3 Relation to Other Chapters

This chapter discusses the protection of multimedia data using DRM. It also positions DRM in the Multimedia Information Retrieval System architecture presented in Chapter 1. In this extended architecture both the content server and the client are extended with DRM functionality. DRM introduces the concept of licenses, which may be regarded as metadata. The concept of metadata is introduced in Chapter 2, which provides an overarching framework to ensure interoperability of digital multimedia objects, including protection and management of rights.

### 12.1.4 Outline

In the remainder of this paper we concentrate on preventive DRM systems. The next section discusses the context in which DRM operates such as the legal framework and the applications areas for DRM. Section 12.3 describes the general DRM architectural principles. Section 12.4 discusses a case to highlight a number of technical aspects relating to DRM. As an example the Personal Entertainment Domain (PED) DRM concept is chosen. We focus on the person-based and domain-based aspects of PED-DRM. We conclude with further reading and a summary.

## 12.2 DRM Context and Application Areas

### 12.2.1 DRM and the Legal Framework

It is important to note that DRM is more than technology alone. DRM technology functions in the context of a legal framework that outlines the regulations that DRM technology supports to enforce. Examples of such legal frameworks are copyright laws, privacy laws and antitrust laws.

Copyright law differs per jurisdiction although mostly the same principles are present. The background of these principles can be found in an international treaty called the Berne Convention for the Protection of Literary and

Artistic Works. In daily life most relevant are the Digital Millennium Copyright Act (DMCA) in the United States, and the European Union Copyright Directive that is used as a basis for copyright law in the EU countries. New provisions in the DMCA and EUCD also address DRM technology by outlawing circumvention technology.

## 12.2.2 DRM for Secure Audio and Video Content Management

The secure management of audio and video content is an important application area for DRM. The fact that digital audio and video content can be easily transported over electronic networks opens the way for electronic delivery of music and movies. Both consumers and content owners are interested in exploiting this new way of content distribution. For example a networked version of a video rental store would be advantageous to both consumers (that do not need to drive to the rental store) and content owners (that will rent more videos due to a lower threshold). However, in this example there is one issue: how to make sure that the consumer does not watch the video any longer after the rental period is over? Of course this problem also exists with physical distribution, since the consumer can make a copy of the video at home before returning the original to the shop. However, due to the ease of digital content distribution, the impact of such behavior is much larger in a digital world, something that was clearly demonstrated by the peer-to-peer networks already mentioned before. As a result the development of electronic music and video distribution services is taking up slowly.

## 12.2.3 Standardization and Products

There are several activities going on around the standardization of DRM technology. Important activities are taking place in DVB (Digital Video Broadcasting) for the secure delivery of digital TV and for the secure sharing of this in home networks [32], in OMA (Open Mobile Alliance) for the secure delivery of music and video to devices including mobile phones [22], in Marlin JDA (Joint Development Association) [21] focusing on efficient implementation of DRM in consumer electronics devices, in the Coral Consortium focusing on DRM interoperability (i.e., solving the problem of content exchange between different DRM systems) [5], and in MPEG-21 focusing more broadly on the secure exchange of digital items [16].

Next to standardization a number of proprietary DRM systems exist, the best known currently is FairPlay that comes with Apple iTunes, but also Microsoft with its Windows Media DRM (WM DRM) technology is offering DRM functionality as well as Sony with its Open Magic Gate system and RealNetworks with its Helix DRM.

## 12.2.4 DRM in Other Areas

Although the current application focus of DRM is on secure delivery of music and movies, DRM can be used in a much wider range of applications. It can be used to protect any digital document, and as such it can be used to implement secure document management or workflow systems for example.

Enterprise DRM is one of such applications. The focus lies on protecting company documents such that only authorized people have access to their contents. Important players are Microsoft with its extensible Windows Rights Management Services, which is also used by other companies as a technology platform, and Adobe with its Adobe Live Cycle Policy Server product.

Another interesting application domain is healthcare. Healthcare has strict regulations with respect to privacy of medical data, e.g., the Health Insurance Portability and Accountability Act (HIPAA) in the US. At the moment we see a starting digitization in healthcare. Increasingly, medical information is becoming available in digital form. Already inside hospitals medical information is managed by departmental information systems, and hospital information systems emerge. The next step will be the exchange of medical information between hospitals and all kinds of parties involved in the healthcare processes, leading to the creation of electronic health records containing a lot of privacy sensitive information. DRM technology has the potential of becoming a key technology for the secure exchange of all kinds of medical information. Research in this field is emerging [27] and some DRM vendors start to address this. For example Microsoft presents their Windows Rights Management Services as a solution for protecting electronic content in Healthcare, and Sealed-Media offers a similar proposition with its solutions targeted at healthcare applications. Both solutions advertise their audit facilities next to preventive DRM methods.

Different DRM applications share the basic technical principles, although aspects may differ. For example DRM for audio/video content is often device oriented meaning that certain devices are authorized to access content, while enterprise DRM is often more identity or user oriented, and medical DRM typically has special measures to support emergency cases.

## 12.3 DRM Architecture and Technology

Figure 12.1 depicts the generic DRM system architecture. The essential information exchanged between components are content and licenses. The policies that control content use are defined by the rules of the DRM system itself and by the licenses.

Separation between content and licenses is a core characteristic of DRM. This characteristic is present in all major commercial systems like WM DRM and OMA DRM. That said, many systems support embedding of licenses in the content container to make content use more convenient. The main benefit of separating licenses and content is that it allows for a wide variety of distribution and business models, while still having an efficient system with respect to bandwidth, storage and processing requirements at servers and networks.

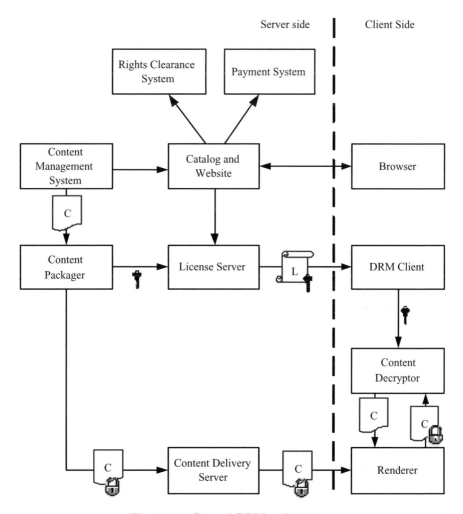

**Fig. 12.1.** General DRM architecture.

Content packager, license server, DRM client and content decryptor are the main DRM components. Content packager is responsible for protecting the content and fitting it in a DRM format. License server issues licenses after content is bought. DRM client interprets a license and makes the content key available to the content decryptor to decrypt the content for the renderer.

Next to the core DRM components, front-end components play a role such as Web browsers and Web shops with a catalog and ordering system. Also backend systems play a role such as rights or royalty clearing systems that facilitate payment of the copyright holders, and payment services that serve as intermediaries for payments by end-users.

In reality the client side is more complex than illustrated in the figure. Instead of just one DRM client people have multiple devices with heterogeneous capabilities. For example, some devices such as a PC can buy licenses, while other devices such as portable music players cannot. Naturally, users want to use their content on all their devices. This implies that content and licenses must be distributed to these devices and use of the content on these devices must be authorized. To address these issues concepts are introduced like domains, tethered devices, and person-based DRM. Section 12.4 elaborates on a number of these aspects.

From now on we mainly focus on the DRM functionality at the client and server side. Commercial front-ends as shops and payment are not considered further, while backend DRM functionality like content packaging only get minimal attention.

Figure 12.2 depicts the DRM functions and the relation between content and licenses. This approach achieves enforcement of the intended policy set by the content shop. From a data management perspective content has the role of data, while all supporting information such as licenses, keys and identifiers are metadata. The metadata facilitates data management and policy enforcement on the data. The following sections describes in more detail how content management and license management achieves content security and enforcement of the intended policy.

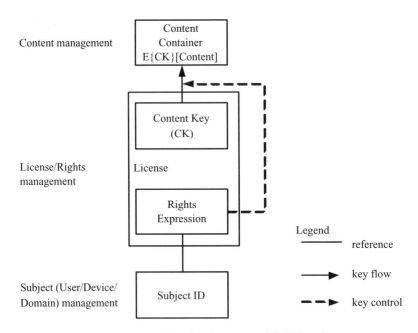

**Fig. 12.2.** Functional and informational DRM architecture.

### 12.3.1 Content Management

Content management in the context of DRM comprises the protection of content, the handling of content through the system, e.g., moving, copying and accessing audio/video/text assets, and the insertion of new content in the system.

Content protection has as a goal to prevent unauthorized access to content. One method is content protection during storage or transmission. The content is embedded in a secure content container by a process called content packaging. The main purpose of the content container is to offer confidentiality by means of encryption of the content using a content encryption key. Many content container definitions exist, typically one for each proprietary DRM system, but also standards exist such as ISMACryp [14], MPEG-2 Transport Streams (TS) [6] and OMA DCF (DRM Content Format) [23]. IS-MACryp is intended for streaming content and makes use of the secure RTP (Real-Time Protocol) on top of IP for the content, and RTSP (Real-Time Streaming Protocol) and SDP (Session Description Protocol) for control and key management. Encryption is applied on packets with MPEG content, while authentication is done at transport level. MPEG-2 TS as defined by DVB is typically used for conditional access pay TV and also encrypts at the content level. DCF is a content file format that contains the encrypted content, some content metadata such as identifiers, and metadata related to DRM such as licenses. DCF has a profile for discrete media such as pictures which can be used for any type of content, and a profile for continuous or streaming content such as audio and video content. DCF also offers integrity protection to the content. Integrity and authentication of protected content may serve the end-user who is assured that he gets what he paid for, but also the content and service providers who have a means to control who can insert content into the DRM system infrastructure.

The handling of protected content is not much different than the handling of unprotected content, because licenses and content are separated. The same protocols to move, copy and stream content are typically used with sometimes small extensions to improve user convenience. For example UPnP AV [31] may be used to move content around in a home network. DRM metadata extensions indicate to the user and the receiving system that it is DRM protected content.

Insertion of new content happens frequently, for example when music labels release new music albums. Insertion of new content involves content protection by the content packager component. The content key is distributed to the license server, and the availability of new content is signaled to the catalog and Website to make it available for sale.

### 12.3.2 Rights/License Management

In a classic DRM system a license defines the rights that are issued for the content. A license is a signed statement by a content provider that indicates under what conditions it is allowed to use the content encryption key and access a piece of content. A typical license has a structure like:

License = { ContentID, ContentKey, Subject, RightsExpression,
SignatureContentProvider }.

The content identifier forms the link between the license and the content to find the right license for some content and vice versa. For this purpose it is necessary that the content can be uniquely identified. If the content identifier is also used for other purposes such as rights clearing then often standards are used like DOI (Digital Object Identifier) [13] and MPEG-21 DII [15].

The rights expression indicates how the subject may use the content. Typical examples for rights expressions include unlimited play (a user "owns" the content, see Figure 12.3), play for one month (a user has a subscription), play three times, copy once and write to CD. The rights expression format can be ranging from copy control bits to XML rights expression languages (REL) such as ODRL [12], XrML [4] and MPEG21-REL [17]. Most full-fledged DRM systems nowadays use a REL, although still systems exist that use implicit rights such as FairPlay in which the rights are defined by the system. All main RELs are based on a model that relates assets (content), subjects or principles, permissions, constraints on permissions, and conditions, although the exact terminology differs per standard.

Security of licenses relates to three main aspects, namely integrity of the rights expression, confidentiality of the content key and integrity of the state for so-called stateful licenses, e.g., ensuring that a play-three-times license is not played four times. Integrity of the rights expression is typically addressed by a signature of the content provider. Confidentiality of the content key is realized by protecting the content key using some other key, e.g., encrypting the license with the public key of the target device or by a domain key. The management for these keys is system specific and therefore we will give one example in Section 12.4. Integrity of license state is the responsibility of the DRM client, which will typically maintain the state in some secure license storage.

### 12.3.3 User, Device and Domain Management

Granting access to content based on licenses is key to DRM. Access may be granted because a certain device is used. Access could also be granted because a certain person has authenticated and requests access. Alternatively, content access is granted if a device is used that belongs to a certain domain, i.e., a group of devices. Figure 12.2 conveniently summarizes these three cases with the term subject. A license server binds a license to a subject as part of license acquisition after the content is bought.

The above principle requires identification and authentication of devices and users. For this purpose devices get an identity and are certified. Certification has the further advantage that it allows to make distinction between trustworthy compliant devices that follow the rules of the DRM system and devices that do not. Only compliant devices may have access to DRM secrets and keys.

```
<o-ex:rights>
 <o-ex:context>
  <o-dd:version>2.0</o-dd:version><o-dd:uid>RightsObjectID</o-dd:uid>
 </o-ex:context>
 <o-ex:agreement>
  <o-ex:asset>
   <o-ex:context><o-dd:uid>ContentID</o-dd:uid></o-ex:context>
   <o-ex:digest>
    <ds:DigestMethod ds:Algorithm="http://www.w3.org/2000/09/xmldsig#sha1"/>
    <ds:DigestValue>DCFHash</ds:DigestValue>
   </o-ex:digest>
   <ds:KeyInfo>
    <xenc:EncryptedKey>
    <xenc:EncryptionMethod
      xenc:Algorithm="http://www.w3.org/2001/04/xmlenc#kw-aes128"/>
     <xenc:CipherData>
      <xenc:CipherValue>EncryptedCEK</xenc:CipherValue>
     </xenc:CipherData>
    </xenc:EncryptedKey>
    <ds:RetrievalMethod ds:URI="REKReference"/>
   </ds:KeyInfo>
  </o-ex:asset>
  <o-ex:permission><o-dd:play/></o-ex:permission>
 </o-ex:agreement>
</o-ex:rights>
```

**Fig. 12.3.** OMA DRM 2.0 license (simplified) for unlimited play right using ODRL.

## 12.4 Case: Content Management in the Personal Entertainment Domain

The previous section presented the general DRM architecture. We continue with a more detailed discussion for a specific case. We have selected the Personal Entertainment Domain (PED) concept. We sketch the PED-DRM concept and a realization. PED-DRM builds upon two hot topics in DRM, namely domain-based and person-based DRM.

The objective of this case is to give an impression what aspects and considerations play a role if we want to access content on a number of devices and based on user presence. The solutions and mechanisms presented highlight certain aspects rather than that they present a blueprint of a DRM system. The architecture deviates on some aspects from existing approaches such as OMA DRM or WM DRM. This follows mainly from other assumptions and requirements. For this case we assume that DRM functions should be performed on devices instead of servers where possible, and that devices should be able to operate while they are not online.

Content management in PED-DRM for commercial audio/video content is a special case of data management, because of its distribution model and required security. The distribution model of commercial audio/video content is typically characterized by a download from a server to some device over a public channel, followed by small scale distribution in a local network. Securitywise, content in this case requires usage control next to access control.

### 12.4.1 Personal Entertainment Domain concept

Digital Rights Management (DRM) with support for domains [11, 32] needs to fulfill the requirements of both the content owners and the users, which often appear to be conflicting. The general idea is that content can flow freely between the devices that belong to the domain, while content transactions between domains are restricted.

Companies [10, 26, 29] and standardization bodies such as DVB (Digital Video Broadcasting) [32] and OMA (Open Mobile Alliance) are investigating and developing the concept of domains [9, 18]. Traditionally people have taken a device-oriented approach [11], where a domain groups a set of devices that belong to a certain household.

Many of the device-based domain concepts suffer from technological or user convenience problems, e.g., with respect to enabling the user to access content anywhere, at any time and on any device. The PED-DRM concept [20] does not have many of the disadvantages of device-based domains. More important, it starts with a comprehensive concept that users can understand, i.e., a limited number of rules and no differentiation between device classes. This is different compared with current DRM systems like FairPlay and WM DRM that do make this distinction, e.g., between PCs and portables.

PED-DRM is characterized by its structure, i.e., the relationship between various entities such as content, devices and persons, and by its policy, i.e., the rules that govern content access and proliferation. Key characteristics of the PED-DRM structure are that one single person is the member/owner of the domain, that content is bound to that person and that a number of devices is bound to the user (see Figure 12.4). Key characteristics of the PED-DRM policy are that content can be accessed on the domain devices and on all other compliant devices after user authentication. Content access on the set of permanent domain devices without user authentication allows for convenient content usage at home, including the sharing of content among family members. The only thing people must do is to register their device to their domain once. Temporary content access on all other compliant devices after user authentication enables people to access their content anywhere and at any time. Devices may be a member of multiple domains, both permanent and temporary.

Two small scenarios form the foundation of the PED-DRM concept as they illustrate the expected user experience and interaction, namely use of family content at home, and personal content use at another remote place. We assume that a user has a user identity device, such as a smartcard or mobile phone, with which he can authenticate conveniently to other devices. Access to family content at home is typically done on a central device in the living room such as a media center or PVR connected to the TV. A user can operate

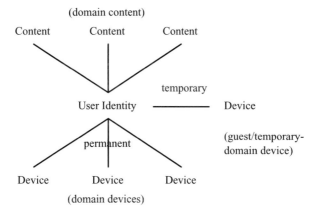

**Fig. 12.4.** PED-DRM concept.

his media center and select a movie bought by another family member using the remote control. The movie starts rendering after he presses play. Access to personal content at a remote location, conveniently called guest access, is typically done in a hotel or at a friend's house. The user decides he wants to render some content stored on his media center at home and he authenticates to the hotel TV using for example his mobile phone. The TV lists his available content and after the user selects some content the TV renders the content, which is streamed from his home over the Internet.

### 12.4.2 Functional PED-DRM Architecture and Design

Figure 12.5 shows a functional and data view of PED-DRM. The typical domain aspects of PED-DRM build upon the user, device and domain management functions (Figure 12.5, right). Domain management concerns the management of the set of permanent devices in the domain. It has a loose coupling to the rest to limit the effect on the traditional DRM functions (Figure 12.5, left). The relation between rights management and domain management is typically realized by means of a user identifier embedded in the license. This relation illustrates that a user owns a piece of content.

### User and Device Management

User and device management in PED-DRM is not different than normal DRM. Users get provisioned with a certificate and corresponding public/private key pair.

Devices in PED-DRM are given a DeviceID certificate and key pair that they can use to prove their compliance. Devices are also given explicit authorization to fulfill certain functions. This limits the effects of a security breach by preventing the certificate and keys of a hacked device from being misused for other functions, e.g., keys from a rendering device cannot be used to register devices to the domain.

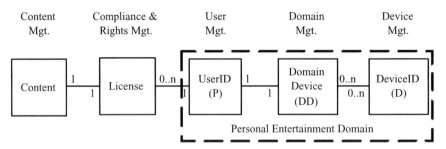

**Fig. 12.5.** PED-DRM functions and data overview.

## Domain Management

Domain management in PED-DRM concerns the relation between users and a number of devices, as depicted in Figure 12.5 where a UserID and a number of DeviceIDs are brought together by a DomainDevices (DD) data object. Here, we present an approach in which DD is a certificate containing a reference to the user of the domain, references to a number of devices, a version number and the signature of the domain manager (DomainManager in Figure 12.6):

$$\text{DD} = \{\text{ DomainID, Version, UserID, DeviceID1, } \dots, \text{ DeviceIDn,}$$
$$\text{SignDomainManager }\}.$$

The first advantage of making DD a certificate is that it shows who issued it. The second advantage of putting all domain members in one certificate is that this allows a simple but secure signaling mechanism to show which devices are in the domain. The third advantage of the DD certificate is the ability to report domain information to the user on any domain device at any time. Alternatively, a device gets a domain membership certificate that only lists itself. This is an option, but it lacks amongst others the latter two advantages.

To make optimal use of the DD certificates devices should exchange each other's DD certificate as part of common DRM operations such as license exchange of licenses belonging to the domain. When a domain device receives a valid DD certificate with a higher version number than its stored DD certificate, it replaces the stored DD with the new DD, provided that it is still contained in the new DD certificate, otherwise it removes its DD completely.

It is typically a security requirement that in case of a hacked device that only content is compromised that was available to the device, i.e., the domain content. To address this requirement domain-based DRM systems often base their security on domain key(s), e.g., SmartRight [29], xCP [26], PERM [10] and OMA DRM 2.0 [22]. In these systems the content key is typically encrypted with the domain key. We address this requirement differently by limiting license distribution to permanent and temporary domain devices.

## System Components and their Interaction

Figure 12.6 presents the main client side DRM components – DomainManager, DRMClient and UserIdentity – that group PED-DRM functionality, and the interaction between them. These components interact with Terminal for interfacing with the end-user, and License Server to acquire licenses for content.

The typical connectivity means that enable interaction between the components are also indicated: combined on the same device (local), connected through a network (IP) or via wired/wireless connection with a limitation on the distance (near-field).

The DomainManager, DRMClient and UserIdentity must run on a compliant device which has a DeviceID certificate because they manage domain or content-related sensitive data. In a typical deployment of components over devices UserIdentity and DomainManager components are combined on one device, e.g., on a smartcard or mobile phone. Alternatively, DomainManager runs as a service on the Internet, an approach similar to OMA DRM 2.0 and Apple's FairPlay. Ideally, the DRMClient and Terminal are combined on one device, allowing straightforward domain management operations using the user interface of the device for interaction with the user. Typical devices include media centers and connected renderers (TVs).

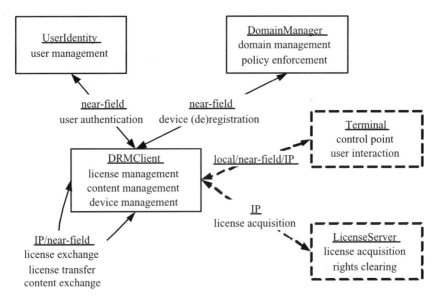

**Fig. 12.6.** PED-DRM client side components and their interaction.

**Domain Policy and Domain Management**

The domain policy specifies under which conditions entities are entitled to be part of the domain and thereby largely defines the scale of content proliferation in a domain-based DRM system. It is evident that end-users prefer a policy with a relaxed regime, while copyright holders prefer more tight regimes. As in most domain-based DRM systems, PED-DRM has a domain policy that is fixed for the system. OMA DRM 2.0 takes a slightly different approach by making solely the license issuer responsible for domain policy enforcement. The drawback of the latter is that a user has to redefine his domain for each shop he wants to buy content from.

We propose a simple and straightforward basic domain policy enforced by the DomainManager. The policy is based on a maximum number of devices per domain. Furthermore, a DomainManager only registers DRMClients that are in direct proximity. This limits the domain size and content proliferation to places that the user visits. Devices may be a member of multiple domains to support sharing of content between people who share devices.

Technically, enforcement of the domain policy by DomainManager is the main part of domain management together with the creation and management of DD certificates. Other aspects are secure domain registration and deregistration protocols. In a successful run of the registration protocol the device is authenticated as a compliant device, the request is evaluated against the domain policy, and the device gets an updated DD certificate with its own identity listed.

**Content and License Management**

The working of a DRM system is largely defined by the protocols and processes for content and license management. This section discusses the PED-DRM protocols for the leading example presented in Figure 12.7.

The leading example starts with some content bought by the user (U1). Figure 12.7 shows that the license server stores the encrypted content (contentB) and the related content key (keyB). The first action is the acquisition of a license for this content by a device containing a DRMClient (A). After that the DRMClients belonging to the domain (D1) exchange the content, and the receiving DRMClient (B) renders the content. Subsequently the content is exchanged with another DRMClient (C) which renders it. The exchange and rendering are both based on authentication of the user (U1). Finally, the user transfers the content ownership to another user (U2). This user has its own domain (D2) that includes his device with DRMClient (C).

The figure also shows that all devices have compliance certificates (certX) and related public/private key pairs (pubKeyX/privKeyX). The DRMClients are member of a domain for which they store a DD certificate. As defined before, DD consists of the domain ID, the version number of the certificate, the domain user, the domain devices and a signature by the domain manager.

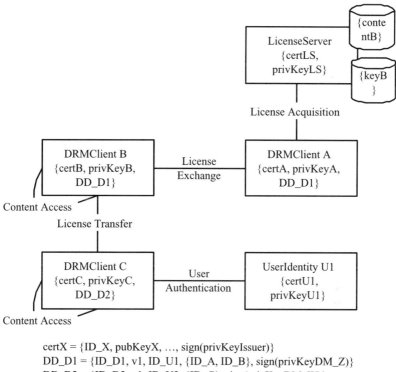

certX = {ID_X, pubKeyX, ..., sign(privKeyIssuer)}
DD_D1 = {ID_D1, v1, ID_U1, {ID_A, ID_B}, sign(privKeyDM_Z)}
DD_D2 = {ID_D2, v1, ID_U2, {ID_C}, sign(privKeyDM_W)}

**Fig. 12.7.** Leading example content and license management.

The protocols follow the general principle that content keys are only distributed to devices that can access the content. This affects the license acquisition and license exchange protocols, because the content key is part of the license. For example, devices distribute the license encrypted by the public key of the target device so that only the target device can decrypt it. Furthermore, devices keep the licenses in their secure storage database. Devices are responsible for sufficiently protecting their secure storage database.

*Content and License Acquisition*
Content acquisition in a DRM context involves buying content, acquiring a license and downloading the content. We assume that the user already bought and paid for the content. Figure 12.8 depicts the starting point and subsequent steps for license acquisition for our example.
The essential part of license acquisition is the binding of the license to the user identity and his domain. Therefore, the license acquisition request contains the license ID and the DD certificate.
The license server must be assured that it delivers the license and content key to a compliant trustworthy DRMClient (A). Therefore, the license server

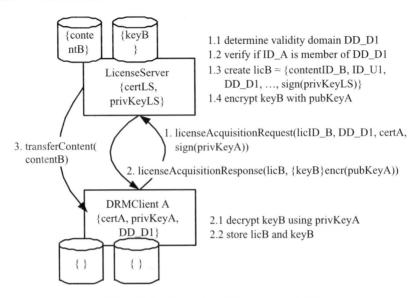

**Fig. 12.8.** Content and license acquisition.

uses the device certificate (certA) to verify that it is compliant. Of course, the license server also verifies that the signature of the request is from the device.

The license server furthermore requires that the domain (D1) has an acceptable policy. The license server verifies the signature on the DD certificate (DD_D1) to determine if it can trust the domain it issues content to. In systems with a fixed domain policy like here any domain created by a trustworthy DomainManager is accepted by a license server. The trustworthiness of the DomainManager follows from its certificate. Alternatively, it is possible to have different domain policies. In that case the domain policy should be indicated in the DD certificate. That enables the license server to determine if it delivers the license, withholds the license, or charges more. Finally, the license server checks if the requesting device is part of the domain. For this purpose it verifies that the device ID from the certificate (ID_A) is listed in the provided DD certificate (DD_D1).

After the checks the license server continues with the creation of a license (licB). This license binds the content (contentB) to the user (U1) and domain (D1), and also identifies the relevant content key (keyB). The license server encrypts the content key with the public key of the requesting device (pubKeyA) before it responds to the request.

The DRMClient of the device (A) verifies that it receives the correct license (licB) for the requested content (contentB), that it is bound to the right domain (D1), and issued by the license issuer to which the request was sent. This helps to detect accidental and malicious errors, and prevents license acquisitions from rogue license servers.

The transfer of the content (contentB) completes the license and content acquisition. Figure 12.8 depicts a simplified case where the content is served by the same server as the license. As explained earlier there is no security related to this transmission from the perspective of the content owner and license issuer. The device can verify that it received the correct content using the metadata in the content container and verifying the integrity of the content using information in the license. As a final step the device stores the license, key and content. This leads to the situation depicted in Figure 12.9.

*Content and License Exchange*

Content and license exchange concerns the organization of content and licenses over devices. This is especially relevant in domain based DRM systems because content may be rendered on any domain device. Content and license exchange only changes the location of content and licenses, but not the ownership. We talk about transfer of ownership later.

The exchange of a user's license between two of his domain devices is depicted in Figure 12.9. The responding DRMClient (A) has the encrypted content (contentB) and the corresponding license (licB) and content key (keyB). These are exchanged with the requesting DRMClient (B), which afterwards holds a copy as depicted in Figure 12.10.

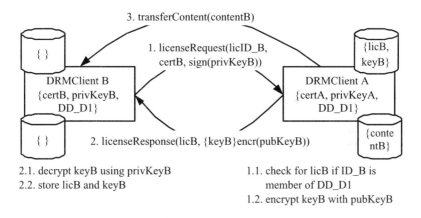

**Fig. 12.9.** Content exchange between domain devices.

The license exchange protocol starts with a license request. The request indicates the desired license and contains the necessary proof to convince the responder (A) to send the license. The proof consists of the requesters certificate and signature. The responding DRMClient (A) uses the certificate and signature in the request to determine that the requesting DRMClient (B) is compliant. Furthermore, it must be assured that both DRMClients belong to the same domain. For this purpose the responding DRMClient (A) retrieves the license (licB) from its license store, compares the domain indicated in the license (DD_D1) with the DD certificate (DD_D1) it possesses, and verifies that the request or's ID (ID_B) is also listed in the DD certificate.

After the responding DRMClient (A) has done all checks it encrypts the content key (keyB) with the request or's public key (pubKeyB), and sends the response including the license (licB) and encrypted content key. The requesting DRMClient (B) decrypts the content key and stores both the license and the content key after verifying that it received the requested license.

The protocol above only shows the basic steps. In a more elaborate version the DRMClients exchange their DD certificate to ensure that both possess the latest version. This ensures that both have the same view on the domain, which may have changed since recent domain changes. Another improvement is to sign the response to convince the requesting DRMClient that the license originates from the intended responder. Also, a challenge/response should be included to prevent that an old response is replayed. Finally, revocation should be taken into account, i.e., the responding DRMClient checks that the requesting DRMClient is not listed on a certificate revocation list.

The above protocol assumes that the receiving device is member of the user's domain to which the license is bound. Alternatively, the user could have authenticated to the receiving device, which is depicted in Figure 12.11 and also discussed in more detail in the next section.

*Content Access*

Content access is the general term for usage of content such as rendering and printing. This involves DRM processing like license evaluation and content decryption. It takes the secure content container and the license as input. Furthermore, context is an important parameter, e.g., date/time for subscription based licenses, but also current authentication sessions.

The process for content access only involves the device itself as depicted in Figure 12.10. In our example the DRMClient (B) has knowledge of the license (licB), its device identity (certB), domain information for the domain (DD_D1), and has access to the content key (keyB). The DRMClient verifies that it may use the license based on the user ID (ID_U1) listed in the license. This user ID must match the user ID in the DD certificate (DD_D1). In addition, the domain ID (ID_D1) in the license and DD certificate must also match. The DRMClient verifies that its identifier (ID_B) is listed in the corresponding DD certificate (DD_D1). One may question why this verification is still necessary, since licenses can only be distributed to devices after they have proven to be member of the domain as described for the license exchange protocol. However, time may have passed after the distribution of licenses. In the meantime the device could be deregistered from the domain. Therefore, it is verified upon content access that a device is still member of the domain. To complete the evaluation also the other conditions stated in the rights expression of the license are verified. After that the DRMClient releases the proper content decryption keys to enable decrypting and rendering of the content.

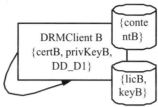

1. accessRequest(contentID_B)
1.1. evaluate licB license expression
1.2. check if ID_B is member of DD_D1
1.3. use keyB to decrypt contentB

**Fig. 12.10.** Content access on a domain device.

An alternative course of action for license exchange and content access is based on user authentication instead of domain membership of the DRMClient. The main difference is that the necessary proof now comes from the UserIdentity device and not from the DD certificate. Figure 12.11 depicts the relevant protocols for our example.

The first protocol is the authentication protocol (steps 1–3). To ensure presence of the user, a proximity verification is performed between the user's authentication token and the device. An unilateral challenge/response authentication convinces the DRMClient (C) that UserIdentity (U1) is present. Furthermore, the authentication response can serve as proof to other components that the DRMClient authenticated the user's token. This solution is just a basic version of the protocol and some extensions can improve security. An example is mutual authentication where UserIdentity also authenticates DRMClient and includes the identity in the response. Another security improvement is the inclusion of the validity time of the authentication in the proof.

The license exchange protocol works slightly different when based on user authentication (see Figure 12.11, step 4). The requesting DRMClient (C) includes the proof from the UserIdentity (U1). The responding DRMClient (B) uses this instead of the DD certificate. The responding DRMClient (B) verifies that the authentication proof it gets contains a reference to the same user ID (ID_U1) as the license (licB). The proof may be any signed statement, for example the authentication response message. If the proof contains a validity period then the DRMClient must verify that it is not expired to prevent that the authentication happened too far in the past. The DRMClient (B) also performs the other standard checks and responds with the license, key and content. The requesting DRMClient (C) stores these for the subsequent content access.

Content access follows the standard steps described before and depicted in Figure 12.10, except that the proof is used from the UserIdentity token (Figure 12.11, step 6). Next to the standard checks, it suffices for the DRMClient

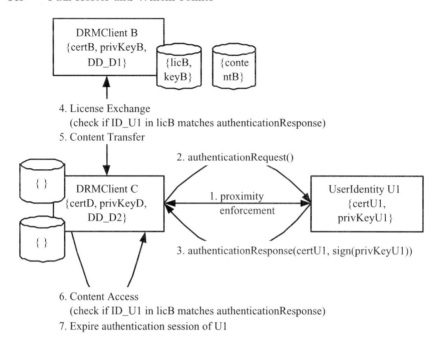

**Fig. 12.11.** License exchange and content access after user authentication.

(C) to check that the authenticated user ID (ID_U1) matches with the license (licB).

Finally, the authentication session on the DRMClient (C) expires (step 7). After this no licenses can be obtained from other devices for the domain (D1) or the user (U1), and the content cannot be rendered anymore. Securitywise it is no problem to keep the license and content on the DRMClient for future use.

As a closing note we should mention that the figure shows a basic version of identities and certificates stored on UserIdentity. In a flexible solution the token has separate certificates for compliance and user identity. This allows for example that users later obtain a token by buying a token and register it with their identity. These organizational and infrastructural aspects of user authentication and identity management have been largely omitted here.

*Content Transfer*

Content ownership transfer enables giving away or trading of multimedia content. The typical means to realize content transfer in a DRM system is to bind the license to a new user, which we call license transfer. License transfer is technically more challenging than license exchange, because it is not enough to distribute the license to another device. Instead, a new license must be created or the old license must be amended. Both approaches have to deal with trust issues. We take the approach to let the current owner (or one of his devices) create a transfer license, which has the advantage that it works offline. This transfer license declares that the owner transfers a license to another user. This transfer license can only be used in conjunction with the original license. This approach maintains the integrity of the old license. Thereby trust issues stay limited to the transfer itself performed by the device. This avoids attacks where standalone devices create new licenses. In such an attack not only the owner could be changed but also the conditions in the rights expression. A possible extension is to exchange the transfer license together with the original license at the license server for a new license. After that the transfer license can be discarded.

The license transfer protocol for our example is depicted in Figure 12.12. The interaction is very similar to license acquisition. The major differences are the creation of the transfer license and the revocation of the license on the domain devices of the old owner. The protocol starts when the requesting DRMClient (C) requests the license (licID_B) to be transferred and provides the new domain (DD_D2) including the user information (ID_U2). The responding DRMClient (B) verifies that the requesting DRMClient (C) is compliant, and that the domain (DD_D2) is genuine. It also verifies that it is entitled to transfer the license, for which we adhere to the rule that it must belong to the domain of the license. After that it creates the transfer license (transferLic), which rebinds the license from the owner (U1) to the new owner (U2). Furthermore, it should initiate revocation of the licenses (licB) in the old domain (D1), because those should not be used anymore after the ownership has been transferred. After that, it sends the license, the transfer license, and the content key (keyB) to the requesting DRMClient (C). As for the other protocols the content key is encrypted with the public key of the requesting DRMClient (C). The requesting DRMClient (C) receives and stores the licenses and key. As an additional check the requesting DRMClient (C) verifies if the other DRMClient is entitled to transfer it. Here, this check consists of checking if the responding DRMClient belongs to the domain at the moment of transfer. This is verified using the DD certificate (DD_D1). To complete the transfer also the content is sent to the requesting DRMClient.

Rendering of the content is now possible on the requesting DRMClient (C). However, the evaluation process now also requires the evaluation and interpretation of the transfer license. For example, a rendering DRMClient must check that the transfer license is issued by a compliant device. Exchange of this content and license with other domain devices in the domain (D2) is possible using the license exchange protocol. This license exchange should also include the transfer license. For efficiency reasons it is best if the license and transfer license are kept closely together from this point onwards since they cannot be used apart.

License revocation is essential for license transfer because content may only be rendered by the new owner and not by the former. For license revocation no good general solution has been found yet. Also current commercial DRM

1.1. verify compliance of C
1.2. verify that B is member of DD_D1
1.3. create transferLic = {licID_B, ID_U1, ID_U2, sign(privKeyB)}
1.4. encrypt keyB with pubKeyC
(1.5. revoke licB on devices of DD_D1)

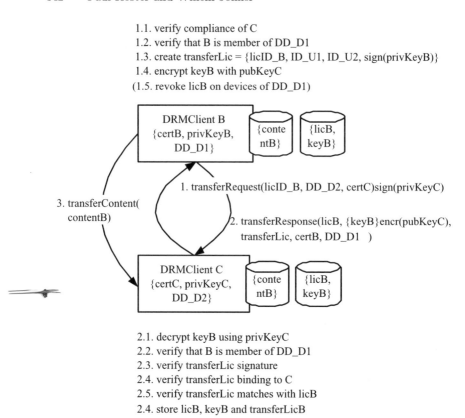

2.1. decrypt keyB using privKeyC
2.2. verify that B is member of DD_D1
2.3. verify transferLic signature
2.4. verify transferLic binding to C
2.5. verify transferLic matches with licB
2.4. store licB, keyB and transferLicB

**Fig. 12.12.** Content transfer between users and their domains.

systems do not support license revocation. Therefore, license revocation is a topic that still requires research.

## 12.5 Summary

In this chapter the foundations of DRM have been introduced. DRM is based on copyright law. However, DRM goes further since it also covers content usage. The scope of DRM ranges from protecting audio/video entertainment content to enterprise rights management to protect business data, e.g., in the area of healthcare.

A general principle found in the DRM architecture is the separation between content and licenses, where the former can be characterized as data and the latter as essential metadata. The DRM architecture assumes trustworthy compliant devices to enforce the security of licenses and content. This provides the foundation for preventive DRM in which only allowed actions on content are possible.

A case on person-based and domain-based DRM showed that users need a clear DRM concept. The PED-DRM concept enables fair scenarios such as accessing family content at home and accessing personal content anywhere. Key management is also important in DRM and has been illustrated in a number of protocols for license and content management.

## 12.6 Further Reading

More information on DRM architecture, technology, research and news can be found in the following sources. Several books [1, 30] provide an introduction to DRM and various architectural and technological aspects. To get an insight in the structure and engineering side of DRM one could read the OMA DRM version 2 architecture overview and DRM specifications [22]. Scientific conferences and workshops in the field of DRM are the annual ACM DRM workshop which exists since 2001, the annual IEEE workshop on DRM Impact on Consumer Communications since 2005, the annual IFIP Conference on Communications and Multimedia Security (CMS), and the conference on Digital Rights Management: Technology, Issues, Challenges and Systems (DRMtics) which had its first edition in 2005. For DRM news, technological developments and accessible overview information one can access online Internet sources like DRMWatch [8], DRM News Blog [7] and the Wikipedia's article on DRM [34].

DRM is a topic that has gone through a long history already and is still being researched and standardized. A number of current research topics are introduced below together with some references to existing work. A first topic is research in the field of person and identity-based DRM, e.g., the Personal Entertainment Domain concept [20], and in the OPERA project [33]. Closely related to this is the further work on domain research, e.g., secure content exchange in OMA DRM [24], domain management, and license state management in domains. The introduction of person identities in DRM also raises privacy and user control issues in the area of DRM [2, 3, 28]. DRM interoperability [19] gets higher on the agenda now actual DRM systems are getting introduced in the market, giving momentum to initiatives like Coral [5]. Furthermore, DRM systems start to allow import from and export to other content protection systems. For example in OMA work is ongoing to unify secure flash storage with DRM [25]. A final topic that requires further research is the transfer of ownership of content, e.g., to give it away or to trade, which raises issues like license revocation.

## References

1. E. Becker, W. Buhse, D. Günnewig, and N. Rump (Eds.). *Digital Rights Management: Technological, Economic, Legal and Political Aspects*, LNCS2770, Springer-Verlag, 2003.

2. C. Conrado, F.L.A.J. Kamperman, G.J. Schrijen, and W. Jonker. Privacy in an Identity-based DRM System, *Fourteenth International Workshop on Database and Expert Systems Applications,* 1–5 September 2003, Prague, pp. 389–395, 2003.
3. C. Conrado, M. Petkovic, and W. Jonker. Privacy-Preserving DRM, *Secure Data Management (SDM) 2004,* Toronto, Canada, LNCS 3178, Springer, 2004.
4. ContentGuard. *eXtensible rights Markup Language (XrML),* 2003. http://www.xrml.org/.
5. Coral Consortium Corporation. *Coral Consortium Architecture Specification: version 1.0,* March 2005. http://www.coral-interop.org/
6. Digital Video Broadcasting (DVB). *Support for use of scrambling and Conditional Access (CA) within digital broadcast systems,* ETR 289, ETSI, 1996.
7. DRM News Blog. http://www.drmblog.com, 2007.
8. DRMWatch. http://www.drmwatch.com, 2007.
9. A.M. Eskicioglu and E.J. Delp. An overview of multimedia content protection in consumer electronic devices, *Signal Processing: Image Communication,* Elsevier, 2001.
10. J. Gildred, A. Andreasyan, R. Osawa, and T. Stahl. *Protected Entertainment Rights Management (PERM): Specification Draft v0.54,* Pioneer Research Center USA Inc, Thomson, 9-2-2003.
11. S.A.F.A.van den Heuvel, W.Jonker, F.L.A.J.Kamperman, and P.J.Lenoir. Secure Content Management in Authorised Domains, *IBC Conference Publication,* pp. 467–474, Amsterdam, IBC2002, 15-9-2002.
12. R. Iannella. *Open Digital Rights Language (ODRL) Version 1.1,* W3C, 2003.
13. International DOI Foundation. *The DOI Handbook,* 2005.
14. Internet Streaming Media Alliance. *ISMA Encryption and Authentication Specification 1.0,* Feb. 2004.
15. MPEG-21. *Information technology – Multimedia framework – Part 3: Digital Item Identification,* ISO/IEC 21000-3, 2003.
16. MPEG-21. *Information technology – Multimedia framework – Part 4: Intellectual Property Management and Protection Components,* ISO/IEC 21000-4, 2006.
17. MPEG-21. *Information Technology – Multimedia Framework – Part 5: Rights Expression Language,* ISO/IEC 21000-5, 2004.
18. W. Jonker and J.P. Linnartz. Digital Rights Management in Consumer Electronics Products, *IEEE Signal Processing Magazine, Special Issue on Digital Rights Management,* 2004.
19. R.H. Koenen, J. Lacy, M. Mackay, and S. Mitchell. The Long March to Interoperable Digital Rights Management, *Proceedings of the IEEE,* vol. 92, issue 6, pp. 883–97, June 2004.
20. R.P. Koster, F.L.A.J. Kamperman, P.J. Lenoir, K.H.J. Vrielink, Identity-based DRM: Personal Entertainment Domain, *Transactions on Data Hiding and Multimedia Security I, LNCS 4300,* Springer-Verlag, Berlin Heidelberg, pp. 104–122, 2006.
21. Marlin Developer Community. *Marlin Architecture Overview,* 2006.
22. Open Mobile Alliance. *DRM Architecture: Approved Version 2.0,* 3-3-2006.
23. Open Mobile Alliance. *DRM Content Format V2.0,* April 2005.
24. Open Mobile Alliance. *Secure Content Exchange (SRE),* Work Item Document, 2005.

25. Open Mobile Alliance. *Secure Removable Media Profile (SRMProfile)*, Work Item Document, 2005.
26. F. Pestoni, J.B. Lotspiech, and S. Nusser. xCP:peer-to-peer content protection, *IEEE Signal Processing Magazine, vol. 21, issue 2, pp. 71–81, March* 2004.
27. M. Petkovic, M. Hammouténe, C. Conrado, and W. Jonker. Securing Electronic Health Records using Digital Rights Management, *10th International Symposium for Health Information Management Research (iSHIMIR)*, Greece 2005.
28. M. Petkovic and R.P. Koster. User Attributed Rights in DRM, *First International Conference on Digital Rights Management: Technology, Issues, Challenges and Systems,* 31 October–2 November 2005, Sydney, Australia, LNCS 3919, pp. 75–89, 2006.
29. Thomson Multimedia. *SmartRight: Technical white paper, version 1.7,* January 2003.
30. B. Rosenblatt, B. Trippe, and S. Mooney. *Digital Rights Management: Business and Technology,* M&T Books, 2002.
31. UPnP Forum. *UPnP AV Architecture,* June 12 2002.
32. R.Vevers and C.Hibbert. Copy Protection and Content Management in the DVB, *IBC Conference Publication,* pp. 458–466, Amsterdam, IBC2002, 15-9-2002.
33. S. Wegner (ed.). *OPERA – Interoperability of Digital Rights Management (DRM) Technologies,* OPERA Eurescom Project 1207, August 2003.
34. Wikipedia. *Digital rights management,* http://en.wikipedia.org/wiki/Digital_rights_management, 2007.

# Evaluation of Multimedia Retrieval Systems

Djoerd Hiemstra[1] and Wessel Kraaij[2]

[1] University of Twente
[2] TNO Information and Communication Technology

## 13.1 Introduction

In this chapter, we provide the tools and methodology for comparing the effectiveness of two or more multimedia retrieval systems in a meaningful way. Several aspects of multimedia retrieval systems can be evaluated without consulting the potential users or customers of the system, such as the query processing time (measured for instance in milliseconds per query) or the query throughput (measured for instance as the number of queries per second). In this chapter, however, we will focus on aspects of the system that influence the *effectiveness* of the retrieved results. In order to measure the effectiveness of search results, one must at some point consult the potential user of the system. For, what are the correct results for the query "black jaguar"? Cars, or cats? Ultimately, the user has to decide.

Doing an evaluation involving real people is not only a costly job, it is also difficult to control and therefore hard to replicate. For this reason, methods have been developed to design so-called test collections. Often, these test collections are created by consulting potential users, but once they are created they can be used to evaluate multimedia retrieval systems without the need to consult the users during further evaluations. If a test collection is available, a new retrieval method or system can be evaluated by comparing it to some well-established methods in a controlled experiment. Hull [15] mentions the following three ingredients of a controlled retrieval experiment:

1. a test collection consisting of (1) multimedia data, (2) a task and data needed for that task, for instance image search using example images as queries, and (3) ground truth data or so-called relevance judgments (i.e., the correct answers);
2. one or more suitable evaluation measures that assign values to the effectiveness of the search;
3. a statistical methodology that determines whether the observed differences in performance between the methods investigated are statistically significant.

Multimedia retrieval systems typically combine many components and tools. For instance, for a video retrieval system, a component might be a large-vocabulary speech recognition system; other components might detect low-level feature representations such as color histograms and Gaussian mixtures; the system might have a component that performs shot detection and key frame selection based on the low-level features, to allow the user to search for video shots, etc. We assume that a system component is an input-output device: feed in a video and get out some annotation of the video data. We also assume that components may be pipelined: some components will input the output of one or more other components to produce annotations. The quality of a system component will affect the quality of the system as a whole. So, there are two approaches to test the effectiveness of complex systems such as multimedia search systems [13]:

1. *glass box* evaluation, i.e., the systematic assessment of every component of a system; and
2. *black box* evaluation, i.e., testing the system as a whole.

For some of the components mentioned above, it is easy to define a clear task, and it is possible to come up with meaningful ground truth data. For instance, for the speech recognition subtask, we can ask a human annotator to define the ground truth speech transcript of the test data; we can run our large-vocabulary speech recognition system on the data; and we can compute the word-error rate (the percentage of words that was wrongly recognized). Similarly, for the shot detection task, we can ask a human annotator to mark the shot boundaries; we can run our shot detector; and report precision and recall of the shot detection component (see Section 13.3 and 13.5). For complex systems that are composed of such components, glass box evaluation is a good option. An advantage of a glass box evaluation procedure is that it easily pinpoints the parts of the systems that should be improved.

For other components it is less clear what the ground truth data should be. For instance, for a component that extracts color histograms or Gaussian mixture models, it is impossible to say what constitutes a good histogram or mixture. The only way to evaluate a low-level feature extraction component, is to do a black box evaluation: Test the system as a whole with component $A$; then test a system as a whole with component $B$; and see if there is a significant difference. Even components for which we seem to be able to do a meaningful evaluation – such as the speech recognition and shot detection components mentioned above – we do not know upfront what the effect of the component's quality will be on the overall system quality. In general, a better speech recognition component will result in a better system, however, a 100% improvement in word error rate does in practice not result in a 100% improvement of precision and recall (see Section 13.3) of the overall system [12].

In this chapter, we will discuss the evaluation of multimedia retrieval systems by following the three ingredients of Hull: a test collection, an evaluation measure, and a statistical methodology. In Section 13.2, we will discuss some multimedia test collections and the retrieval tasks or subtask that can be evaluated with them. In Section 13.3, some well known evaluation measures are introduced. Section 13.4 briefly introduces significance testing. Finally, Section 13.5 will discuss the TRECVID collection and evaluation workshop in more depth.

## 13.2 Test Collections and Evaluation Workshops

The scientific evaluation of multimedia search systems is a costly and laborious job. Big companies, for instance Web search companies such as Yahoo and Google, might perform such evaluations themselves, but for smaller companies and research institutions a good option is often to take a test collection that is prepared by others. In order to share resources, test collections are often created by the collaborative effort of many research groups in so-called evaluation workshops of conferences. This approach was first taken in the Text Retrieval Conferences (TREC) [31]. The TREC-style evaluation approach is now taken by many smaller workshops that aim at the evaluation of multimedia search systems. An evaluation workshop typically follows a yearly cycle like the following: (1) the cycle starts with a call for participation in which an evaluation task and data is announced; (2) groups that participate receive the data and possibly some ground truth training data; (3) groups receive the test data (for instance queries) perform the test and send their results to the workshop organizers; (4) the organizers merge the results of all participants into one big pool create new ground truth data for those results; (5) the participants meet to discuss the evaluation results; (6) participants publish the results as workshop proceedings. Often, an important side-effect of the evaluation workshop is the creation of a test collection that can be used later on without the need to create new ground truth data or relevance judgments.

For black-box evaluations, people are involved in the process of deciding whether a multimedia object is relevant for a certain query. The results of this process are the so-called *relevance judgments* or *relevance assessments*. The people involved in this process are usually called *assessors*. For glass-box evaluations, for instance an evaluation of a shot boundary detection algorithm, the process of deciding whether a sequence of frames contains a shot boundary involves people as well (for instance, for TRECVID 2004 almost 5000 shot transitions in the test data were identified and classified by a single student that worked at the US National Institute of Standards and Technology [17]). The results of this process are the so-called *ground truth data* or *reference data*.

In the following subsections, we briefly review a number of test collections that are publicly available, most of which are developed in evaluation workshops. The sections are meant to be illustrative. Workshops change their tasks regularly, workshops might stop their activities after a number of years and new workshops might emerge depending on trends in research.

## 13.2.1 The Corel Set

The Corel test collection is a set of stock photographs, which is divided into subsets of images each relating to a specific theme (e.g., Arabian horses, sunsets, or English pub signs, see Figure 13.1). The collection is used to evaluate the effectiveness of content-based image retrieval systems in a large number of publications [3, 4, 5, 9, 16, 18, 30] and has become a de-facto standard in the field. Usually, Corel is used as follows: (1) from the test collection, take out one image and use it as a query-by-example; (2) relevant images for the query are those that come from the same theme; and (3) compute precision and recall for a number of queries.

**Theme**: Arabic Horses

**Fig. 13.1.** Example images from the Corel database.

A problem with evaluation using Corel is that a single "Corel set" does not exist. The data is sold commercially on separate thematic CDs, and different publications use different CDs and different selections of themes. Müller et al. [20] showed that evaluations using Corel are highly sensitive to the subsets and evaluation measures used. Another problem is that the data can be qualified as "easy" because of the clear distinctions between themes and the high similarity within a theme because they usually come from one source (e.g., one professional photographer). Westerveld and De Vries [32] showed that good results on Corel do not guarantee good results in a more realistic setting, such as the TRECVID collection described below.

## 13.2.2 The MIREX Workshops

The Music Information Retrieval Evaluation eXchange (MIREX) was organized for the first time in 2005 as a direct descendant of the Audio Description Contest organized in 2004 as part of the International Symposium on Music Information Retrieval (ISMIR). The MIREX test collections consist of data from record labels that allow to publish tracks from their artists' releases, for instance from Internet record labels like Epitonic [10] and Magnatune [19] that feature music by independent artists.

MIREX uses a glass box approach to the evaluation of music information retrieval by identifying various subtasks an musing retrieval system would have to perform and allow the participants to build components that perform those tasks. In 2005, the workshop identified the following tasks: Artist

**Composer**: Anonymous
**Title**: Roslin Castle
**Signature**: 000.109.446

**Fig. 13.2.** Example symbolic music from the MIREX RISM A/II database.

identification, Drum detection, Genre classification, Melody extraction, Onset detection, Tempo extraction, Key finding, Symbolic genre classification, Symbolic melodic similarity. The tasks are performed on CD-quality audio except for the last two tasks which operate on symbolic music as shown in Figure 13.2 [8].

### 13.2.3 TRECVID: The TREC Video Retrieval Workshops

An important evaluation workshop for this chapter is TRECVID: the TREC Video evaluation workshop. Section 13.5 discusses this one in detail. The workshop emerged as a special task of the Text Retrieval Conference (TREC) in 2001 and was later continued as an independent workshop collocated with TREC. The workshop has focused mostly on news videos, from US, Chinese and Arabic sources, such as CNN Headline News, and ABC World News Tonight. Figure 13.3 shows some TRECVID example data.

```
<VideoSegment id="shot88-16">
  <MediaTime>
    <MediaTimePoint>T00:02:48:16051F30000</MediaTimePoint>
    <MediaDuration>PT9S18288N30000F</MediaDuration>
  </MediaTime>
  <TextAnnotation confidence="0.581549">
    <FreeTextAnnotation>KNOW HOW I'LL A FAMILIAR SONG AND
DANCE SAY TO THE RUSSIAN PRESIDENT</FreeTextAnnotation>
  </TextAnnotation>
</VideoSegment>
```

**Fig. 13.3.** Example data from TRECVID with an MPEG-7 annotation.

TRECVID provides several black box evaluation tasks such as: Shot boundary detection, Story segmentation, and High-level feature extraction. The workshop series also provides a black-box evaluation framework: a Search task that may include the complete interactive session of a user with the system. We will describe the TRECVID tasks in depth in Section 13.5.

### 13.2.4 The Multimedia Tasks of the CLEF Workshops

CLEF stands for Cross-Language Evaluation Forum, a workshop series mainly focusing on multilingual retrieval, i.e., retrieving data from a collection of documents in many languages, and cross-language retrieval, i.e., querying data using one natural language and retrieving documents in another language. Like TRECVID, CLEF started as a cross-language retrieval task in TREC in 1997. It became independent from TREC in 2000 and is currently run in

Europe. Within CLEF, several image search tasks were organized starting
in 2003. The goal of ImageCLEF is to investigate the effectiveness of combining text and image for retrieval [7]. Interestingly, a cross-language image search
task is easier evaluated than a cross-language text search task: Whatever the
language skills of the user, the relevance of an image is easily determined independently of the language of the caption or the language of the surrounding
text.

There is a CLEF image databases consisting of historic photographs from
the library at St. Andrews University [7], for which all images are accompanied
by a caption consisting of several distinct fields, see Figure 13.4 for an example.

**Short title**: Rev William Swan.
**Location**: Fife, Scotland
**Description**: Seated, 3/4 face studio portrait of a man.
**Photographer**: Thomas Rodger
**Categories**: [ ministers ][ identified male ] [dress - clerical ]
**Notes**: ALB6-85-2 jf/ pcBIOG: Rev William Swan () ADD: Former own-
ers of album: A Govan then J J? Lowson. Individuals and other subjects
indicative of St Andrews provenance. By T. R. as identified by Karen A.
Johnstone "Thomas Rodger 1832-1883. A biography and catalog of se-
lected works".

**Fig. 13.4.** An example image from the CLEF St. Andrews database.

CLEF also provides an evaluation task for a medical image collection consisting of medical photographs, X-rays, CT-scans, MRIs, etc. provided by the
Geneva University Hospital in the Casimage project. Casimage is the fusion
of the words "case" and "image". The goal of the project is to help the development of databases for teaching purposes. A database is a collection of
cases, for instance diseases. Each case contains several images with textual
descriptions [24]; Figure 13.5 shows an example. CLEF provides black-box
evaluations for these databases in the form of a several search tasks.

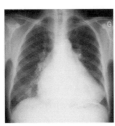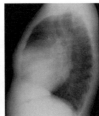

**Chapter**: Pathologie cardiaque
**Diagnosis**: Insuffisance mitrale
**Clinical Presentation**: Dyspné d'effort. Souf-
fle systolique au foyer mitral
**Description**: Dilatation de l'oreillette gauche
qui reste inscrite dans l'oreillette droite. Dilatation du ventricule gauche (arc infrieur gauche).
Arc moyen gauche à double bosse: auricule
gauche et tronc de l'artère pulmonaire dilatés
**Commentary**: L'insuffisance mitrale entrane
une surcharge en volume de l'oreillette et du
ventricule gauches responsable d'une dilatation de ces deux cavités. Le retentissement
en amont explique la dilatation secondairedes
cavités droites.

**Fig. 13.5.** An example case from the CLEF Casimage database.

### 13.2.5 The Multimedia Tasks of the INEX Workshops

The Initiative for the Evaluation of XML Retrieval (INEX) aims at evaluating
the retrieval performance of XML retrieval systems. The INEX multimedia
track differs from other approaches in multimedia information retrieval, in the
sense that it focuses on using the structure of the document to extract, relate
and combine the relevance scores of different multimedia fragments.

```
<article> <name id="797481">Beurs van Berlage</name>
<figure>
  <image ...href=".../Amsterdam_Stock_Exchange.JPG">
  Amsterdam_Stock_Exchange.JPG</image>
  <caption>Beurs van Berlage</caption>
</figure><p>
The <emph3>Beurs van Berlage</emph3> is a building
on the Damrak, in the center of Amsterdam.
It was designed as a commodity exchange by
  <collectionlink ... xlink:href="775874.xml">
  Hendrik Petrus Berlage
  </collectionlink>
and constructed between 1896 and 1903.
...
</article>
```

**Fig. 13.6.** Example data from the INEX Wikipedia database.

INEX 2006 had a modest multimedia task that involved data from the
Wikipedia. A search query might for instance search for images by combining
information from its caption text, its links, and from the article that contains the image; see Figure 13.6. Queries might also include example images
to specify the search for similar images [34].

## 13.3 Evaluation Measures

The effectiveness of a system or component is often measured by the combination of *precision* and *recall*. Precision is defined by the fraction of the retrieved
or detected objects that is actually relevant. Recall is defined by the fraction
of the relevant objects that is actually retrieved:

$$\text{precision} = \frac{r}{n}$$

$r$ : number of relevant documents retrieved

$n$ : number of documents retrieved

$$\text{recall} = \frac{r}{R}$$

$R$ : total number of relevant documents.

Precision and recall are defined on sets of objects, not on ordered lists of
objects. If the system ranks the objects in decreasing order of some score
value, then the precision and recall measures should somehow be averaged over
the number of objects retrieved. Several average precision and average recall
measures have been suggested that model the behavior of a user walking down
a ranked list of objects. The idea is to give a number of evaluation measures for

different types of users. At one end of the spectrum is the user that is satisfied with any relevant object, for instance a user that searches a Web page on last night's football results. At the other end of the spectrum is the user that is only satisfied with most or all of the relevant objects, for instance a lawyer searching for jurisprudence. We present four different evaluation measures that combine precision and recall in this section: precision at fixed levels of recall, precision at fixed points in the ranked list, the average precision over the ranks of relevant documents, and the $F$ measure [14].

### 13.3.1 Precision at Fixed Recall Levels

For this evaluation a number of fixed recall levels are chosen, for instance 10 levels: $\{0.1, 0.2, \cdots, 1.0\}$. The levels correspond to users that are satisfied if they find respectively 10%, 20%, $\cdots$, 100% of the relevant documents. For each of these levels the corresponding precision is determined by averaging the precision on that level over the tests that are performed, for instance over a set of test queries. The resulting precision points are often visualized in a recall–precision graph. Figure 13.7 shows an example. The graph shows the typical behavior of information retrieval systems. Increasing the recall of a search implies decreasing the precision of the search. Or, by walking down a ranked list in search for more relevant documents, the chance to encounter irrelevant documents will grow faster than the chance to encounter relevant documents.

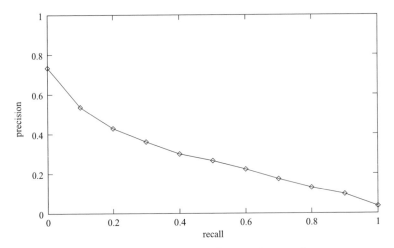

**Fig. 13.7.** Example recall–precision graph.

In practice, the levels of recall might not correspond with natural recall levels. For instance, if the total number of relevant documents $R$ is 3, then the natural recall levels are 0.33, 0.67 and 1.0. Other recall levels are determined by using interpolation. A simple but often used interpolation method determines the precision at recall level $l$ by the maximum precision at all points larger than $l$. For example, if the three relevant documents were retrieved at rank 4, 9 and 20, then the precision at recall points $0.0, \cdots, 0.3$ is 0.25, at recall points 0.4, 0.5 and 0.6 the precision is 0.22 and at $0.7, \cdots, 1.0$ the precision is 0.15 [14]. Interpolation might also be used to determine the precision at recall 0.0, resulting in a total of 11 recall levels. Sometimes one average measure, the so-called 11 points interpolated average precision, is calculated by averaging the average precision values over the 11 recall points.

### 13.3.2 Precision at Fixed Points in the Ranked List

Recall is not necessarily a good measure of user equivalence. For instance if one query has 20 relevant documents while another has 200. A recall of 50% would be a reasonable goal in the first case, but unmanageable for most users in the second case [15]. A more user oriented method would simply choose a number of fixed points in the ranked list, for instance nine points at: 5, 10, 15, 20, 30, 100, 200, 500 and 1000 documents retrieved. These points correspond with users that are willing to read 5, 10, 15, etc. documents of a search. For each of these points in the ranked list, the precision is determined by averaging the precision on that level over the queries. Similarly, the average recall might be computed for each of the points in the ranked list. A potential problem with these measures however is that, although precision and recall theoretically range between 0 and 1, they are often restricted to a small fraction of the range for many cut-off points. For instance, if the total number of relevant documents $R = 3$, then the precision at 10 will be 0.3 at maximum. One point of special interest from this perspective is the precision at $R$ documents retrieved. At this point the average precision and average recall do range between 0 and 1. Furthermore, precision and recall are by definition equal at this point. The $R$-precision value is the precision at each (different) $R$ averaged over the queries [14].

### 13.3.3 Mean Average Precision

The average precision measure is a single value that is determined for each request and then averaged over the requests. The measure corresponds with a user that walks down a ranked list of documents that will only stop after he/she has found a certain number of relevant documents. The measure is the average of the precision calculated at the rank of each relevant document retrieved. Relevant documents that are not retrieved are assigned a precision value of zero. For the example above where the three relevant documents are retrieved at ranks 4, 9 and 20, the average precision would be computed as $(0.25 + 0.22 + 0.15)/3 = 0.21$. This measure has the advantages that it does not need the interpolation method and that it uses the full range between 0 and 1 [14].

### 13.3.4 Combining Precision and Recall: The F-Measure

For many glass box evaluations, there is no ranked list that needs to be considered. For instance, a tool that detects video shot boundaries (see Section 13.5.1) does not really rank anything: It either detects a shot boundary or not. In such cases, we need to choose between two systems based on the raw precision and recall measures. Suppose that on a shot boundary detection task one system achieves a precision of 0.8 and a recall of 0.95, and another system achieves a precision of 0.99, but a recall of only 0.7. What system would we prefer? Obviously that depends on our preferences: do we want a system that detects shot boundaries accurately or thoroughly? If we are equally interested in precision *and* recall, we might use the following measure:

$$ F = \frac{2 \cdot \text{precision} \cdot \text{recall}}{\text{precision} + \text{recall}}. \tag{13.1} $$

The F-measure combines precision and recall with an equal weight. In the example above, the first system achieves $F = 0.87$, whereas the second system achieves $F = 0.82$. So, we better choose the first system if we are equally interested in precision and recall.

### 13.3.5 Problems with Measuring Recall

The computation of recall is a well-known problem in retrieval system evaluation, because it involves the manual assessment or estimation of the total number of relevant items in the database for each query. Assessment of each document is too costly for large collections and estimation by assessing a sample with sufficient reliability would still require large samples [28]. A common way to get around this problem is to use the *pooling method* which is applied in TREC. This method computes *relative* recall values instead of *absolute* recall. It is assumed that if we have a "pool" of diverse retrieval systems, the probability that a relevant document will be retrieved by one of the systems is high. So a merged list of document rankings is assumed to contain most relevant documents. The pool assumption is actually a bit more precise: we assume that most relevant documents are contained in a pool consisting of the merged top $D$ documents of several different high quality retrieval systems. Here $D$ is the *pool depth*, i.e., the number of retrieved items taken from the top of a retrieval run. At TREC usually a pool depth of 100 documents has been applied. So, for each query, the top 100 documents from the submissions that contribute to the pool are merged in a set of which a list of unique document identifiers is extracted. These documents are subjected to a (manual) relevance assessment procedure.

In the previous sections we already mentioned that systems are often evaluated on existing test collections. There are two potential problems with "reusing" a test collection: (i) it takes more discipline to perform a really blind experiment and extra care not to tune on the data; (ii) post–hoc runs are unjudged runs by definition. An unjudged run is a run that did not contribute to the pool. For judged runs we know that at least the top 100 (the most common pool depth) is judged. For unjudged runs, this will not be the case. The percentage of judged documents (the judged fraction) will be lower. However, presenting results of unjudged runs is very common. Even at TREC not every run is judged. Participants can submit runs and because of the limited capacity and budget, the pool is based on a selection of the submitted runs, usually one run per participating site. For judged runs, the number of judged documents in the top 100 is exactly 100, for unjudged runs this number is lower. That means that the calculated performance measures are more reliable for judged runs. The difference in reliability between judged and unjudged runs has been studied by Zobel [33] as follows: recompute the average precision of every run that contributed to the pool based on a pool without the judged documents that were uniquely contributed by the very same run. Finally, compute the averages of the average differences or improvements in performance over the runs. He reported an average improvement of 0.5% over 61 runs with a maximum of 3.5% for the TREC-5 collection. The fact whether a run is judged or not thus seems to play a minor role in the TREC-5 dataset.

## 13.4 Significance Tests

Simply citing percentage improvements of one method over another is helpful, but it does not tell if the improvements were in fact due to differences of the two methods. Instead, differences between two methods might simply be due to random variation in the performance, that is, the difference might occur by chance even if the two methods perform equally well. To make significance testing of the differences applicable, a reasonable amount of queries is needed. When evaluation measures are averaged over a number of queries, one can obtain an estimate of the error associated with the measure [15].

Often, a technique called *cross-validation* is used to further prevent biased evaluation results. The data and ground truth data is split in two disjoint sets: the *training set* and the *test set*. The training set is used for development and tuning of the system and, if applicable, to train learning algorithms like classifiers. Then, the test set is used to measure the effectiveness of the system. These three steps (dividing the data, training and testing) might be repeated for different sizes of the sets and different random selections of training set and test set for each size.

### 13.4.1 Assumptions of Significance Tests

Significance tests are designed to disprove the null hypothesis $H_0$. For retrieval experiments, the null hypothesis will be that there is no difference between method $A$ and method $B$. The idea is to show that, given the data, the null hypothesis is indefensible, because it leads to an implausibly low probability. Rejecting $H_0$ implies accepting the alternative hypothesis $H_1$. The alternative hypothesis for the retrieval experiments will be that either method $A$

consistently outperforms method $B$, or method $B$ consistently outperforms method $A$.

A test statistic is a function of the data. It should have the following two properties. Firstly, it should behave differently under $H_0$ than under $H_1$. Secondly, it should be possible to calculate its probability distribution under $H_0$. For information retrieval, there is usually much more variation in the performance per query than in the performance per system. Therefore, the test statistics used are paired tests which are based on the performance differences between two systems for each query. The methods assume that the performance differences consist of a mean difference $\mu$ and an error $\varepsilon_i$ for each query $i$, where the errors are independent. The null hypothesis is that $\mu = 0$. The following three paired tests have been used in the Smart retrieval experiments [25, page 171]:

- **The paired t-test** assumes that errors are normally distributed. Under $H_0$, the distribution is Student's t with $\#queries - 1$ degrees of freedom.
- **The paired Wilcoxon signed ranks test** is a non-parametric test that assumes that errors come from a continuous distribution that is symmetric around 0. The statistic uses the ranks of the absolute differences instead of the differences themselves.
- **The paired sign test** is a non-parametric test that only uses the sign of the differences between method $A$ and $B$ for each query. The test statistic is the number of times that the least frequent sign occurs. It assumes equal probability of positive and negative errors. Under $H_0$, the distribution is binomial.

So, in order to use the $t$-test the errors must be normally distributed, and in order to use Wilcoxon's test the errors have to be continuous. However, precision and recall are discrete and bounded and therefore neither normally distributed nor continuous. Still, the average of a reasonable number of discrete measures, like the average precision measure presented in Section 13.3.3, might behave similar to continuous measures and approximate the normal distribution quite well. Before the tests can be applied, the researcher has to make a qualitative judgment of the data, to check if indeed the normality assumption is reasonable [15]. If not, the sign test can be used as an alternative. Some researchers, for instance Van Rijsbergen [29], argue that only the sign test can be considered valid for information retrieval experiments.

### 13.4.2 Example: Performing a Significance Test

As an example consider the following experiment. We compare the effectiveness of two content-based image retrieval systems $A$ and $B$ that, given an example query image, return a ranked lists of images from a standard benchmark test collection. For each system, we run 50 queries from the benchmark. Using the benchmark's relevance judgments, we compute the average precision for each query on both systems. Suppose the mean average precision is

0.208 for system $A$ and 0.241 for system $B$. Are these differences significant? To test this, we might use a two-tailed pair-wise sign test and only report differences at a 1% level as significant, that is, the probability that differences are contributed to chance should be less than 1%.

To apply the test, we determine for each query the sign of the difference between the average precision of both systems: $-1$ if system $A$ outperforms system $B$ on the query, and 1 if system $B$ outperforms system $A$. Assume that it turns out that for 16 queries system $A$ produced the highest average precision, and for 34 queries system $B$ produced the highest average precision. Under $H_0$, the probability of observing these numbers can be computed by the binomial distribution. However, it would be incorrect to only calculate the probability of getting exactly 16 successes for system $A$. Instead, we should calculate the probability of getting a deviation from the null hypothesis as large as, or larger than, the observed result. The probability of getting $k$ or less successes in $n$ trials with probability $p$ is given by the cumulative binomial distribution function $F$:

$$F(k; n, p) = \sum_{j=1}^{k} \frac{n!}{j!(n-j)!} p^j (1-p)^{n-j}. \qquad (13.2)$$

In this case, $F(16; 50, 0.5) = 0.00767$. So, the probability of observing 16 or less successes for system $A$ is 0.00767, which is less than 1%. But we are not done yet! The above calculation gives the total probability of getting 16 or less successes for system $A$. However, the alternative hypothesis $H_1$ states that the probability of success for system $A$ is not equal to the probability of success of system $B$. If there had been 34 successes for system $A$, then that would have been an equally extreme deviation from the expected number of successes under the null hypothesis. To account for both tails of the probability distribution – hence the name *two-tailed* test – the probability has to be multiplied by 2, resulting in a probability of 0.0153. Therefore, we cannot reject the null hypothesis. Despite the substantial difference between the mean average precision of both systems, this might still be contributed to chance. The two-tailed pair-wise sign test was unable to detect a significant difference at the 1% level.

## 13.5 A Case Study: TRECVID

In 2004, there were four main tasks in TRECVID: shot boundary detection; story segmentation; high-level feature extraction; and search. We will describe each of these four tasks below.

### 13.5.1 Shot Boundary Detection

When you see a film in the theater or on television, you see moving images, but actually the film consists of still pictures, called *frames*. If enough different frames are projected within each second, typically 25 or 30 per second, the human brain smears them together and we get the illusion of motion or change. Because there are many nearly identical frames each second, it does not make much sense to index each single frame when building a video search system. The system would typically index video at some higher granularity, for instance by grouping frames together into *shots*. Traditionally, a shot marks the complete sequence of frames starting from the moment that the camera was switched on, and stopping when it was switched off again, or a subsequence of that selected by the movie editor. Shot detection is a crucial step in many video search systems. Shot retrieval is for instance useful in a scenario where a user has the desire to re-use video material, or in a scenario where a user wants very precise points into the video stream.

A shot detector is a tool that inputs digital video and outputs the shot boundaries, i.e., the positions in the video stream that contain the transitions from one shot to the next shot. Usually, at least two types of shot transitions are distinguished: *hard cuts* and *soft cuts*. A hard cut is an abrupt change from one shot to the next shot: One frame belongs to the first shot, and the next frame to the second shot. Hard cuts are relatively easy to detect because there is usually a relatively large difference between the two frames. A soft cut, or *gradual transition*, uses several frames to establish the cut, that is, there is a sequence of frames that belongs to both the first shot and the second shot. These are much harder to detect, because there are no obvious points in the video with a big difference between consecutive frames that mark the shot boundary. Gradual transitions are sometimes further classified as *dissolves*, *fades* and *wipes*.

The TRECVID shot boundary task is defined as follows: identify the shot boundaries with their location and type (hard or soft) in the given video clips. The performance of a system is measured by precision and recall of detected shot boundaries, where the detection criteria require only a single frame overlap between the submitted transitions and the reference transition. This is done to make the detection independent of the accuracy of the detected boundaries. For the purposes of detection, a hard cut transition is treated as if it includes both the frame before the cut and after the cut, making the length of a hard cut effectively two frames instead of zero frames.

The TRECVID 2004 test data consists of 618,409 frames in total containing 4806 shot transitions of which about 58% are hard cuts and 42% are soft cuts, mostly dissolves. The best performing systems perform very well on hard cuts: around 95% precision and 95% recall, but considerably worse on soft cuts, which perform around 80% precision and 80% recall [17].

### 13.5.2 Story Segmentation

A digital video retrieval system with shots as the basic retrieval unit might not be desirable in situations in which users are searching an archive of video assets that consist of a compilation of different topics, such as news shows and news magazines. In such a case, retrieval of a complete topical unit is usually preferred over retrieval of shots. However, reverse-engineering the structure of, e.g., a television news show in a general fashion is not always straightforward, since news shows have widely differing formats. The segmentation of a news show into its constituting news items has been studied under the names of *story boundary detection* and *story segmentation*. Story segmentation of multimedia data can potentially exploit visual, audio and textual cues present in the data. Story boundaries often but not always occur at shot boundaries, since an anchor person can conclude a story and introduce the subsequent story in a single shot. A news item often spans multiple shots, starting with an anchor person, switching, e.g., to a reporter on-site or a split screen interview.

Story segmentation of digital video was evaluated at TRECVID in 2003 and 2004 based on a collection of ABC/CNN news shows. These news shows consist of a series of news items interspersed with publicity items. The story segmentation task was defined as follows: given the story boundary test collection, identify the story boundaries with their location (time) in the given video clip(s). The definition of the story segmentation task was based on manual story boundary annotations made by Linguistic Data Consortium (LDC) for the Topic Detection and Tracking (TDT) project [11] and thus LDC's definition of a story was used in the task. A news story was defined as a segment of a news broadcast with a coherent news focus which contains at least two independent, declarative clauses. Other coherent non-news segments were labeled as *miscellaneous*, merged together when adjacent, and annotated as one single story. These non-news stories cover a mixture of footage: commercials, lead-ins and reporter chit-chat.

With the TRECVID 2003 and 2004 story segmentation task, the goal was to show how video information can enhance or completely replace existing story segmentation algorithms based on text, in this case Automatic Speech Recognition (ASR) transcripts and/or Closed Captions (CC). In order to concentrate on this goal there were several required experiments (called *runs* in TRECVID) for participants in this task:

- Video + Audio (no ASR/CC);
- Video + Audio + ASR/CC;
- ASR/CC (no Video + Audio).

Additional optional runs using other ASR and/or CC-based transcripts were also allowed to be submitted. Since story boundaries are rather abrupt changes of focus, story boundary evaluation was modeled on the evaluation of shot boundaries (the hard cuts, not the gradual boundaries). A story boundary was expressed as a time offset with respect to the start of the video file in seconds, accurate to nearest hundredth of a second. Each reference boundary was expanded with a fuzziness factor of five seconds in each direction, resulting in an evaluation interval of 10 seconds. A reference boundary was detected when one or more computed story boundaries lay within its evaluation interval. If a computed boundary did not fall in the evaluation interval of a reference boundary, it was considered a false alarm. In addition, the $F$-measure (see Section 13.3.4) was used to compare performance across conditions and across systems.

### 13.5.3 High-level Feature Extraction

One way to bridge the semantic gap between video content and textual representations is to annotate video footage with *high-level features*. The assumption is (and evidence is accumulating [1, 27]) that features describing generic concepts such as **indoor/outdoor** or **people** could help search and navigation. It is easy to understand the plausibility of this assumption, when a collection of video assets is annotated (at the shot level) with a lexicon of (high-level) features, these features can be used to constrain the search space by conditioning the result set to include or exclude a certain feature. High-level features can thus complement search in speech recognition transcripts/closed captions. A sufficiently rich and structured feature lexicon could strongly enhance the possibilities for faceted navigation, i.e., navigation where a user interactively selects features from different concept classes.

In TRECVID, the high-level feature detection task is modeled as a ranking task. Systems have to assign to each shot (taken from a standard collection) the probability that a certain feature is present. The top 2000 shots for each feature are submitted for manual evaluation, based on the pooling principle described in Section 13.3.5. This approach has the advantage that the number of manual judgments that has to be done is limited. The presence/absence of a feature is taken to be a binary property, if a feature holds for just one frame in a shot, it is assumed the feature is present for the whole shot. For each feature, the average precision is computed as described in Section 13.3.3 using the standard TREC evaluation package [6]. Since the test features in TRECVID cannot be thought of as a random draw from the space of possible features (the features represent fixed rather than random factors), average precision is reported per feature and no *mean* average precision is calculated.

### 13.5.4 Video Search

The shot detection, story segmentation and high-level feature extraction tasks discussed up till now are glass box evaluations. The purpose of the *video search* task however, is to evaluate the system as a whole, i.e., to do a black-box evaluation of the system. The task is as follows: Given the search test collection and a multimedia statement of a user's information need (called *topic* in TRECVID), return a ranked list of at most 1000 shots from the test collection that best satisfy the need. A topic consists of a textual description of the user's need, for instance: "Find shots of one or more buildings with flood waters around it/them." and possibly one or more example frames or images. Researchers might use the topics to automatically generate queries from, for instance the textual description might be used to generate a text query which is run on automatic speech recognition transcripts and each example frame might be used directly as a query-by-example, i.e., it might be used to retrieve shots that contain frames that are in some sense similar to the examples. However, the topics are intended to be used by human searchers who either manually formulate their queries, or interactively use the system to formulate and reformulate the queries. These two search tasks are shown in Figure 13.8 which was taken from the TRECVID guidelines [22].

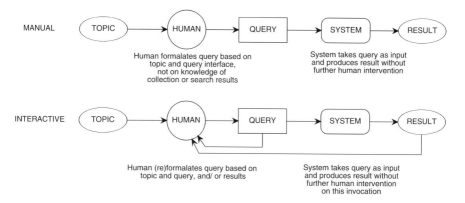

**Fig. 13.8.** Two video search tasks: manual and interactive.

The searcher should have no experience of the topics beyond the general world knowledge of an educated adult. The maximum total elapsed time limit for each topic (from the time the searcher sees the topic until the time the final result set for that topic is returned) in an interactive search run is 15 minutes. For manual runs the manual effort (topic to query translation) for any given topic is limited to 15 minutes as well. To make the search results of different systems better comparable, all systems use exactly the same shot boundaries provided by TRECVID, the so-called *common shot boundary reference.* This way, the shots act as pre-defined units of retrieval just as in ordinary (text) document retrieval. Retrieval methods are evaluated by comparing their mean average precision or by comparing the precision at several recall points.

## 13.6 Summary

Evaluation is a crucial element of multimedia retrieval research, since it is important to validate whether a certain idea or theoretical model is effective (and efficient) in practice. Test collections play an important role for the advancement of the field as a whole because they provide common reference points for measuring progress. Several rigorous evaluation methods exist for the performance measurement of fully automatic systems. Evaluation of systems that include user interaction is much more complicated, efficient evaluation methodology schemas are still under development for this area.

## 13.7 Further Reading

Retrieval system evaluation methodology is described is many books on information retrieval. For instance, Keith van Rijsbergen [29] extensively discusses evaluation methodology. More up-to-date is the book by Ricardo Baeza-Yates and Berthier Ribeiro-Neto [2]. David Hull [15] wrote a well-cited paper on significance testing, discussing amongst others interactive search scenarios that include relevance feedback. Stephen Robertson [23] wrote an excellent evaluation tutorial for the European Summer School on Information Retrieval, ESSIR. John Smith [26] as well as Henning Müller et al. [21] wrote interesting notes on the specific issues for image and video retrieval.

## References

1. A. Amir, J. Argillandery, M. Campbellz, A. Hauboldz, G. Iyengar, S. Ebadollahiz, F. Kangz, M.R. Naphadez, A. Natsevz, J.R. Smithz, J. Tesicz, and T. Volkmer. IBM Research TRECVID-2005 Video Retrieval System. In *Proceedings of the TRECVID 2005 workshop*, 2005.
2. R. Baeza-Yates and B. Ribeiro-Neto, editors. *Modern Information Retrieval*. Addison-Wesley, 1999.
3. K. Barnard, P. Duygulu, D. Forsyth, N. de Freitas, D. M. Blei, and M. I. Jordan. Matching words and pictures. *Journal of Machine Learning Research*, 3:1107–1135, 2003.
4. S. Belongie, C. Carson, H. Greenspan, and J. Malik. Color- and texture-based image segmentation using em and its application to content-based image retrieval. In *Proceedings of the sixth International Conference on Computer Vision*, 1998.
5. D.M. Blei and M.I. Jordan. Modeling annotated data. In *Proceedings of the 26th ACM SIGIR Conference on Research and Development in Information Retrieval (SIGIR)*, 2003.
6. C. Buckley. trec_eval: TREC evaluation software. In *Provided to participants of the Text Retrieval Conferences (TREC)*, 2006. http://trec.nist.gov/trec_eval/.
7. P. Clough, H. Müller, and M. Sanderson. The CLEF cross-language image retrieval track (ImageCLEF) 2004. In *Proceedings of the fifth Workshop of the Cross Language Evaluation Forum (CLEF)*, Lecture Notes in Computer Science (LNCS). Springer, 2005.
8. J.S. Downie, K. West, A. Ehmann, and E. Vincent. The 2005 music information retrieval evaluation exchange (MIREX 2005): preliminary overview. In *Proceedings of the Lnternational Conference on Music Information Retrieval*, 2005.
9. P. Duygulu, K. Barnard, N. de Freitas, and D. Forsyth. Object recognition as machine translation: Learning a lexicon for a fixed image vocabulary. In *Proceedings of the seventh European Conference on Computer Vision*, pages 97–112, 2002.
10. Epitonic. http://www.epitonic.com.
11. J.G. Fiscus, G. Doddington, J.S. Garofolo, and A. Martin. NIST's 1998 Topic Detection and Tracking Evaluation (TDT2). In *Proceedings of the DARPA Broadcast News Workshop*, 1999.

12. J. Garfolo, C. Auzanne, and E.M. Voorhees. The TREC SDR track: A success story. In *Proceedings of the eighth Text Retrieval Conference (TREC)*, pages 107–129, 2000.

13. E.E.W. Group. Evaluation of natural language processing systems. Technical report, ISSCO, 1996.

14. D.K. Harman. Appendix B: Common evaluation measures. In *Proceedings of the 13th Text Retrieval Conference (TREC)*, 2005.

15. D. Hull. Using statistical testing in the evaluation of retrieval experiments. In *Proceedings of the 16th ACM Conference on Research and Development in Information Retrieval (SIGIR'93)*, pages 329–338, 1993.

16. J. Jeon, V. Lavrenko, and R. Manmatha. Automatic image annotation and retrieval using cross-media relevance models. In *Proceedings of the 26th ACM SIGIR Conference on Research and Development in Information Retrieval (SIGIR)*, 2003.

17. W. Kraaij, A.F. Smeaton, P. Over, and J. Arlandis. Trecvid — an introduction. In *Proceedings of TRECVID 2004*, 2004. http://www-nlpir.nist.gov/projects/trecvid/.

18. J. Li and J.Z. Wang. Automatic linguistic indexing of pictures by a statistical modeling approach. *IEEE Transactions on Pattern Analysis and Machine Intelligence*, 25 (9), 1075–1088, 2003. http://infolab.stanford.edu/~wangz/project/imsearch/ALIP/PAMI03/01227984.pdf.

19. Magnatune. http://magnatune.com.

20. H. Müller, S. Marchand-Maillet, and T. Pun. The truth about Corel – evaluation in image retrieval. In *Proceedings of The Challenge of Image and Video Retrieval (CIVR)*, 2002.

21. H. Müller, W. Müller, D. McG.Squire, S. Marchand-Maillet, and T. Pun. Performance evaluation in content-based image retrieval: Overview and proposals. *Pattern Recognition Letters*, 22:593–601, 2001.

22. P. Over, A. Smeaton, and W. Kraaij. Guidelines for the TRECVID 2004 evaluation. 2004. http://www-nlpir.nist.gov/projects/tv2004/tv2004.html.

23. S.E. Robertson. Evaluation in information retrieval. In M. Agosti, F. Crestani, and G. Pasi, editors, *European Summer School on Information Retrieval (ESSIR)*, number 1980 in Lecture Notes in Computer Science, pages 81–92. Springer-Verlag, 2000.

24. A. Rosset, O. Ratib, A. Geissbuhler, and J.P. Vallé. Integration of a multimedia teaching and reference database in a PACS environment. *RadioGraphics*, 22:1567–1577, 2002.

25. G. Salton and M.J. McGill. *Introduction to Modern Information Retrieval*. McGraw-Hill, 1983.

26. J. Smith. Image retrieval evaluation. In *Proceedings of the IEEE Workshop on Content-Based Access of Image and Video Libraries (CBAIVL)*, 1998.

27. C.G.M. Snoek, J.C. van Gemert, J.M. Geusebroek, B. Huurnink, D.C. Koelma, G.P. Nguyen, O. de Rooij, F.J. Seinstra, A.W.M. Smeulders, C.J. Veenman, and M. Worring. The MediaMill TRECVID 2005 Semantic Video Search Engine. In *Proceedings of the 2005 TRECVID workshop*, 2005.

28. J.M. Tague. The pragmatics of information retrieval experimentation. In K. Sparck-Jones, editor, *Information Retrieval Experiment*, pages 59–102. Butterworths, 1981.

29. C.J. van Rijsbergen. *Information Retrieval, 2nd edition*. Butterworths, 1979. http://www.dcs.gla.ac.uk/Keith/Preface.html.

30. N. Vasconcelos and A. Lippman. A probabilistic architecture for content-based image retrieval. In *Proceedings of the IEEE Conference on Computer Vision and Pattern Recognition (CVPR)*, pages 216–221, 2000.

31. E.M. Voorhees and D. Harman, editors. *TREC: Experiment and Evaluation in Information Retrieval.* MIT Press, 2005.

32. T. Westerveld and A.P. de Vries. Experimental evaluation of a generative probabilistic image retrieval model on 'easy' data. In *Proceedings of the Multimedia Information Retrieval Workshop*, 2003.

33. J. Zobel. How reliable are the results of large-scale information retrieval experiments? In *Proceedings of the 21st ACM Conference on Research and Development in Information Retrieval (SIGIR'98)*, pages 307–314, 1998.

34. T. Westerveld and R. van Zwol. INEX 2006 Multimedia Track. In *Advances in XML Information Retrieval and Evaluation: Fifth International Workshop of the Initiative for the Evaluation of XML Retrieval, INEX 2006*, Lecture Notes in Computer Science (LNCS) / Lecture Notes in Artificial Intelligence (LNAI), *to appear*, Springer, 2007.

# Index

$\Theta$, 194
$\theta$, 183
$\phi$, 185
$\kappa$, 193
$\lambda$, 192

AAM, *see* active appearance model
acoustic
  adaptation, 219
  modeling, 202
active appearance model (AAM), 172
active shape model (ASM), 172
activity recognition
  automatic, 54
AdaBoost, 67
ADC, analog-to-digital conversion, 4
amplitude–time sequence, 9
analog-to-digital conversion (ADC), 4
analysis
  multimodal, 236
annotation, 8, 53
  assigned terms, 98
ASM, *see* active shape model
assigned terms, *see* annotation
autocorrelation
  analysis, 274
  function, 274
average energy, 9

background model, 191
backward selection, *see* feature
bag-of-words, 186
Baum–Welch algorithm, 263
Bayes' classifier, 59

Bayesian
  averaging, 66
  bagging, 66
  dynamic Baysesian network (DBN),
    278
  dynamic network (DBN), 277
  network (BN), 277
binarization, 286
black box, 348
BN, *see* Bayesian network
Boolean model, 100
boosting, 66

catalog, 98
classification
  discriminative model, 178
  generative model, 179
  iterative style, 239
  multimodal, 236
  pixel, 137, 150
  speaker, 199
classifier, 54, 60
  Bayes', 59
  support vector, 63
CLEF, 351
clustering
  hierarchical, 76
  soft, 189
co-occurrence matrix, 142
codebook, 260
collection model, 191
color histogram, 9
common shot boundary reference, 363

Printing: Krips bv, Meppel
Binding: Stürtz, Würzburg